3

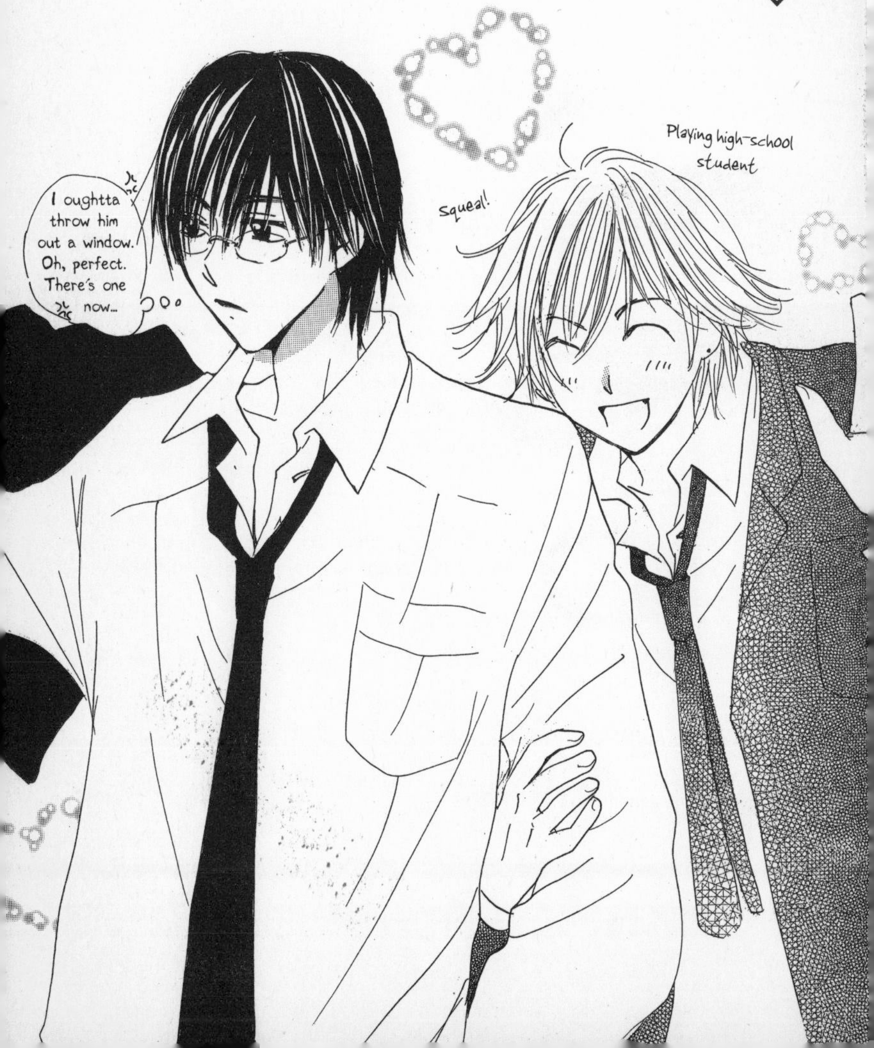
Playing high-school student
squeal!
I oughtta throw him out a window. Oh, perfect. There's one now...

Translation – Kathy Schilling
Adaptation – Audry Taylor
Lettering & Design – Eva Han
Production Assistant – Mallory Reaves
Production Manager - James Dashiell
Editor – Jake Forbes

A Go! Comi manga

Published by Go! Media Entertainment, LLC

Crossroad Volume 3

Originally published in Japan in 2004 by Akita Publishing Co., Ltd., Tokyo.
English translation rights arranged with Akita Publishing Co., Ltd.
through TOHAN CORPORATION, Tokyo.

This edition is struck from the original Japanese film for the best possible reproduction. Absolutely no artwork has been censored.

Visit us online at www.gocomi.com
e-mail: info@gocomi.com

ISBN 1-933617-00-4

First printed in April 2006

1 2 3 4 5 6 7 8 9

Manufactured in the United States of America

crossroad

Story and Art by
Shioko Mizuki

Volume 3

go!comi

Concerning Honorifics

At Go! Comi, we do our best to ensure that our translations read seamlessly in English while respecting the original Japanese language and culture. To this end, the original honorifics (the suffixes found at the end of characters' names) remain intact. In Japan, where politeness and formality are more integrated into every aspect of the language, honorifics give a better understanding of character relationships. They can be used to indicate both respect and affection. Whether a person addresses someone by first name or last name also indicates how close their relationship is.

Here are some of the honorifics you might encounter in reading this book:

-san: This is the most common and neutral of honorifics. The polite way to address someone you're not on close terms with is to use "-san." It's kind of like Mr. or Ms., except you can use "-san" with first names as easily as family names.

-chan: Used for friendly familiarity, mostly applied towards young girls. "-chan" also carries a connotation of cuteness with it, so it is frequently used with nick-names towards both boys and girls (such as "Na-chan" for "Natsu").

-kun: Like "-chan," it's an informal suffix for friends and classmates, only "-kun" is usually associated with boys. It can also be used in a professional environment by someone addressing a subordinate.

-sama: Indicates a great deal of respect or admiration.

Sempai: In school, "sempai" is used to refer to an upperclassman or club leader. It can also be used in the workplace by a new employee to address a mentor or staff member with seniority.

Sensei: Teachers, doctors, writers or any master of a trade are referred to as "sensei." When addressing a manga creator, the polite thing to do is attach "-sensei" to the manga-ka's name (as in Mizuki-sensei).

Onii: This is the more casual term for an older brother. Usually you'll see it with an honorific attached, such as "onii-chan."

Onee: The casual term for older sister, it's used like "onii" with honorifics.

[blank]: Not using an honorific when addressing someone indicates that the speaker has permission to speak intimately with the other person. This relationship is usually reserved for close friends and family.

crossroad

— Table of Contents —

— Bonus Manga —

The Story So Far...

Kajitsu, Taro, Natsu, and Satsuki are four step-siblings living with their irresponsible step-mom Rumiko. As Kajitsu and Natsu struggle against their deepening affections for each other, Kajitsu decides that she must find someone other than her own brother to love, and sets out to find someone who can purge him from her mind. The steamy substitute teacher of the calligraphy class seems perfect for the job, and before Kajitsu has had time to think, she finds herself on a date...with her hot, (and potentially dangerous) teacher...

Cast of Characters

Nitta Mano	Imanakajima Tokihito	Akai-sensei	Natsu	Kajitsu Toda
Kajitu's classmate and best friend. She has a crush on Tokihito, but knows that Tokihito has a crush on Kajitsu, making the situation more complicated than she would like.	The son of a once distinguished family, now in ruins. He has a secret crush on Kajitsu.	The substitute teacher for Kajitsu's calligraphy class. He doesn't exactly play by the rules, since he smokes on school grounds and flirts mercilessly with his student, Kajitsu.	Kajitsu's "younger" brother, also 16. The highest-ranking student at school, he gets a lot of unwanted attention from teachers and other students.	A 16-year old girl who constantly struggles to improve her pessimistic outlook on life.

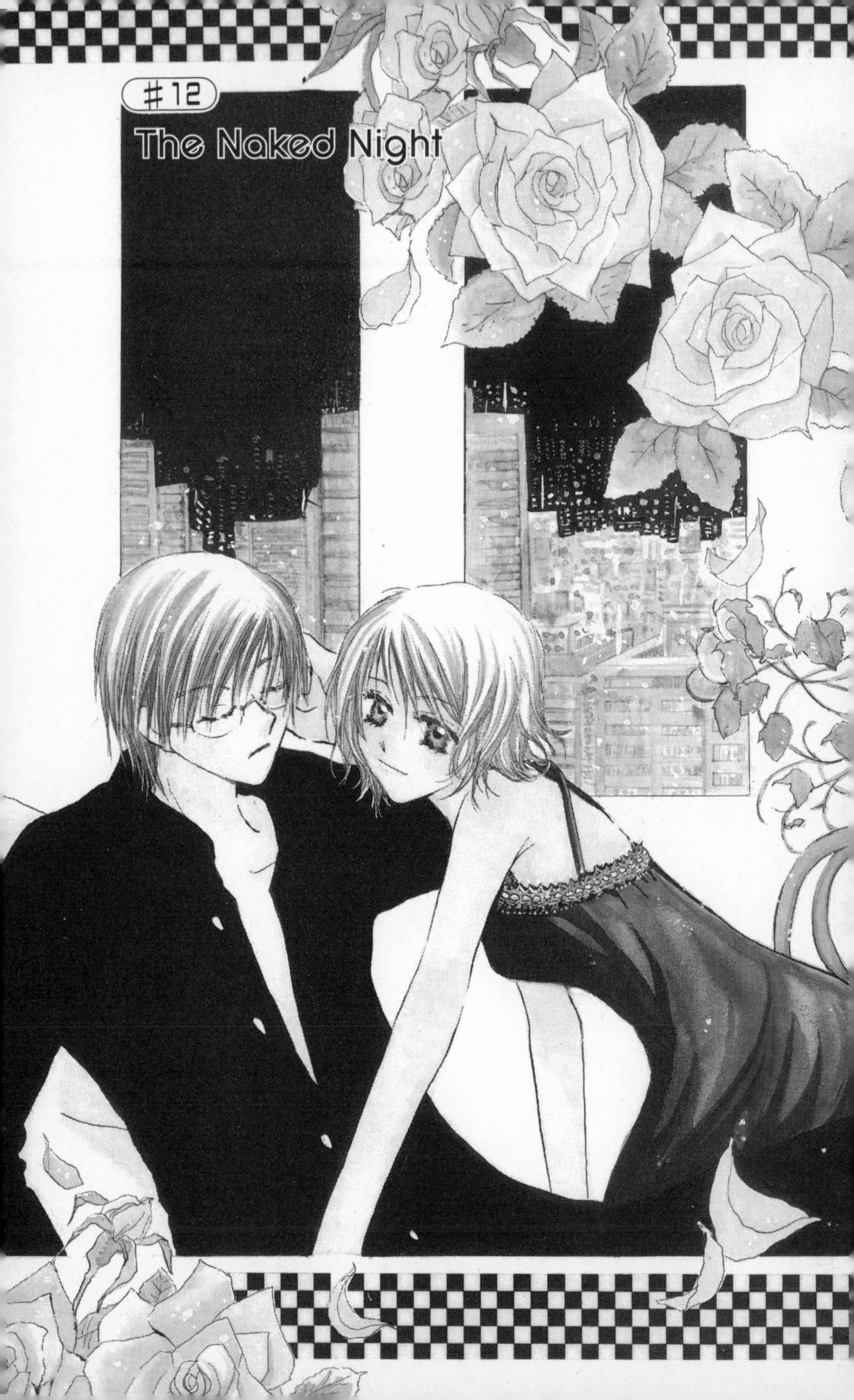
#12
The Naked Night

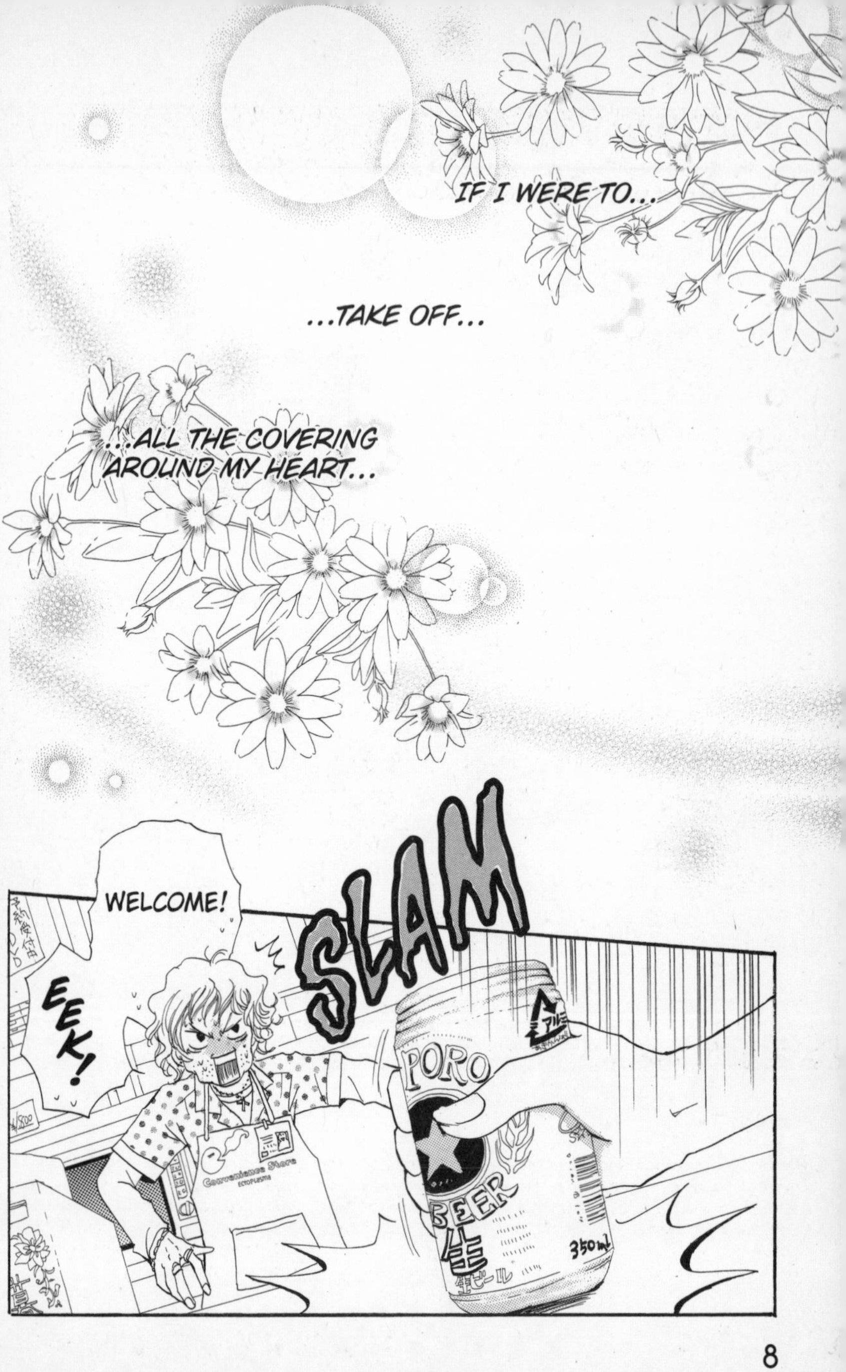
IF I WERE TO...
...TAKE OFF...
...ALL THE COVERING AROUND MY HEART...
SLAM
WELCOME!
EEK!
PORO
BEER
350ml

crossroad Chapter 12: The Naked Night

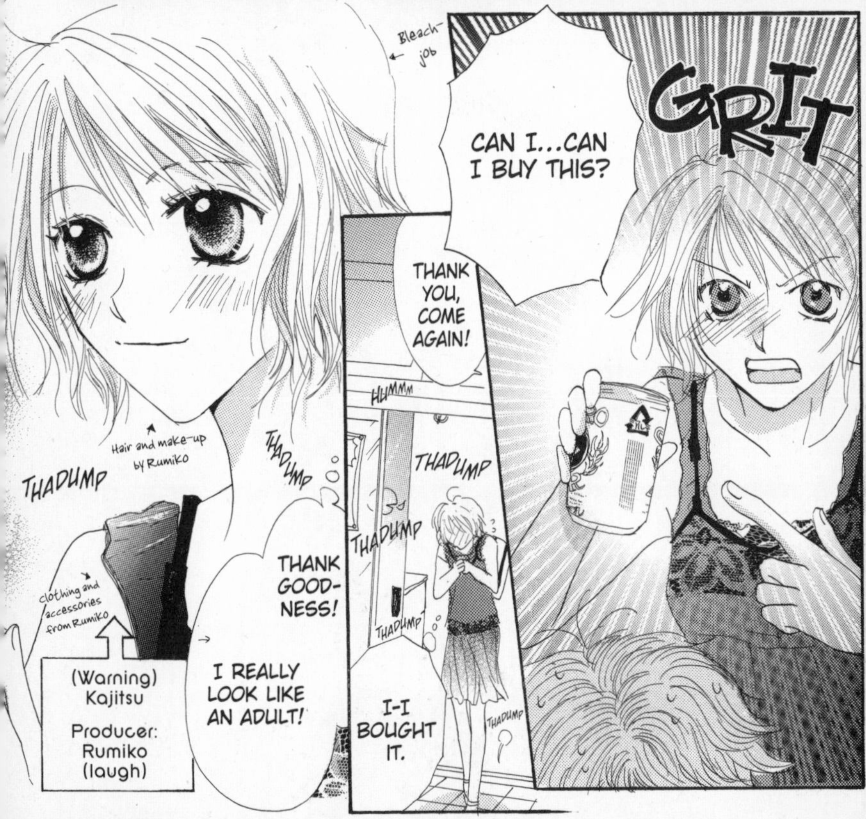
GRIT
CAN I...CAN I BUY THIS?
THANK YOU, COME AGAIN!
HUMMM
THADUMP
THADUMP
THANK GOODNESS!
THADUMP
I-I BOUGHT IT.
THADUMP
Bleach-job
Hair and make-up by Rumiko
THADUMP
THADUMP
clothing and accessories from Rumiko
I REALLY LOOK LIKE AN ADULT!
(Warning) Kajitsu
Producer: Rumiko (laugh)

Nostalgia Time 1

I'm the kind of person who likes drawing night scenes, but this time around it was pretty hard. I wanted Kajitsu's clothing to look like something Rumiko would wear, so I kept muttering to myself, "Think Rumiko!" as I drew her. Later on, I was surprised to see the actor Sugimoto Sai-san wearing practically the same thing! Rumiko and Sai-san...I can totally see the resemblance (laugh). Kajitsu usually spends all her time complaining, and only at times like these (when she desperately needs feminine advice) does she listen to her step-mother. That's just how Kajitsu is (laugh).

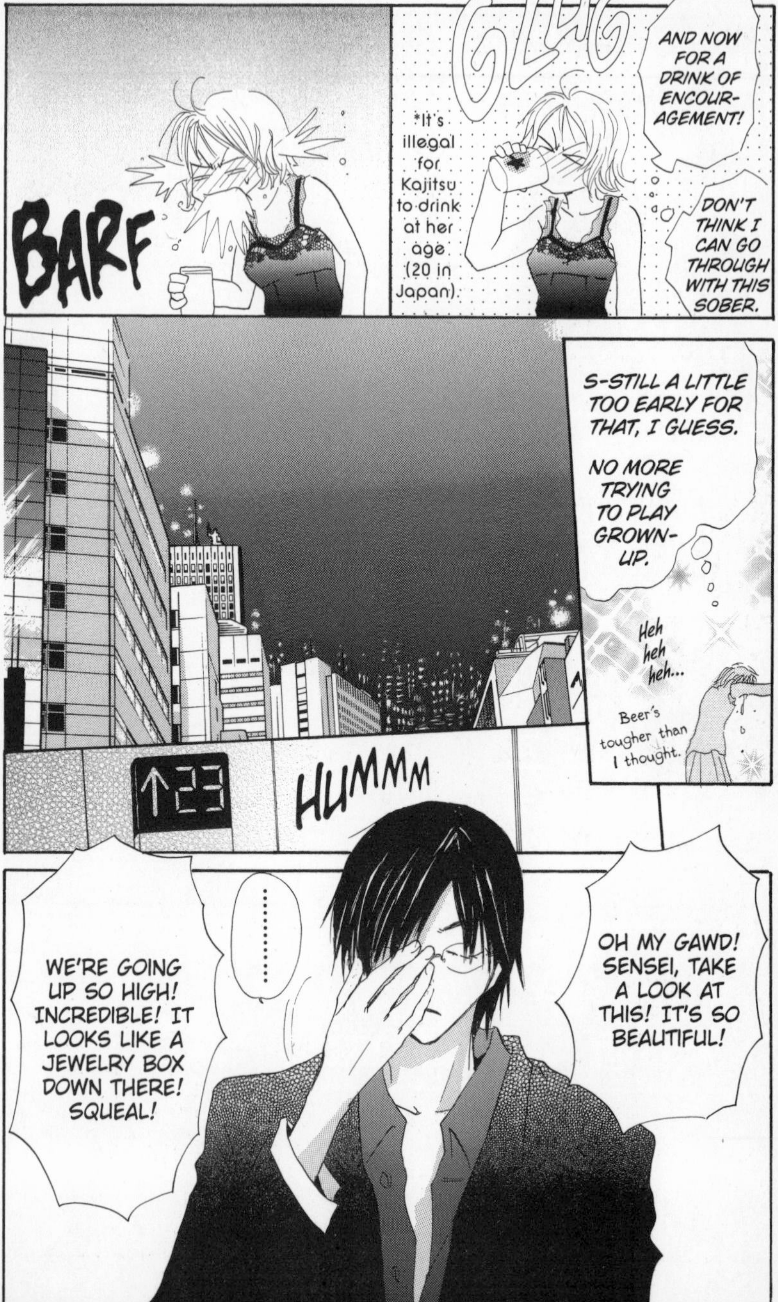
GLUG
AND NOW FOR A DRINK OF ENCOUR-AGEMENT!
DON'T THINK I CAN GO THROUGH WITH THIS SOBER.
*It's illegal for Kajitsu to drink at her age (20 in Japan).
BARF
S-STILL A LITTLE TOO EARLY FOR THAT, I GUESS.
NO MORE TRYING TO PLAY GROWN-UP.
Heh heh heh...
Beer's tougher than I thought.
↑23
HUMMM
OH MY GAWD! SENSEI, TAKE A LOOK AT THIS! IT'S SO BEAUTIFUL!
......
WE'RE GOING UP SO HIGH! INCREDIBLE! IT LOOKS LIKE A JEWELRY BOX DOWN THERE! SQUEAL!

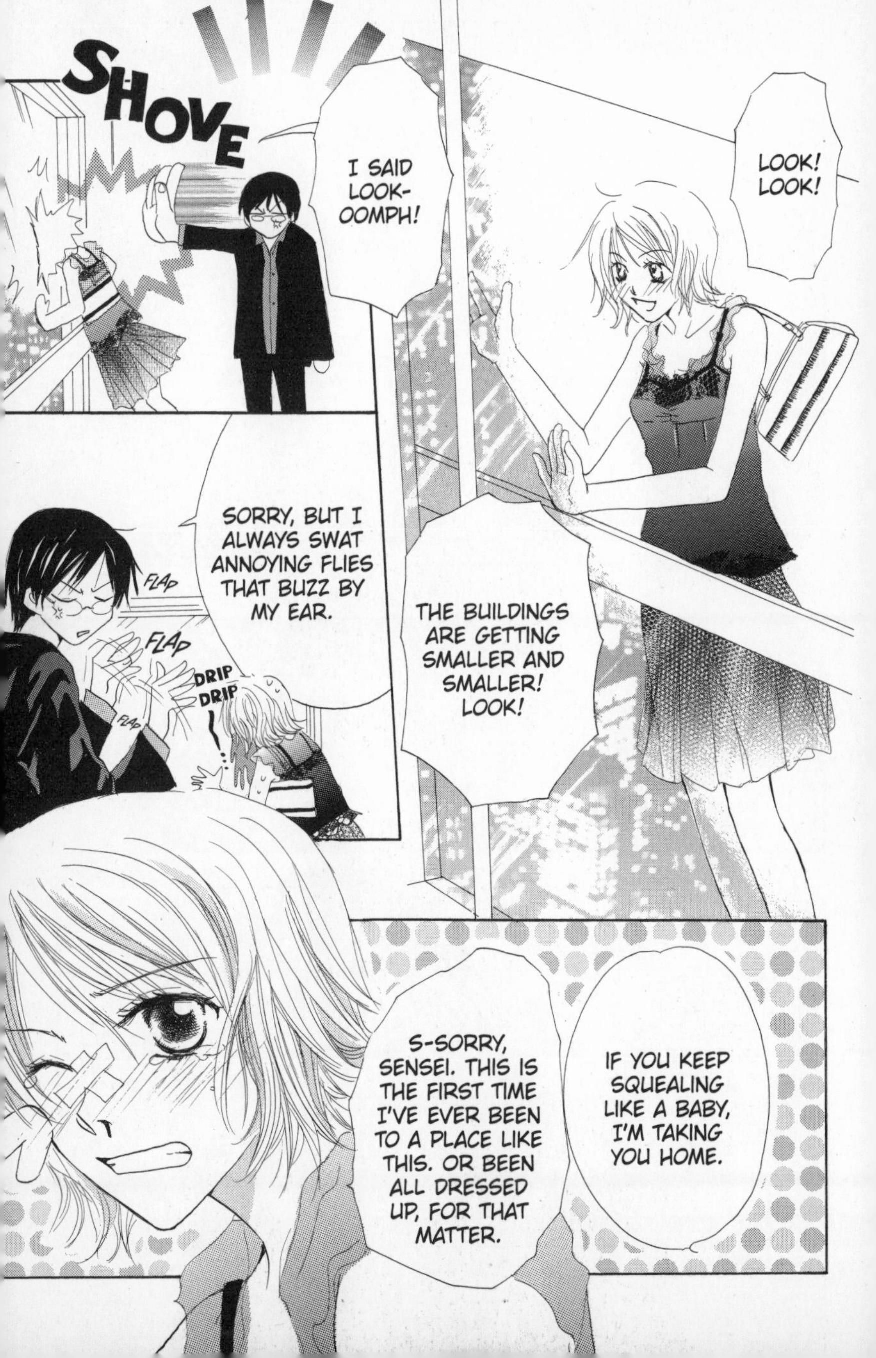

LOOK! LOOK!
THE BUILDINGS ARE GETTING SMALLER AND SMALLER! LOOK!
I SAID LOOK-OOMPH!
SHOVE
SORRY, BUT I ALWAYS SWAT ANNOYING FLIES THAT BUZZ BY MY EAR.
FLAP
FLAP
DRIP DRIP
FLAP
IF YOU KEEP SQUEALING LIKE A BABY, I'M TAKING YOU HOME.
S-SORRY, SENSEI. THIS IS THE FIRST TIME I'VE EVER BEEN TO A PLACE LIKE THIS. OR BEEN ALL DRESSED UP, FOR THAT MATTER.

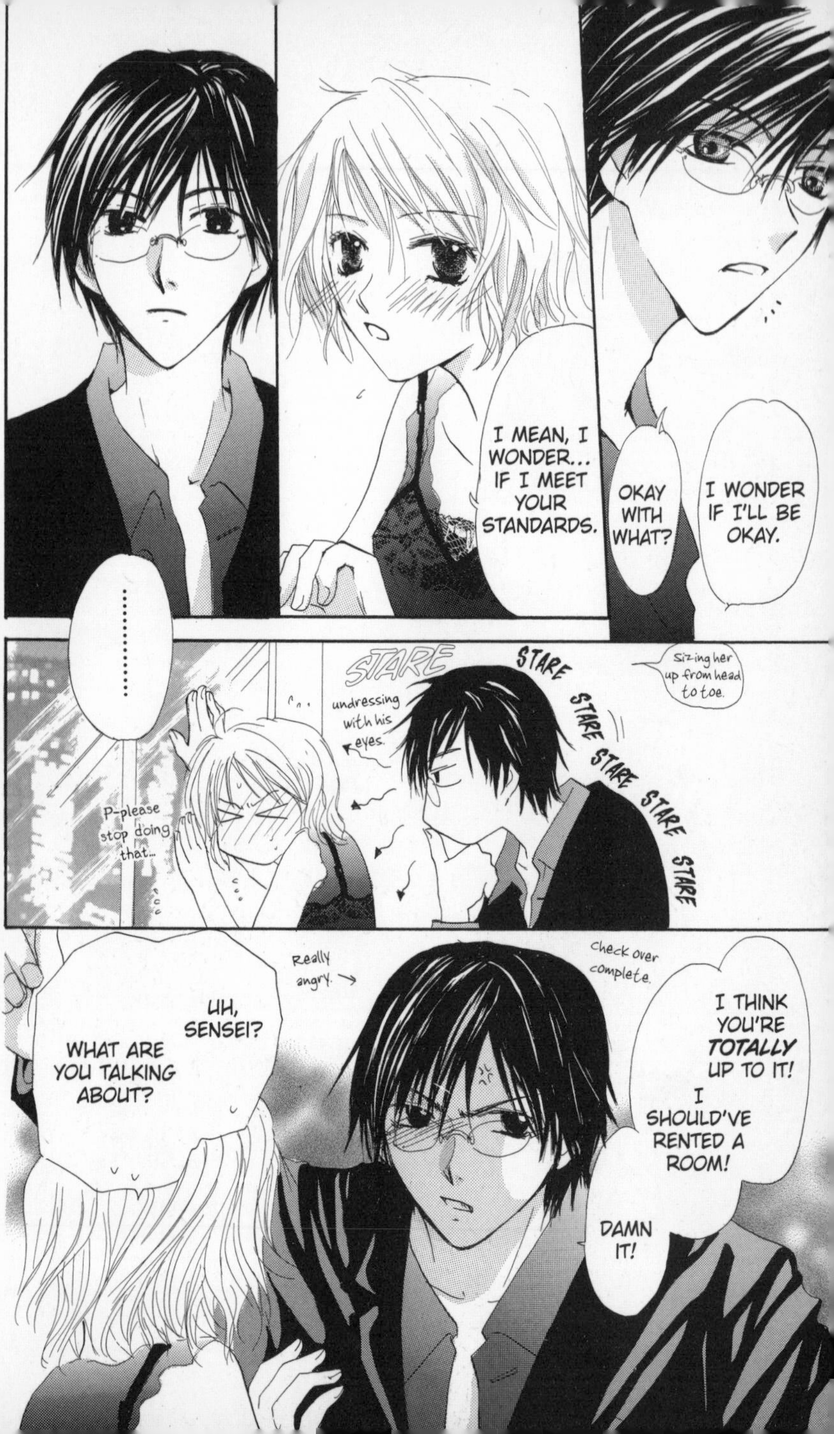
I WONDER IF I'LL BE OKAY.
OKAY WITH WHAT?
I MEAN, I WONDER... IF I MEET YOUR STANDARDS.
......
Sizing her up from head to toe.
STARE
STARE
STARE
STARE
STARE
STARE
undressing with his eyes.
P-please stop doing that...
I THINK YOU'RE ***TOTALLY*** UP TO IT!
I SHOULD'VE RENTED A ROOM!
DAMN IT!
Check over complete.
Really angry.
UH, SENSEI?
WHAT ARE YOU TALKING ABOUT?

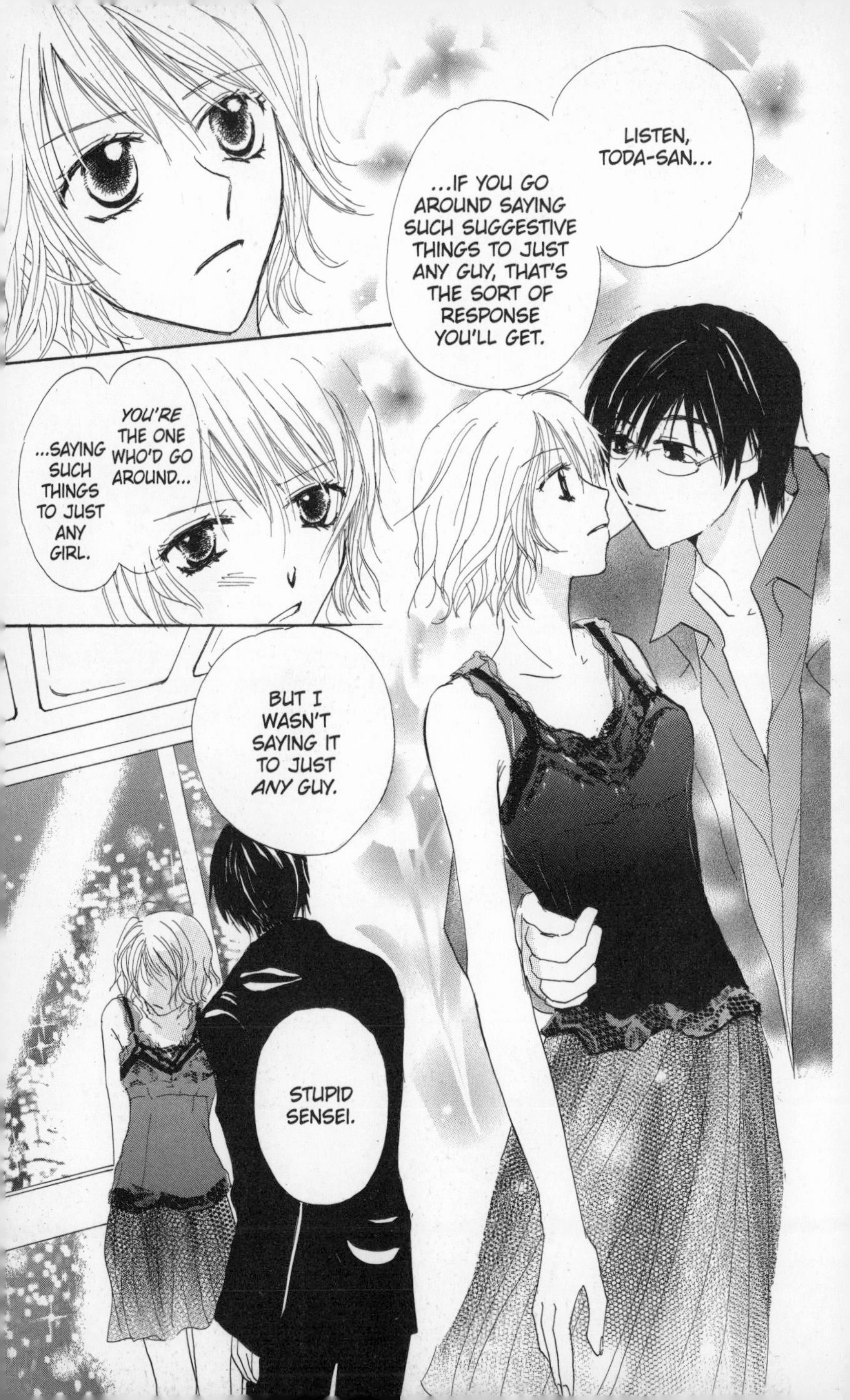
LISTEN, TODA-SAN...
...IF YOU GO AROUND SAYING SUCH SUGGESTIVE THINGS TO JUST ANY GUY, THAT'S THE SORT OF RESPONSE YOU'LL GET.
YOU'RE THE ONE WHO'D GO AROUND... ...SAYING SUCH THINGS TO JUST ANY GIRL.
BUT I WASN'T SAYING IT TO JUST *ANY GUY.*
STUPID SENSEI.

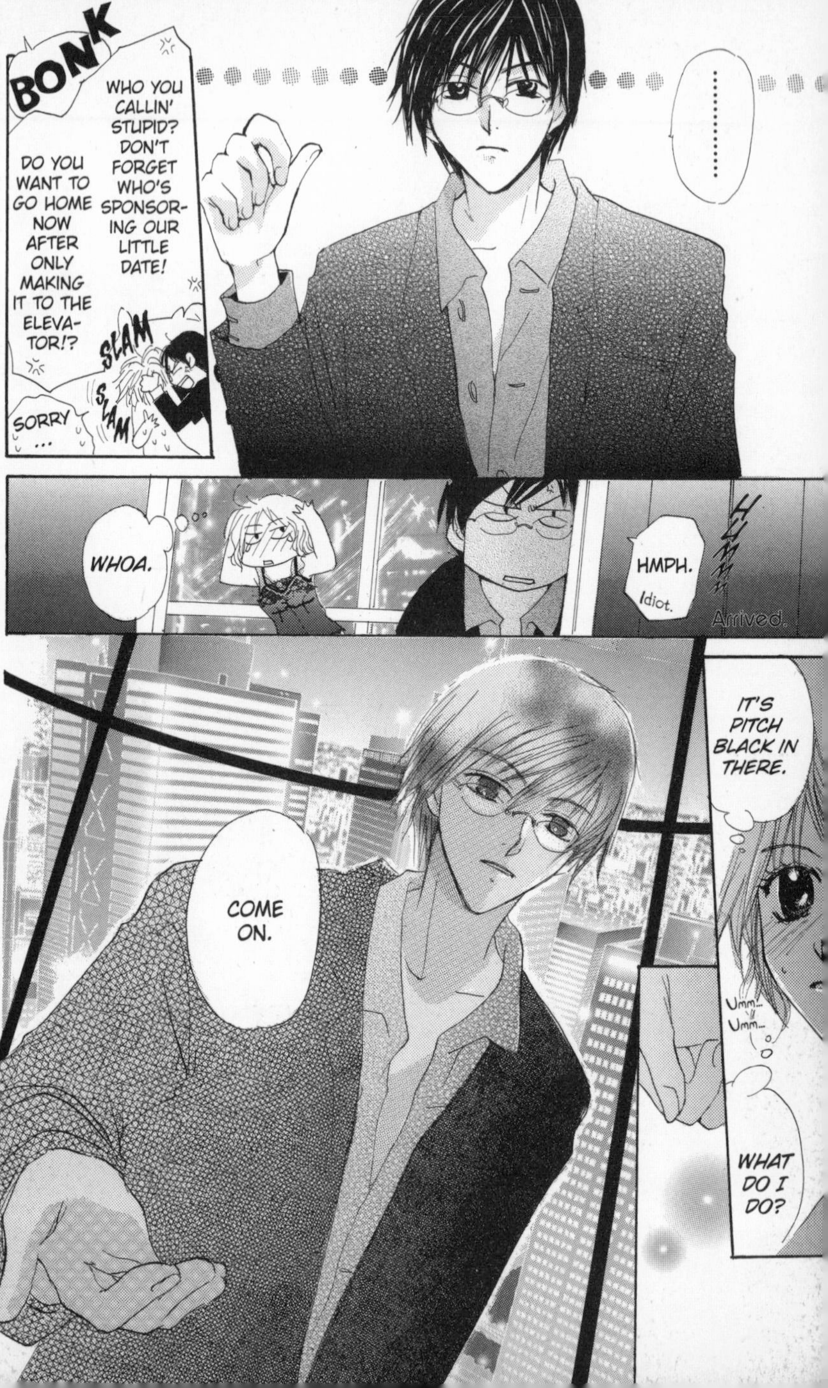
......
BONK
WHO YOU CALLIN' STUPID? DON'T FORGET WHO'S SPONSORING OUR LITTLE DATE!
DO YOU WANT TO GO HOME NOW AFTER ONLY MAKING IT TO THE ELEVATOR!?
SLAM
SLAM
SLAM
SORRY ...
HUMMM
Arrived.
HMPH.
Idiot.
WHOA.
IT'S PITCH BLACK IN THERE.
Umm... Umm...
WHAT DO I DO?
COME ON.

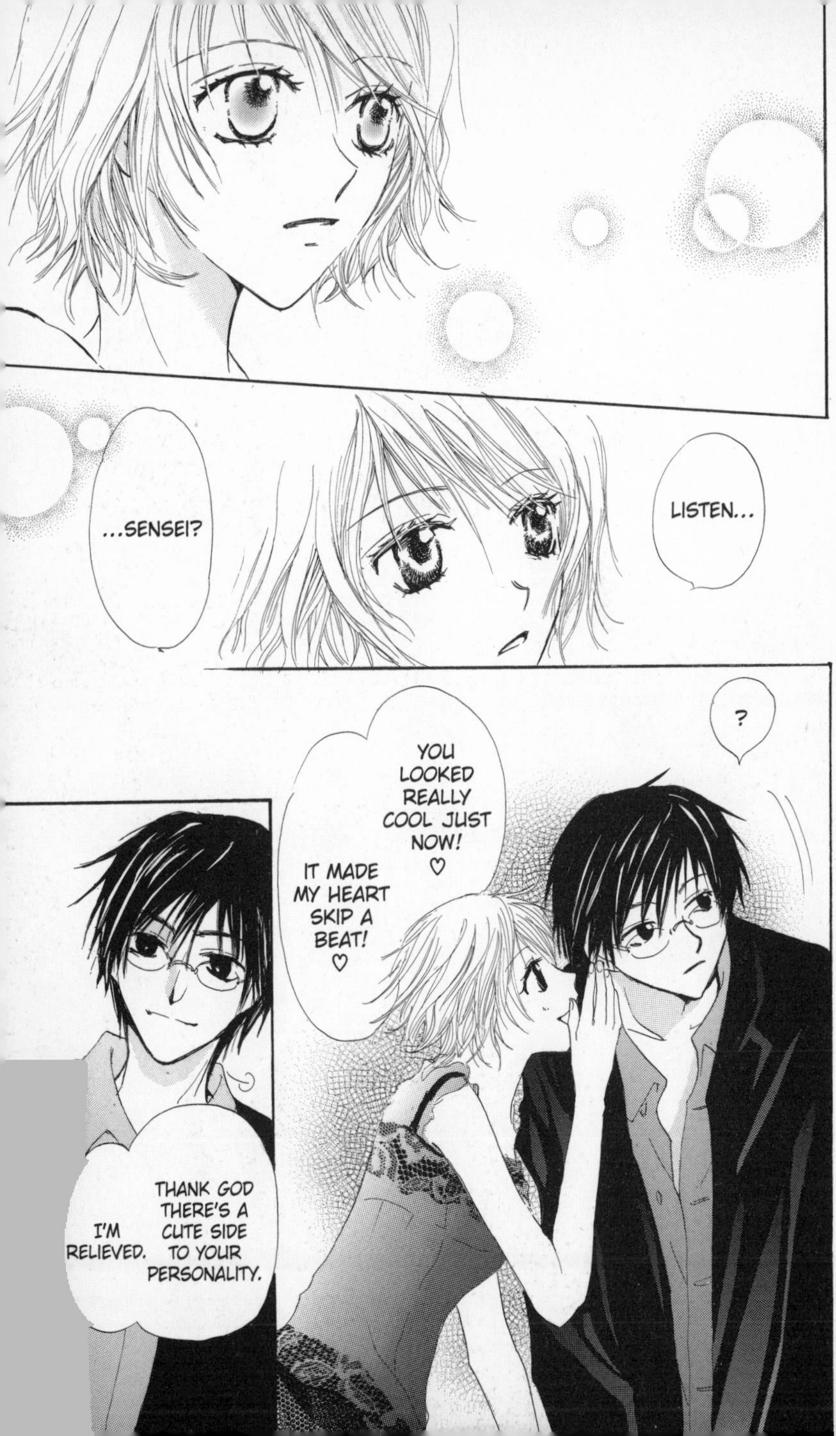
LISTEN...
...SENSEI?
?
YOU LOOKED REALLY COOL JUST NOW! ♡ IT MADE MY HEART SKIP A BEAT! ♡
THANK GOD THERE'S A CUTE SIDE TO YOUR PERSONALITY.
I'M RELIEVED.

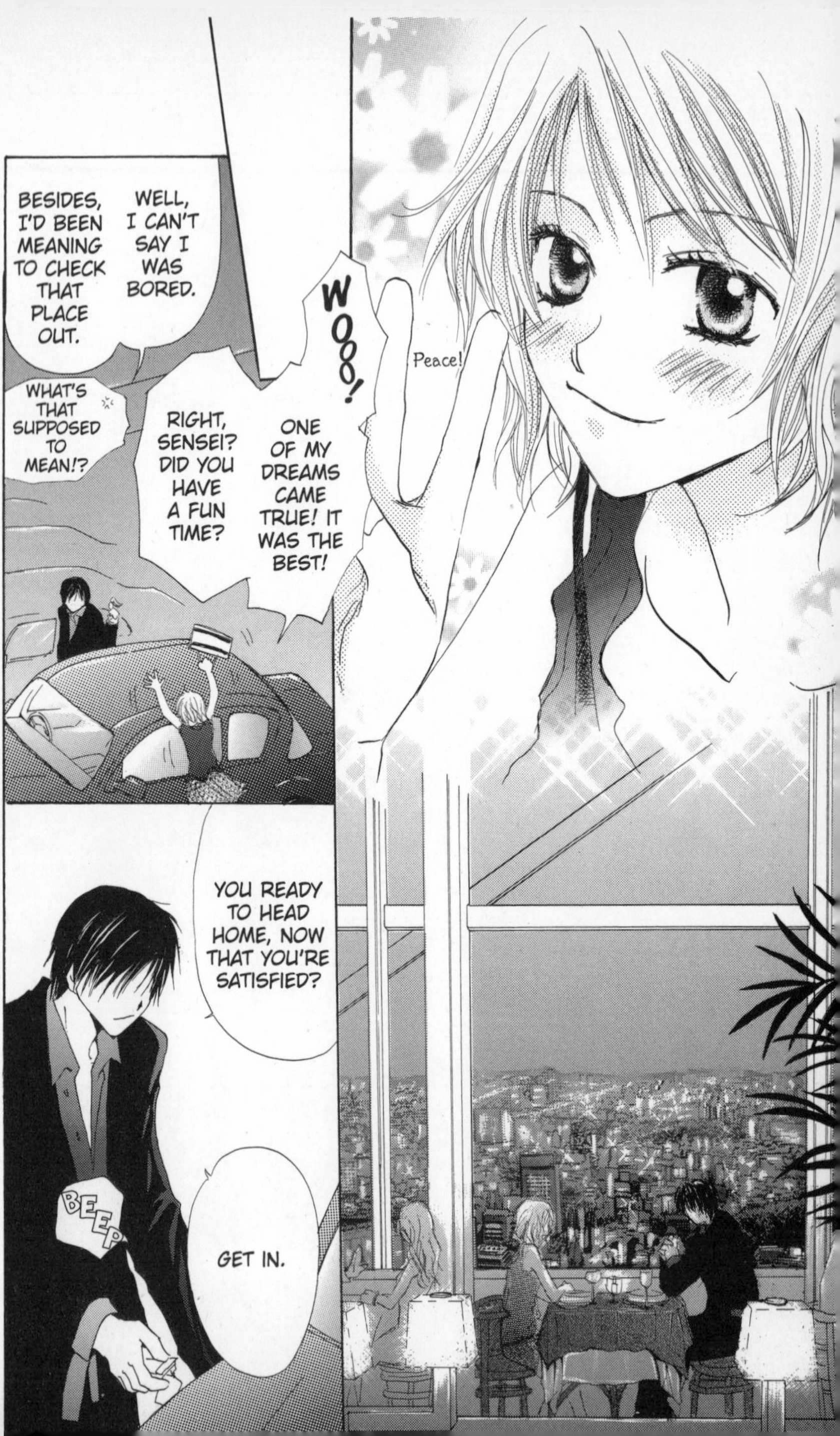
WOOOO!
Peace!
ONE OF MY DREAMS CAME TRUE! IT WAS THE BEST!
RIGHT, SENSEI? DID YOU HAVE A FUN TIME?
WELL, I CAN'T SAY I WAS BORED.
BESIDES, I'D BEEN MEANING TO CHECK THAT PLACE OUT.
WHAT'S THAT SUPPOSED TO MEAN!?
YOU READY TO HEAD HOME, NOW THAT YOU'RE SATISFIED?
BEEP
GET IN.

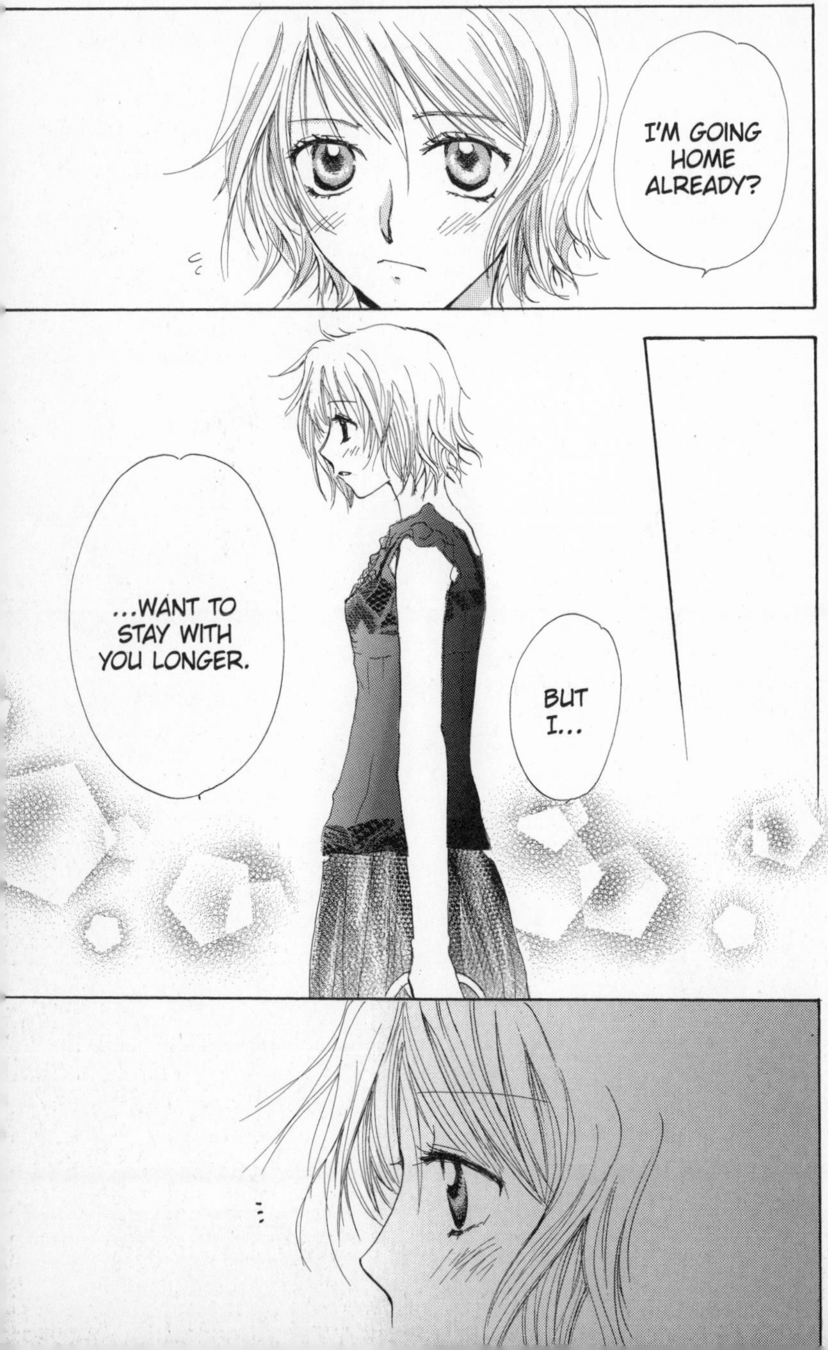
I'M GOING HOME ALREADY?
BUT I...
...WANT TO STAY WITH YOU LONGER.

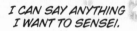

I CAN SAY ANYTHING I WANT TO SENSEI.

AND HE JUST LISTENS QUIETLY AS I TALK.

YOU'RE A GOOD KID.

I KEEP CONFESSING EVERYTHING TO HIM.

IT'S LIKE I'M TAKING OFF MY CLOTHES...

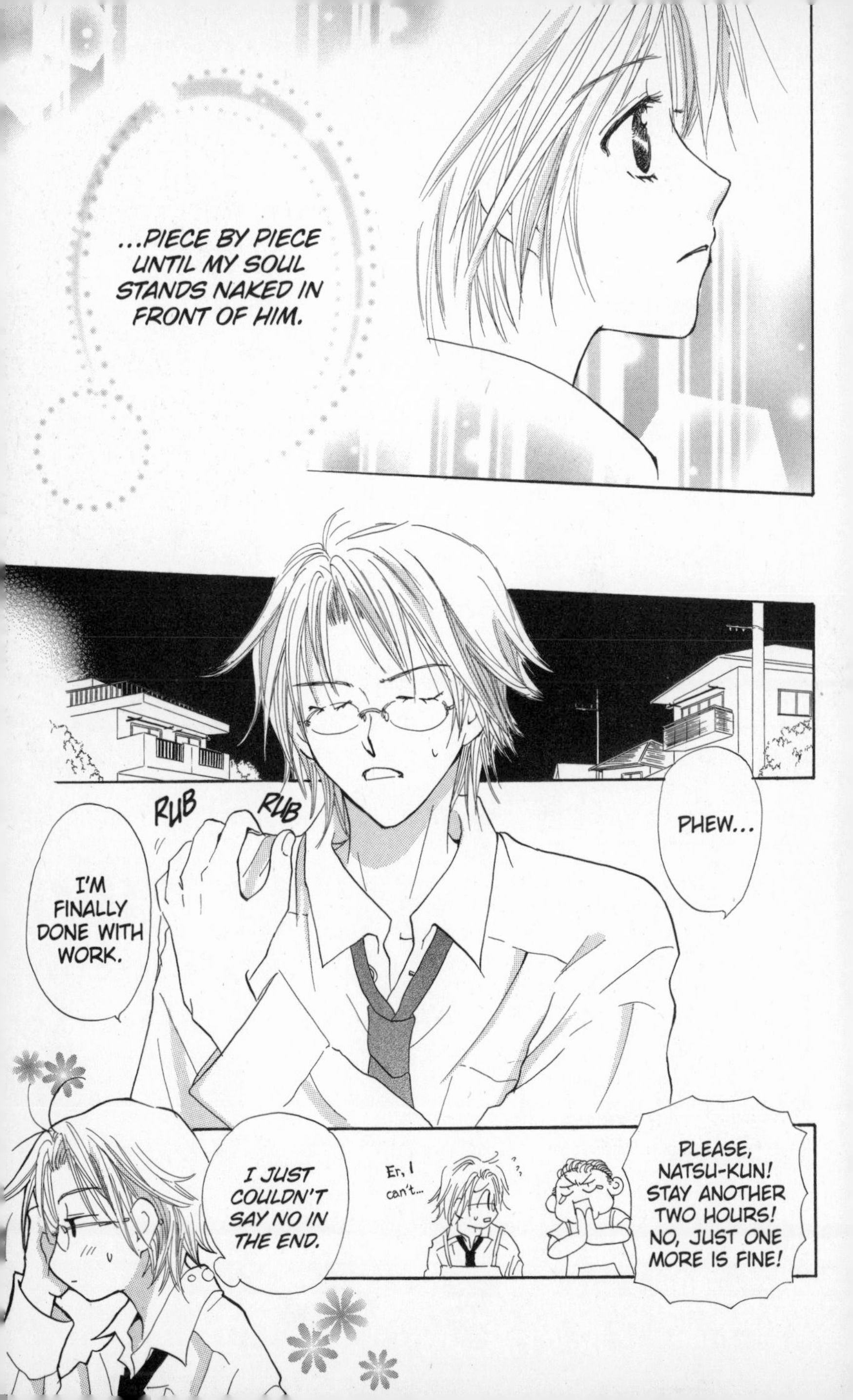
...PIECE BY PIECE UNTIL MY SOUL STANDS NAKED IN FRONT OF HIM.
PHEW...
RUB RUB
I'M FINALLY DONE WITH WORK.
PLEASE, NATSU-KUN! STAY ANOTHER TWO HOURS! NO, JUST ONE MORE IS FINE!
Er, I can't...
I JUST COULDN'T SAY NO IN THE END.

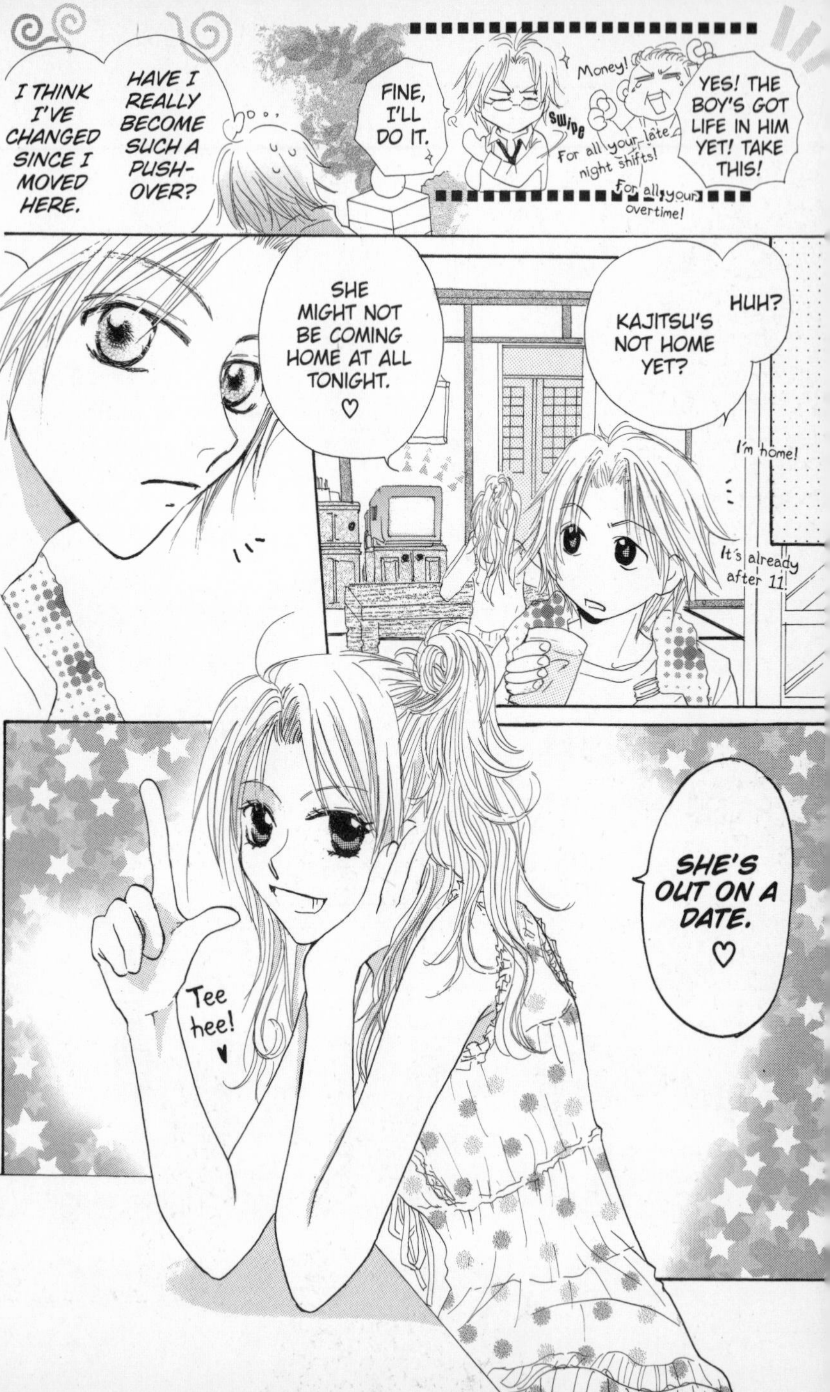
YES! THE BOY'S GOT LIFE IN HIM YET! TAKE THIS!
Money!
For all your late night shifts!
For all your overtime!
Swipe
FINE, I'LL DO IT.
HAVE I REALLY BECOME SUCH A PUSH-OVER?
I THINK I'VE CHANGED SINCE I MOVED HERE.
I'm home!
HUH?
KAJITSU'S NOT HOME YET?
It's already after 11!
SHE MIGHT NOT BE COMING HOME AT ALL TONIGHT. ♡
SHE'S OUT ON A DATE. ♡
Tee hee! ♥

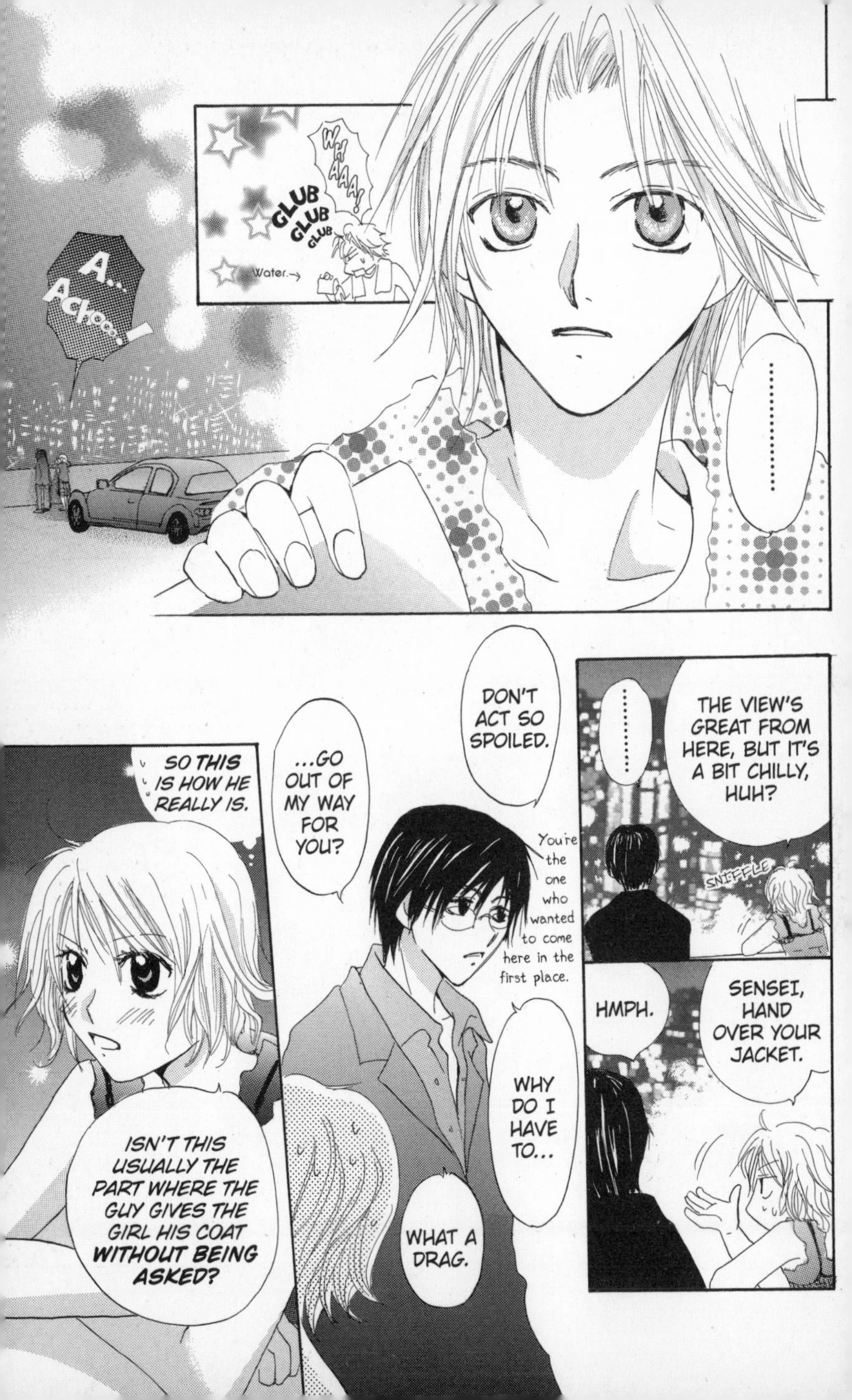
......
WHAAAA!
GLUB GLUB GLUB
Water.→
A... Achooo...!
THE VIEW'S GREAT FROM HERE, BUT IT'S A BIT CHILLY, HUH?
......
SNIFFLE
SENSEI, HAND OVER YOUR JACKET.
HMPH.
WHY DO I HAVE TO...
WHAT A DRAG.
ISN'T THIS USUALLY THE PART WHERE THE GUY GIVES THE GIRL HIS COAT WITHOUT BEING ASKED?
DON'T ACT SO SPOILED.
...GO OUT OF MY WAY FOR YOU?
You're the one who wanted to come here in the first place.
SO THIS IS HOW HE REALLY IS.

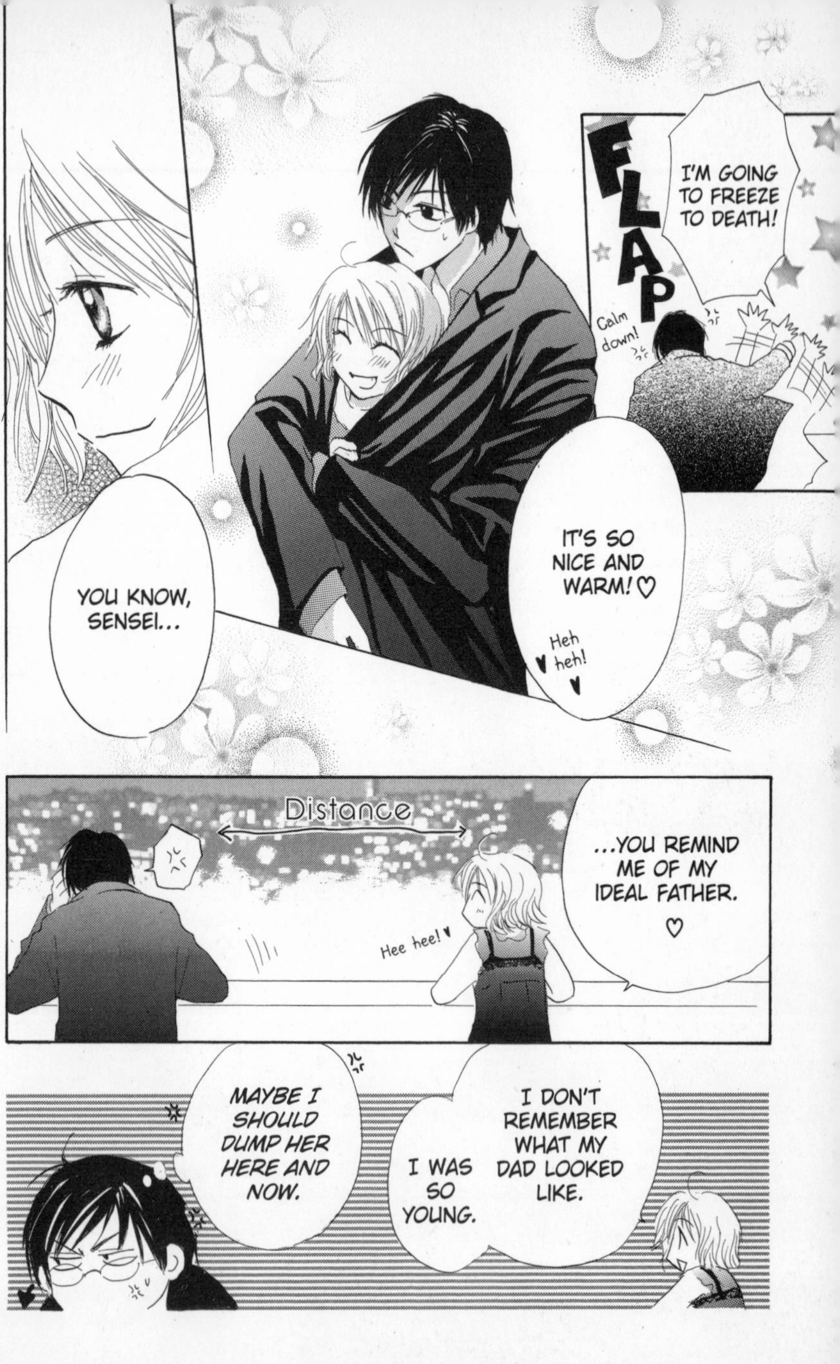
I'M GOING TO FREEZE TO DEATH!
FLAP
Calm down!
IT'S SO NICE AND WARM! ♡
Heh heh!
YOU KNOW, SENSEI...
...YOU REMIND ME OF MY IDEAL FATHER. ♡
Distance
Hee hee!
I DON'T REMEMBER WHAT MY DAD LOOKED LIKE.
I WAS SO YOUNG.
MAYBE I SHOULD DUMP HER HERE AND NOW.

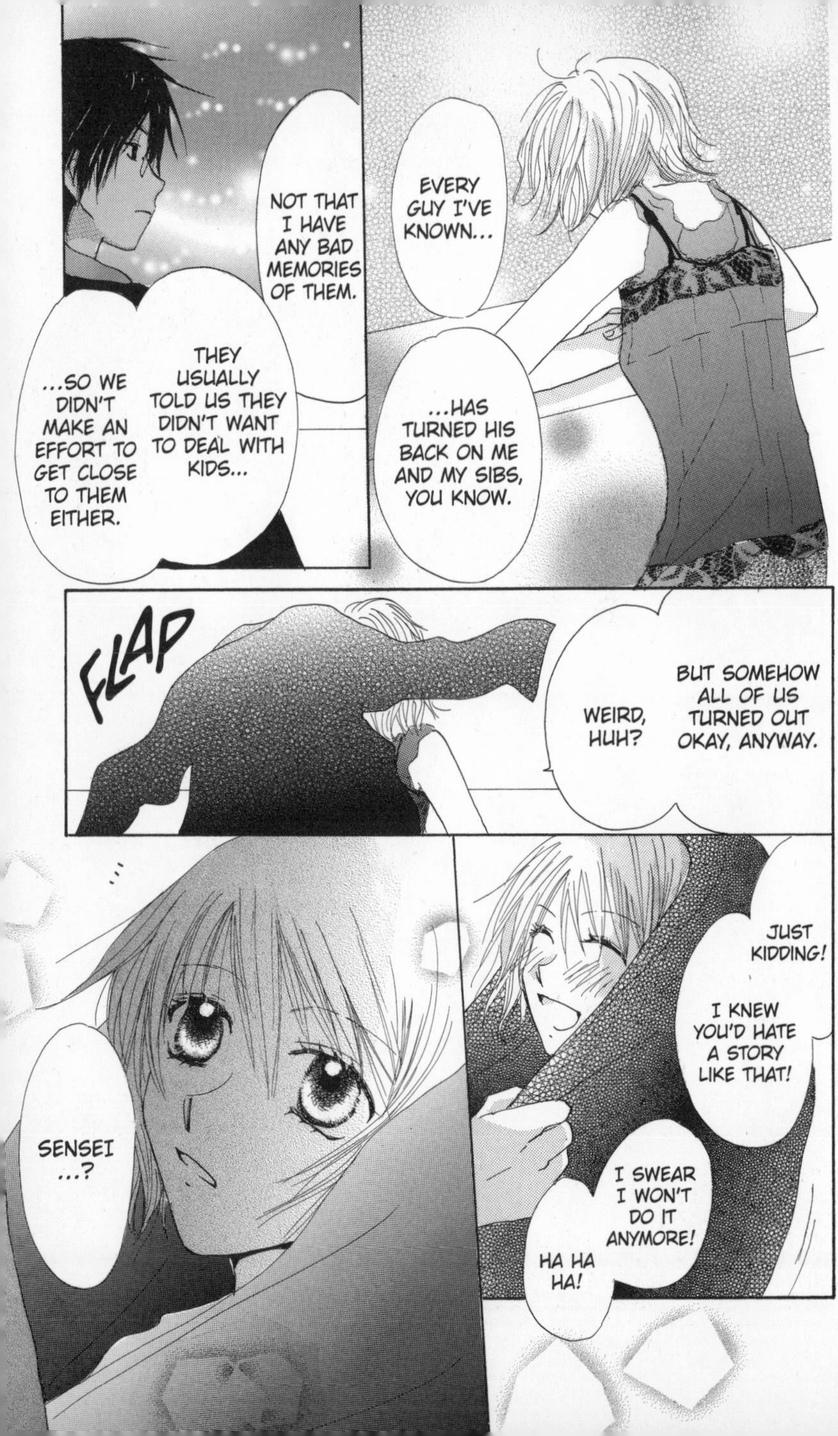
EVERY GUY I'VE KNOWN...
...HAS TURNED HIS BACK ON ME AND MY SIBS, YOU KNOW.
NOT THAT I HAVE ANY BAD MEMORIES OF THEM.
THEY USUALLY TOLD US THEY DIDN'T WANT TO DEAL WITH KIDS...
...SO WE DIDN'T MAKE AN EFFORT TO GET CLOSE TO THEM EITHER.
BUT SOMEHOW ALL OF US TURNED OUT OKAY, ANYWAY.
WEIRD, HUH?
FLAP
JUST KIDDING!
I KNEW YOU'D HATE A STORY LIKE THAT!
I SWEAR I WON'T DO IT ANYMORE!
HA HA HA!
...
SENSEI ...?

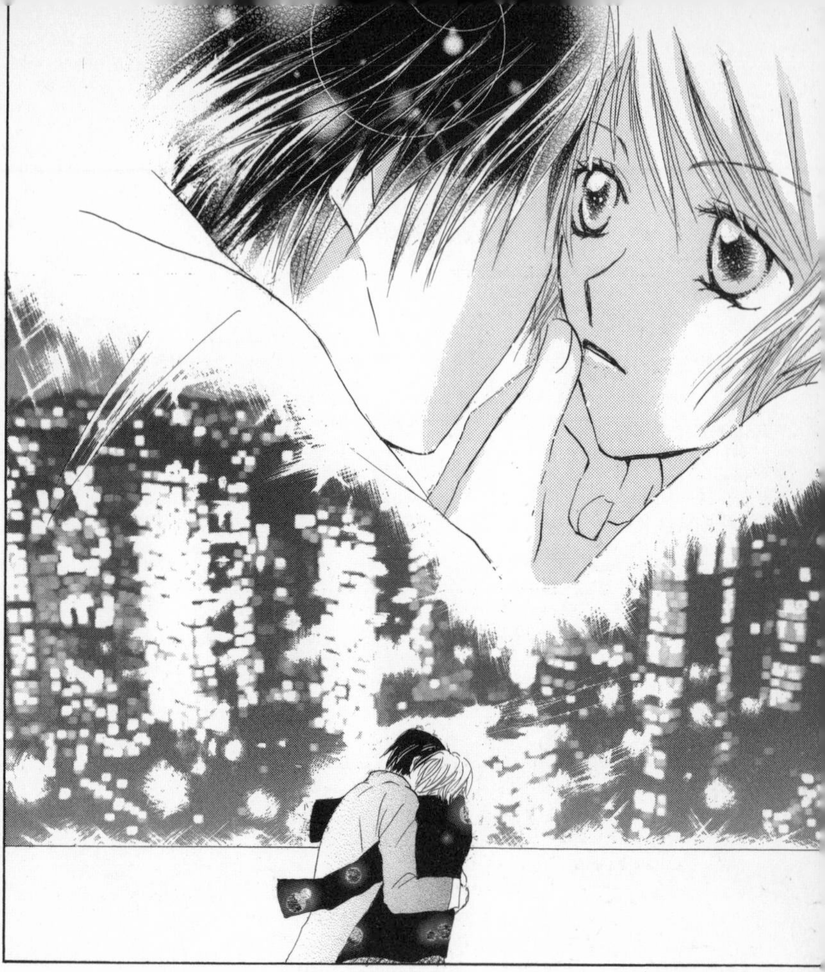

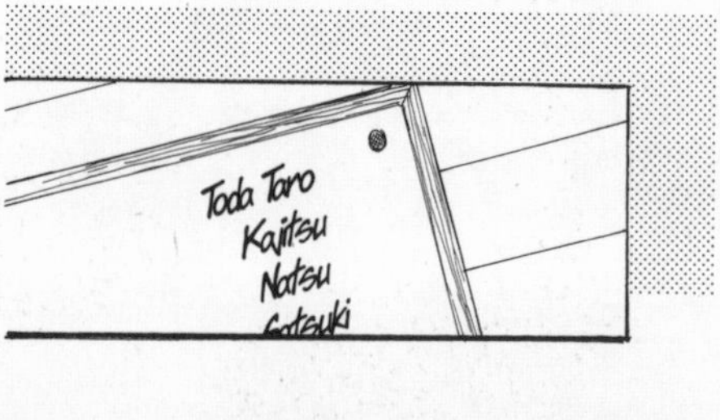
Toda Taro
Kajitsu
Natsu
Gotsuki

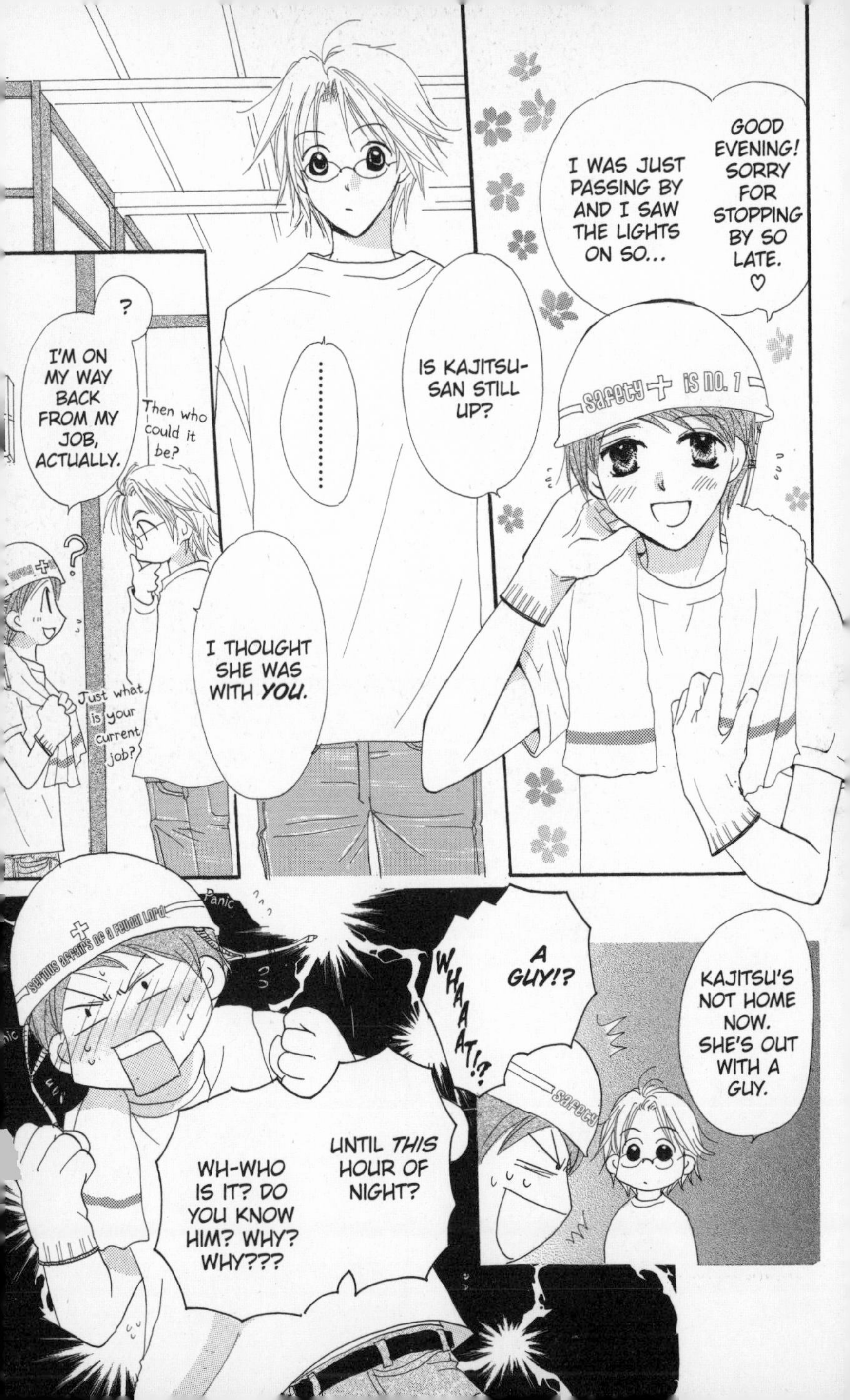
GOOD EVENING! SORRY FOR STOPPING BY SO LATE. ♡
I WAS JUST PASSING BY AND I SAW THE LIGHTS ON SO...
safety + is no. 1
IS KAJITSU-SAN STILL UP?
......
I THOUGHT SHE WAS WITH *YOU*.
?
I'M ON MY WAY BACK FROM MY JOB, ACTUALLY.
Then who could it be?
Just what is your current job?
KAJITSU'S NOT HOME NOW. SHE'S OUT WITH A GUY.
A GUY!?
safety
WHAAAAT!?
Panic
+ serious affairs of a feudal lord
UNTIL *THIS* HOUR OF NIGHT?
WH-WHO IS IT? DO YOU KNOW HIM? WHY? WHY???

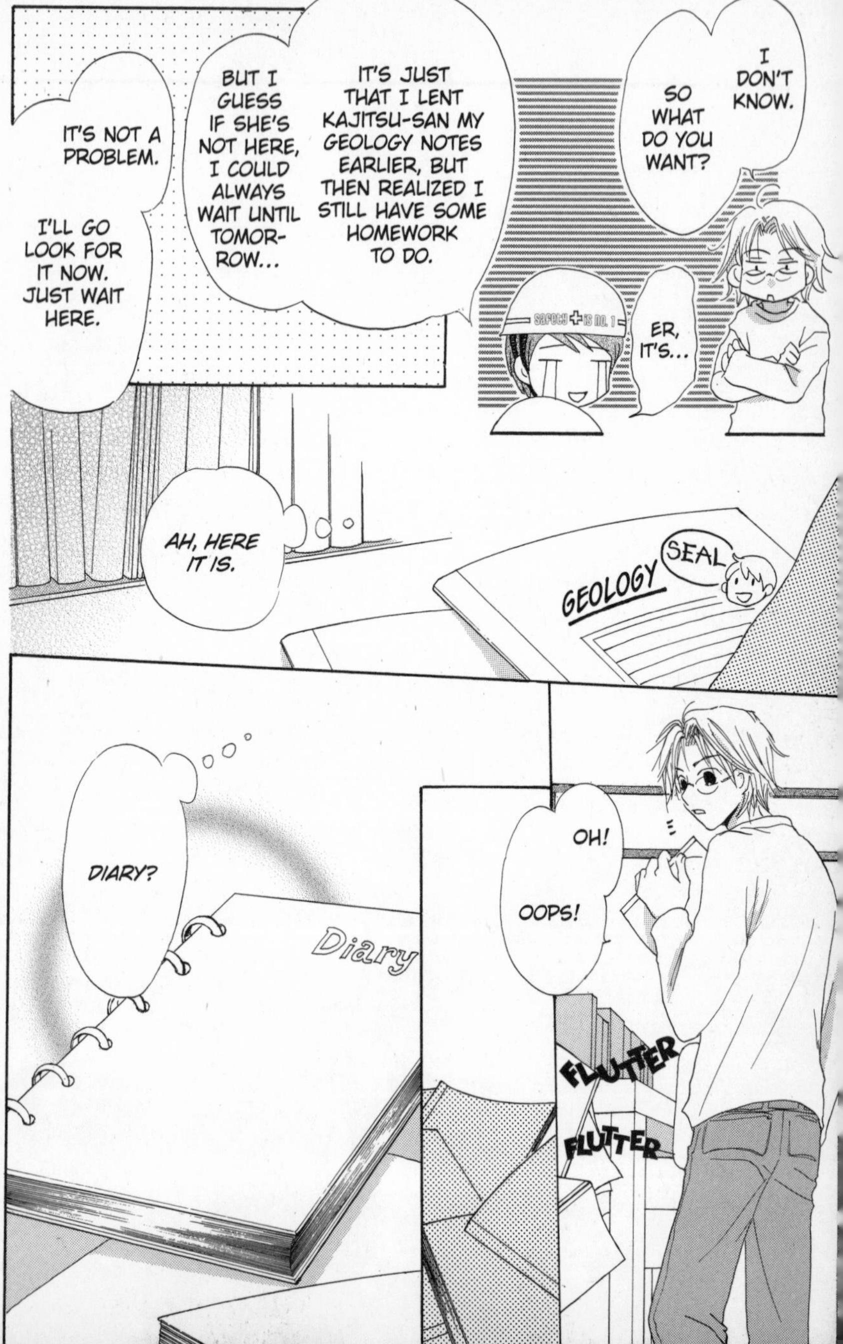
I DON'T KNOW.
SO WHAT DO YOU WANT?
safety is no. 1
ER, IT'S...
IT'S JUST THAT I LENT KAJITSU-SAN MY GEOLOGY NOTES EARLIER, BUT THEN REALIZED I STILL HAVE SOME HOMEWORK TO DO.
BUT I GUESS IF SHE'S NOT HERE, I COULD ALWAYS WAIT UNTIL TOMOR-ROW...
IT'S NOT A PROBLEM.
I'LL GO LOOK FOR IT NOW. JUST WAIT HERE.
SEAL
GEOLOGY
AH, HERE IT IS.
OH!
OOPS!
FLUTTER
FLUTTER
DIARY?
Diary

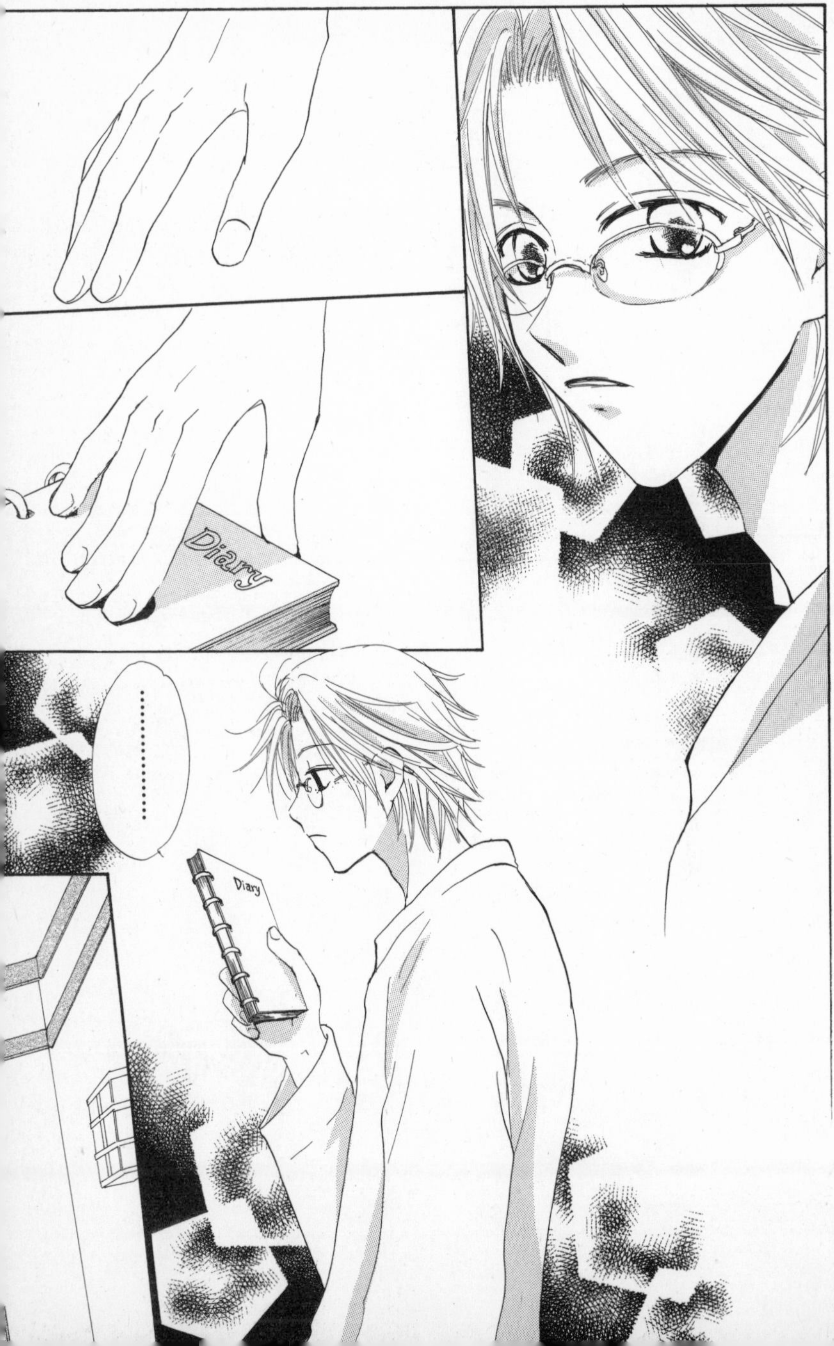
Diary
…………
Diary

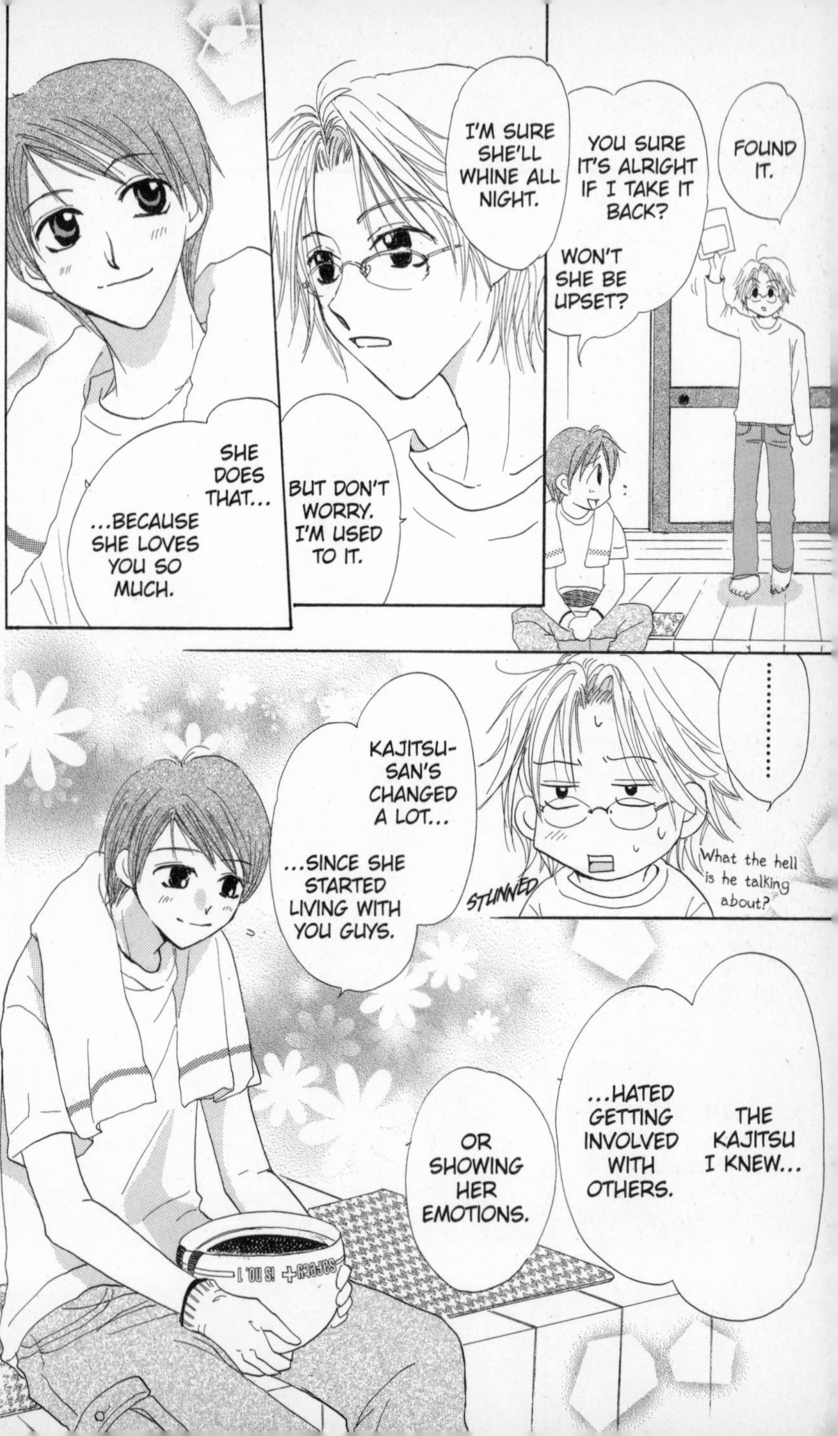
FOUND IT.
YOU SURE IT'S ALRIGHT IF I TAKE IT BACK?
WON'T SHE BE UPSET?
I'M SURE SHE'LL WHINE ALL NIGHT.
BUT DON'T WORRY. I'M USED TO IT.
SHE DOES THAT...
...BECAUSE SHE LOVES YOU SO MUCH.
......
What the hell is he talking about?
STUNNED
KAJITSU-SAN'S CHANGED A LOT...
...SINCE SHE STARTED LIVING WITH YOU GUYS.
THE KAJITSU I KNEW...
...HATED GETTING INVOLVED WITH OTHERS.
OR SHOWING HER EMOTIONS.

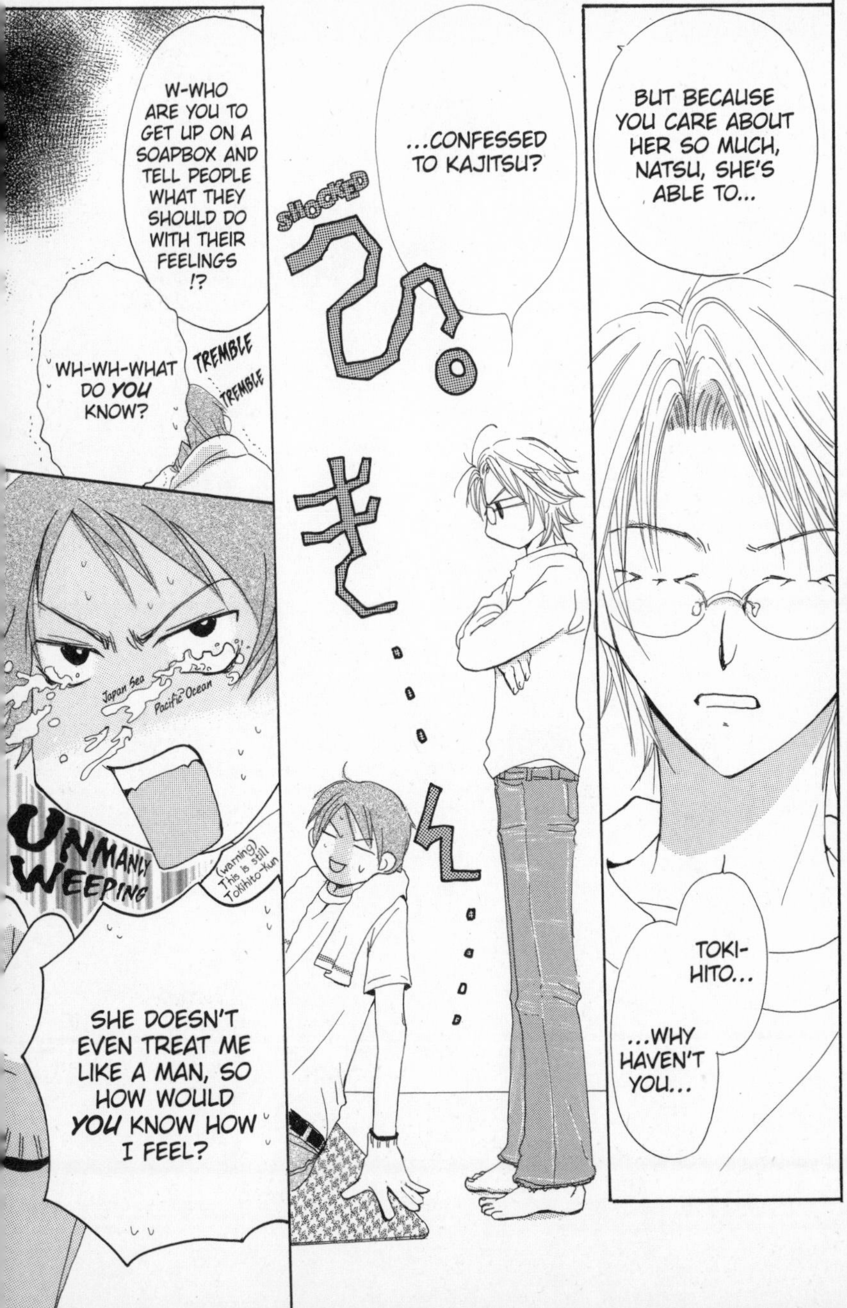
BUT BECAUSE YOU CARE ABOUT HER SO MUCH, NATSU, SHE'S ABLE TO...
TOKI-HITO...
...WHY HAVEN'T YOU...
...CONFESSED TO KAJITSU?
SHOCKED
ぴき……ん
W-WHO ARE YOU TO GET UP ON A SOAPBOX AND TELL PEOPLE WHAT THEY SHOULD DO WITH THEIR FEELINGS!?
WH-WH-WHAT DO *YOU* KNOW?
TREMBLE
TREMBLE
Japan Sea
Pacific Ocean
UNMANLY WEEPING
(warning) This is still Tokihito-Kun
SHE DOESN'T EVEN TREAT ME LIKE A MAN, SO HOW WOULD *YOU* KNOW HOW I FEEL?

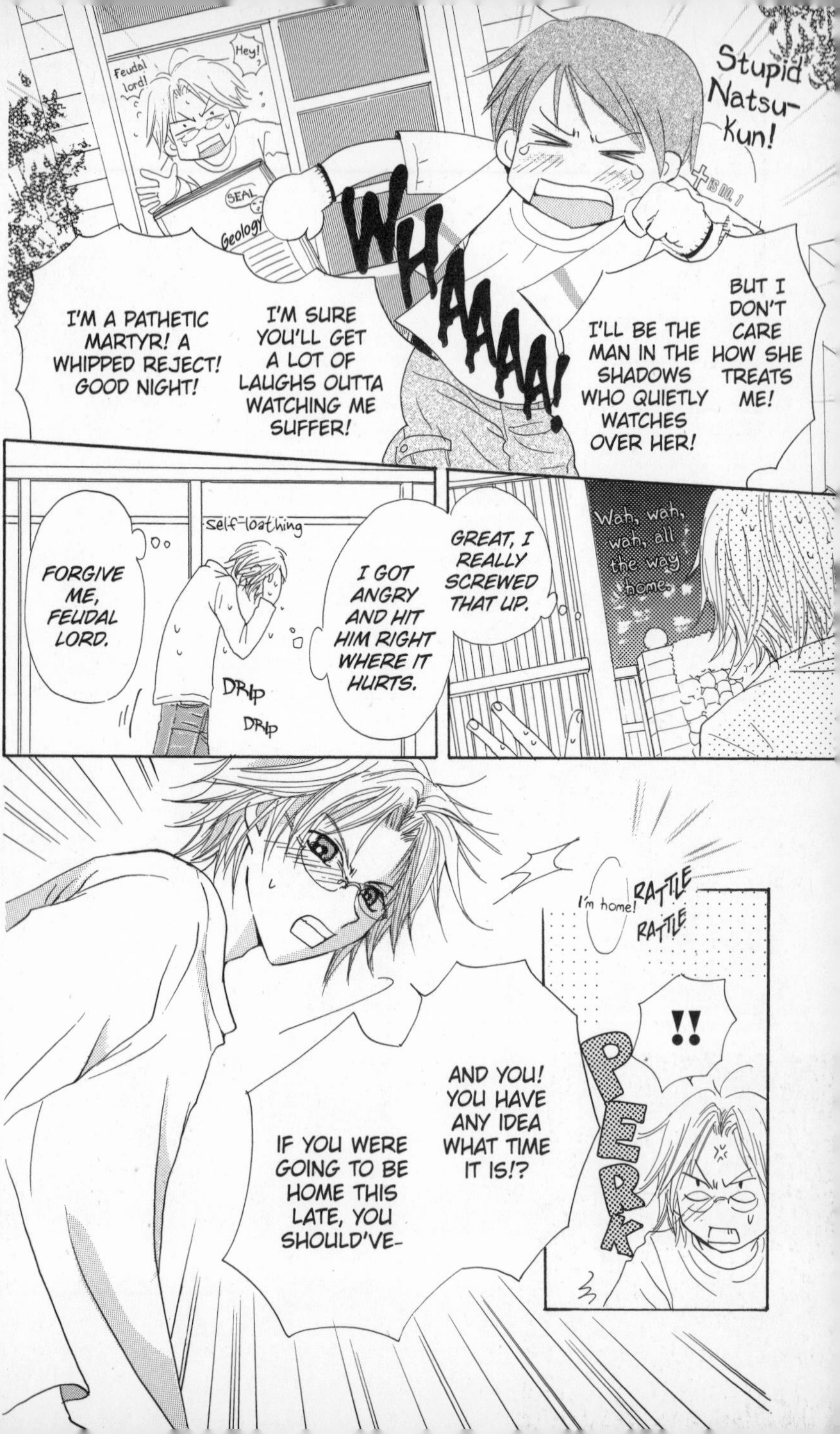

Stupid Natsu-Kun!
BUT I DON'T CARE HOW SHE TREATS ME!
I'LL BE THE MAN IN THE SHADOWS WHO QUIETLY WATCHES OVER HER!
WHAAAAA!
Hey!
Feudal lord!
SEAL
Geology
I'M SURE YOU'LL GET A LOT OF LAUGHS OUTTA WATCHING ME SUFFER!
I'M A PATHETIC MARTYR! A WHIPPED REJECT! GOOD NIGHT!
Wah, wah, wah, all the way home.
GREAT, I REALLY SCREWED THAT UP.
I GOT ANGRY AND HIT HIM RIGHT WHERE IT HURTS.
self-loathing
FORGIVE ME, FEUDAL LORD.
DRIP
DRIP
I'm home!
RATTLE
RATTLE
!!
PERK
AND YOU! YOU HAVE ANY IDEA WHAT TIME IT IS!?
IF YOU WERE GOING TO BE HOME THIS LATE, YOU SHOULD'VE-

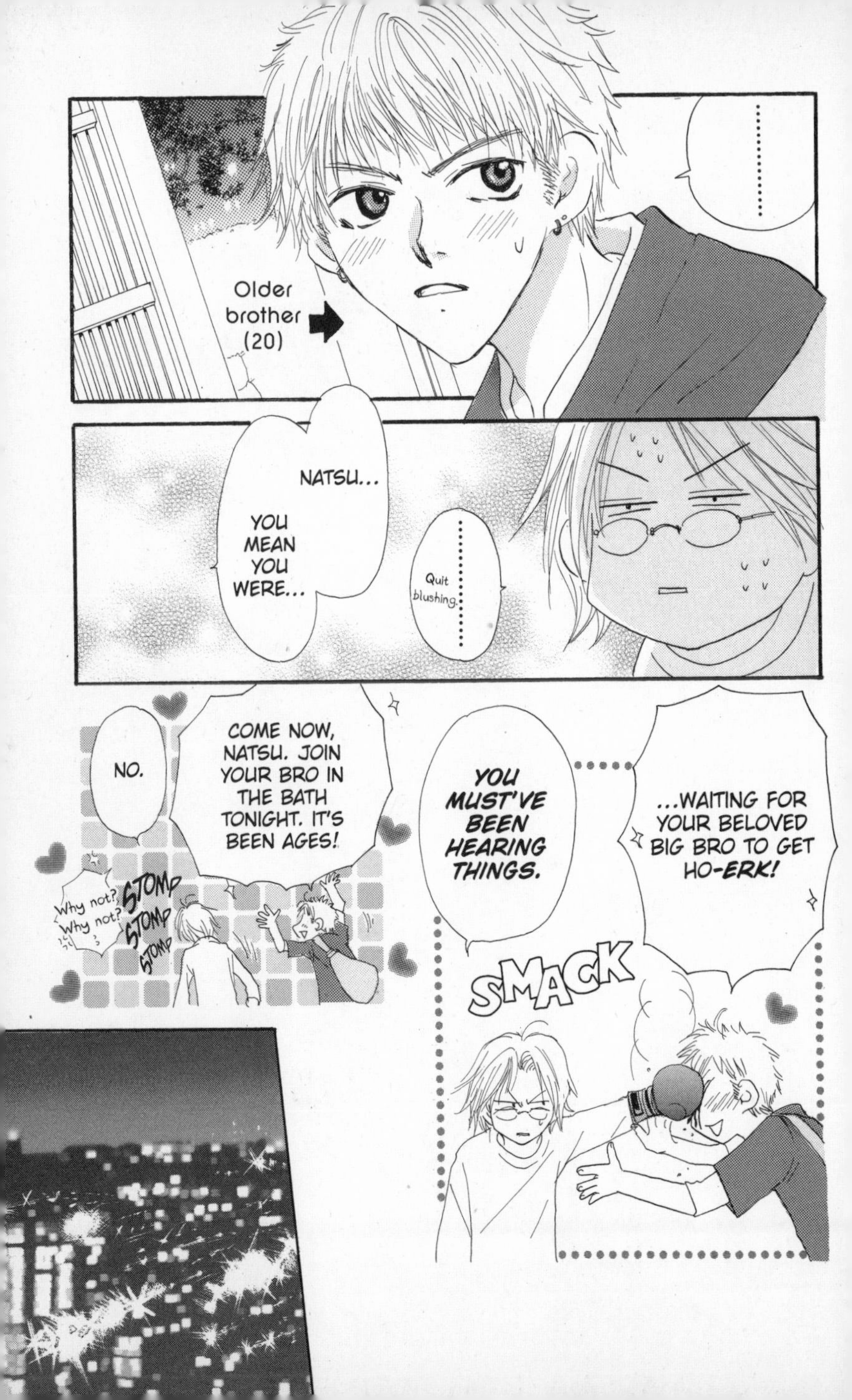

……
Older brother (20)
…… Quit blushing.
NATSU... YOU MEAN YOU WERE...
...WAITING FOR YOUR BELOVED BIG BRO TO GET HO-ERK!
YOU MUST'VE BEEN HEARING THINGS.
SMACK
COME NOW, NATSU. JOIN YOUR BRO IN THE BATH TONIGHT. IT'S BEEN AGES!
NO.
Why not? Why not?
STOMP STOMP STOMP

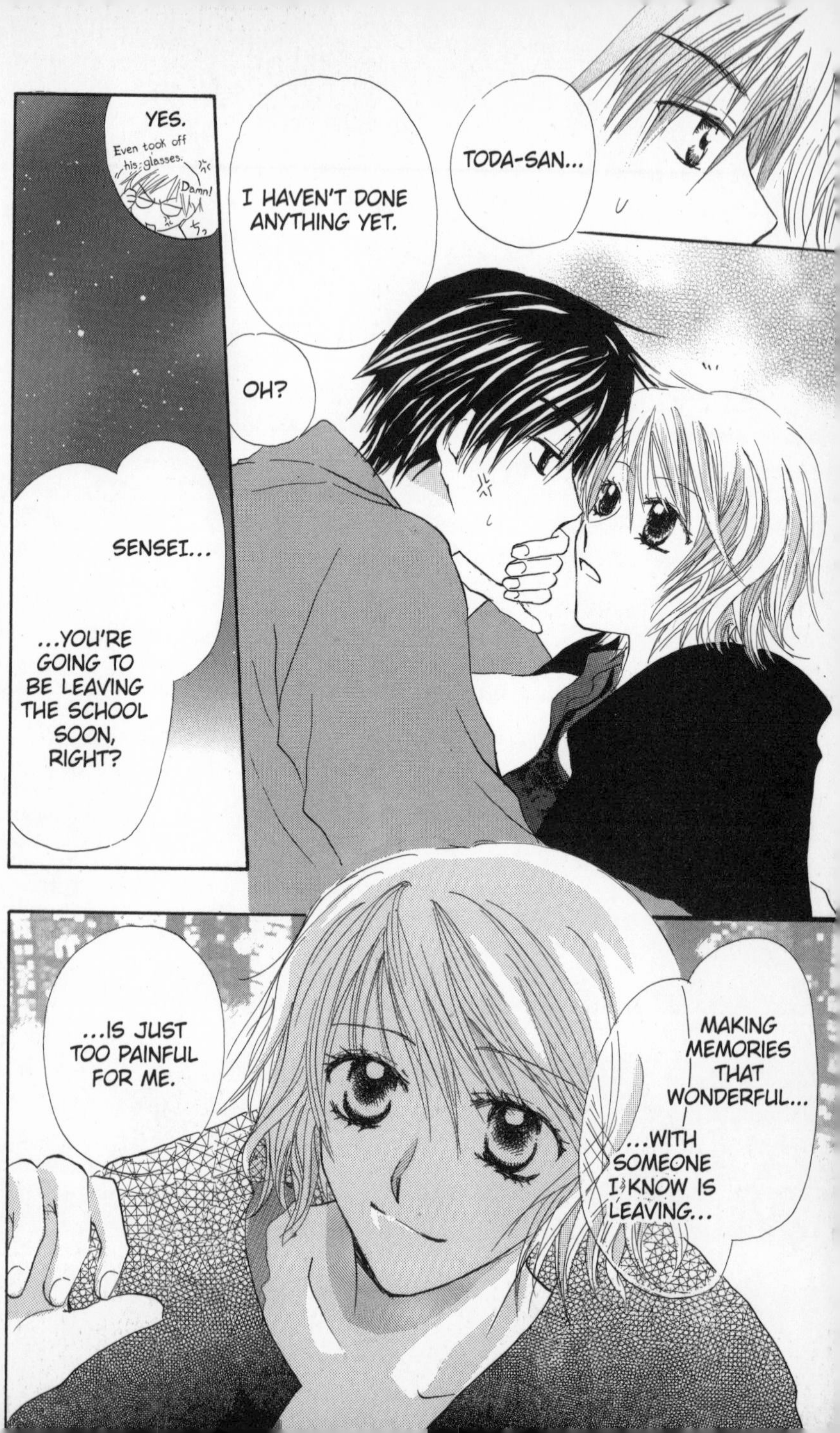
TODA-SAN...
I HAVEN'T DONE ANYTHING YET.
OH?
YES.
Even took off his glasses.
Damn!
SENSEI...
...YOU'RE GOING TO BE LEAVING THE SCHOOL SOON, RIGHT?
MAKING MEMORIES THAT WONDERFUL...
...WITH SOMEONE I KNOW IS LEAVING...
...IS JUST TOO PAINFUL FOR ME.

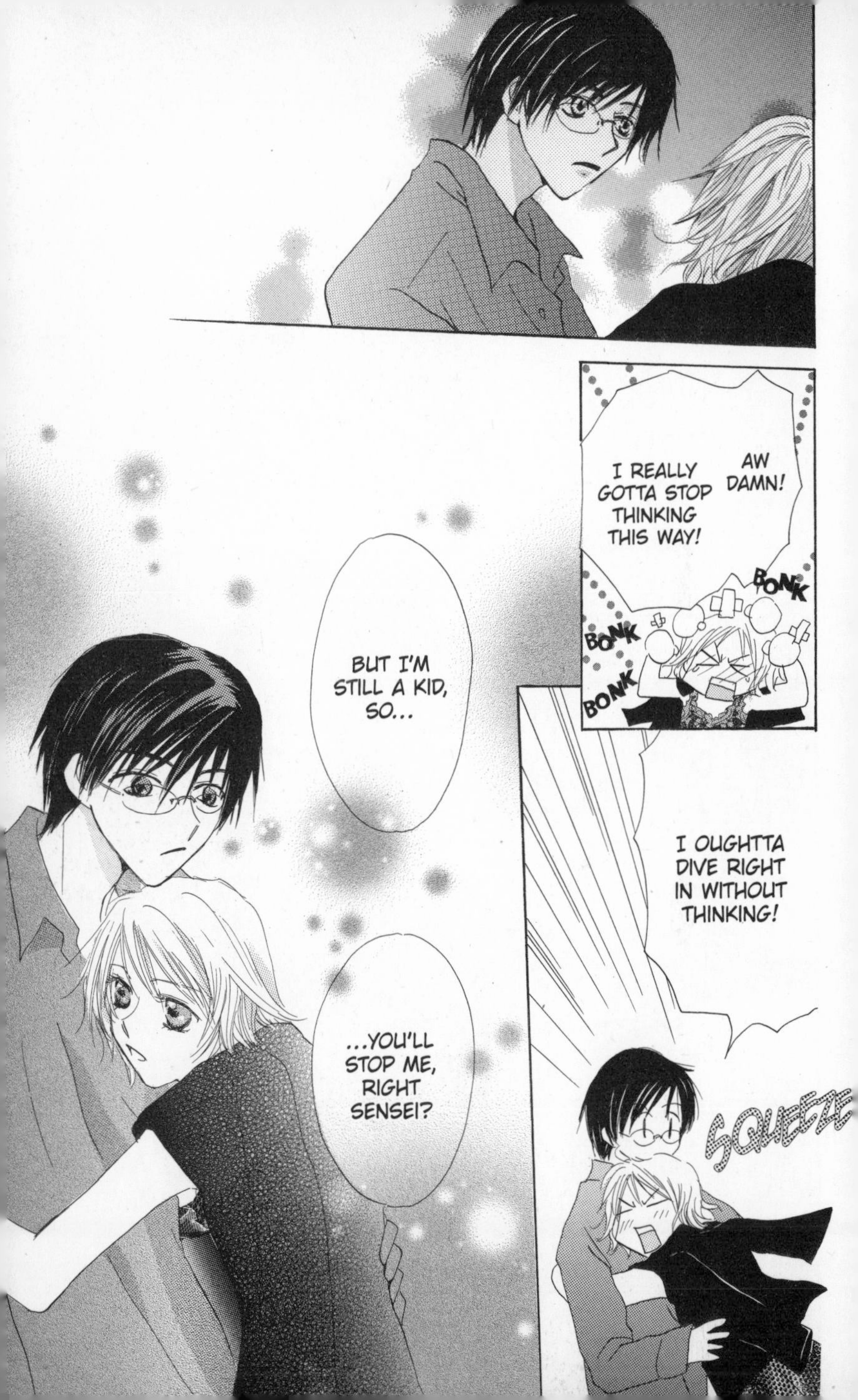
AW DAMN!
I REALLY GOTTA STOP THINKING THIS WAY!
BONK
BONK
BONK
BONK
I OUGHTTA DIVE RIGHT IN WITHOUT THINKING!
SQUEEZE
BUT I'M STILL A KID, SO...
...YOU'LL STOP ME, RIGHT SENSEI?

I'M NOT USED TO ASKING FOR WHAT I WANT...
...SO I'M JUST GONNA SAY WHATEVER COMES INTO MY HEAD.
I DON'T KNOW HOW TO LET MYSELF BE SPOILED, SO PLEASE...
...SCOLD ME FOR WANTING TO BE, OKAY?
IF I COME TO LIKE YOU SO MUCH...
...THAT IT STARTS TO HURT...
...STOP ME.
AND THEN...
...DISAPPEAR FROM MY LIFE IN A BEAUTIFUL, DRAMATIC WAY.

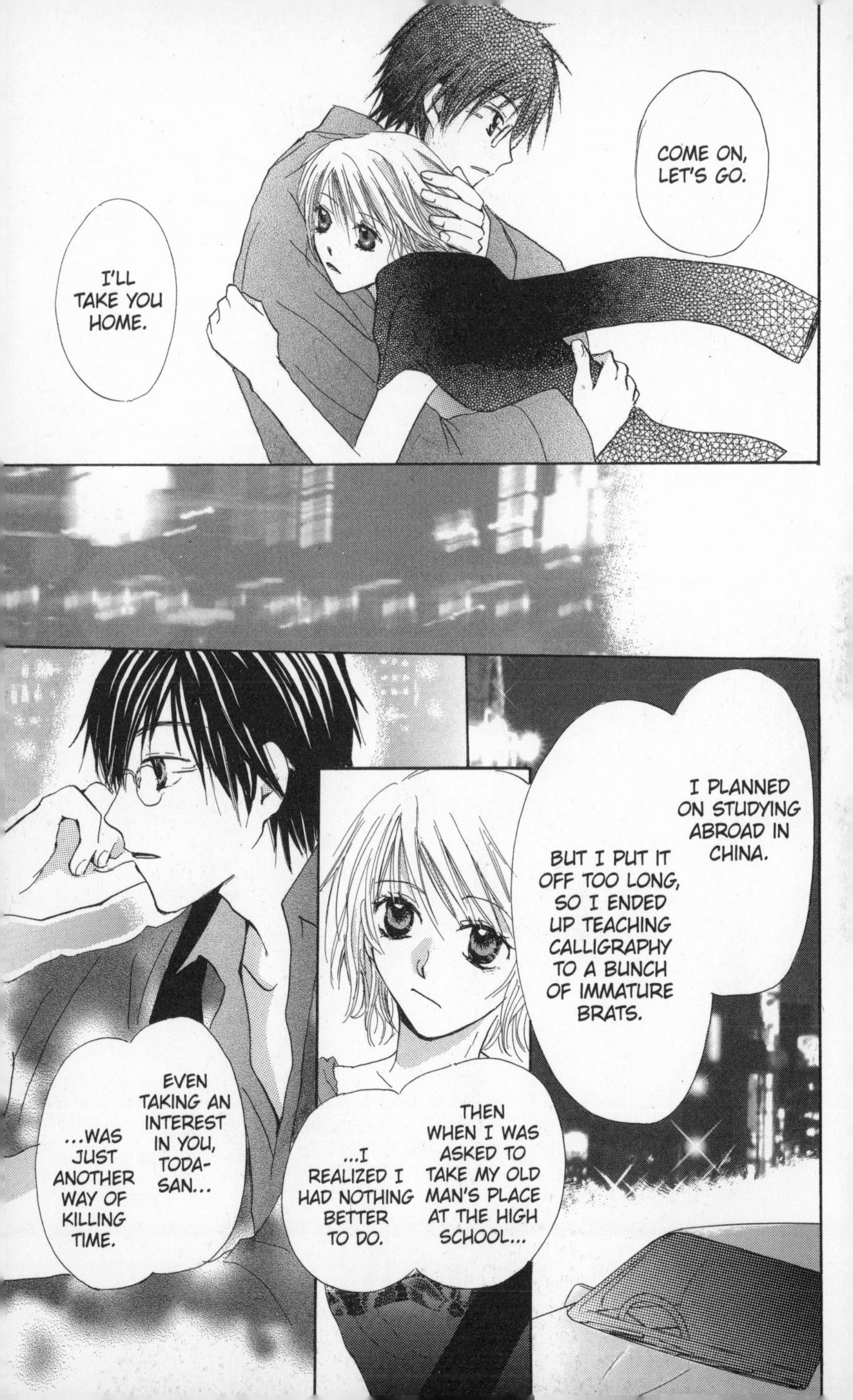
COME ON, LET'S GO.
I'LL TAKE YOU HOME.
I PLANNED ON STUDYING ABROAD IN CHINA.
BUT I PUT IT OFF TOO LONG, SO I ENDED UP TEACHING CALLIGRAPHY TO A BUNCH OF IMMATURE BRATS.
THEN WHEN I WAS ASKED TO TAKE MY OLD MAN'S PLACE AT THE HIGH SCHOOL...
...I REALIZED I HAD NOTHING BETTER TO DO.
EVEN TAKING AN INTEREST IN YOU, TODA-SAN...
...WAS JUST ANOTHER WAY OF KILLING TIME.

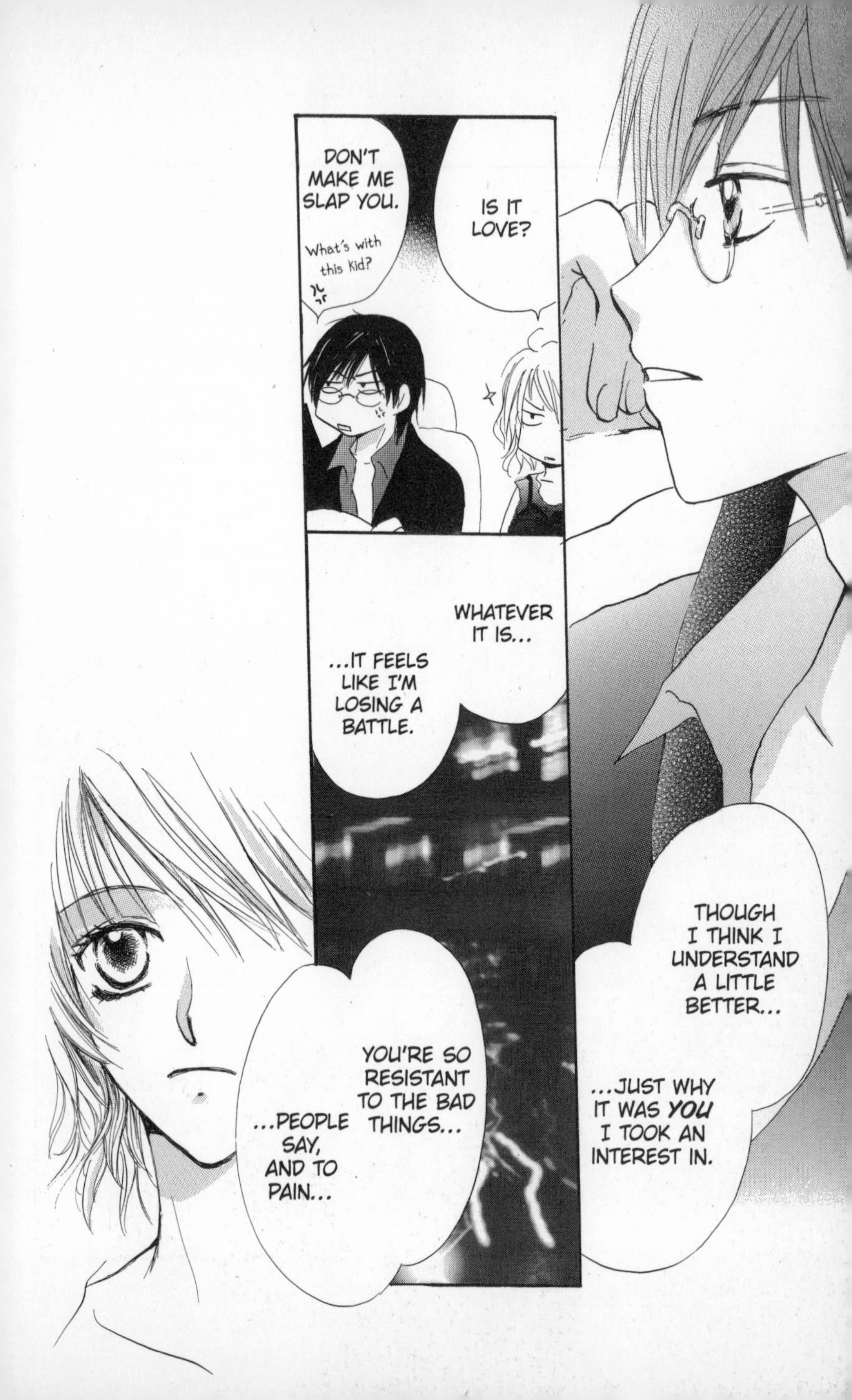
IS IT LOVE?
DON'T MAKE ME SLAP YOU.
What's with this kid?
WHATEVER IT IS...
...IT FEELS LIKE I'M LOSING A BATTLE.
THOUGH I THINK I UNDERSTAND A LITTLE BETTER...
...JUST WHY IT WAS *YOU* I TOOK AN INTEREST IN.
YOU'RE SO RESISTANT TO THE BAD THINGS...
...PEOPLE SAY, AND TO PAIN...

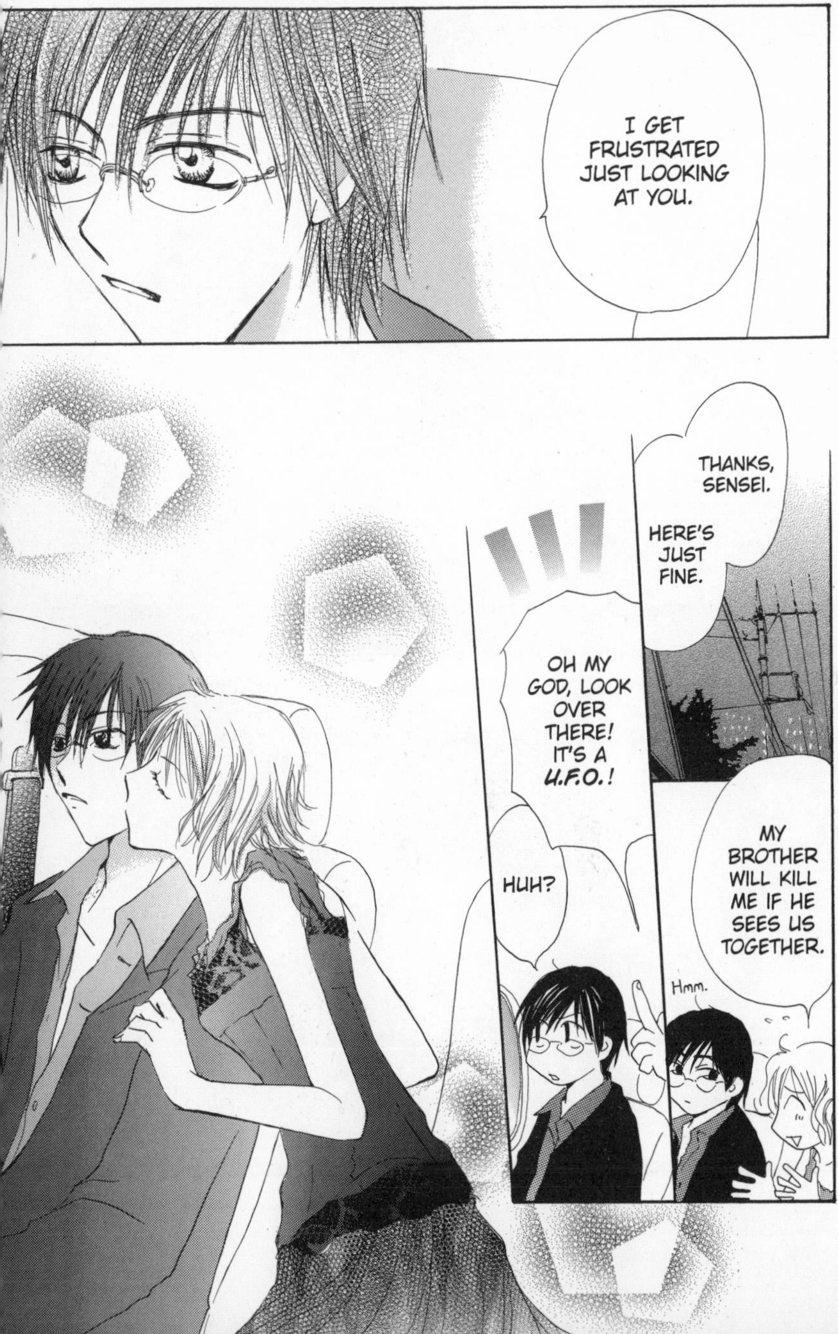
I GET FRUSTRATED JUST LOOKING AT YOU.
THANKS, SENSEI.
HERE'S JUST FINE.
MY BROTHER WILL KILL ME IF HE SEES US TOGETHER.
Hmm.
OH MY GOD, LOOK OVER THERE! IT'S A U.F.O.!
HUH?

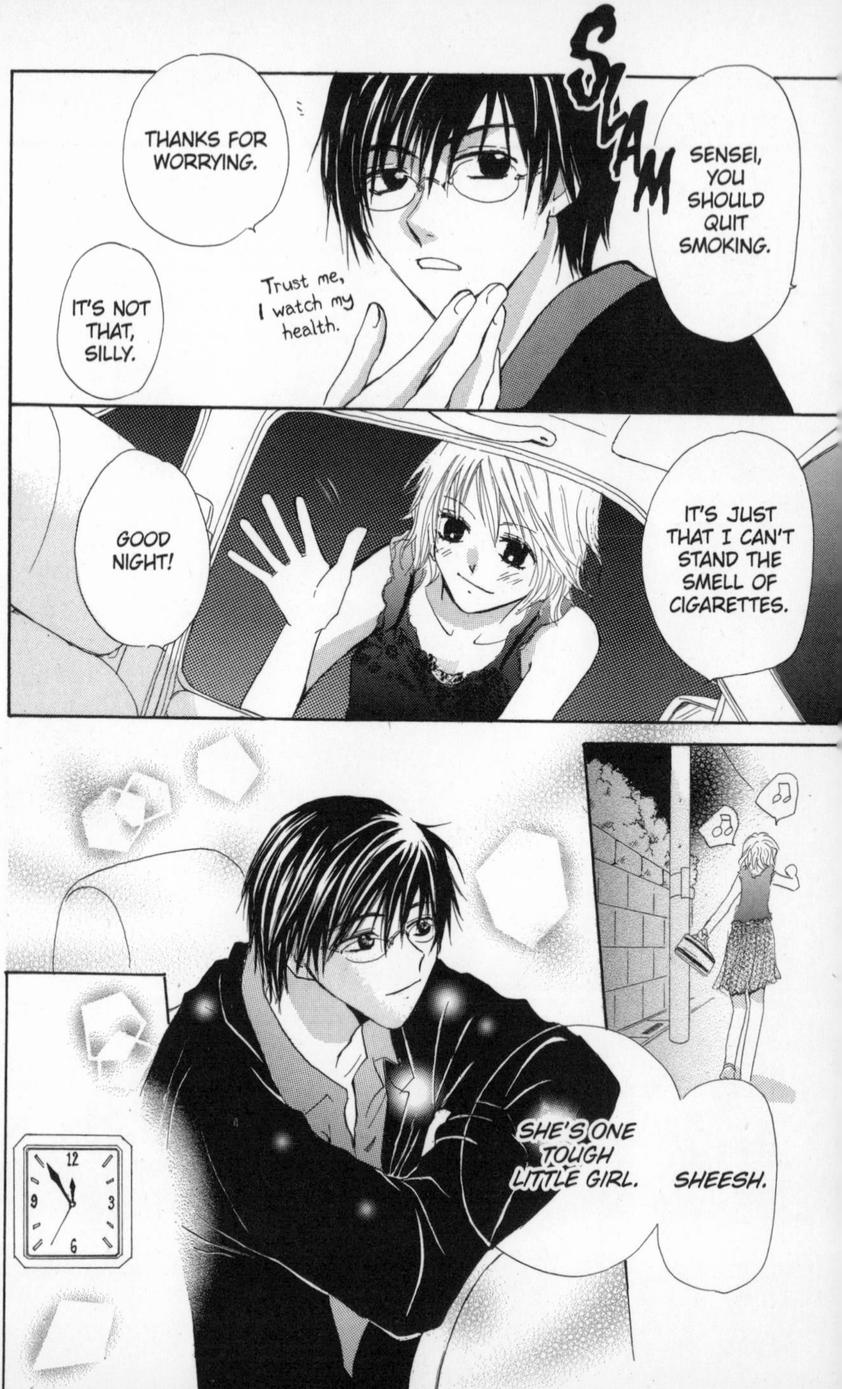
SLAM
SENSEI, YOU SHOULD QUIT SMOKING.
THANKS FOR WORRYING.
Trust me, I watch my health.
IT'S NOT THAT, SILLY.
IT'S JUST THAT I CAN'T STAND THE SMELL OF CIGARETTES.
GOOD NIGHT!
SHEESH.
SHE'S ONE TOUGH LITTLE GIRL.

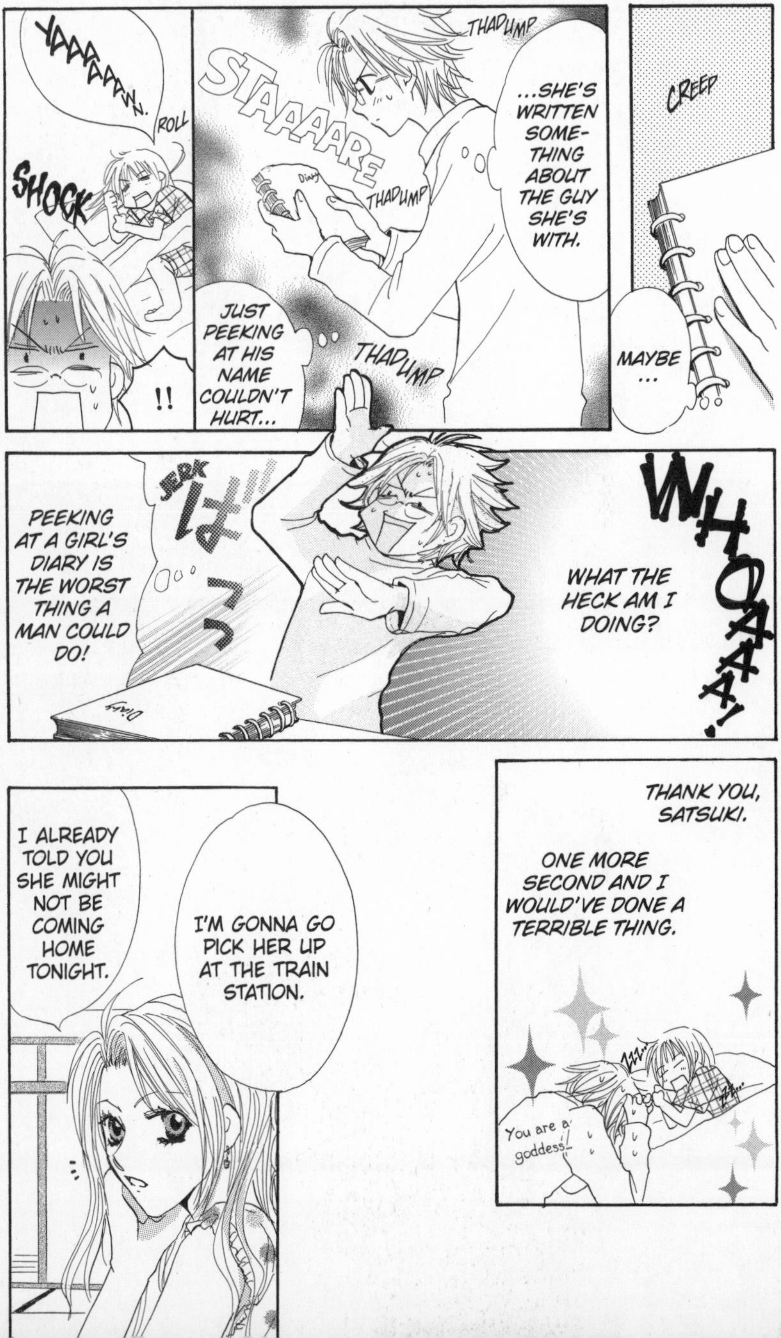
CREEP
MAYBE...
THADUMP
...SHE'S WRITTEN SOMETHING ABOUT THE GUY SHE'S WITH.
STAAAARE
Diary
THADUMP
JUST PEEKING AT HIS NAME COULDN'T HURT...
THADUMP
YAAAAAAWN.
ROLL
SHOCK
!!
WHOAAAA!
WHAT THE HECK AM I DOING?
JERK
ばっ
PEEKING AT A GIRL'S DIARY IS THE WORST THING A MAN COULD DO!
Diary
THANK YOU, SATSUKI.
ONE MORE SECOND AND I WOULD'VE DONE A TERRIBLE THING.
You are a goddess!
I'M GONNA GO PICK HER UP AT THE TRAIN STATION.
I ALREADY TOLD YOU SHE MIGHT NOT BE COMING HOME TONIGHT.

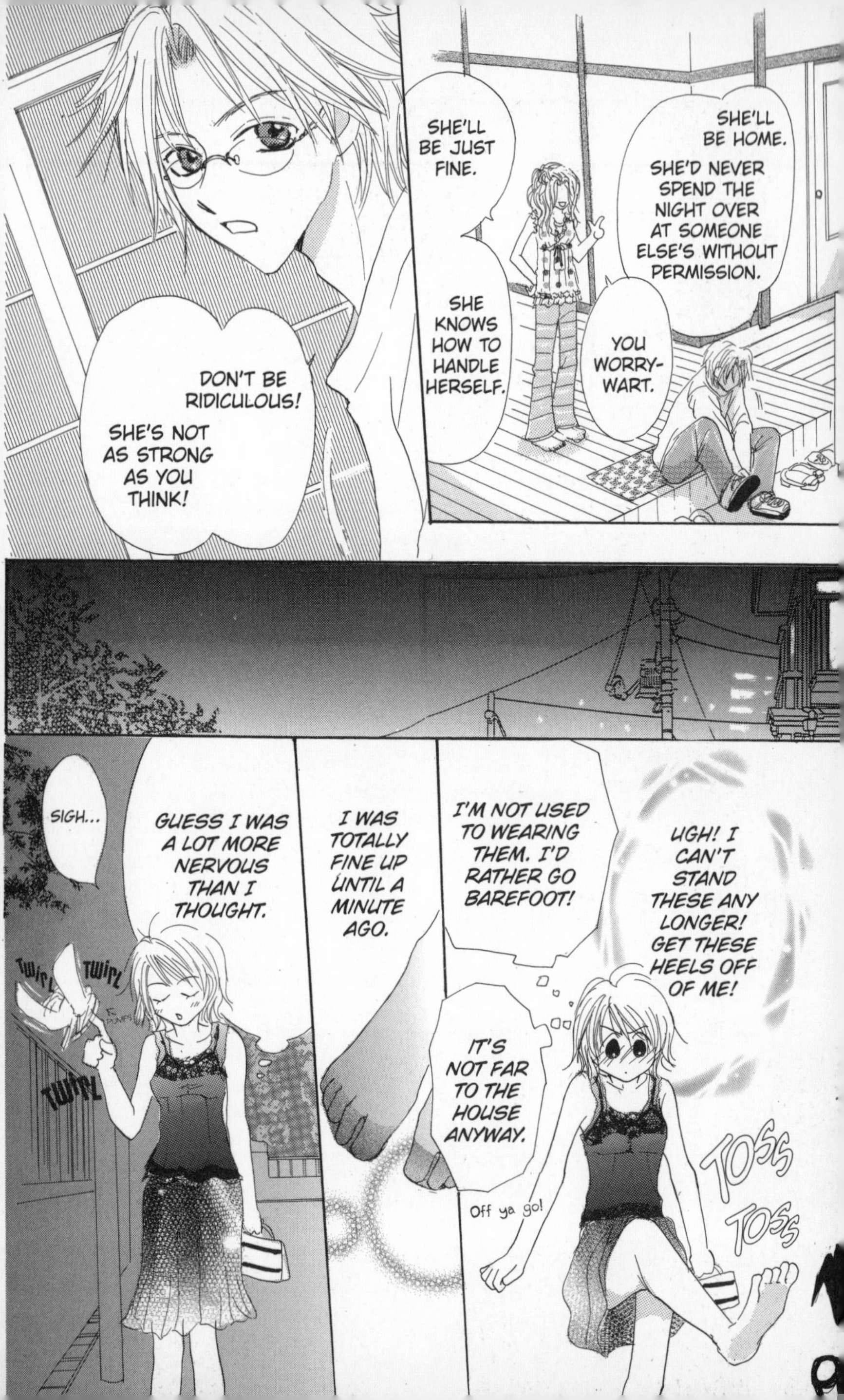
SHE'LL BE HOME. SHE'D NEVER SPEND THE NIGHT OVER AT SOMEONE ELSE'S WITHOUT PERMISSION.
YOU WORRY-WART.
SHE'LL BE JUST FINE.
SHE KNOWS HOW TO HANDLE HERSELF.
DON'T BE RIDICULOUS!
SHE'S NOT AS STRONG AS YOU THINK!
UGH! I CAN'T STAND THESE ANY LONGER! GET THESE HEELS OFF OF ME!
I'M NOT USED TO WEARING THEM. I'D RATHER GO BAREFOOT!
IT'S NOT FAR TO THE HOUSE ANYWAY.
TOSS
TOSS
Off ya go!
I WAS TOTALLY FINE UP UNTIL A MINUTE AGO.
SIGH...
GUESS I WAS A LOT MORE NERVOUS THAN I THOUGHT.
TWIRL
TWIRL
TWIRL

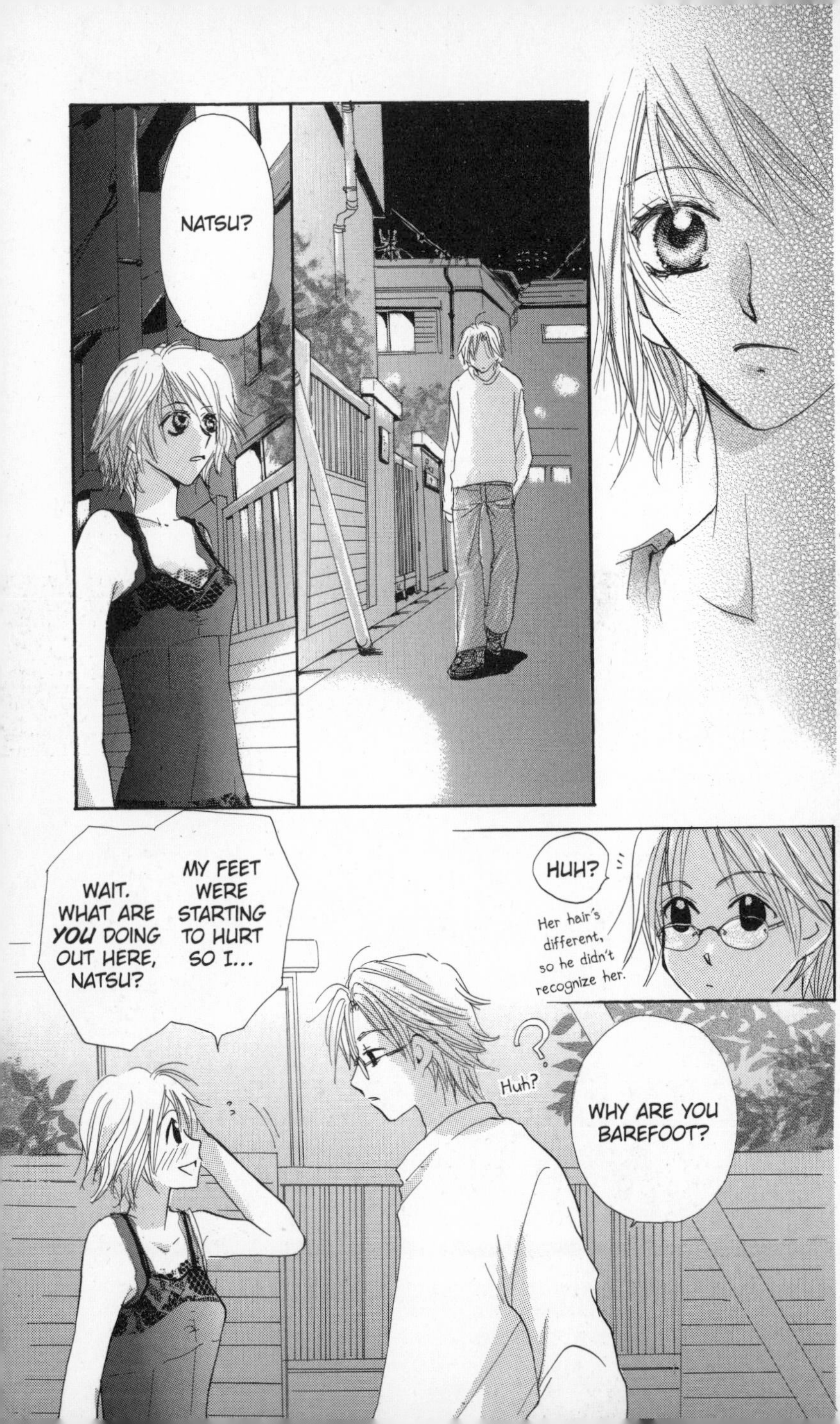
NATSU?
HUH?
Her hair's different, so he didn't recognize her.
WHY ARE YOU BAREFOOT?
Huh?
MY FEET WERE STARTING TO HURT SO I...
WAIT. WHAT ARE YOU DOING OUT HERE, NATSU?

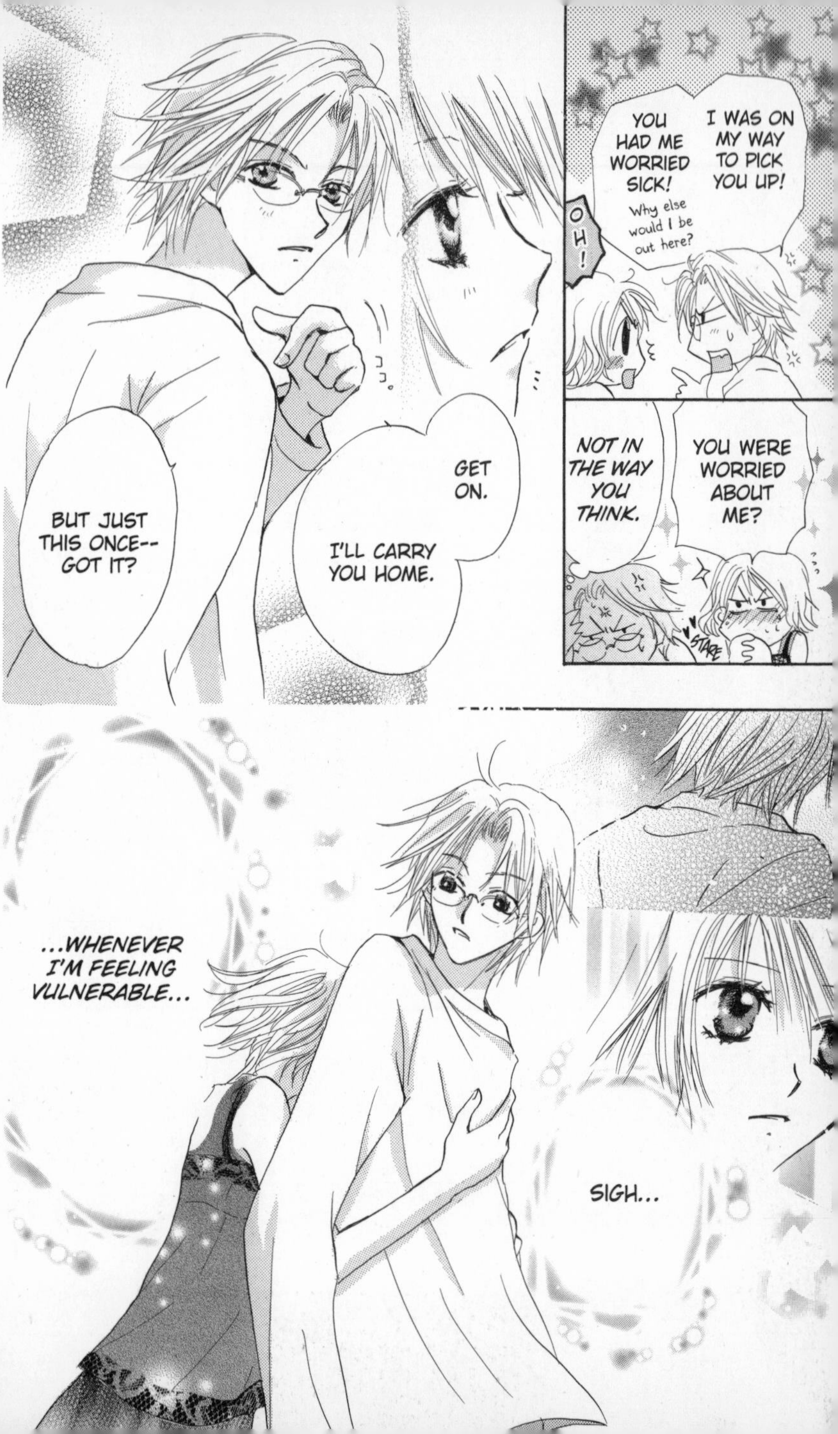
I WAS ON MY WAY TO PICK YOU UP!
YOU HAD ME WORRIED SICK!
Why else would I be out here?
OH!
YOU WERE WORRIED ABOUT ME?
NOT IN THE WAY YOU THINK.
STARE
GET ON.
I'LL CARRY YOU HOME.
BUT JUST THIS ONCE--GOT IT?
SIGH...
...WHENEVER I'M FEELING VULNERABLE...

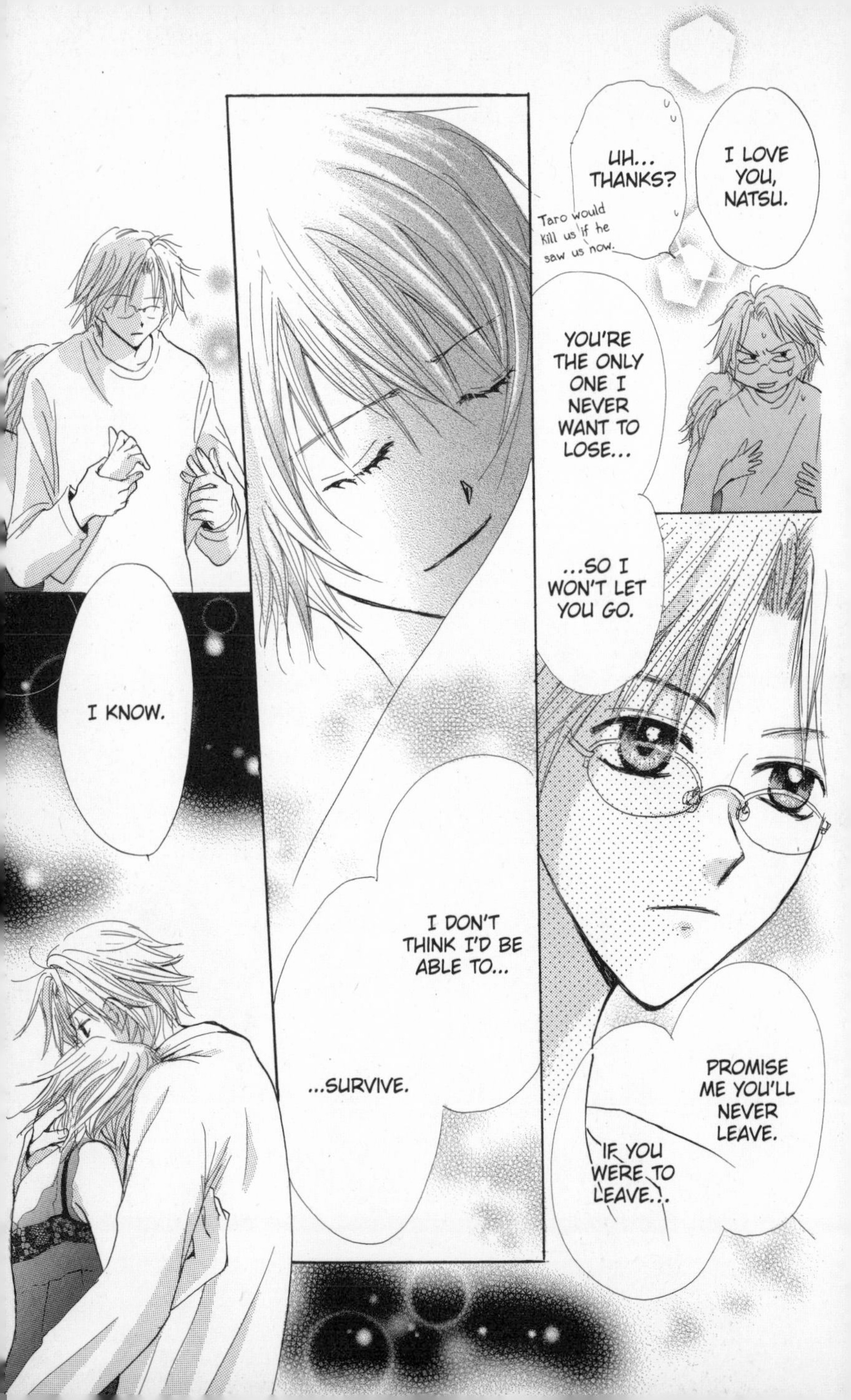

I LOVE YOU, NATSU.
UH... THANKS?
Taro would Kill us if he saw us now.
YOU'RE THE ONLY ONE I NEVER WANT TO LOSE...
...SO I WON'T LET YOU GO.
PROMISE ME YOU'LL NEVER LEAVE.
IF YOU WERE TO LEAVE...
I DON'T THINK I'D BE ABLE TO...
...SURVIVE.
I KNOW.

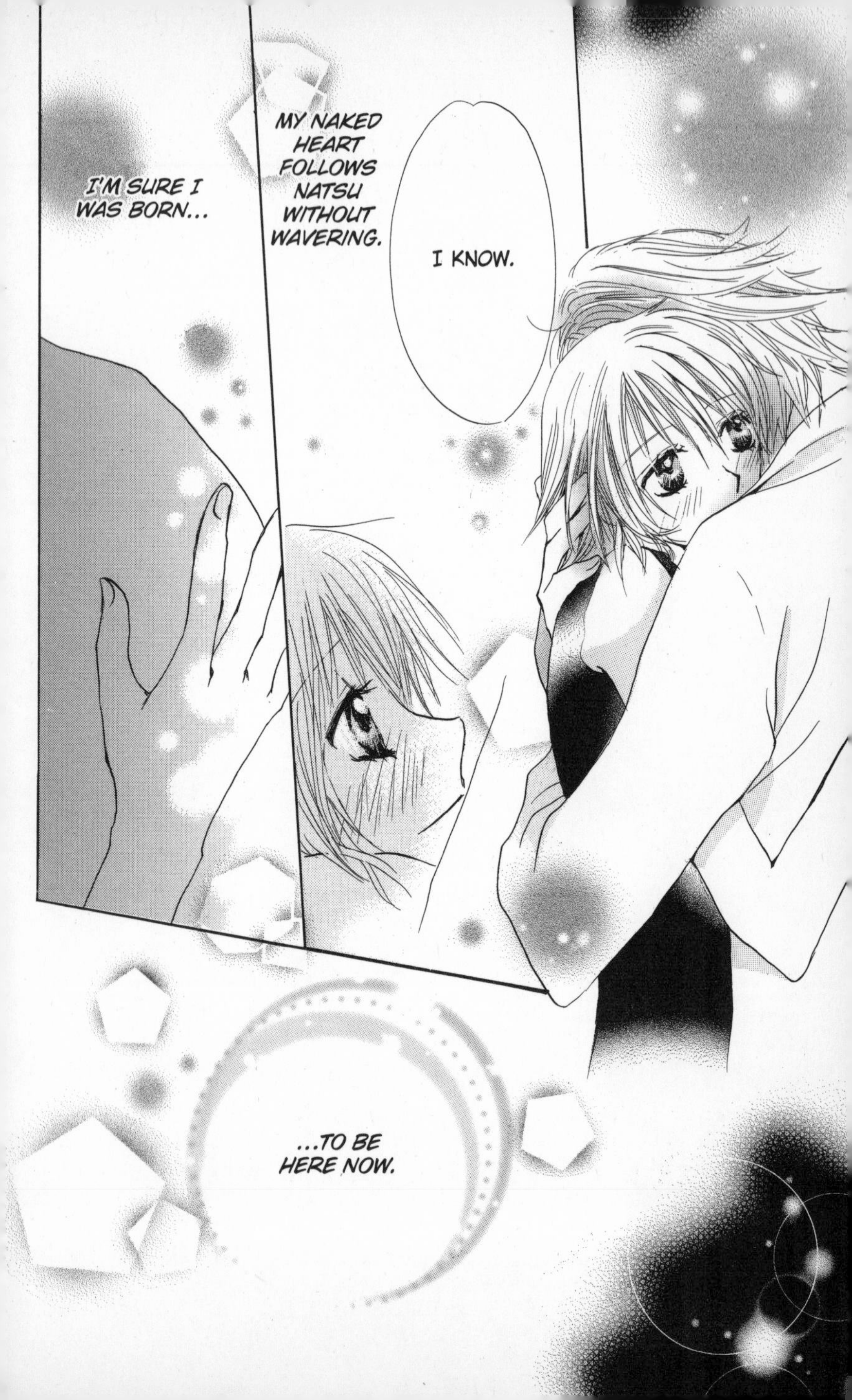
I KNOW.
MY NAKED HEART FOLLOWS NATSU WITHOUT WAVERING.
I'M SURE I WAS BORN...
...TO BE HERE NOW.

#13 Short-Sleeves

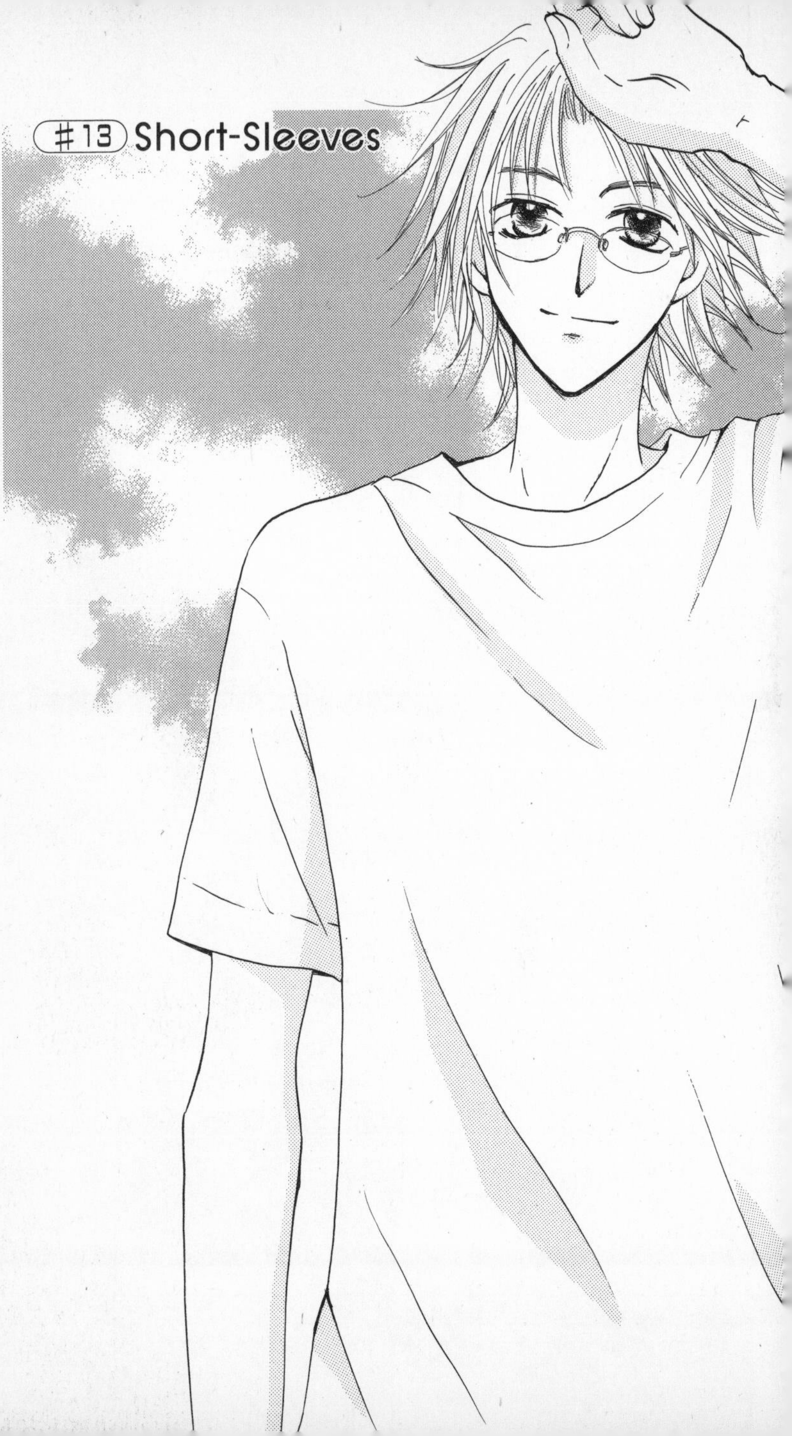

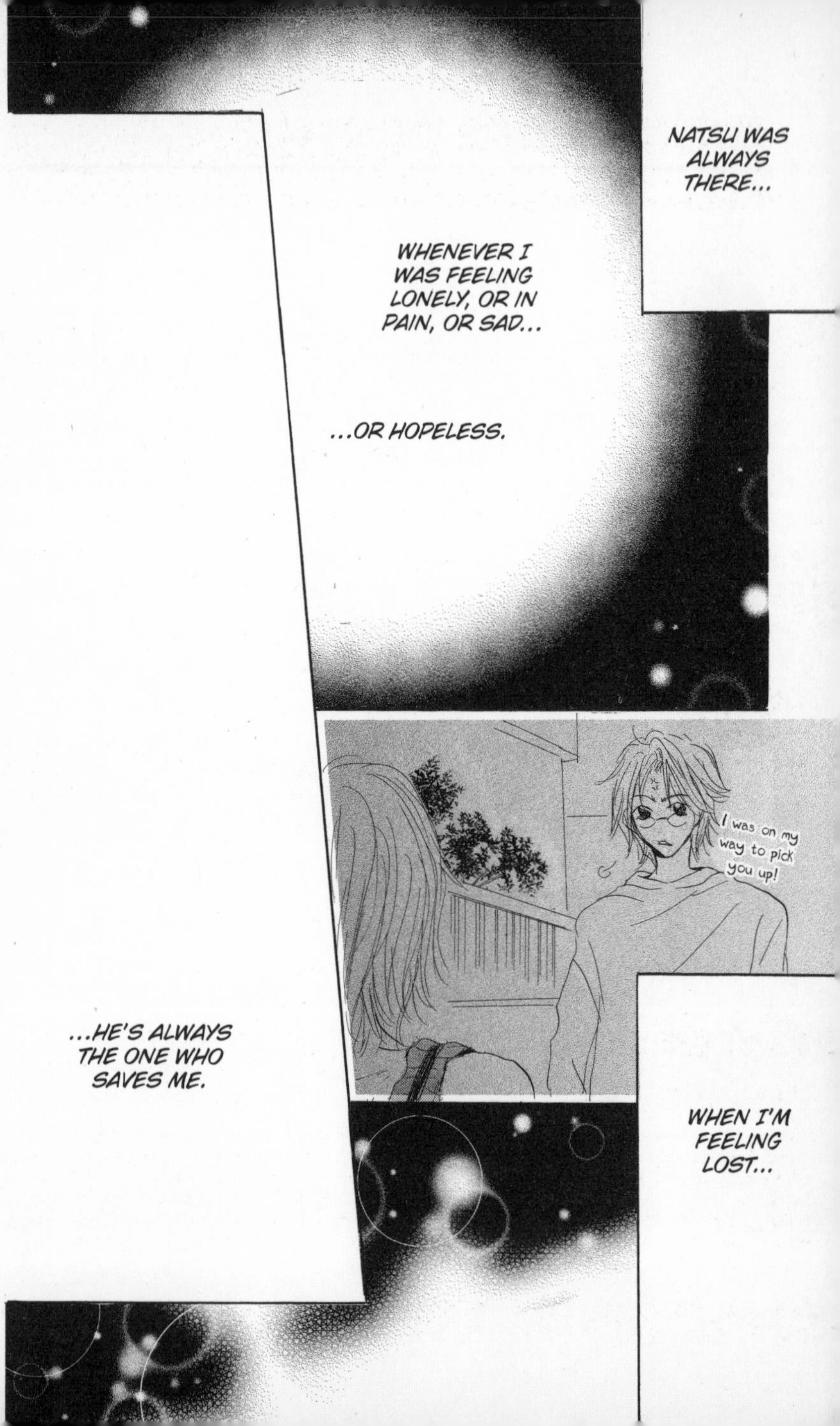
NATSU WAS ALWAYS THERE...
WHENEVER I WAS FEELING LONELY, OR IN PAIN, OR SAD...
...OR HOPELESS.
I was on my way to pick you up!
WHEN I'M FEELING LOST...
...HE'S ALWAYS THE ONE WHO SAVES ME.

crossroad Chapter 13: Short Sleeves

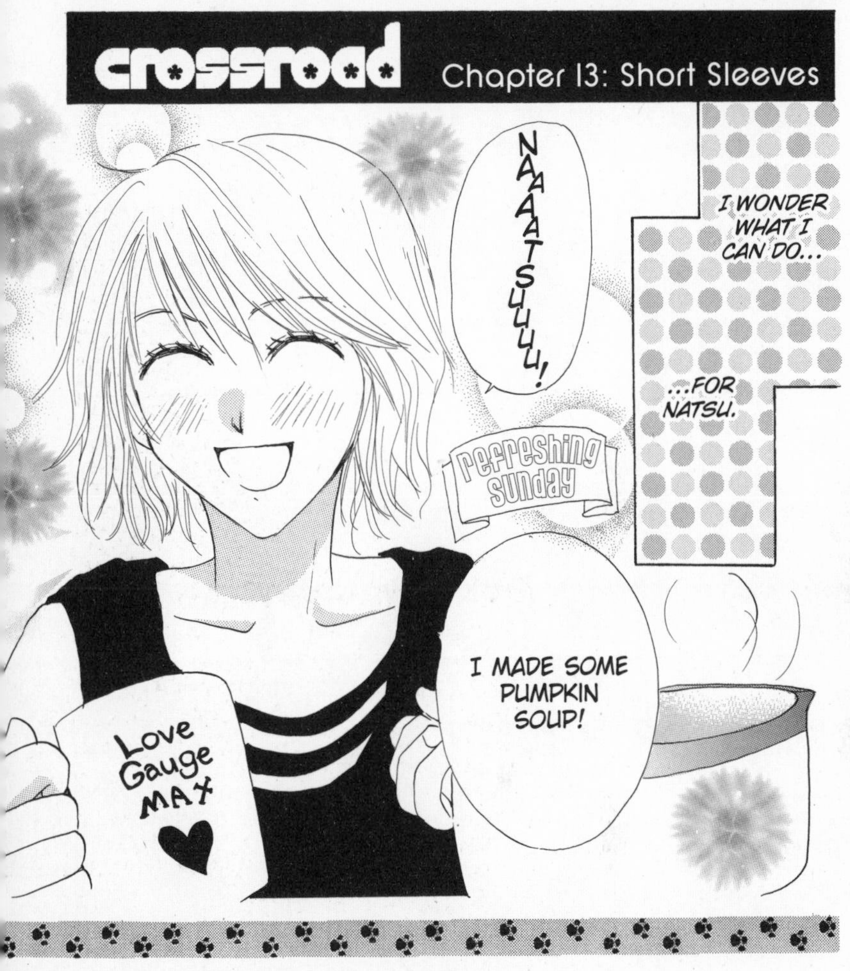
I WONDER WHAT I CAN DO...
...FOR NATSU.
NAAAATSUUUU!
refreshing sunday
I MADE SOME PUMPKIN SOUP!
Love Gauge MAX

Feelings of Nostalgia 2

Why is it that every time I write Subaru and Natsu's conversations, the mood gets virginal? Ever since I used to watch two boys in my neighborhood cling to each other affectionately on the way home from school, my vision of close male relationships has gone way over the top. School uniforms & love... (laugh). To get off-subject, Akita dogs are pretty big and scary and eat a LOT, so I always think of them as the type of dog that could become a police man or civil worker. No doubt being chased by one of them would give you nightmares for weeks. I wonder if you'd die if it bit you? So amazing is the Akita dog... Woof!

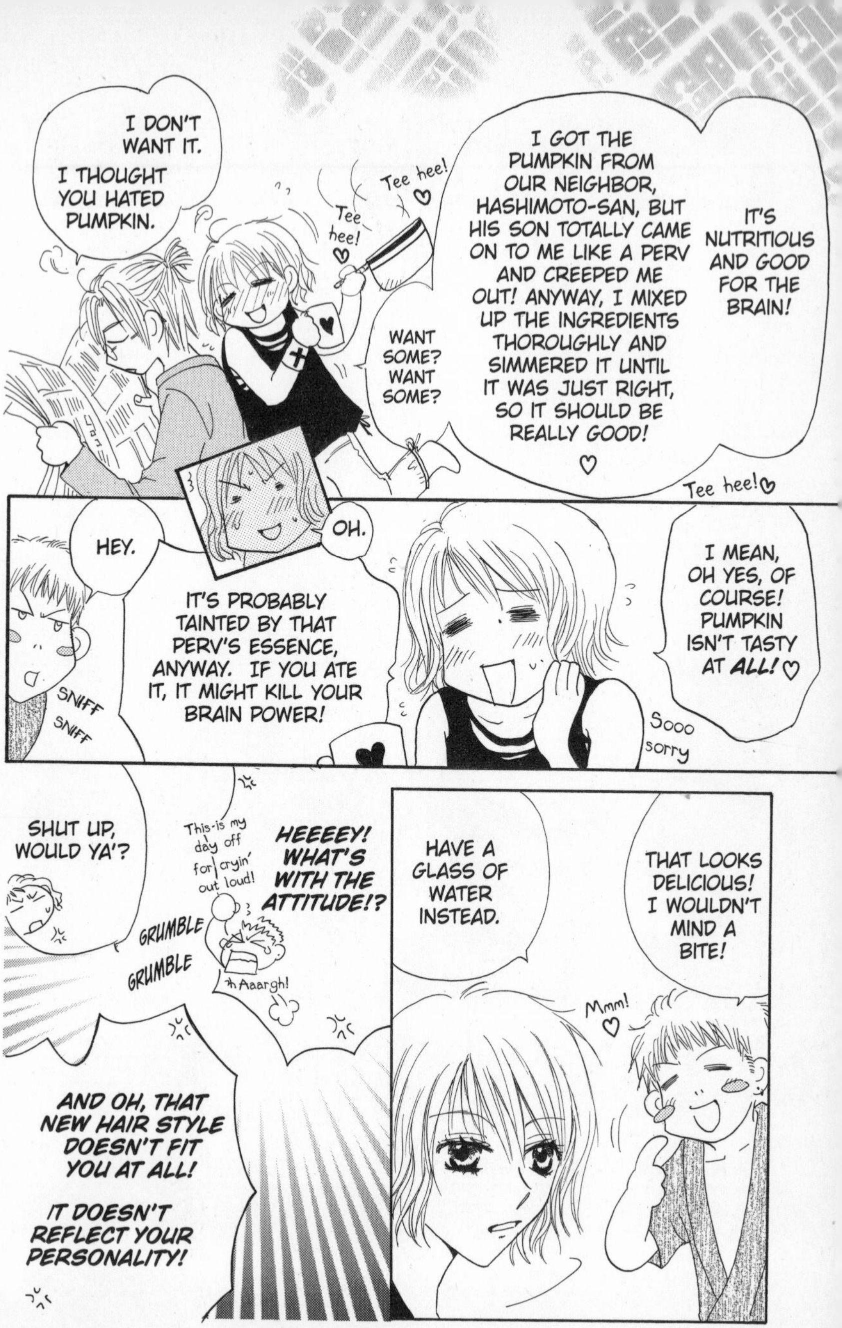
IT'S NUTRITIOUS AND GOOD FOR THE BRAIN!
I GOT THE PUMPKIN FROM OUR NEIGHBOR, HASHIMOTO-SAN, BUT HIS SON TOTALLY CAME ON TO ME LIKE A PERV AND CREEPED ME OUT! ANYWAY, I MIXED UP THE INGREDIENTS THOROUGHLY AND SIMMERED IT UNTIL IT WAS JUST RIGHT, SO IT SHOULD BE REALLY GOOD! ♡
Tee hee!♡
Tee hee! ♡
Tee hee! ♡
WANT SOME? WANT SOME?
I DON'T WANT IT.
I THOUGHT YOU HATED PUMPKIN.
OH.
I MEAN, OH YES, OF COURSE! PUMPKIN ISN'T TASTY AT ALL! ♡
Sooo sorry
IT'S PROBABLY TAINTED BY THAT PERV'S ESSENCE, ANYWAY. IF YOU ATE IT, IT MIGHT KILL YOUR BRAIN POWER!
HEY.
SNIFF SNIFF
THAT LOOKS DELICIOUS! I WOULDN'T MIND A BITE!
HAVE A GLASS OF WATER INSTEAD.
Mmm! ♡
HEEEEY! WHAT'S WITH THE ATTITUDE!?
This is my day off for cryin' out loud!
SHUT UP, WOULD YA'?
GRUMBLE GRUMBLE
Aaargh!
AND OH, THAT NEW HAIR STYLE DOESN'T FIT YOU AT ALL!
IT DOESN'T REFLECT YOUR PERSONALITY!

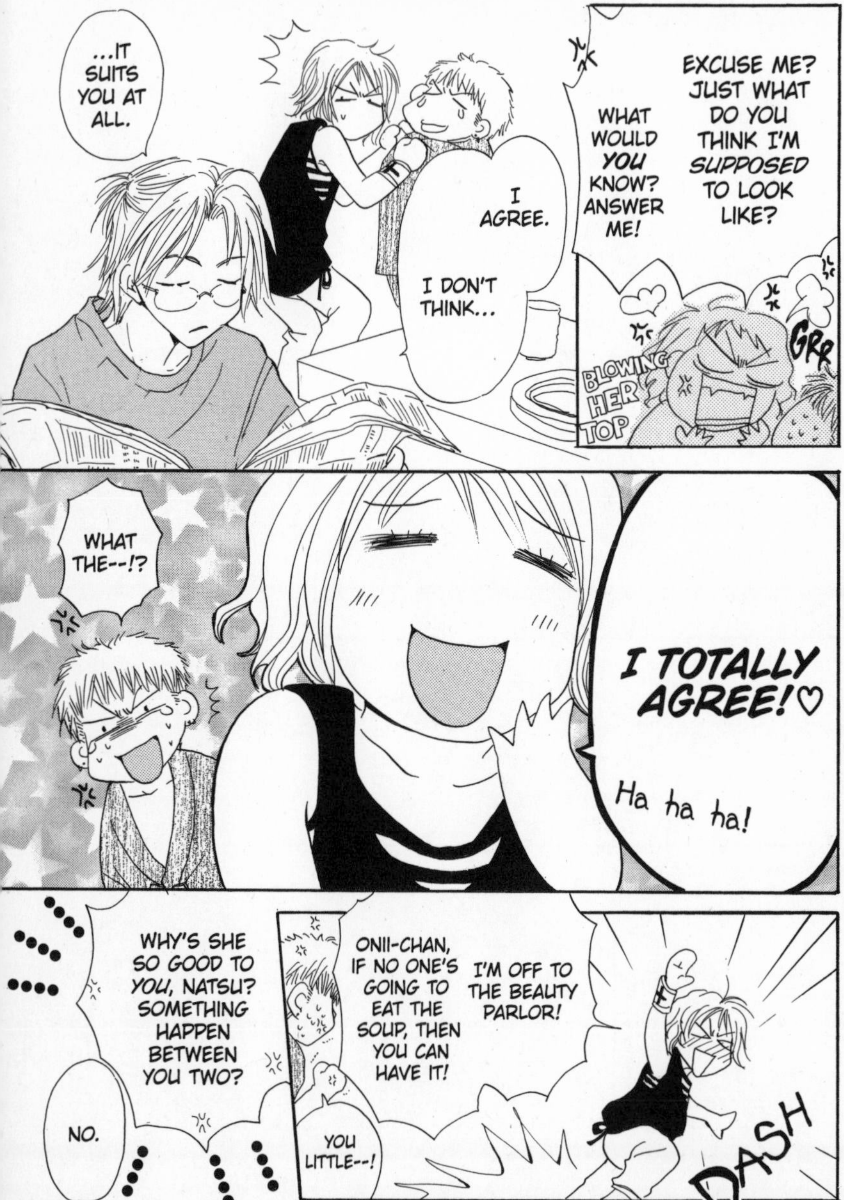
EXCUSE ME? JUST WHAT DO YOU THINK I'M SUPPOSED TO LOOK LIKE?
WHAT WOULD YOU KNOW? ANSWER ME!
GRR
BLOWING HER TOP
I AGREE.
I DON'T THINK...
...IT SUITS YOU AT ALL.
I TOTALLY AGREE! ♡
Ha ha ha!
WHAT THE--!?
I'M OFF TO THE BEAUTY PARLOR!
ONII-CHAN, IF NO ONE'S GOING TO EAT THE SOUP, THEN YOU CAN HAVE IT!
DASH
YOU LITTLE--!
WHY'S SHE SO GOOD TO YOU, NATSU? SOMETHING HAPPEN BETWEEN YOU TWO?
NO.

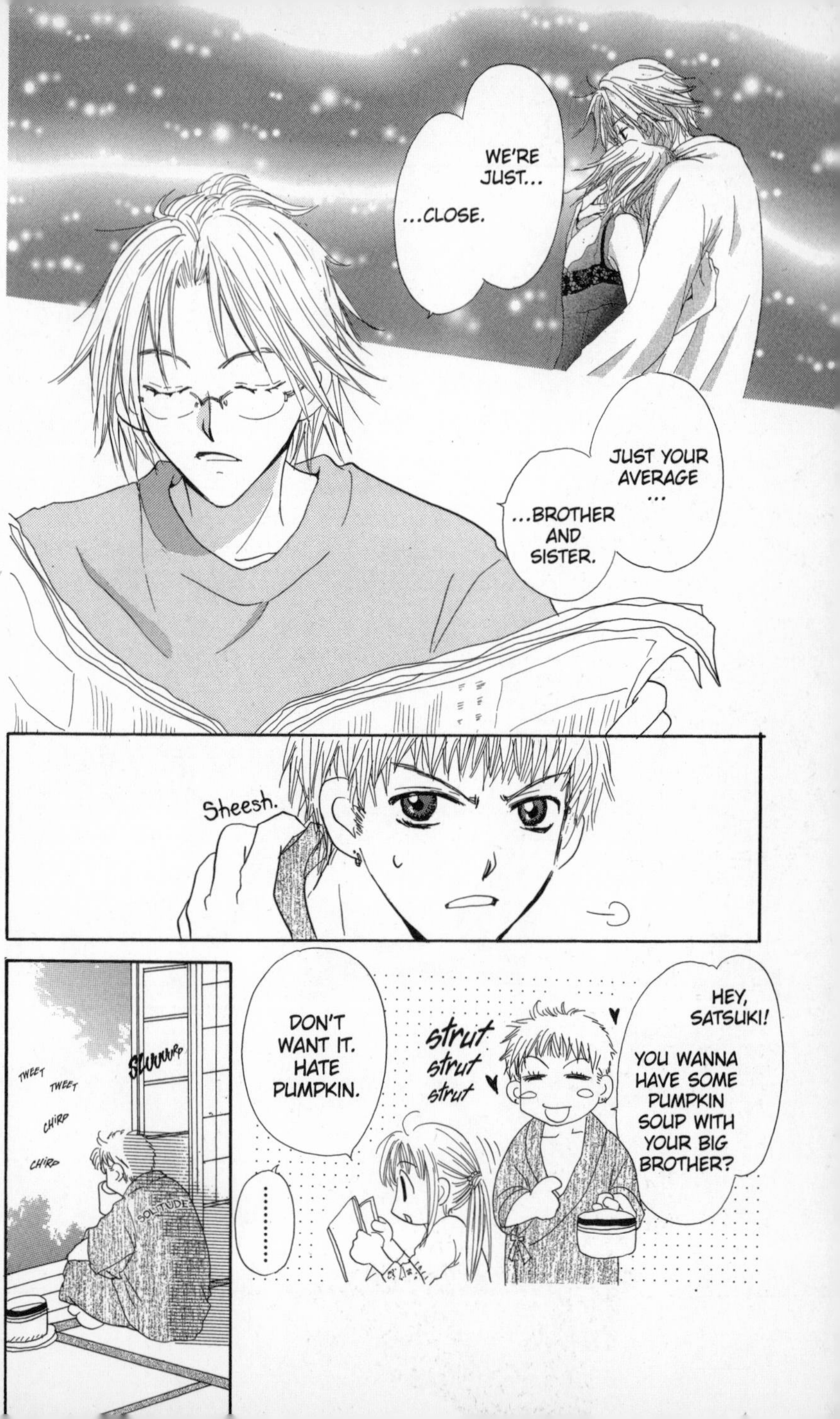
WE'RE JUST...
...CLOSE.
JUST YOUR AVERAGE ...
...BROTHER AND SISTER.
Sheesh.
HEY, SATSUKI!
YOU WANNA HAVE SOME PUMPKIN SOUP WITH YOUR BIG BROTHER?
strut strut strut
DON'T WANT IT. HATE PUMPKIN.
......
SLUUURP
TWEET TWEET
CHIRP
CHIRP
SOLITUDE

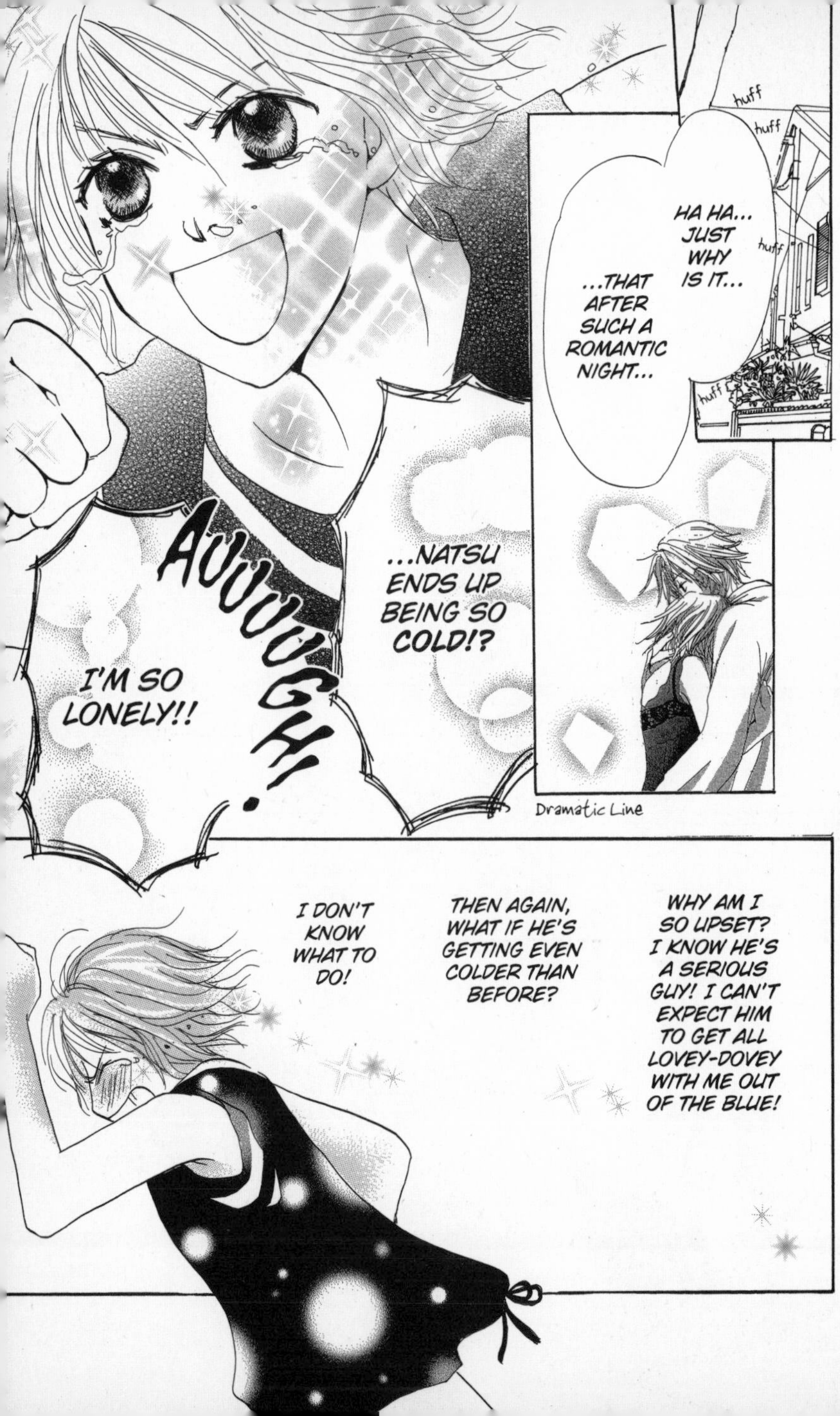
huff
huff
huff
huff
HA HA... JUST WHY IS IT...
...THAT AFTER SUCH A ROMANTIC NIGHT...
Dramatic Line
...NATSU ENDS UP BEING SO COLD!?
AUUUUGH!!
I'M SO LONELY!!
WHY AM I SO UPSET? I KNOW HE'S A SERIOUS GUY! I CAN'T EXPECT HIM TO GET ALL LOVEY-DOVEY WITH ME OUT OF THE BLUE!
THEN AGAIN, WHAT IF HE'S GETTING EVEN COLDER THAN BEFORE?
I DON'T KNOW WHAT TO DO!

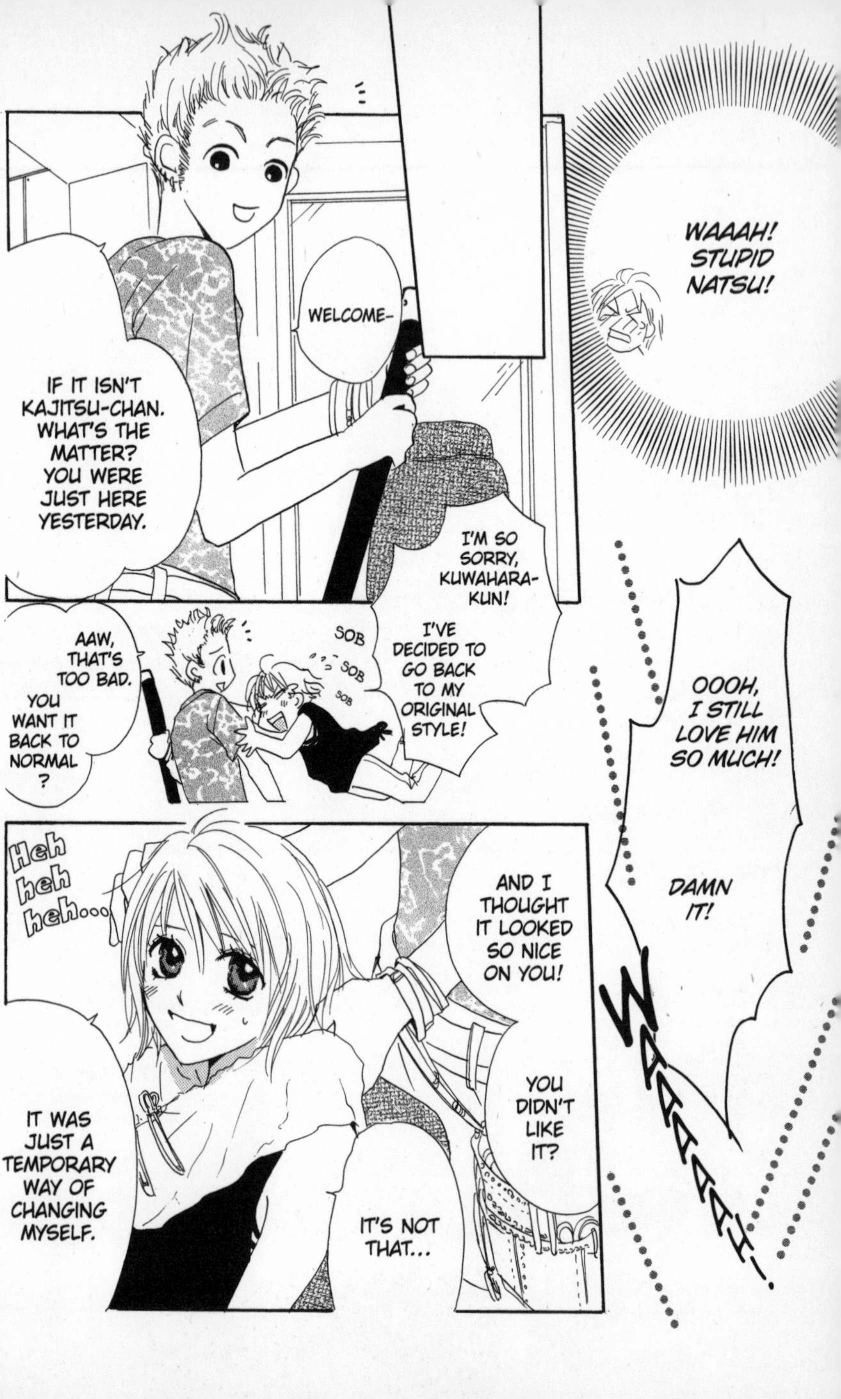
WAAAH! STUPID NATSU!
OOOH, I STILL LOVE HIM SO MUCH!
DAMN IT!
WAAAAAH-!
WELCOME-
IF IT ISN'T KAJITSU-CHAN. WHAT'S THE MATTER? YOU WERE JUST HERE YESTERDAY.
I'M SO SORRY, KUWAHARA-KUN!
I'VE DECIDED TO GO BACK TO MY ORIGINAL STYLE!
SOB SOB SOB
AAW, THAT'S TOO BAD.
YOU WANT IT BACK TO NORMAL?
AND I THOUGHT IT LOOKED SO NICE ON YOU!
YOU DIDN'T LIKE IT?
IT'S NOT THAT...
IT WAS JUST A TEMPORARY WAY OF CHANGING MYSELF.
Heh heh heh...

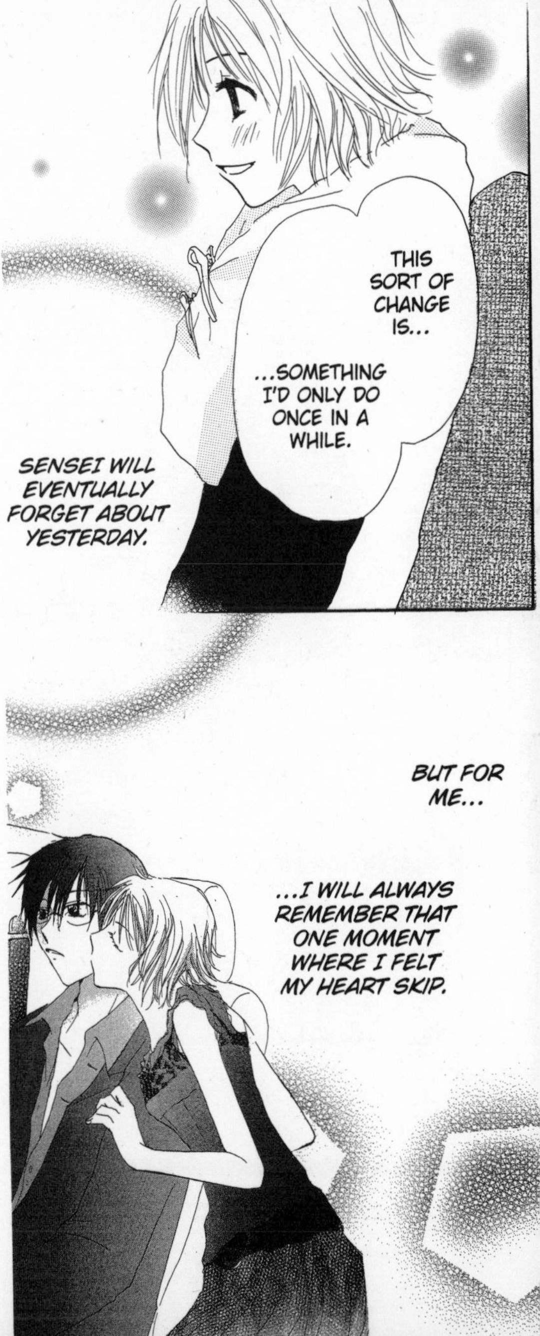
THIS SORT OF CHANGE IS...
...SOMETHING I'D ONLY DO ONCE IN A WHILE.
SENSEI WILL EVENTUALLY FORGET ABOUT YESTERDAY.
BUT FOR ME...
...I WILL ALWAYS REMEMBER THAT ONE MOMENT WHERE I FELT MY HEART SKIP.

Tell us about Crossroad!

"Akai-san and Writing"

Akai-san does Chinese calligraphy.

One would think he'd be bad at it, based on his personality.

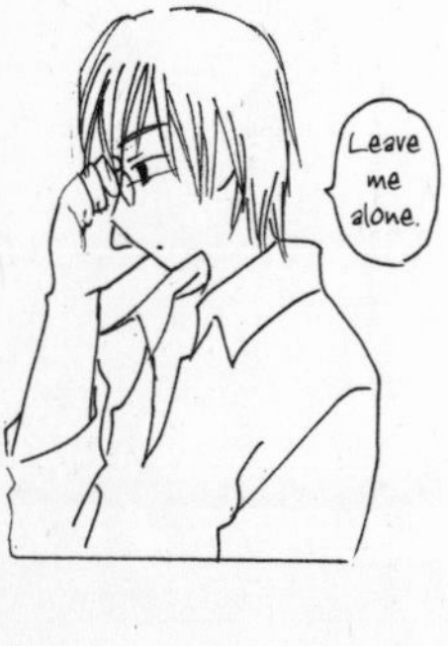
Leave me alone.

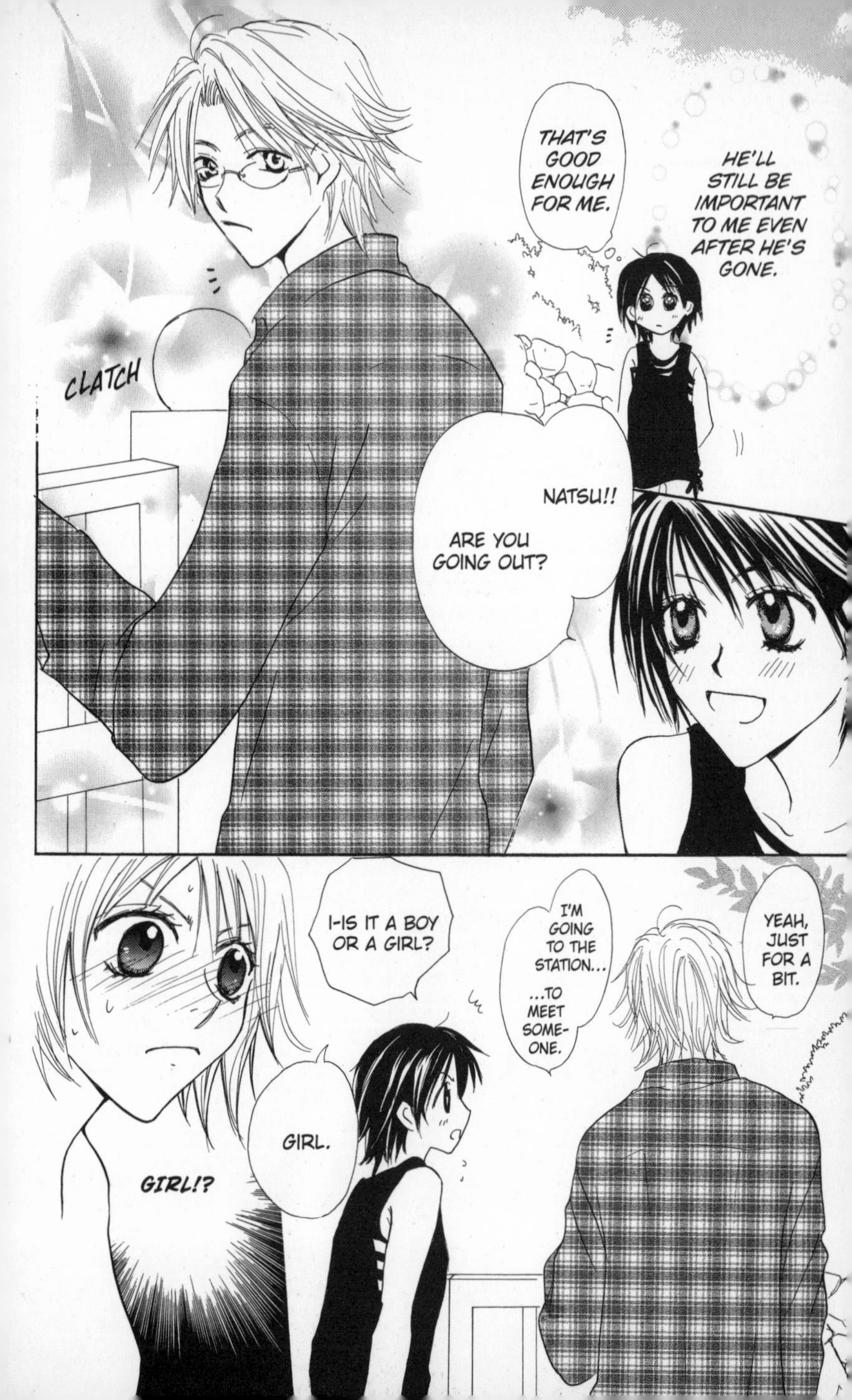
HE'LL STILL BE IMPORTANT TO ME EVEN AFTER HE'S GONE.
THAT'S GOOD ENOUGH FOR ME.
NATSU!!
ARE YOU GOING OUT?
CLATCH
YEAH, JUST FOR A BIT.
I'M GOING TO THE STATION...
...TO MEET SOME-ONE.
I-IS IT A BOY OR A GIRL?
GIRL.
GIRL!?

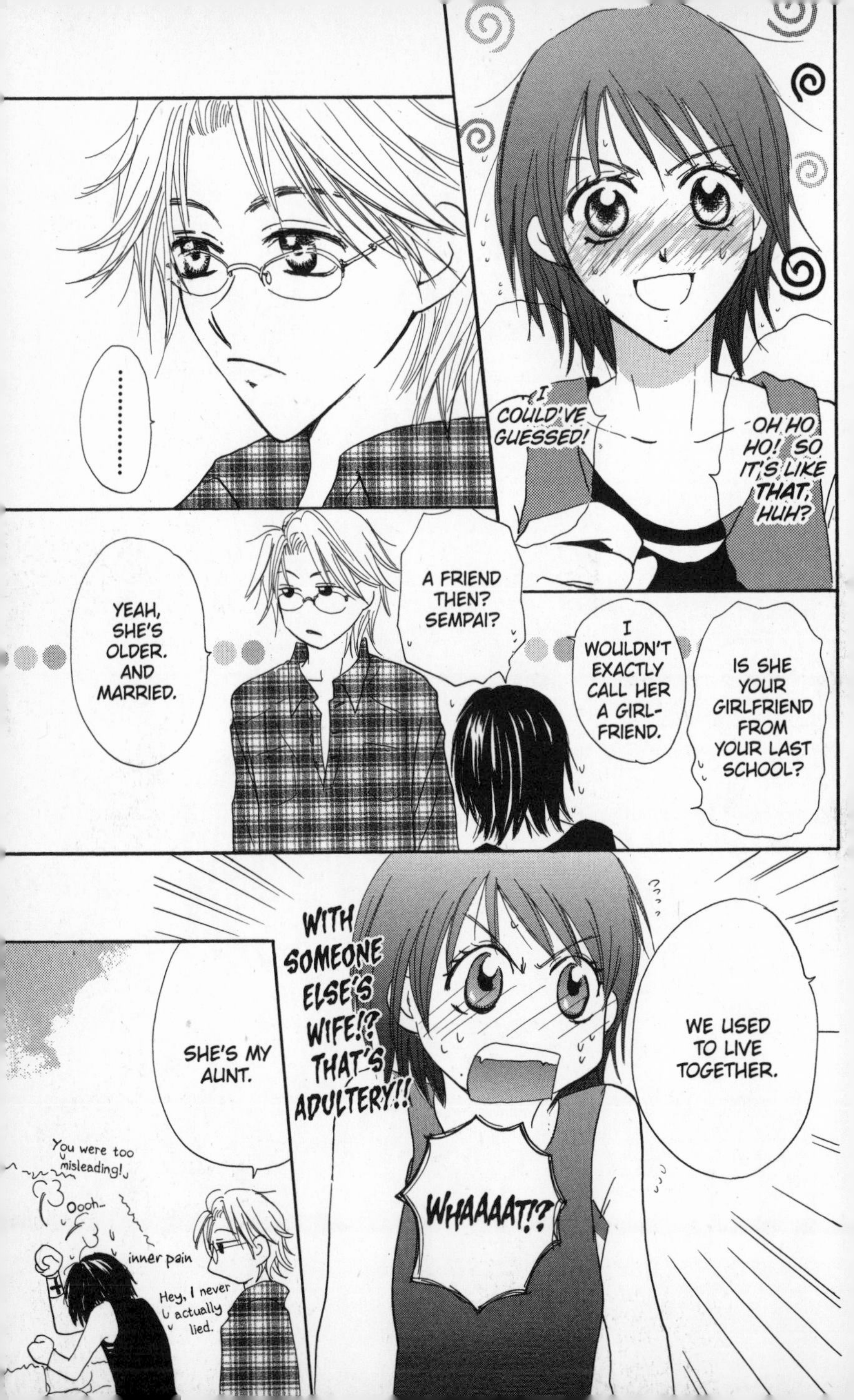

OH HO HO! SO IT'S LIKE THAT, HUH?
I COULD'VE GUESSED!
....
IS SHE YOUR GIRLFRIEND FROM YOUR LAST SCHOOL?
I WOULDN'T EXACTLY CALL HER A GIRL-FRIEND.
A FRIEND THEN? SEMPAI?
YEAH, SHE'S OLDER. AND MARRIED.
WE USED TO LIVE TOGETHER.
WHAAAAT!?
WITH SOMEONE ELSE'S WIFE!? THAT'S ADULTERY!!
SHE'S MY AUNT.
You were too misleading!
Oooh
inner pain
Hey, I never actually lied.

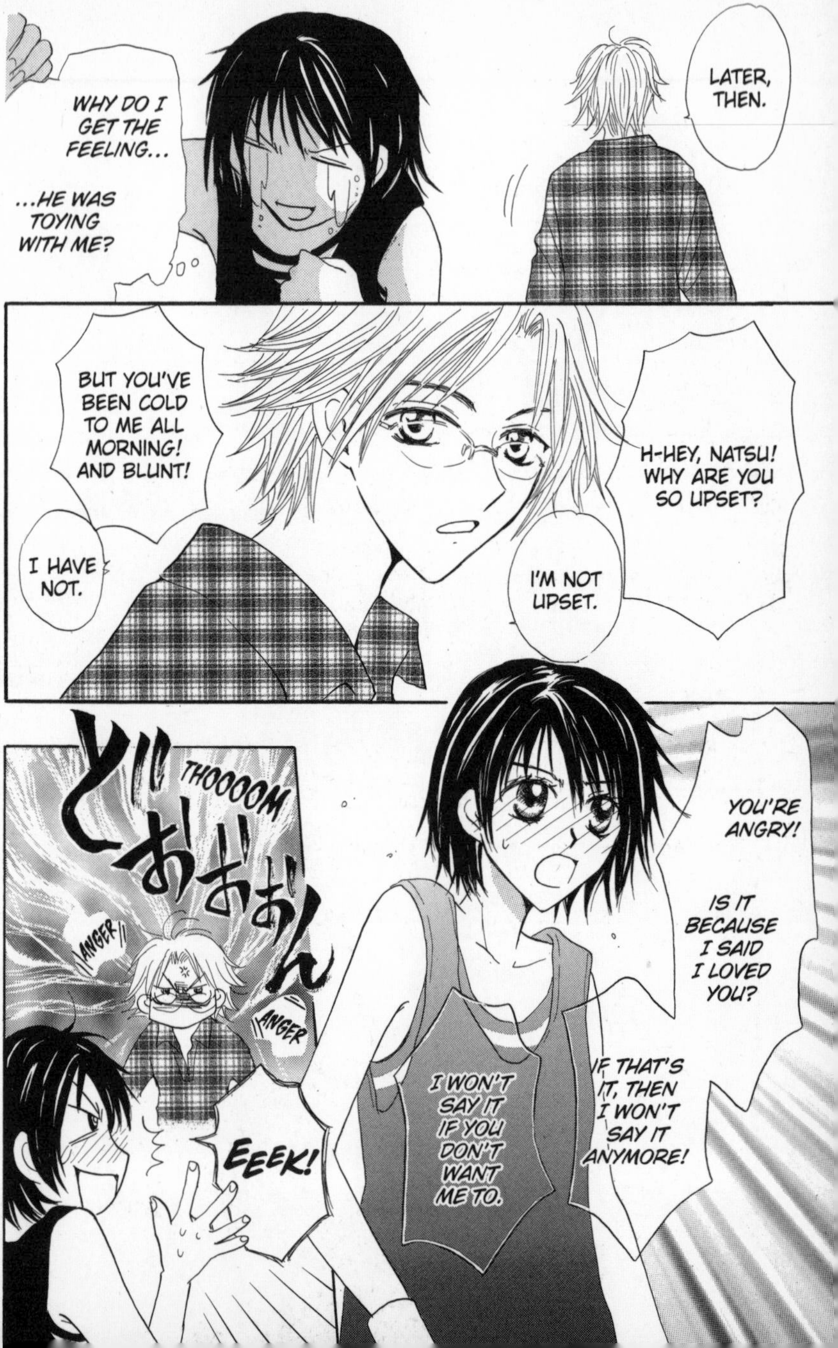

LATER, THEN.
WHY DO I GET THE FEELING...
...HE WAS TOYING WITH ME?
H-HEY, NATSU! WHY ARE YOU SO UPSET?
I'M NOT UPSET.
BUT YOU'VE BEEN COLD TO ME ALL MORNING! AND BLUNT!
I HAVE NOT.
YOU'RE ANGRY!
IS IT BECAUSE I SAID I LOVED YOU?
IF THAT'S IT, THEN I WON'T SAY IT ANYMORE!
I WON'T SAY IT IF YOU DON'T WANT ME TO.
どおおおん
THOOOOM
ANGER
ANGER
EEEK!

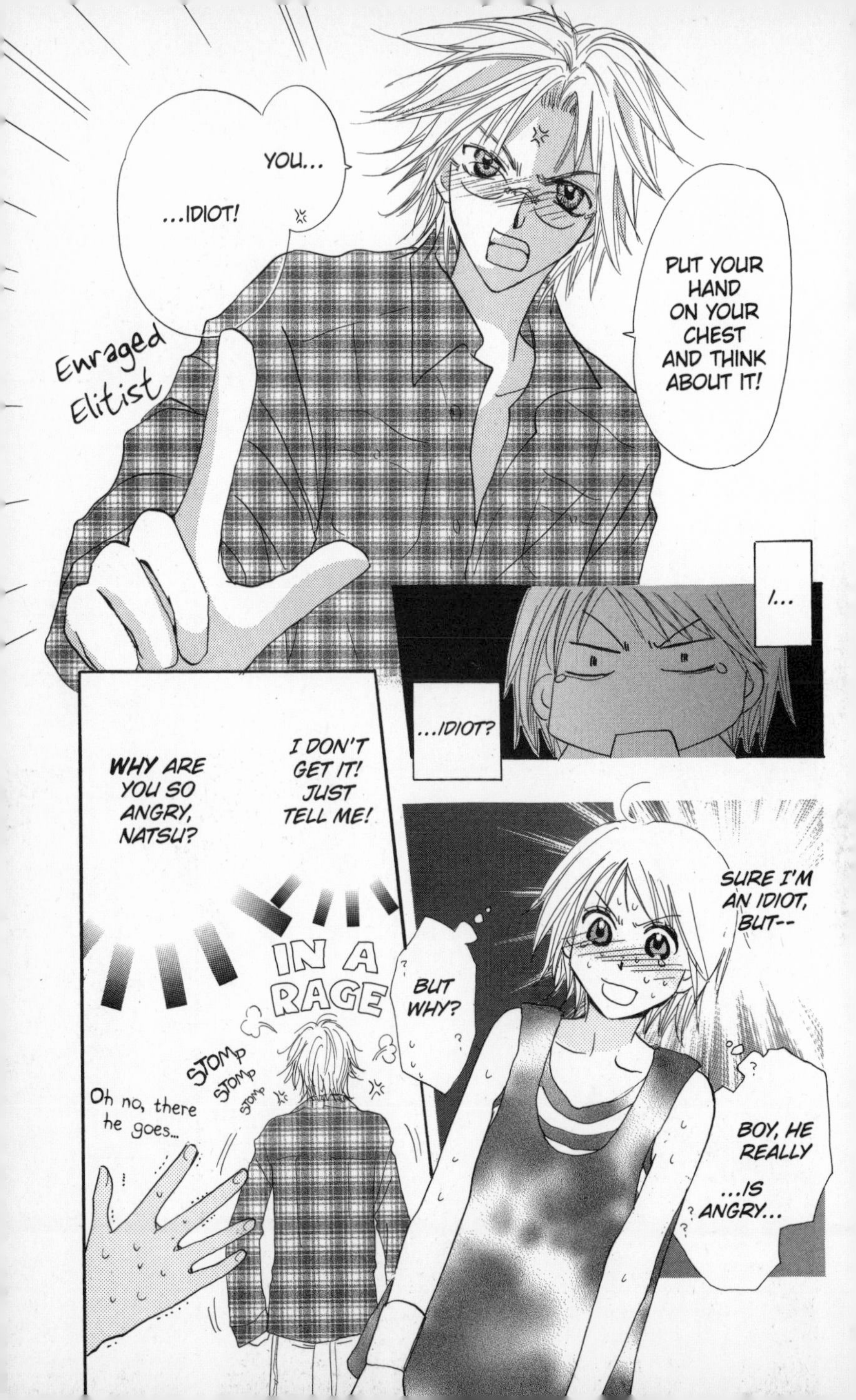
YOU...
...IDIOT!
PUT YOUR HAND ON YOUR CHEST AND THINK ABOUT IT!
Enraged Elitist
I...
...IDIOT?
SURE I'M AN IDIOT, BUT--
BUT WHY?
BOY, HE REALLY
...IS ANGRY...
I DON'T GET IT! JUST TELL ME!
WHY ARE YOU SO ANGRY, NATSU?
IN A RAGE
STOMP STOMP STOMP
Oh no, there he goes...

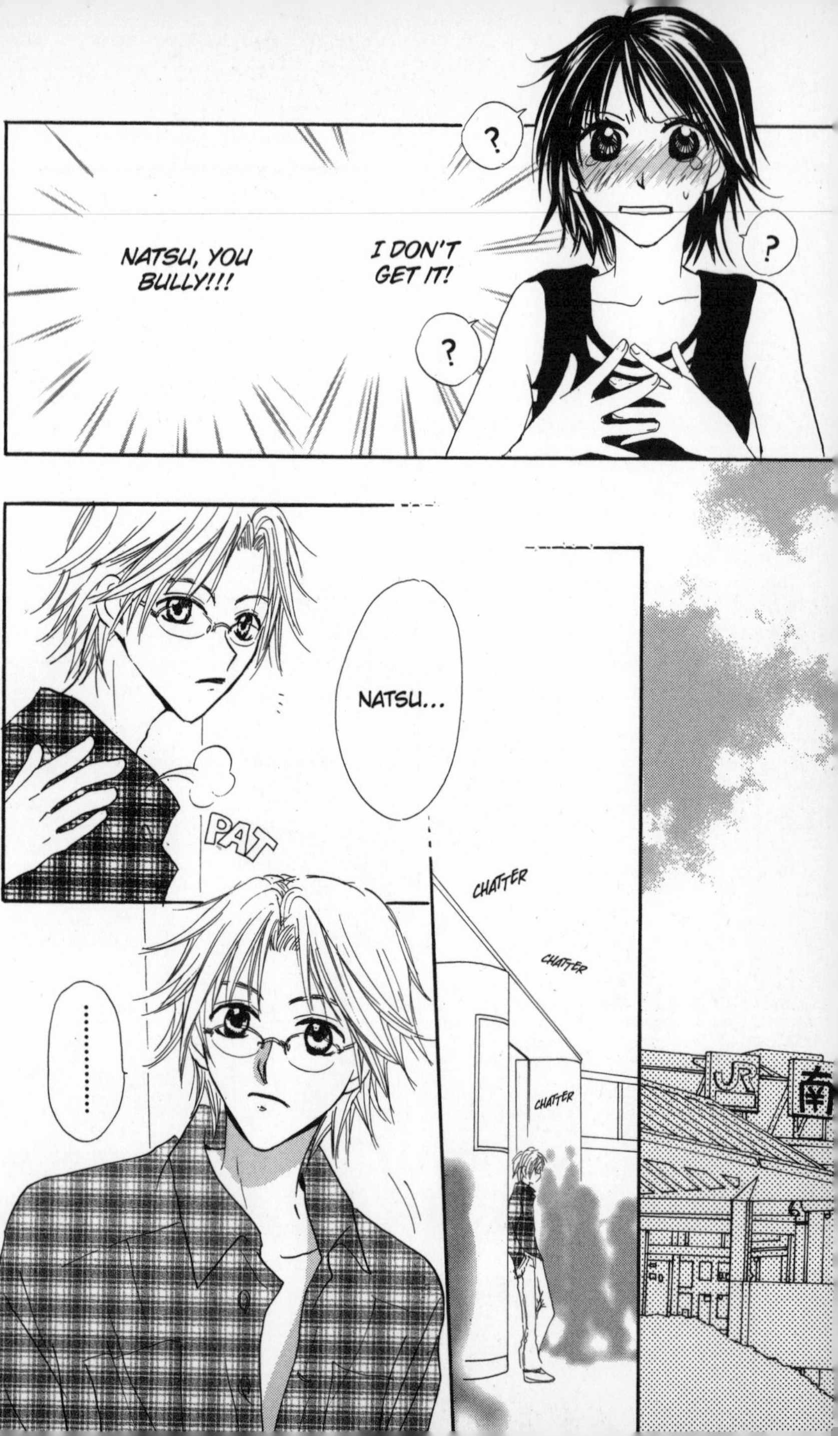
?
?
?
I DON'T GET IT!
NATSU, YOU BULLY!!!
NATSU...
PAT
CHATTER
CHATTER
CHATTER
JR
南
....

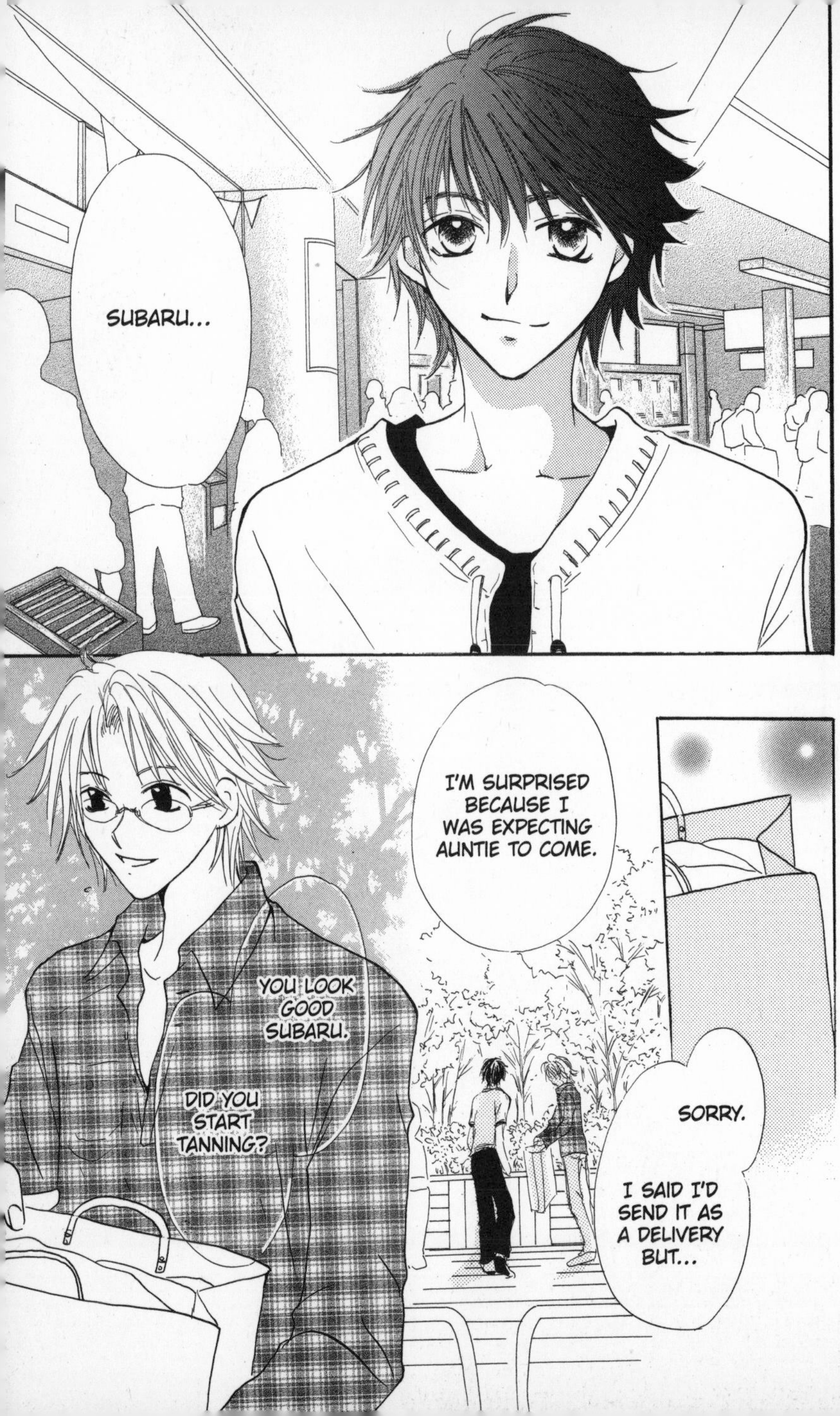
SUBARU...
I'M SURPRISED BECAUSE I WAS EXPECTING AUNTIE TO COME.
SORRY.
I SAID I'D SEND IT AS A DELIVERY BUT...
YOU LOOK GOOD SUBARU.
DID YOU START TANNING?

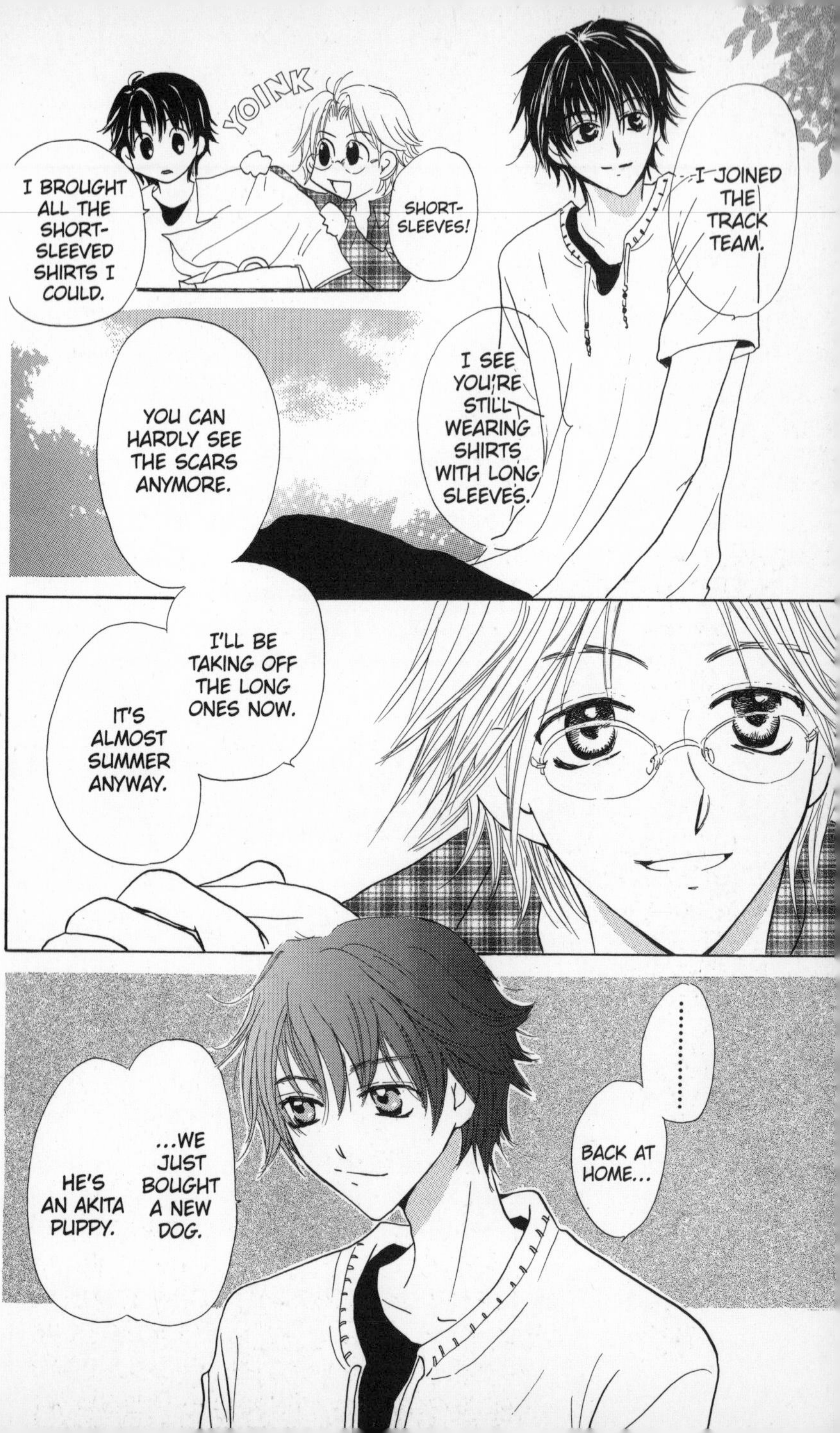
I JOINED THE TRACK TEAM.
I SEE YOU'RE STILL WEARING SHIRTS WITH LONG SLEEVES.
YOINK
SHORT-SLEEVES!
I BROUGHT ALL THE SHORT-SLEEVED SHIRTS I COULD.
YOU CAN HARDLY SEE THE SCARS ANYMORE.
I'LL BE TAKING OFF THE LONG ONES NOW.
IT'S ALMOST SUMMER ANYWAY.
......
BACK AT HOME...
...WE JUST BOUGHT A NEW DOG.
HE'S AN AKITA PUPPY.

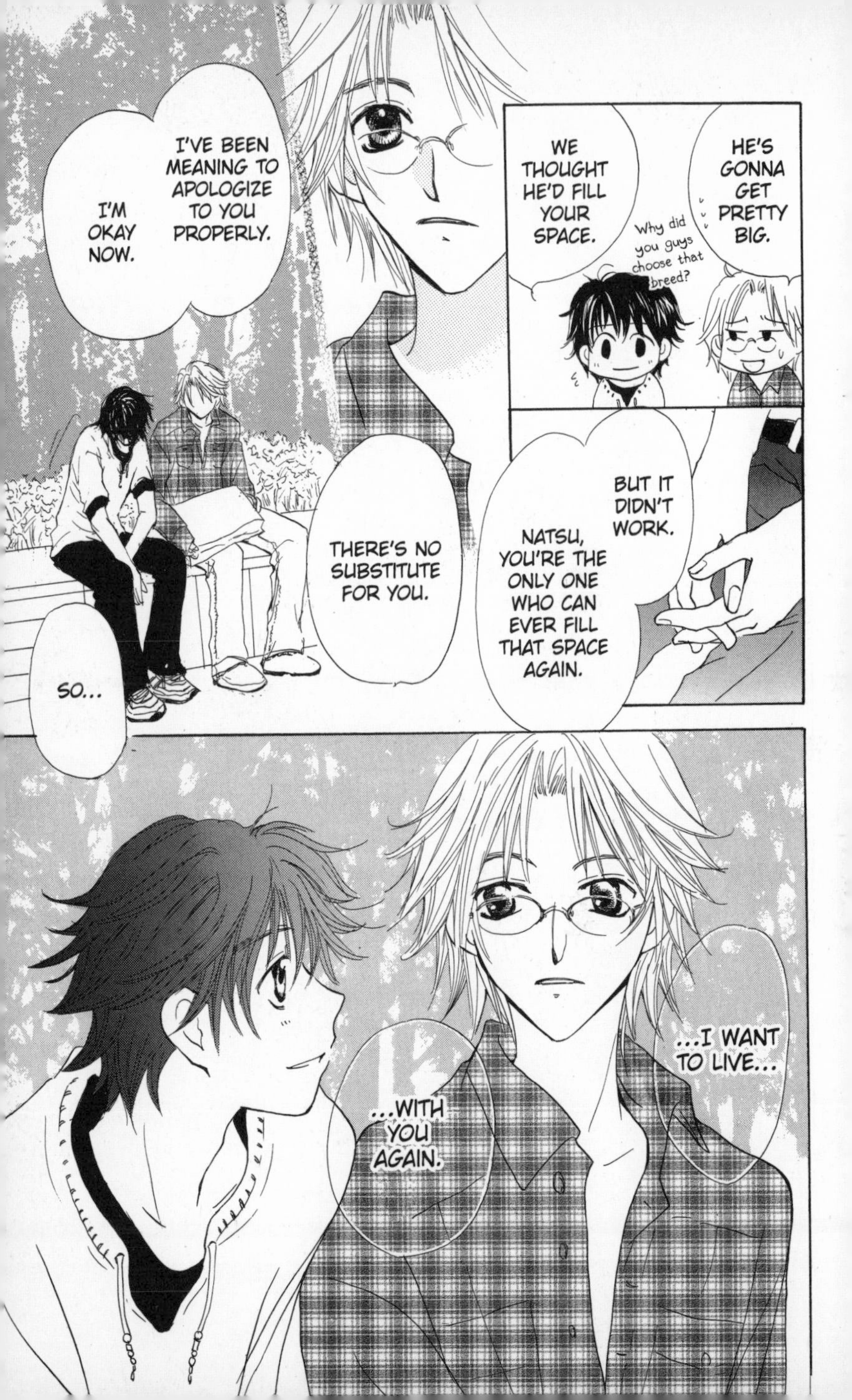
HE'S GONNA GET PRETTY BIG.
WE THOUGHT HE'D FILL YOUR SPACE.
Why did you guys choose that breed?
BUT IT DIDN'T WORK.
NATSU, YOU'RE THE ONLY ONE WHO CAN EVER FILL THAT SPACE AGAIN.
I'VE BEEN MEANING TO APOLOGIZE TO YOU PROPERLY.
I'M OKAY NOW.
THERE'S NO SUBSTITUTE FOR YOU.
SO...
...I WANT TO LIVE...
...WITH YOU AGAIN.

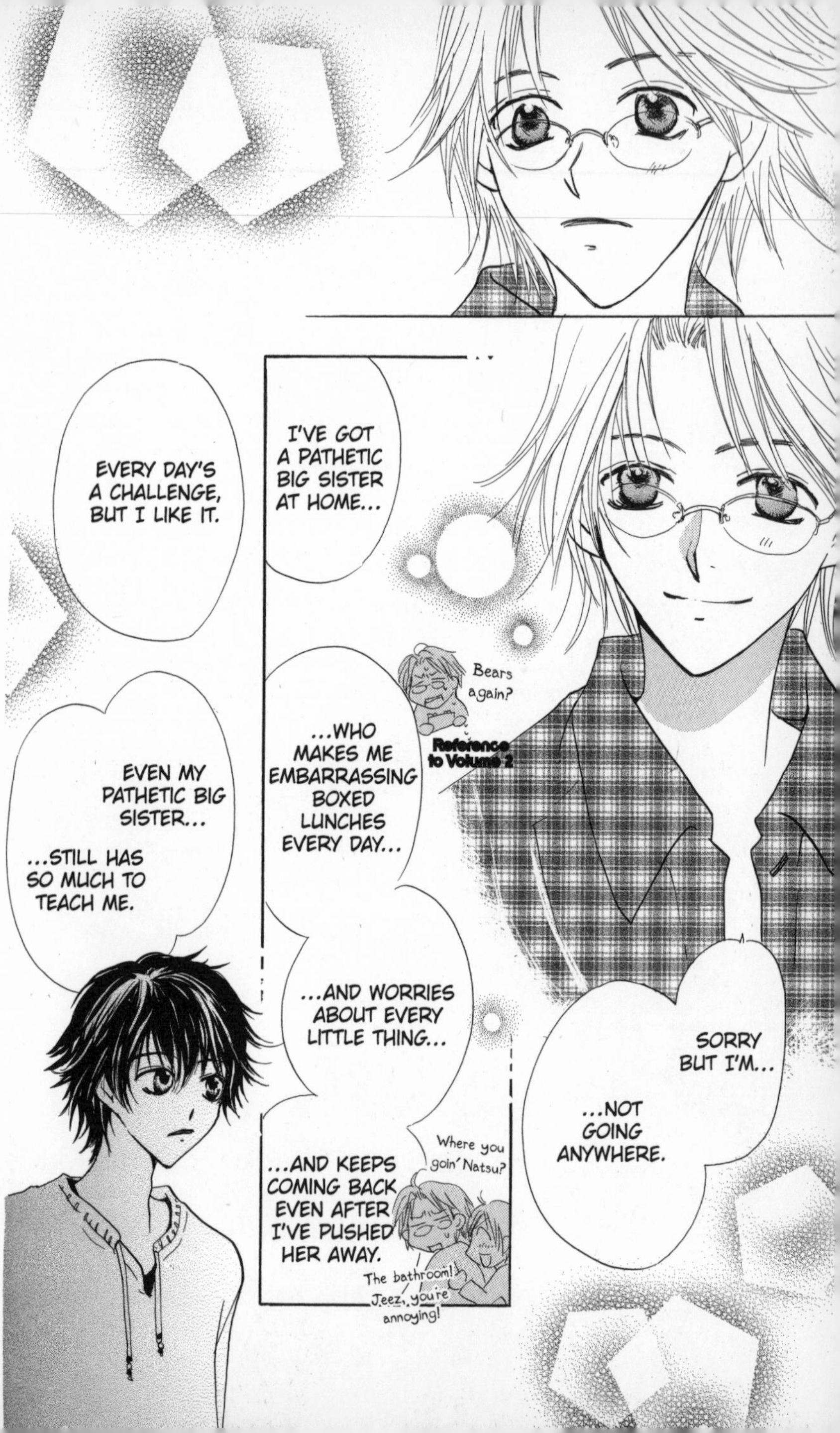
I'VE GOT A PATHETIC BIG SISTER AT HOME...
...WHO MAKES ME EMBARRASSING BOXED LUNCHES EVERY DAY...
Bears again?
Reference to Volume 2
...AND WORRIES ABOUT EVERY LITTLE THING...
...AND KEEPS COMING BACK EVEN AFTER I'VE PUSHED HER AWAY.
Where you goin' Natsu?
The bathroom! Jeez, you're annoying!
EVERY DAY'S A CHALLENGE, BUT I LIKE IT.
EVEN MY PATHETIC BIG SISTER...
...STILL HAS SO MUCH TO TEACH ME.
SORRY BUT I'M...
...NOT GOING ANYWHERE.

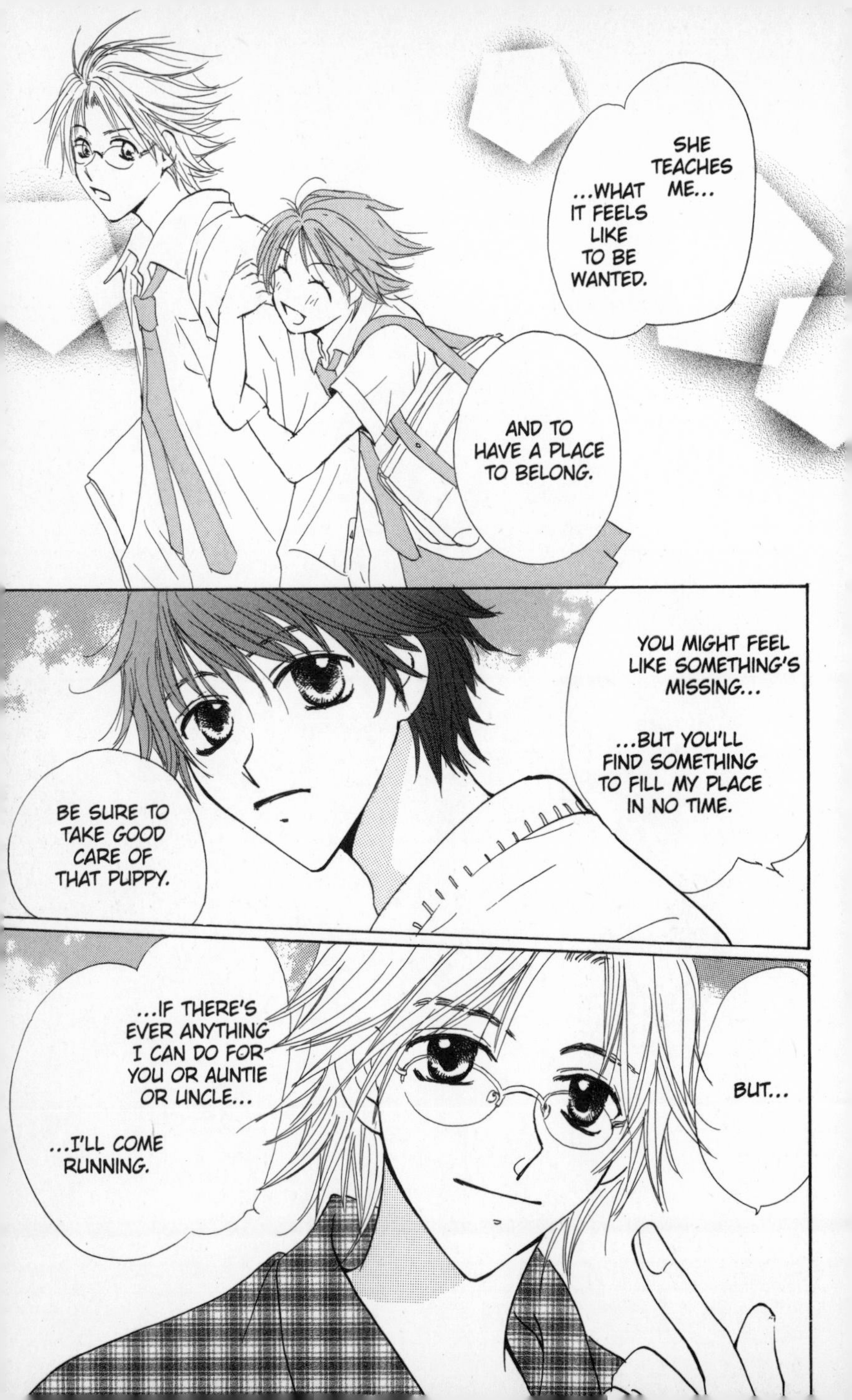
SHE TEACHES ME...
...WHAT IT FEELS LIKE TO BE WANTED.
AND TO HAVE A PLACE TO BELONG.
YOU MIGHT FEEL LIKE SOMETHING'S MISSING...
...BUT YOU'LL FIND SOMETHING TO FILL MY PLACE IN NO TIME.
BE SURE TO TAKE GOOD CARE OF THAT PUPPY.
BUT...
...IF THERE'S EVER ANYTHING I CAN DO FOR YOU OR AUNTIE OR UNCLE...
...I'LL COME RUNNING.

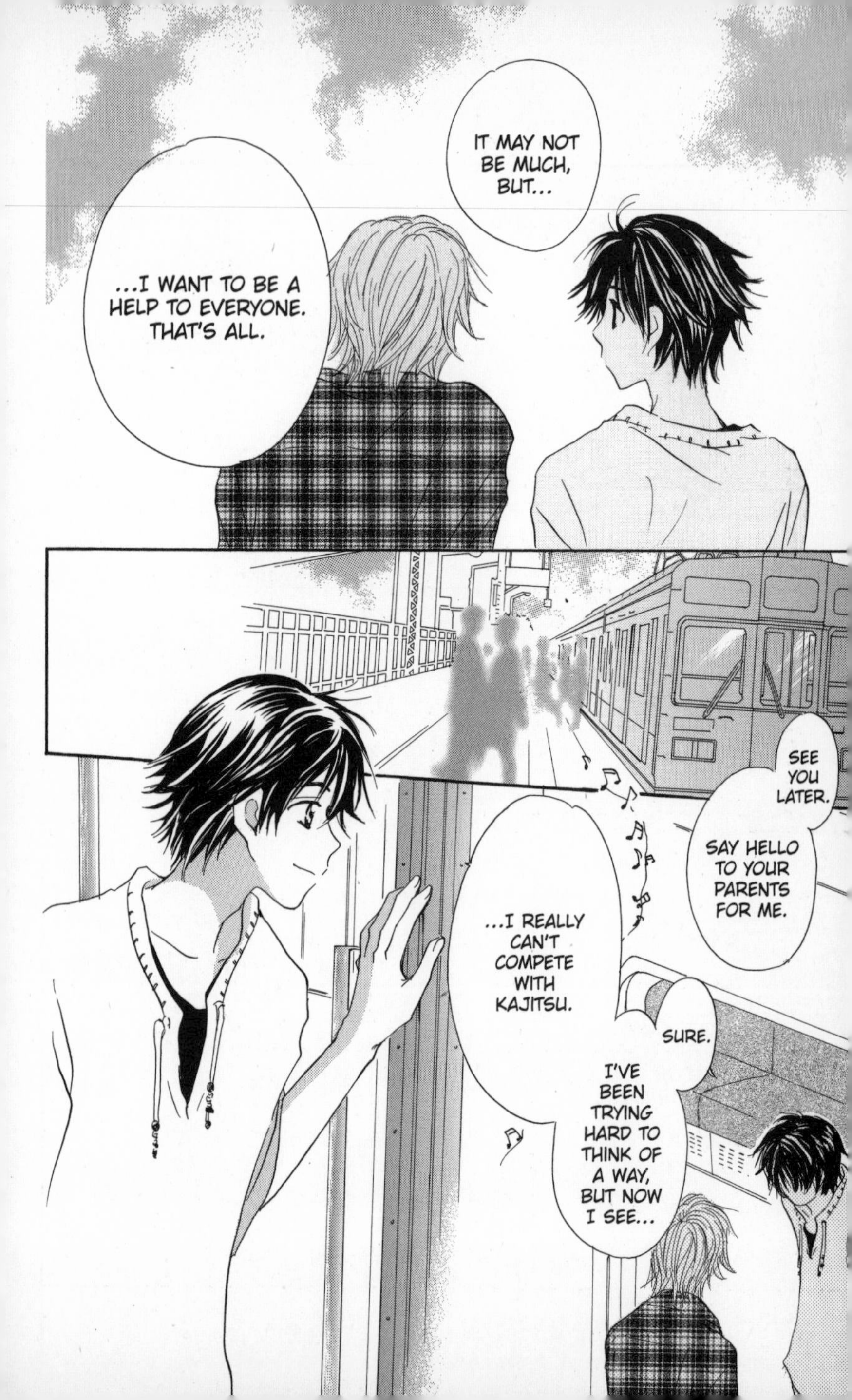
IT MAY NOT BE MUCH, BUT...
...I WANT TO BE A HELP TO EVERYONE. THAT'S ALL.
SEE YOU LATER.
SAY HELLO TO YOUR PARENTS FOR ME.
SURE.
I'VE BEEN TRYING HARD TO THINK OF A WAY, BUT NOW I SEE...
...I REALLY CAN'T COMPETE WITH KAJITSU.

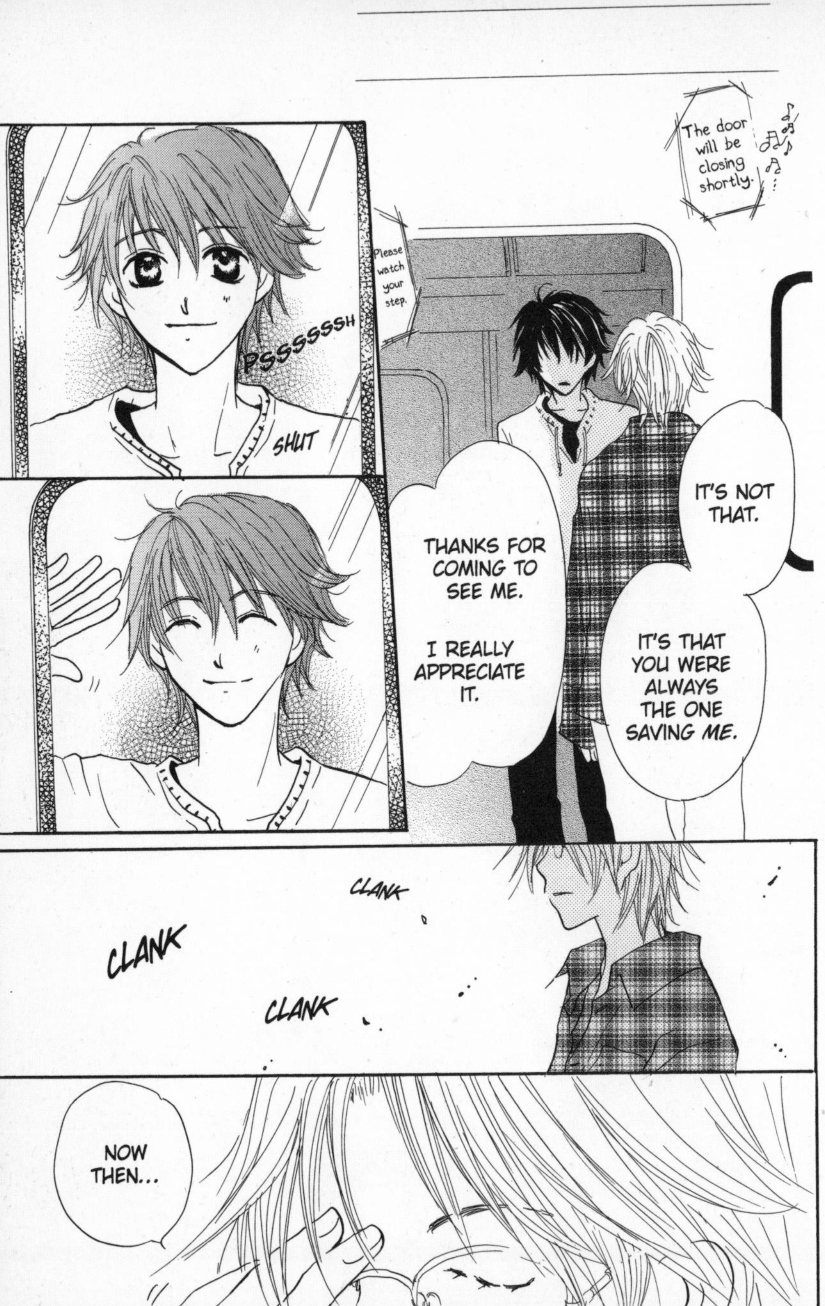
The door will be closing shortly.
Please watch your step.
THANKS FOR COMING TO SEE ME.
I REALLY APPRECIATE IT.
IT'S NOT THAT.
IT'S THAT YOU WERE ALWAYS THE ONE SAVING ME.
PSSSSSSH
SHUT
CLANK
CLANK
CLANK
NOW THEN...

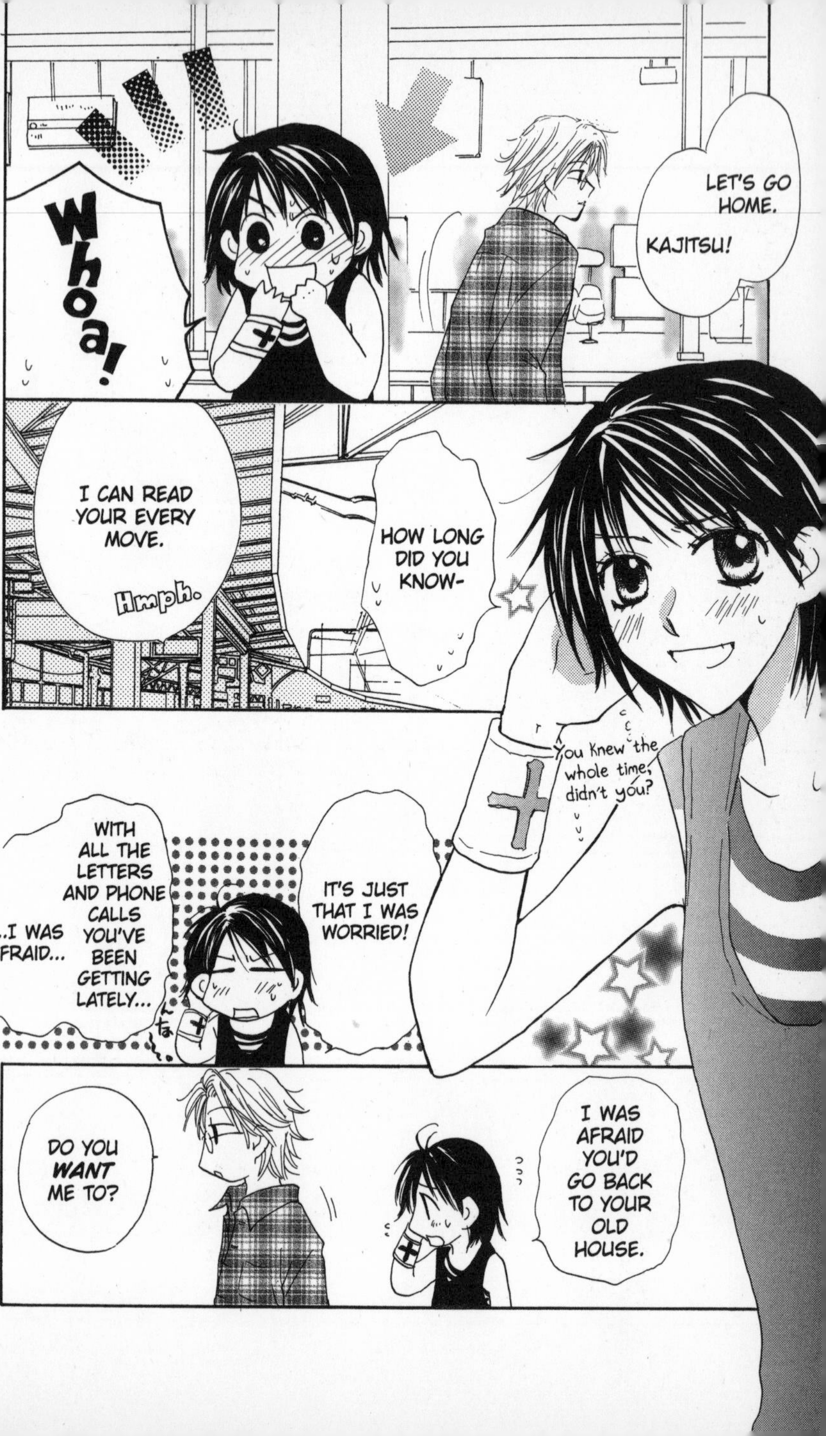
LET'S GO HOME.
KAJITSU!
Whoa!
You knew the whole time, didn't you?
HOW LONG DID YOU KNOW-
I CAN READ YOUR EVERY MOVE.
Hmph.
IT'S JUST THAT I WAS WORRIED!
WITH ALL THE LETTERS AND PHONE CALLS YOU'VE BEEN GETTING LATELY...
...I WAS AFRAID...
I WAS AFRAID YOU'D GO BACK TO YOUR OLD HOUSE.
DO YOU WANT ME TO?

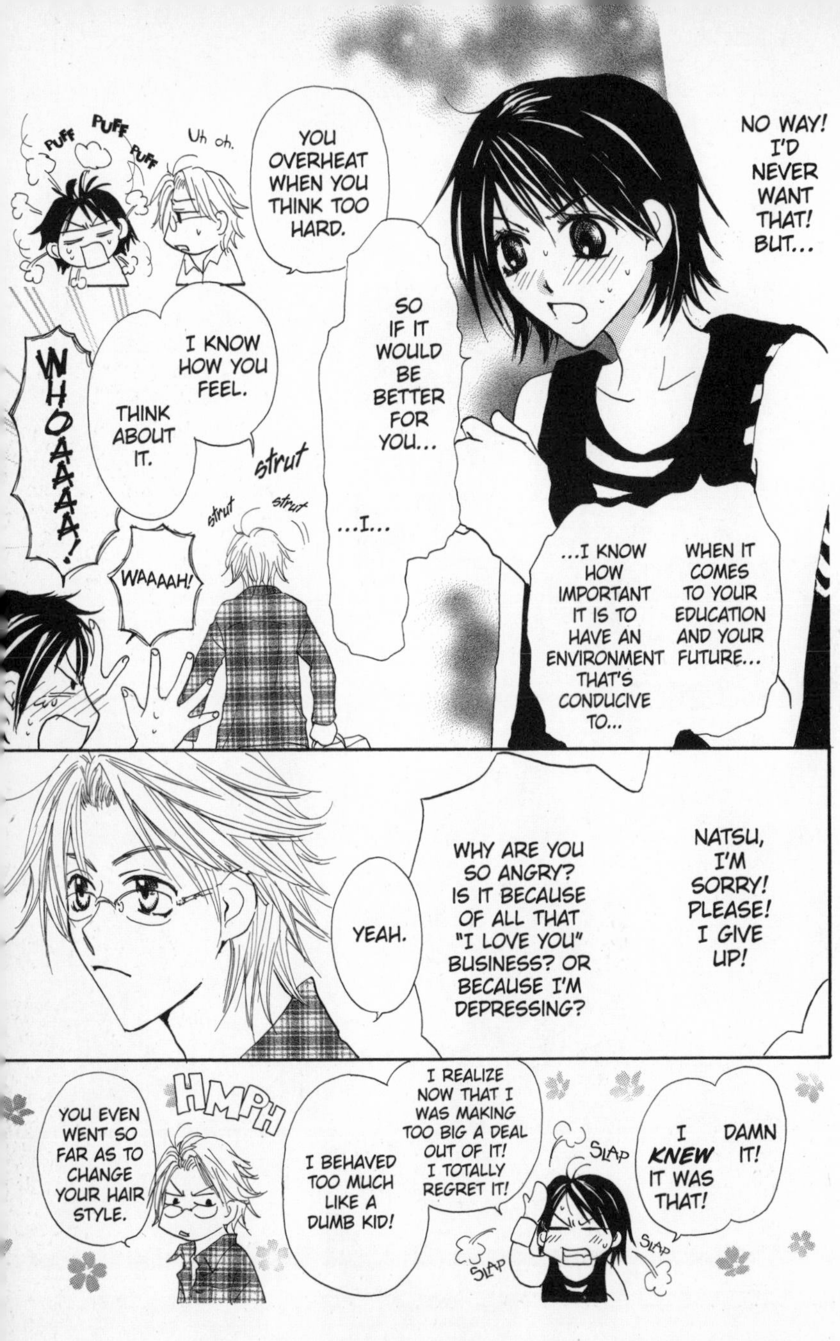
NO WAY! I'D NEVER WANT THAT! BUT...
WHEN IT COMES TO YOUR EDUCATION AND YOUR FUTURE...
...I KNOW HOW IMPORTANT IT IS TO HAVE AN ENVIRONMENT THAT'S CONDUCIVE TO...
SO IF IT WOULD BE BETTER FOR YOU...
...I...
YOU OVERHEAT WHEN YOU THINK TOO HARD.
Uh oh.
PUFF PUFF PUFF
I KNOW HOW YOU FEEL.
THINK ABOUT IT.
strut strut strut
WHOAAAAA!
WAAAAH!
NATSU, I'M SORRY! PLEASE! I GIVE UP!
WHY ARE YOU SO ANGRY? IS IT BECAUSE OF ALL THAT "I LOVE YOU" BUSINESS? OR BECAUSE I'M DEPRESSING?
YEAH.
DAMN IT!
I *KNEW* IT WAS THAT!
SLAP SLAP SLAP
I REALIZE NOW THAT I WAS MAKING TOO BIG A DEAL OUT OF IT! I TOTALLY REGRET IT!
I BEHAVED TOO MUCH LIKE A DUMB KID!
HMPH
YOU EVEN WENT SO FAR AS TO CHANGE YOUR HAIR STYLE.

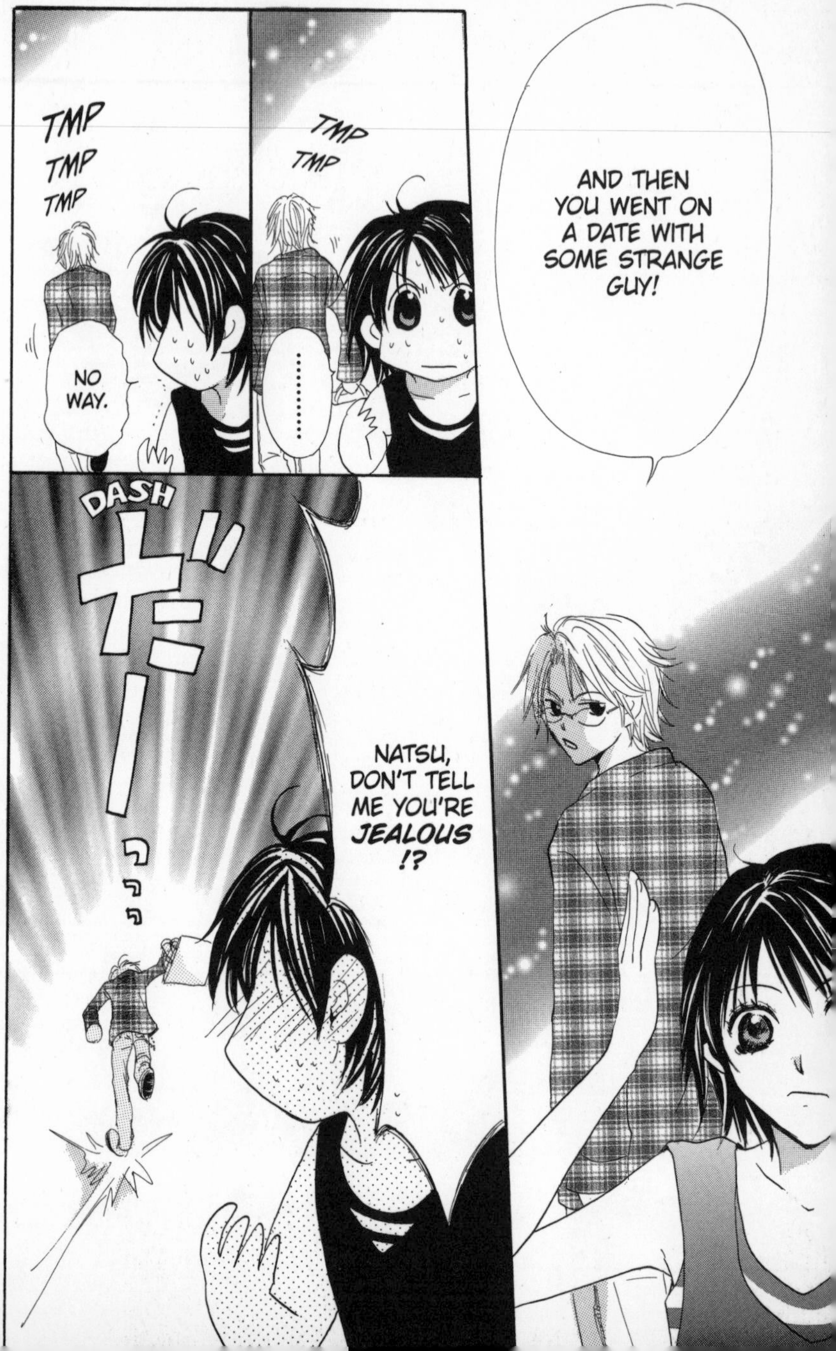
AND THEN YOU WENT ON A DATE WITH SOME STRANGE GUY!
TMP TMP
......
TMP TMP TMP
NO WAY.
DASH
NATSU, DON'T TELL ME YOU'RE JEALOUS!?

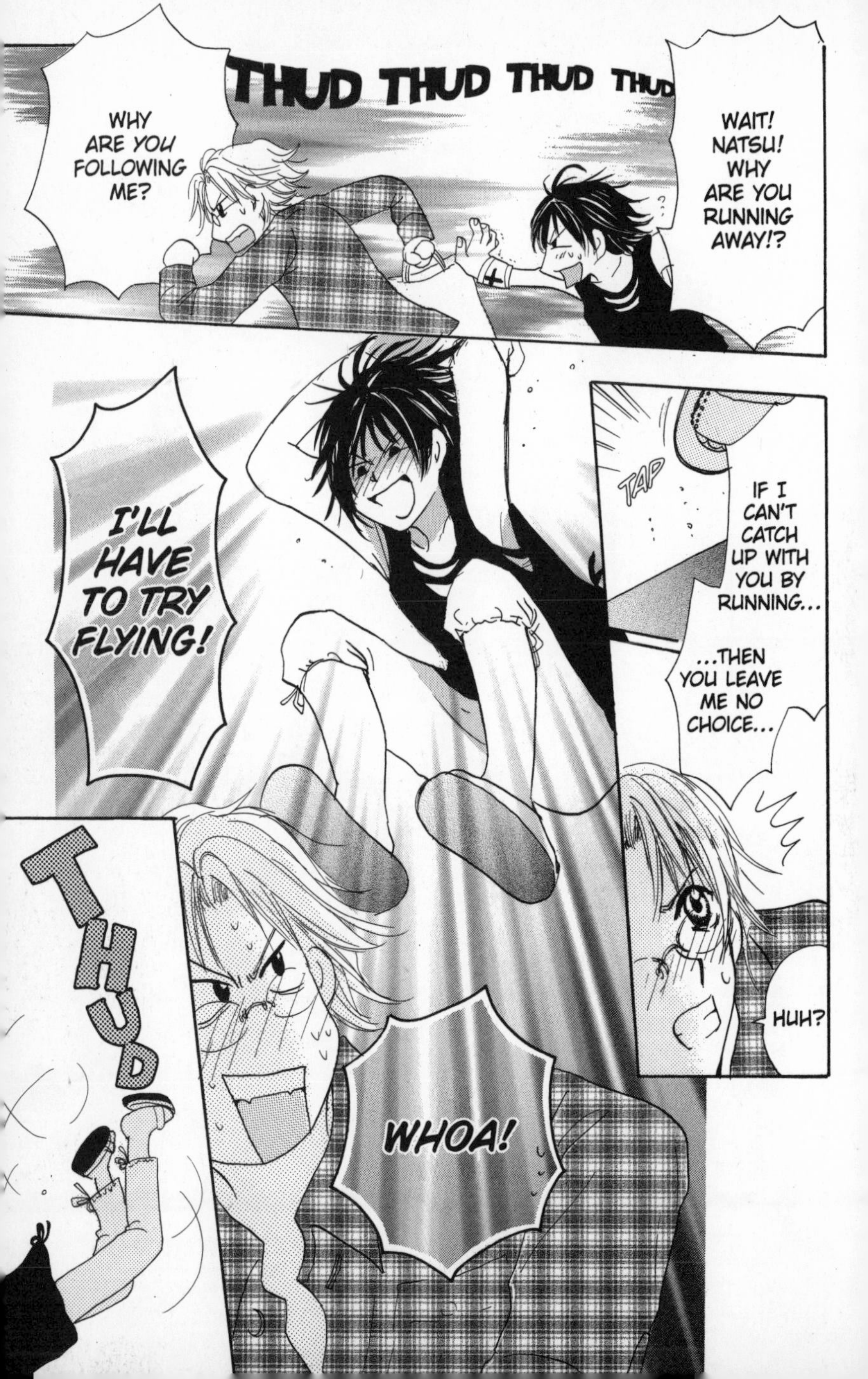
WAIT! NATSU! WHY ARE YOU RUNNING AWAY!?
THUD THUD THUD THUD
WHY ARE YOU FOLLOWING ME?
TAP
IF I CAN'T CATCH UP WITH YOU BY RUNNING...
...THEN YOU LEAVE ME NO CHOICE...
HUH?
I'LL HAVE TO TRY FLYING!
WHOA!
THUD

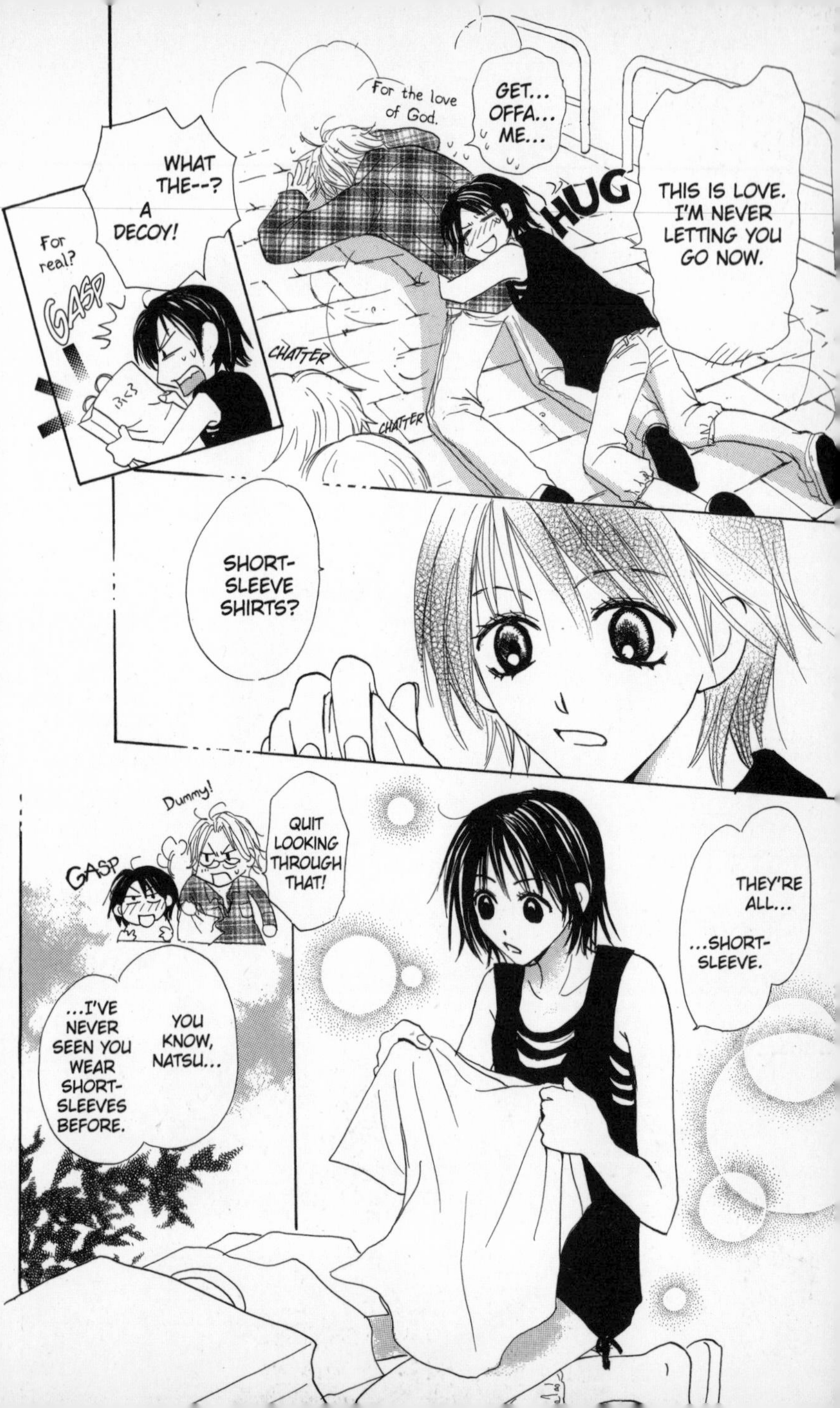

THIS IS LOVE. I'M NEVER LETTING YOU GO NOW.
HUG
GET... OFFA... ME...
For the love of God.
CHATTER
CHATTER
WHAT THE--? A DECOY!
For real?
GASP
SHORT-SLEEVE SHIRTS?
THEY'RE ALL... ...SHORT-SLEEVE.
QUIT LOOKING THROUGH THAT!
Dummy!
GASP
YOU KNOW, NATSU...
...I'VE NEVER SEEN YOU WEAR SHORT-SLEEVES BEFORE.

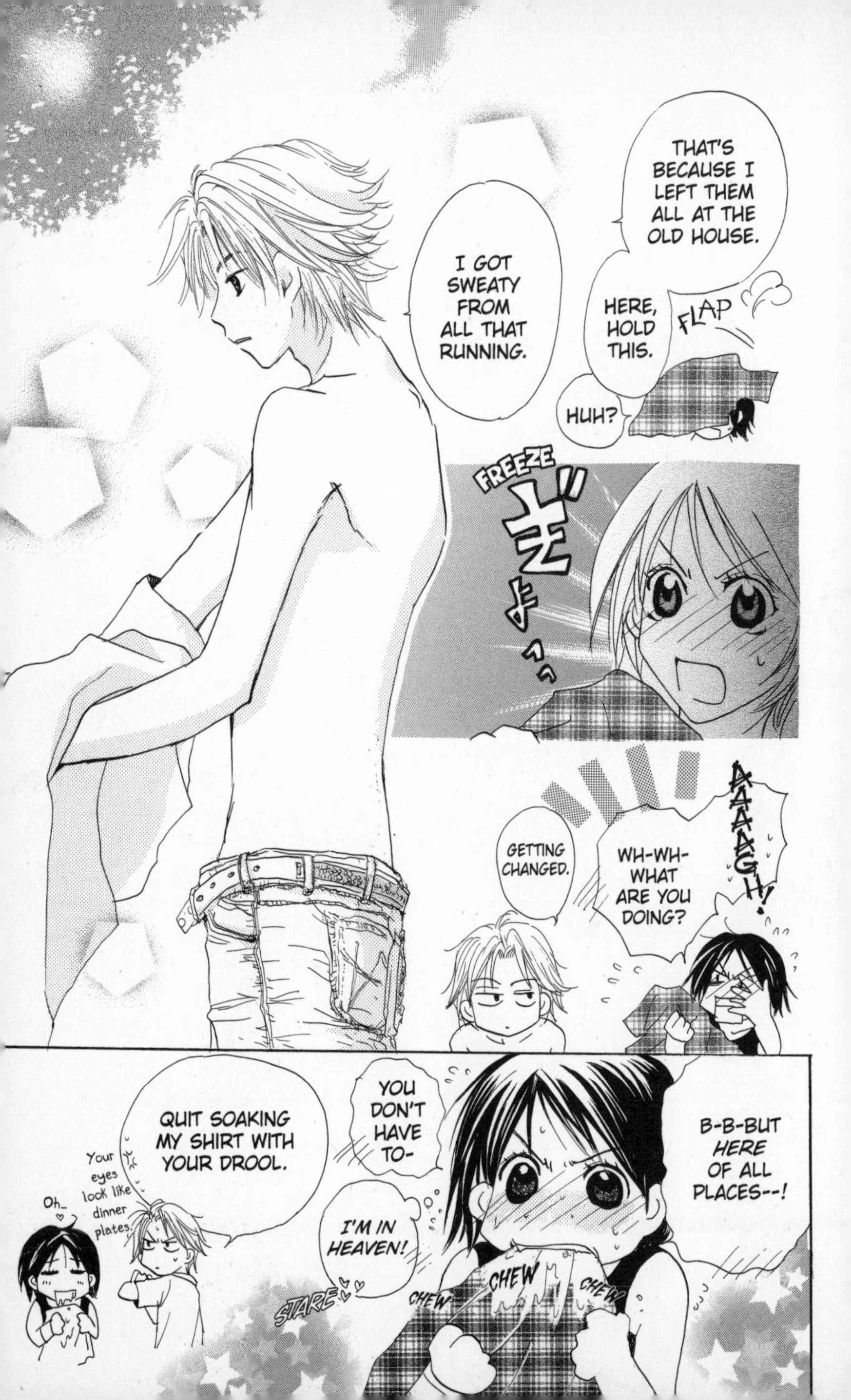

THAT'S BECAUSE I LEFT THEM ALL AT THE OLD HOUSE.
I GOT SWEATY FROM ALL THAT RUNNING.
HERE, HOLD THIS.
FLAP
HUH?
FREEZE
ぎょっ
AAAAGH!
WH-WH-WHAT ARE YOU DOING?
GETTING CHANGED.
B-B-BUT HERE OF ALL PLACES--!
YOU DON'T HAVE TO-
I'M IN HEAVEN!
CHEW
CHEW
CHEW
STARE
QUIT SOAKING MY SHIRT WITH YOUR DROOL.
Your eyes look like dinner plates.
Oh...

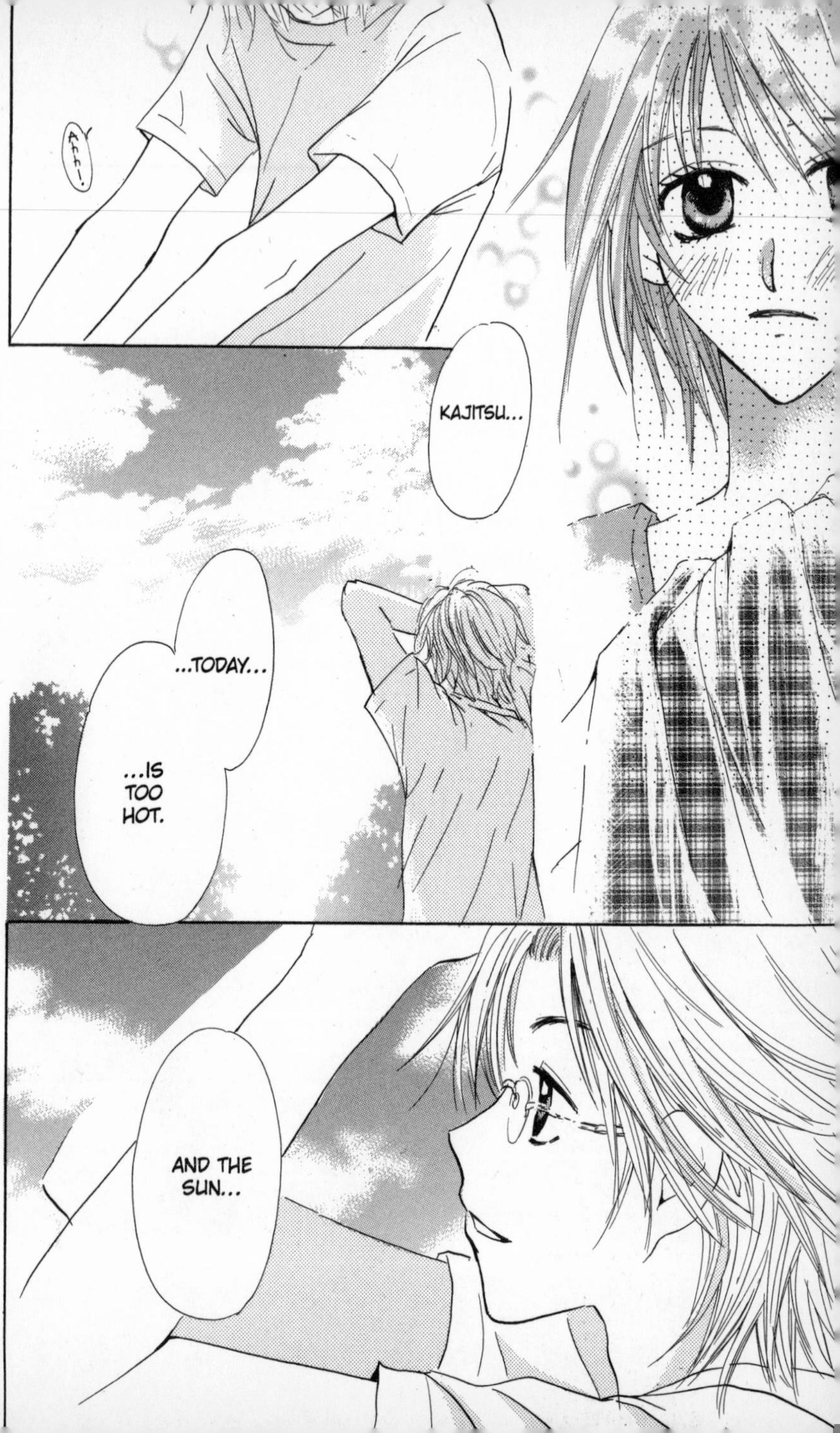
Ahh!
KAJITSU...
...TODAY...
...IS TOO HOT.
AND THE SUN...

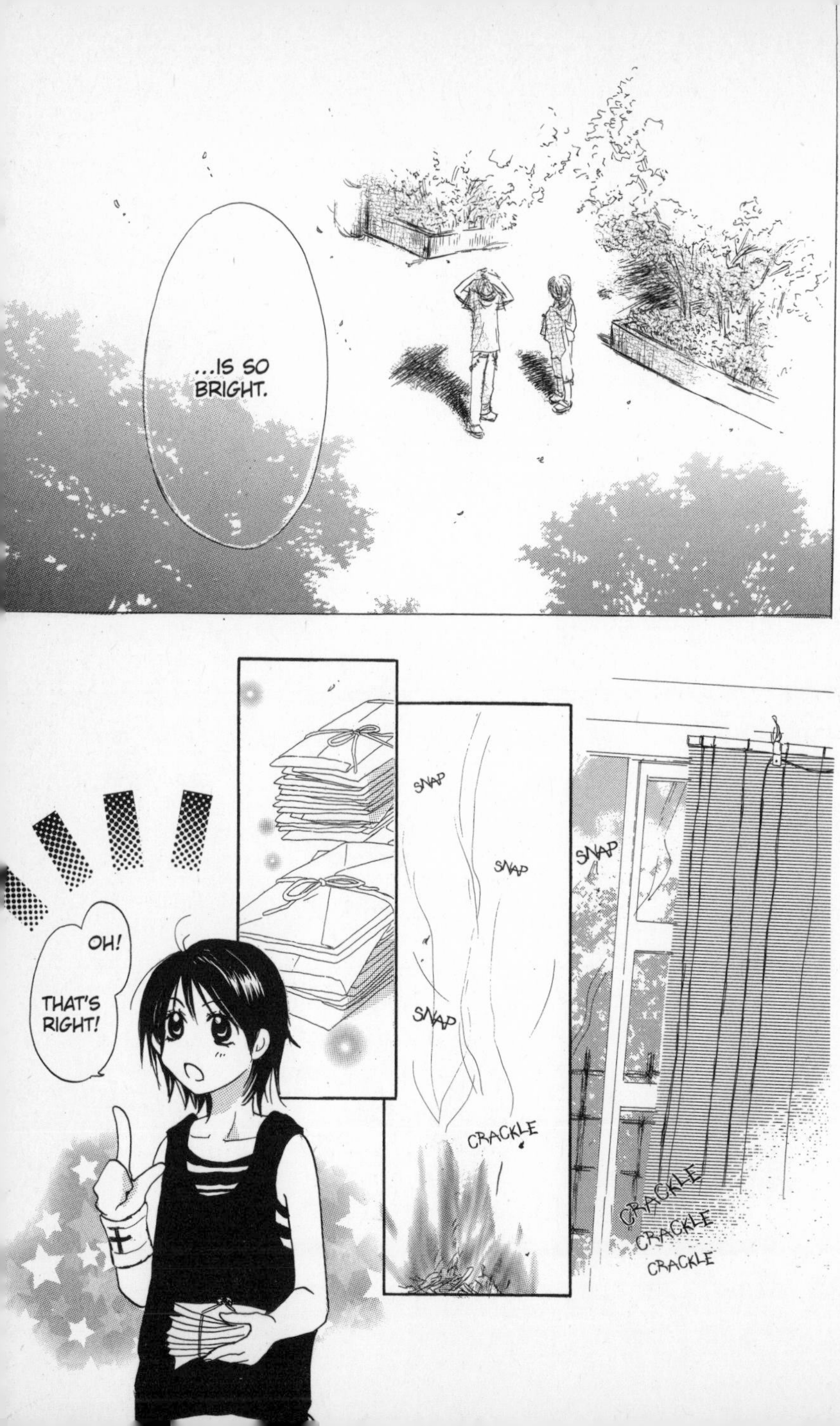
...IS SO BRIGHT.
SNAP
CRACKLE
CRACKLE
CRACKLE
SNAP
SNAP
SNAP
CRACKLE
OH!
THAT'S RIGHT!

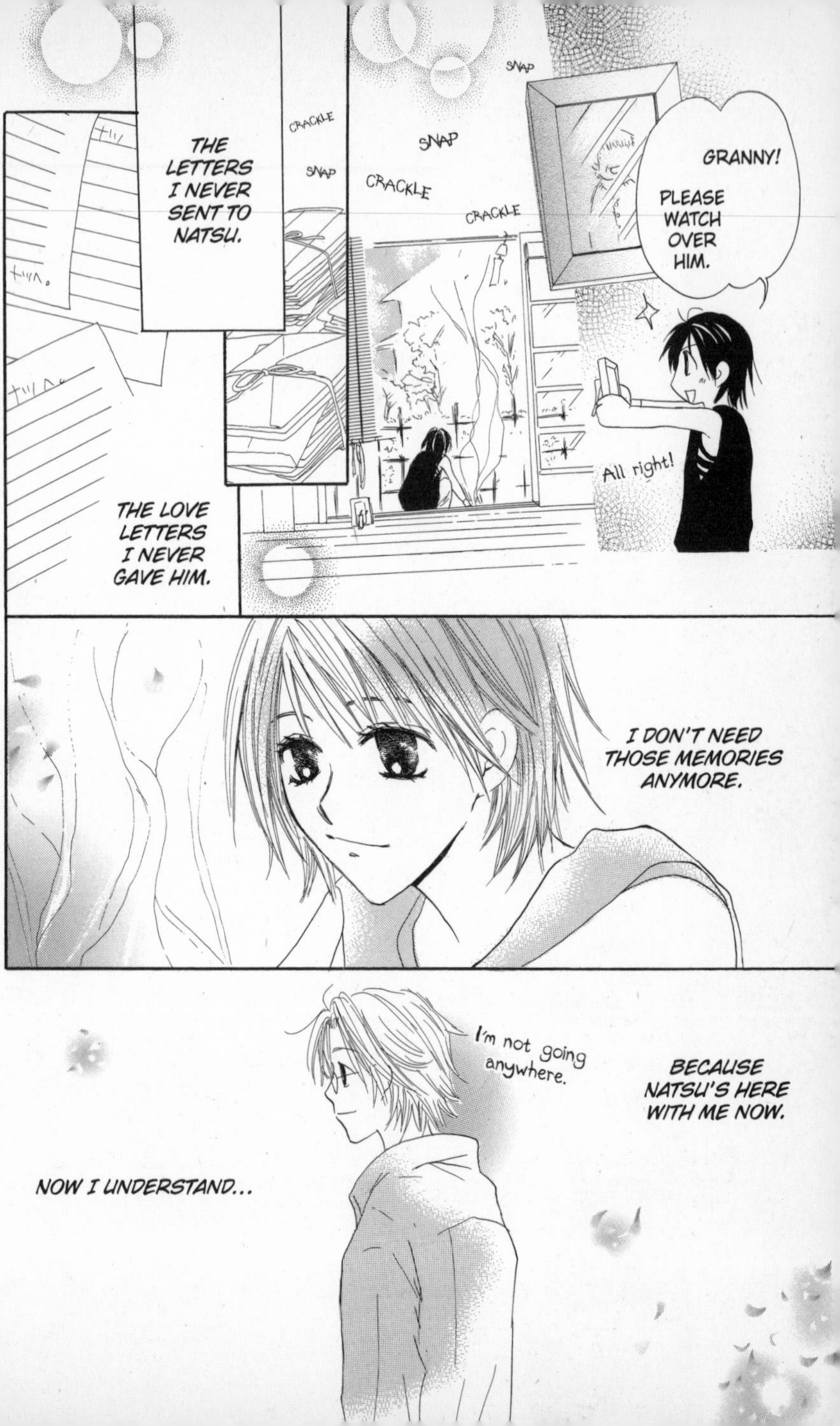
SNAP
GRANNY!
PLEASE WATCH OVER HIM.
All right!
CRACKLE
SNAP
CRACKLE
SNAP
CRACKLE
THE LETTERS I NEVER SENT TO NATSU.
THE LOVE LETTERS I NEVER GAVE HIM.
I DON'T NEED THOSE MEMORIES ANYMORE.
BECAUSE NATSU'S HERE WITH ME NOW.
I'm not going anywhere.
NOW I UNDERSTAND...

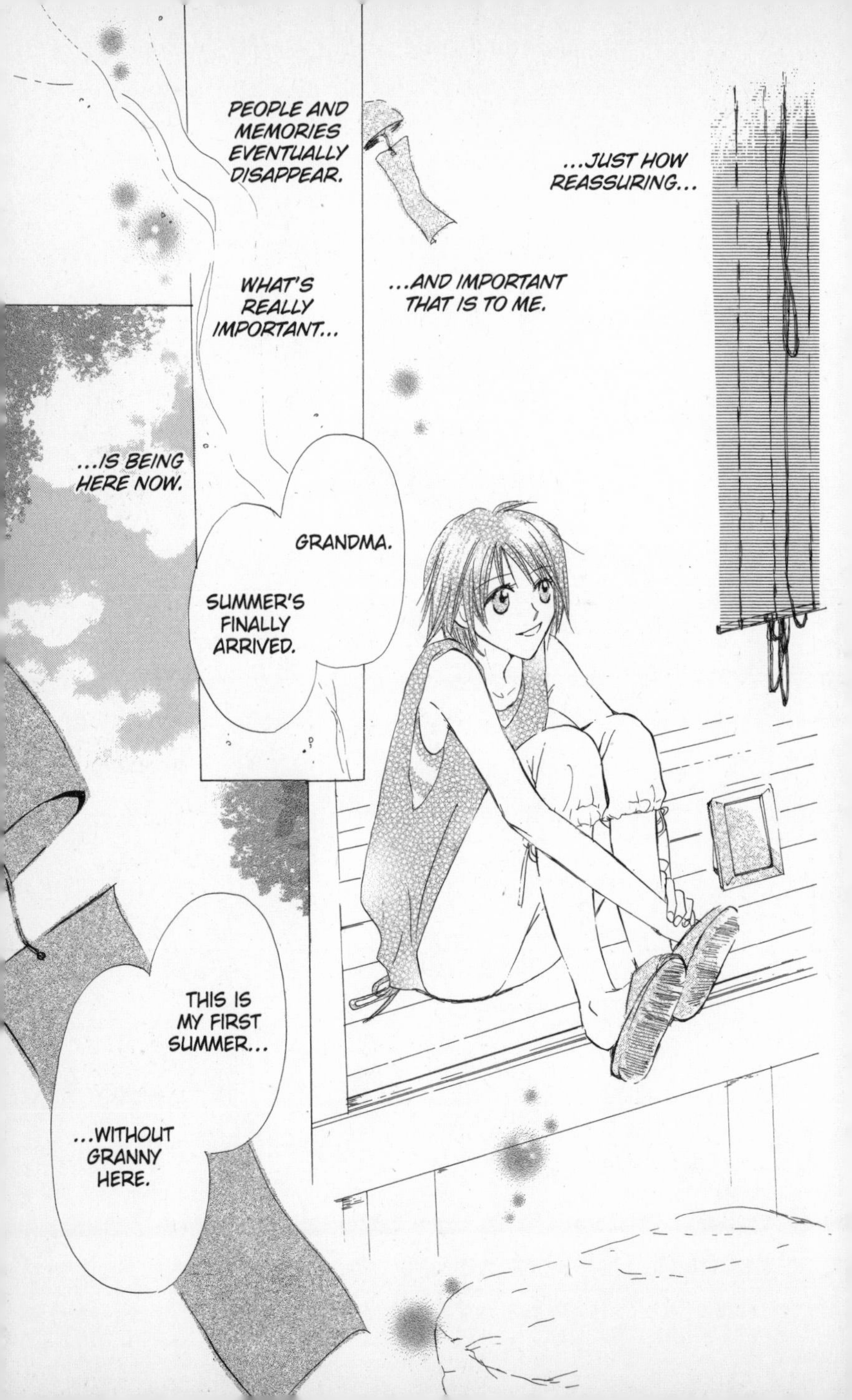
...JUST HOW REASSURING...
...AND IMPORTANT THAT IS TO ME.
PEOPLE AND MEMORIES EVENTUALLY DISAPPEAR.
WHAT'S REALLY IMPORTANT...
...IS BEING HERE NOW.
GRANDMA.
SUMMER'S FINALLY ARRIVED.
THIS IS MY FIRST SUMMER...
...WITHOUT GRANNY HERE.

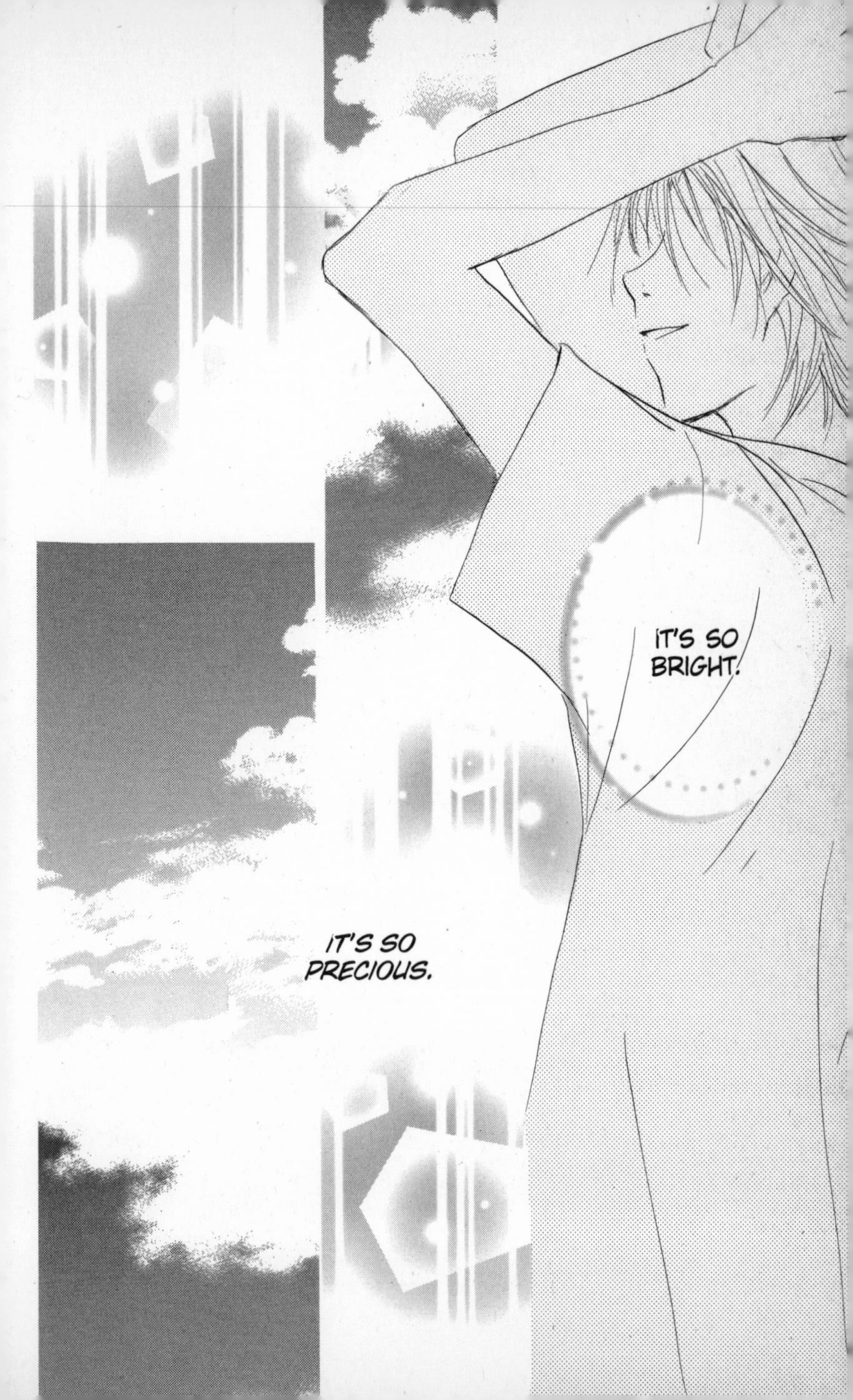
IT'S SO BRIGHT.
IT'S SO PRECIOUS.

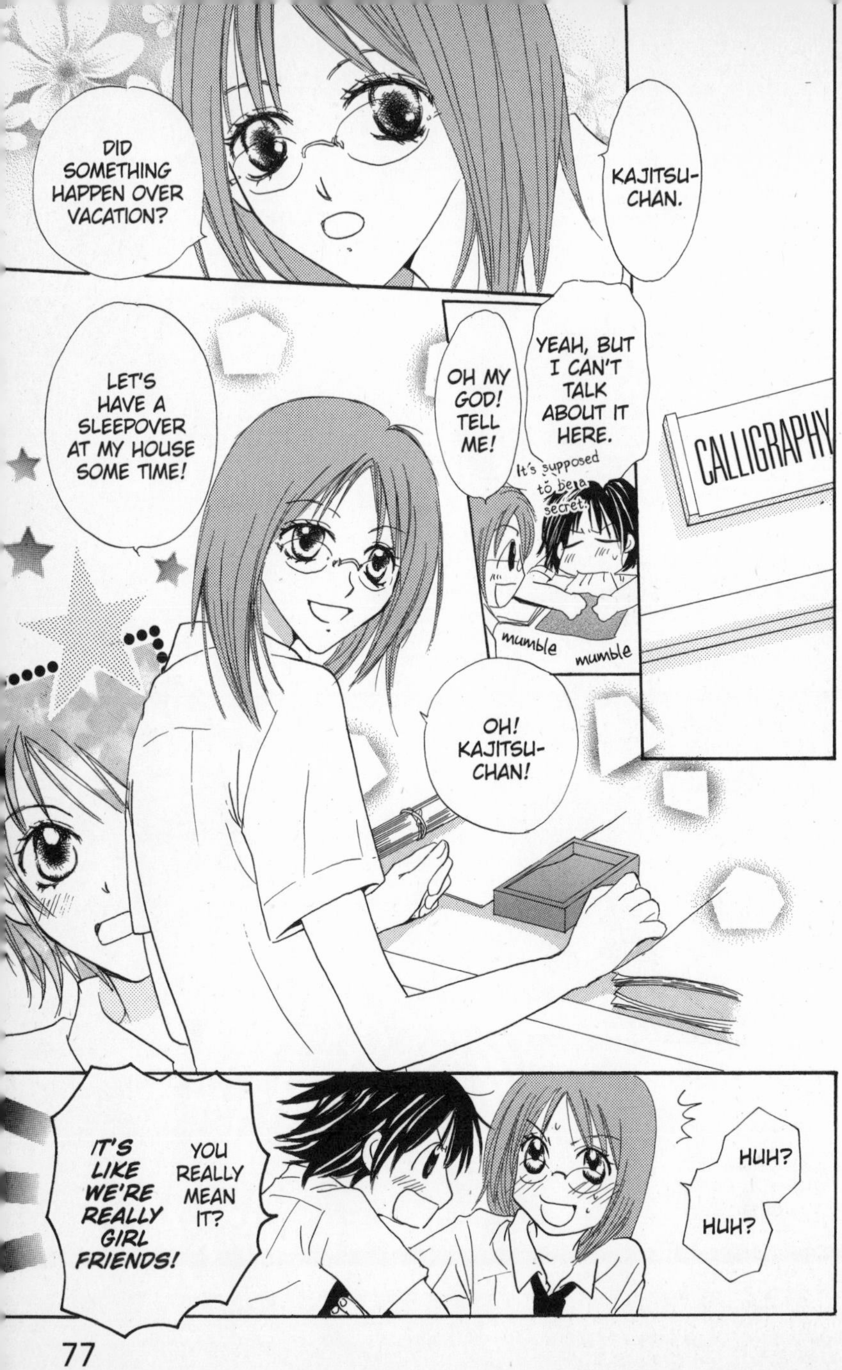
KAJITSU-CHAN.
DID SOMETHING HAPPEN OVER VACATION?
YEAH, BUT I CAN'T TALK ABOUT IT HERE.
OH MY GOD! TELL ME!
CALLIGRAPHY
It's supposed to be a secret!
mumble
mumble
OH! KAJITSU-CHAN!
LET'S HAVE A SLEEPOVER AT MY HOUSE SOME TIME!
HUH?
HUH?
YOU REALLY MEAN IT?
IT'S LIKE WE'RE REALLY GIRL FRIENDS!

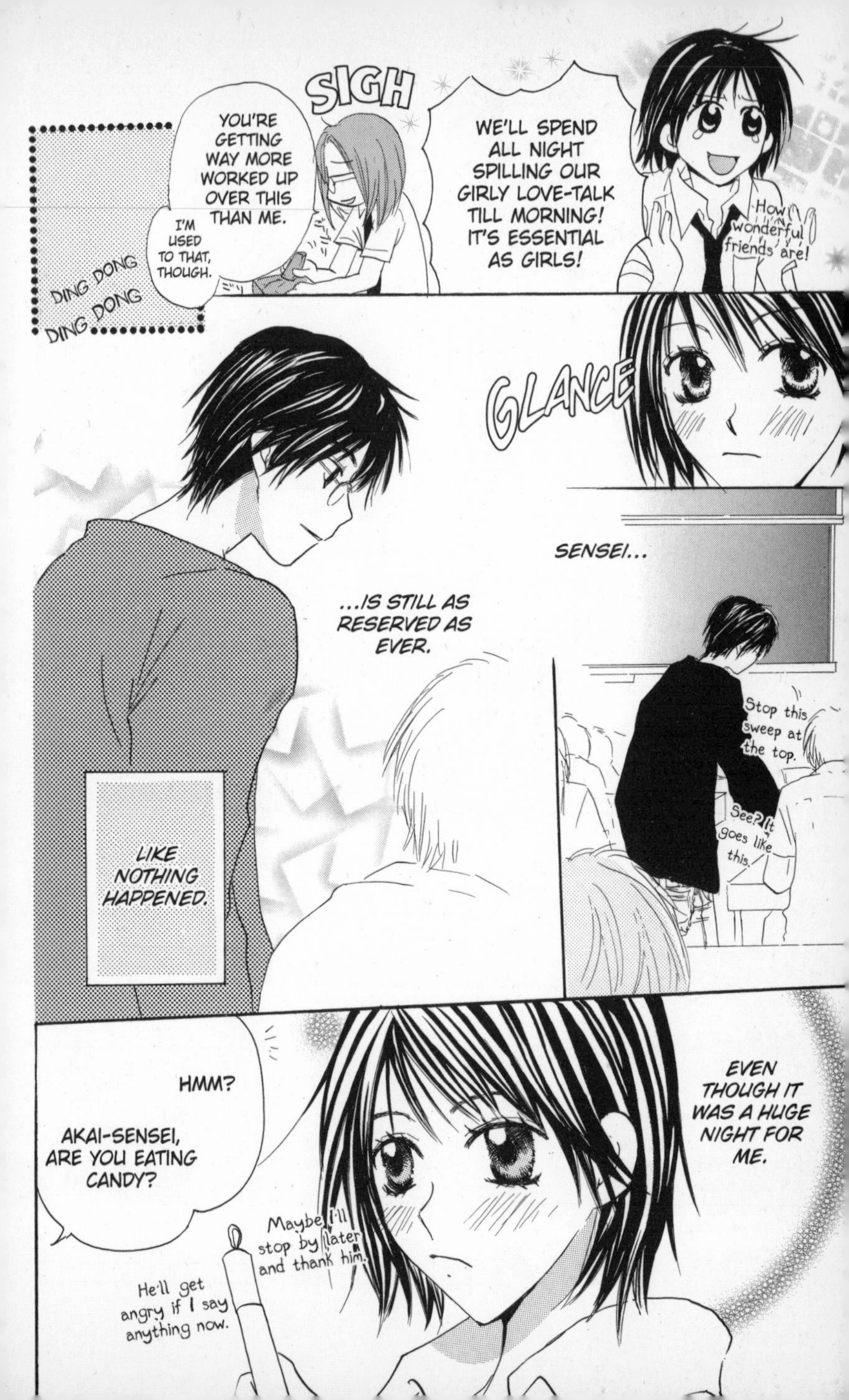
WE'LL SPEND ALL NIGHT SPILLING OUR GIRLY LOVE-TALK TILL MORNING! IT'S ESSENTIAL AS GIRLS!
How wonderful friends are!
SIGH
YOU'RE GETTING WAY MORE WORKED UP OVER THIS THAN ME.
I'M USED TO THAT, THOUGH.
DING DONG DING DONG
GLANCE
SENSEI...
Stop this sweep at the top.
See? It goes like this.
...IS STILL AS RESERVED AS EVER.
LIKE NOTHING HAPPENED.
EVEN THOUGH IT WAS A HUGE NIGHT FOR ME.
Maybe I'll stop by later and thank him.
HMM?
AKAI-SENSEI, ARE YOU EATING CANDY?
He'll get angry if I say anything now.

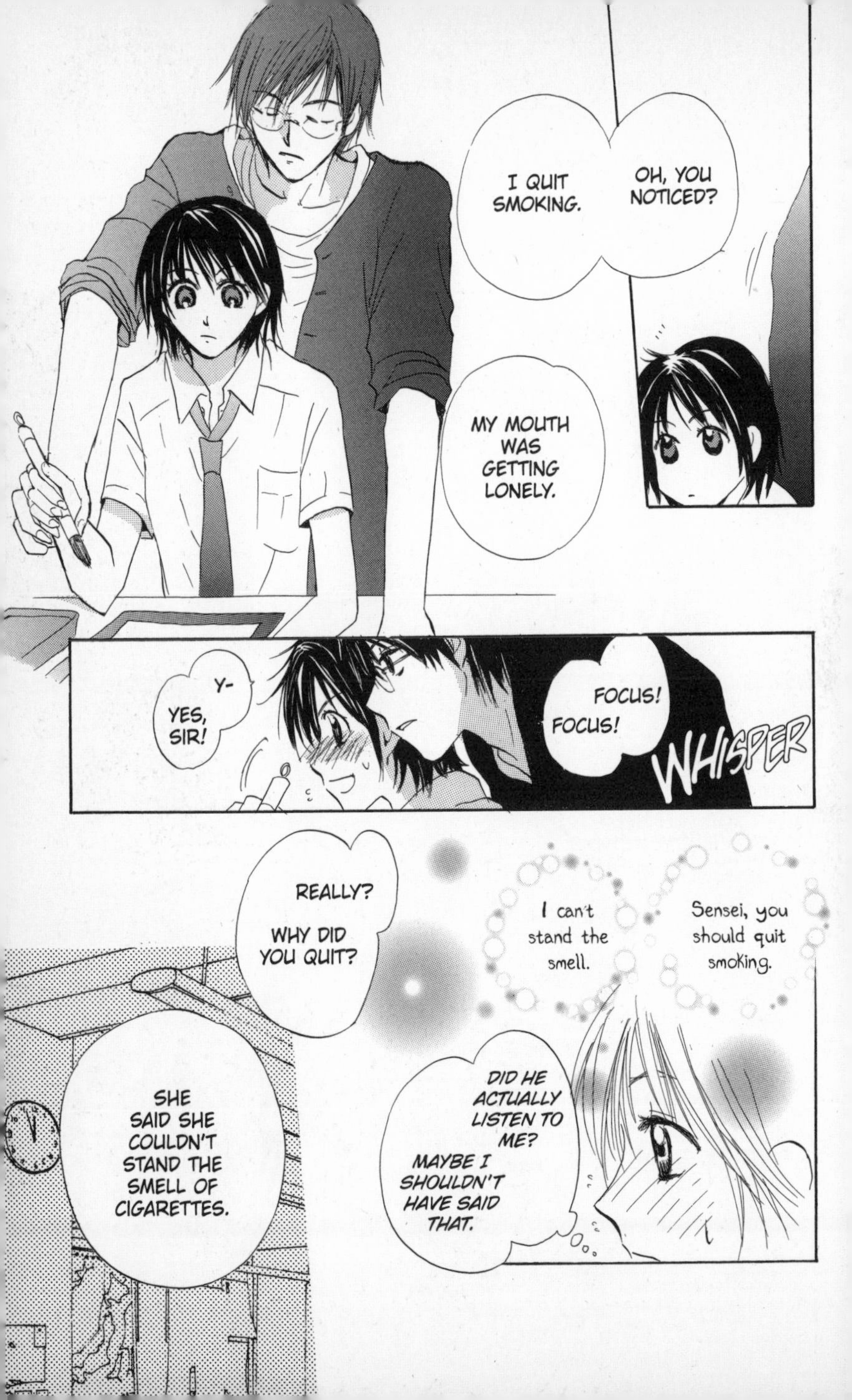
OH, YOU NOTICED?
I QUIT SMOKING.
MY MOUTH WAS GETTING LONELY.
FOCUS! FOCUS!
WHISPER
Y- YES, SIR!
Sensei, you should quit smoking.
I can't stand the smell.
REALLY? WHY DID YOU QUIT?
DID HE ACTUALLY LISTEN TO ME?
MAYBE I SHOULDN'T HAVE SAID THAT.
SHE SAID SHE COULDN'T STAND THE SMELL OF CIGARETTES.

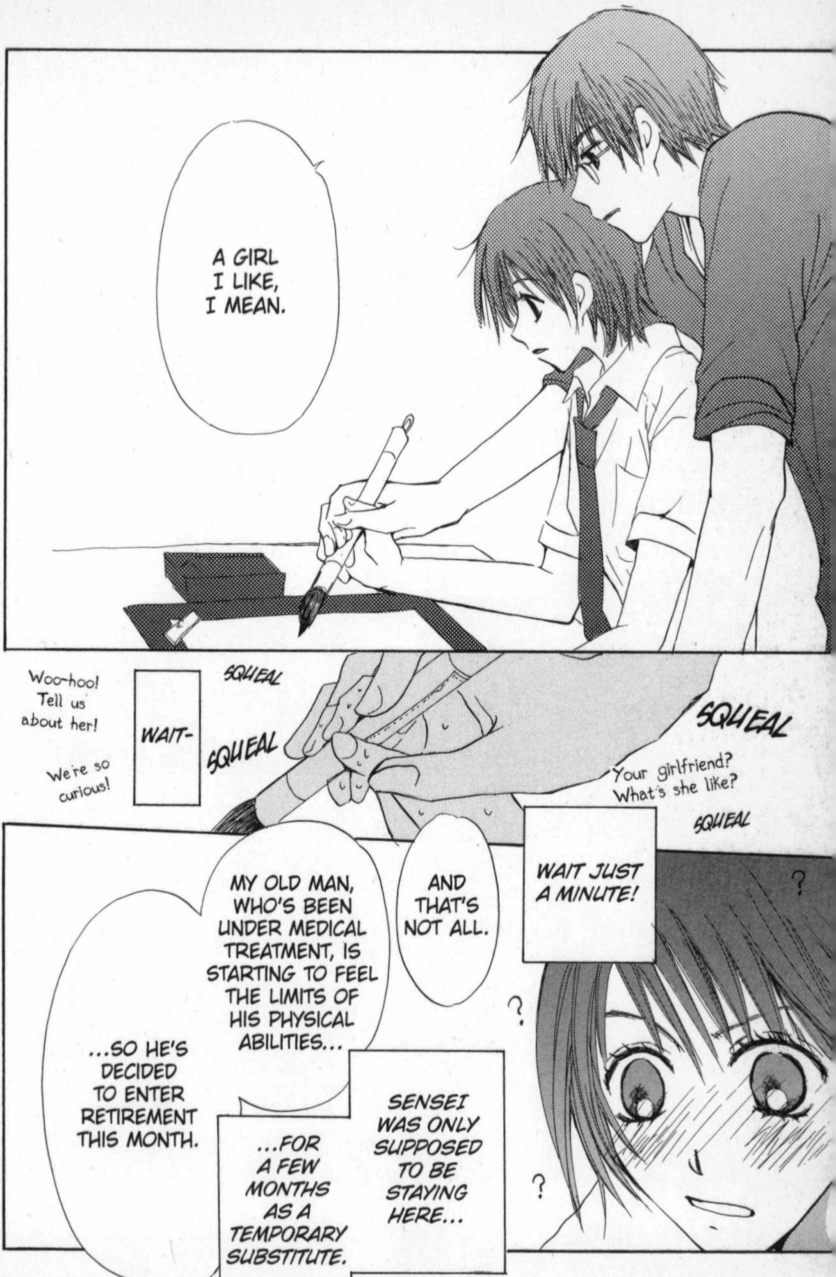
A GIRL I LIKE, I MEAN.
SQUEAL
Your girlfriend? What's she like?
SQUEAL
SQUEAL
SQUEAL
WAIT-
Woo-hoo! Tell us about her!
We're so curious!
WAIT JUST A MINUTE!
AND THAT'S NOT ALL.
MY OLD MAN, WHO'S BEEN UNDER MEDICAL TREATMENT, IS STARTING TO FEEL THE LIMITS OF HIS PHYSICAL ABILITIES...
...SO HE'S DECIDED TO ENTER RETIREMENT THIS MONTH.
SENSEI WAS ONLY SUPPOSED TO BE STAYING HERE...
...FOR A FEW MONTHS AS A TEMPORARY SUBSTITUTE.

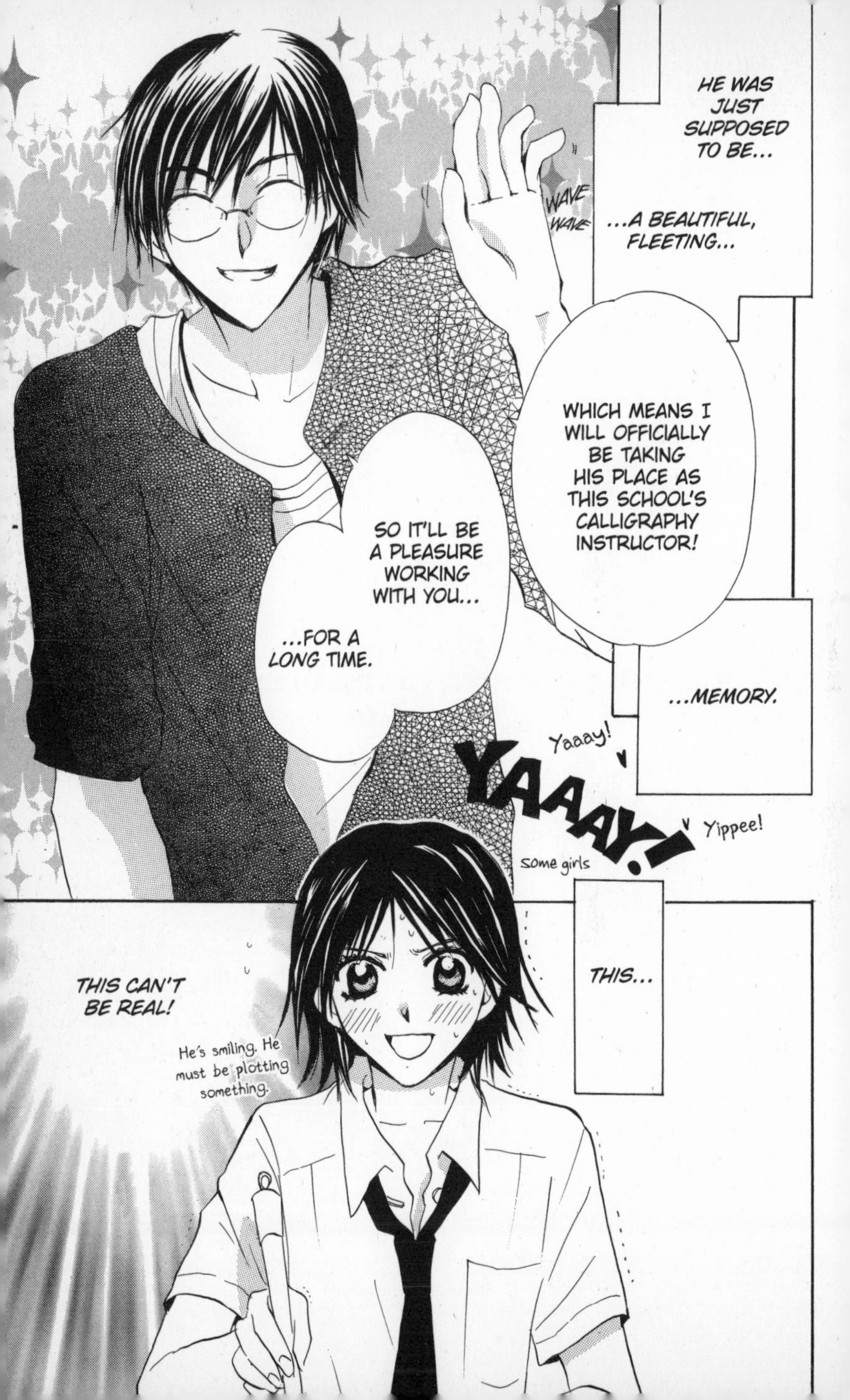
HE WAS JUST SUPPOSED TO BE...
...A BEAUTIFUL, FLEETING...
WAVE WAVE
WHICH MEANS I WILL OFFICIALLY BE TAKING HIS PLACE AS THIS SCHOOL'S CALLIGRAPHY INSTRUCTOR!
SO IT'LL BE A PLEASURE WORKING WITH YOU...
...FOR A LONG TIME.
...MEMORY.
Yaaay!
YAAAY!
Yippee!
Some girls
THIS...
THIS CAN'T BE REAL!
He's smiling. He must be plotting something.

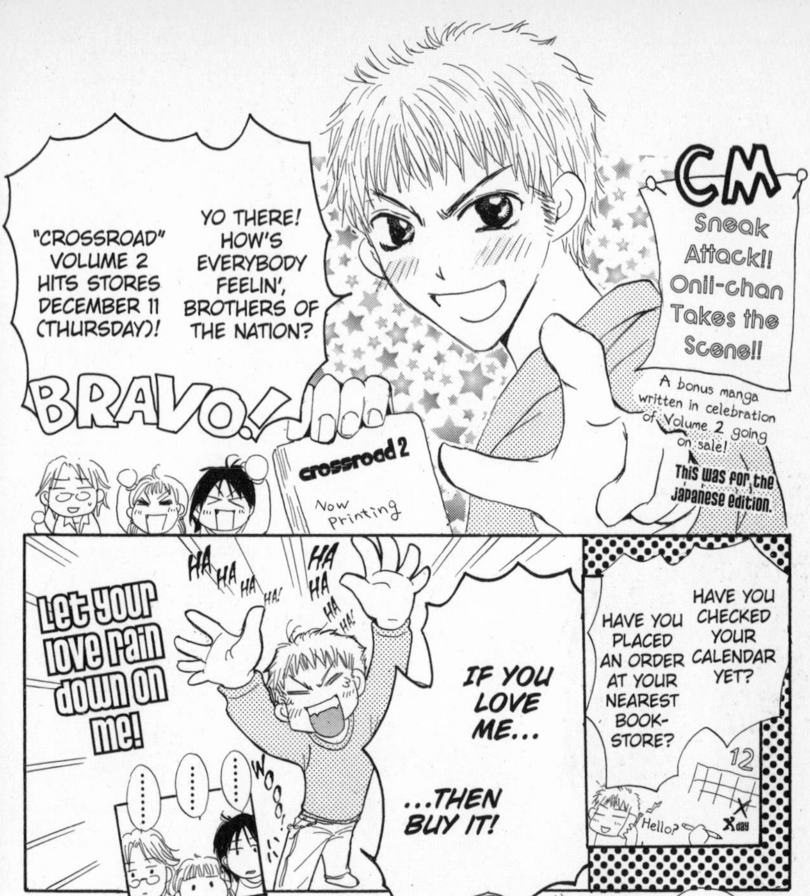
CM
Sneak Attack!! Onii-chan Takes the Scene!!
A bonus manga written in celebration of Volume 2 going on sale!
This was for the Japanese edition.
YO THERE! HOW'S EVERYBODY FEELIN', BROTHERS OF THE NATION?
"CROSSROAD" VOLUME 2 HITS STORES DECEMBER 11 (THURSDAY)!
BRAVO!
crossroad 2
Now Printing
HAVE YOU CHECKED YOUR CALENDAR YET?
HAVE YOU PLACED AN ORDER AT YOUR NEAREST BOOK-STORE?
12
Hello?
X day
IF YOU LOVE ME...
...THEN BUY IT!
HA HA HA HA!
HA HA HA HA!
Let your love rain down on me!
......
......
......

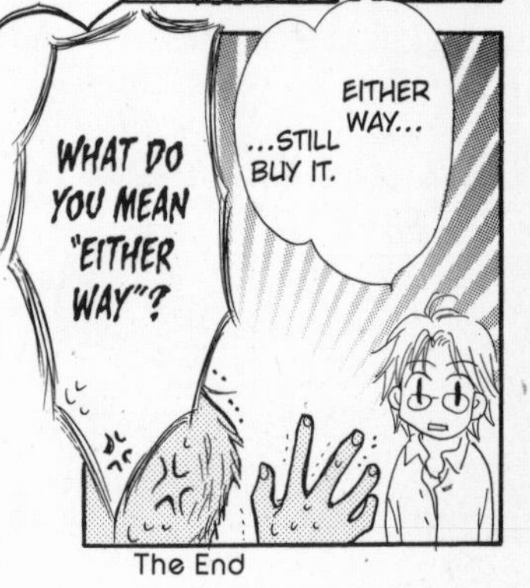
EITHER WAY...
...STILL BUY IT.
WHAT DO YOU MEAN "EITHER WAY"?
The End

shameless promotion

This is the advertisement I wrote for Princess (the magazine that publishes "Crossroad" in Japan). I thought it'd be fun to leave some space here to advertise the release of volume 2 as a tankobon. (I've really been looking forward to it!) I want to do it for volume 3, too, but we'll have to wait and see.

I really liked this one, so I kept it. Heh heh.

Mmm..

#14 Your Blue (Part One)

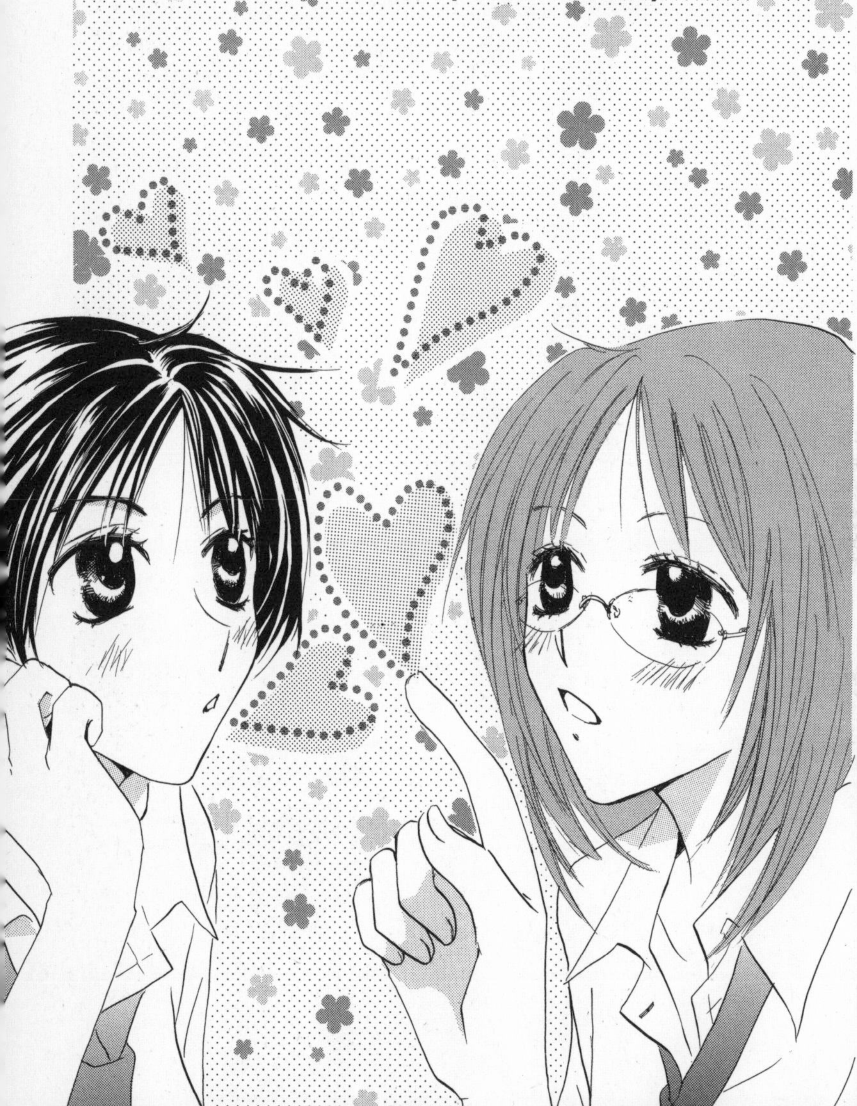

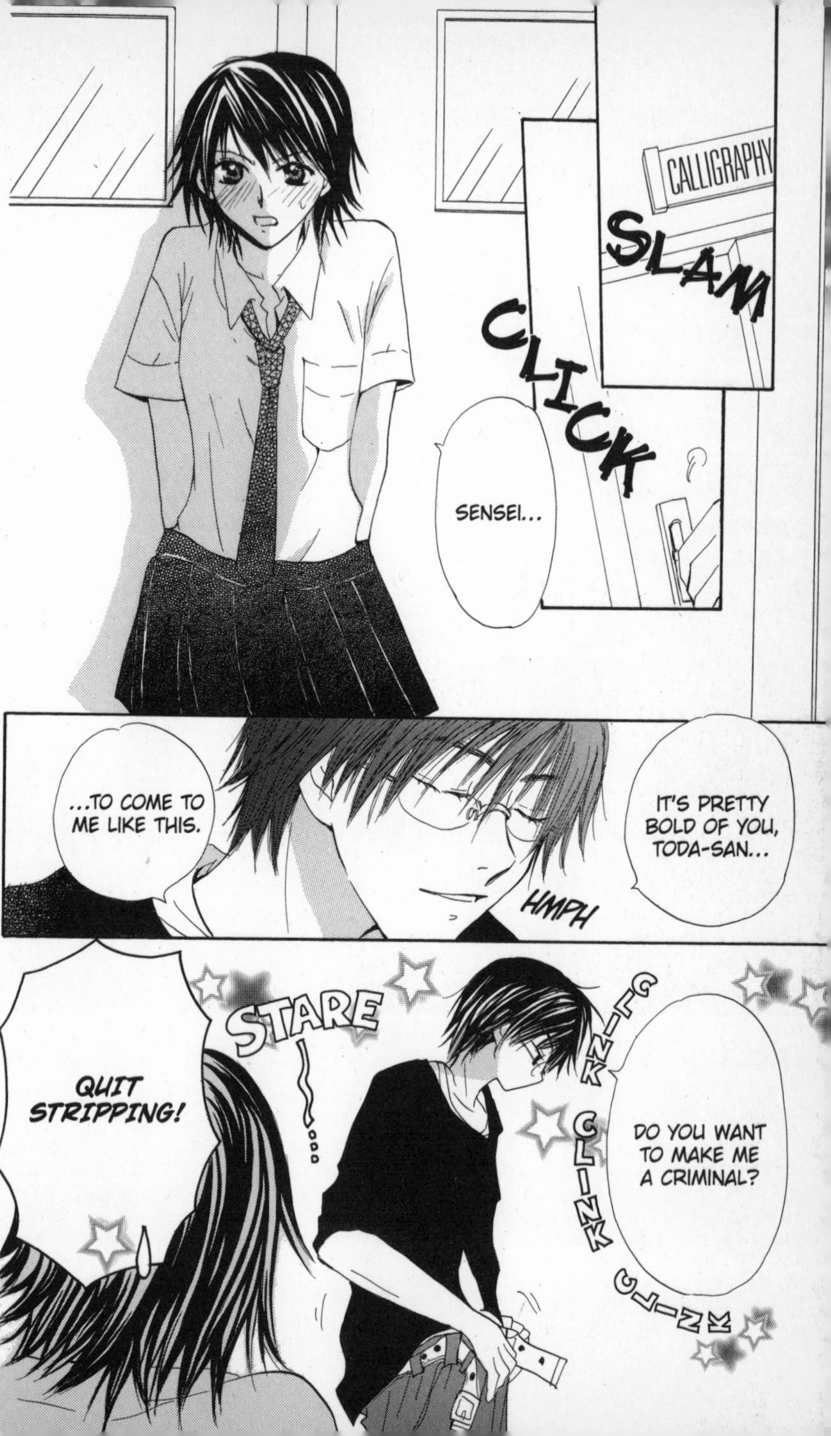
CALLIGRAPHY
SLAM
CLICK
SENSEI...
IT'S PRETTY BOLD OF YOU, TODA-SAN...
HMPH
...TO COME TO ME LIKE THIS.
CLINK
CLINK
DO YOU WANT TO MAKE ME A CRIMINAL?
STARE
QUIT STRIPPING!

crossroad Chapter 16: Your Blue (Part One)

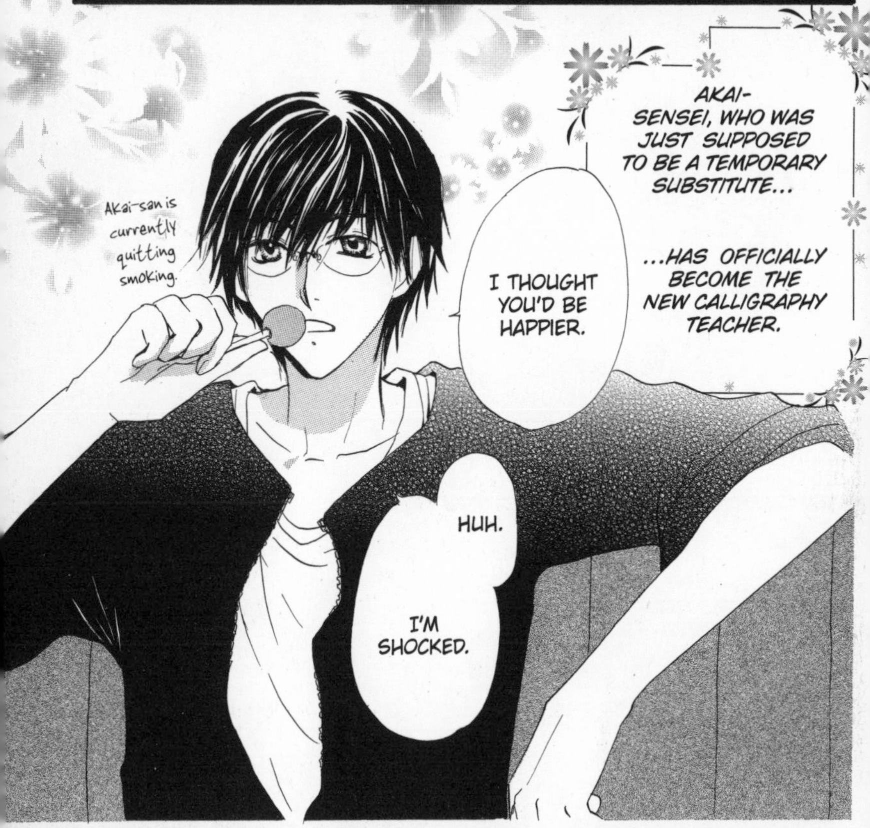
AKAI-SENSEI, WHO WAS JUST SUPPOSED TO BE A TEMPORARY SUBSTITUTE...
...HAS OFFICIALLY BECOME THE NEW CALLIGRAPHY TEACHER.
I THOUGHT YOU'D BE HAPPIER.
Akai-san is currently quitting smoking.
HUH.
I'M SHOCKED.

Feelings of Nostalgia 3

A hole opened up in one of my molars, so after work I stopped by the dentist's office. He told me, "The tooth's set in sideways, so let's take him out." I hate when teeth get like that, so I was happy to see it go. But I still have two like that left in there. Sheesh. Anyway, after he yanked it out, the inside of my mouth was all bloody and it felt gross. But for some reason, I suddenly had the urge to eat meat, and even though I'd been told not to eat while my mouth was still numb, I ran out to the closet Karubi-niku place!* The smell of the plate drew me in. It was like, meat! Meat! Meat!! I'm sure they thought I was a savage or something.

*See translator's notes at the back of the book.

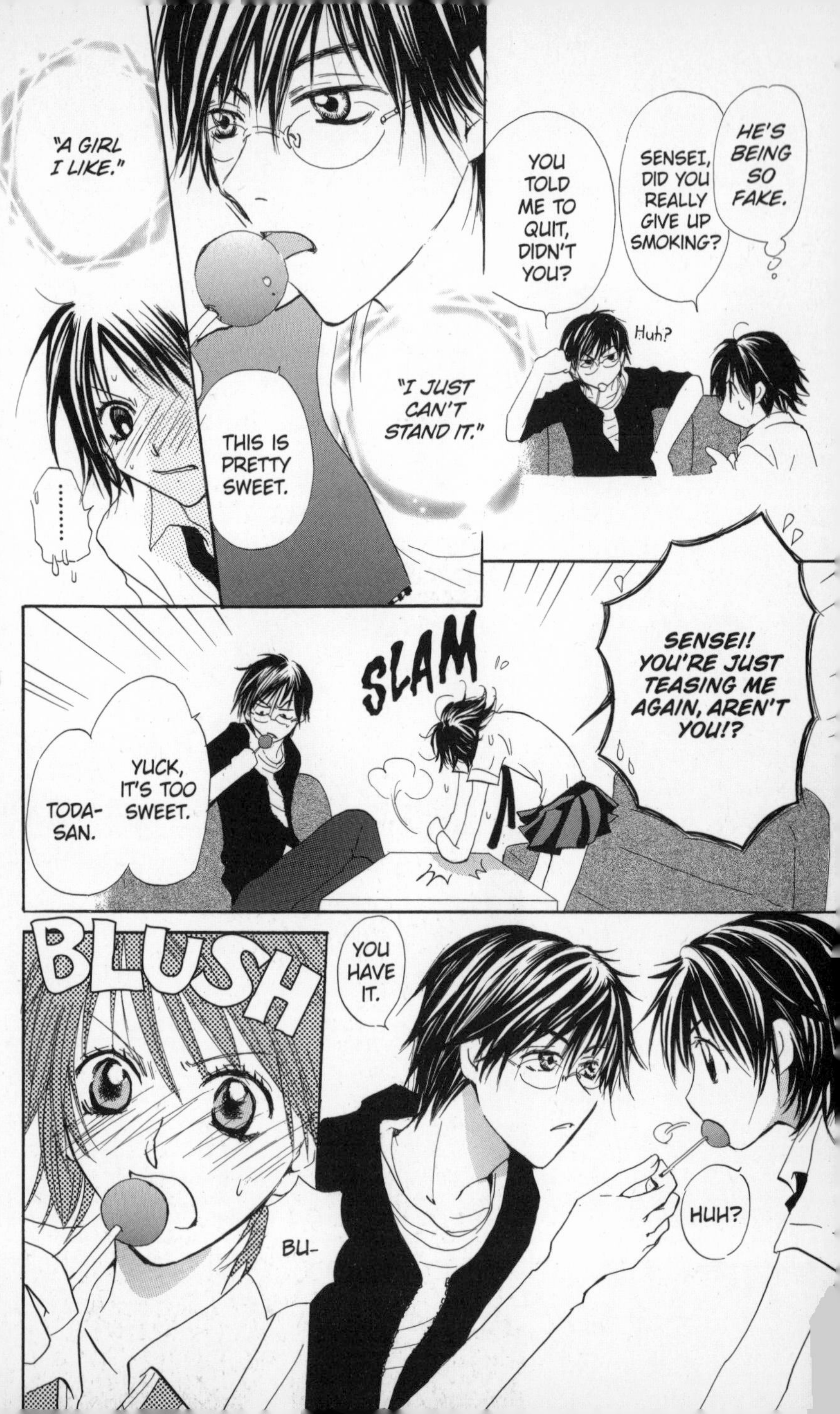
HE'S BEING SO FAKE.
SENSEI, DID YOU REALLY GIVE UP SMOKING?
YOU TOLD ME TO QUIT, DIDN'T YOU?
Huh?
"I JUST CAN'T STAND IT."
THIS IS PRETTY SWEET.
"A GIRL I LIKE."
......
SENSEI! YOU'RE JUST TEASING ME AGAIN, AREN'T YOU!?
SLAM
YUCK, IT'S TOO SWEET.
TODA-SAN.
HUH?
YOU HAVE IT.
BU-
BLUSH

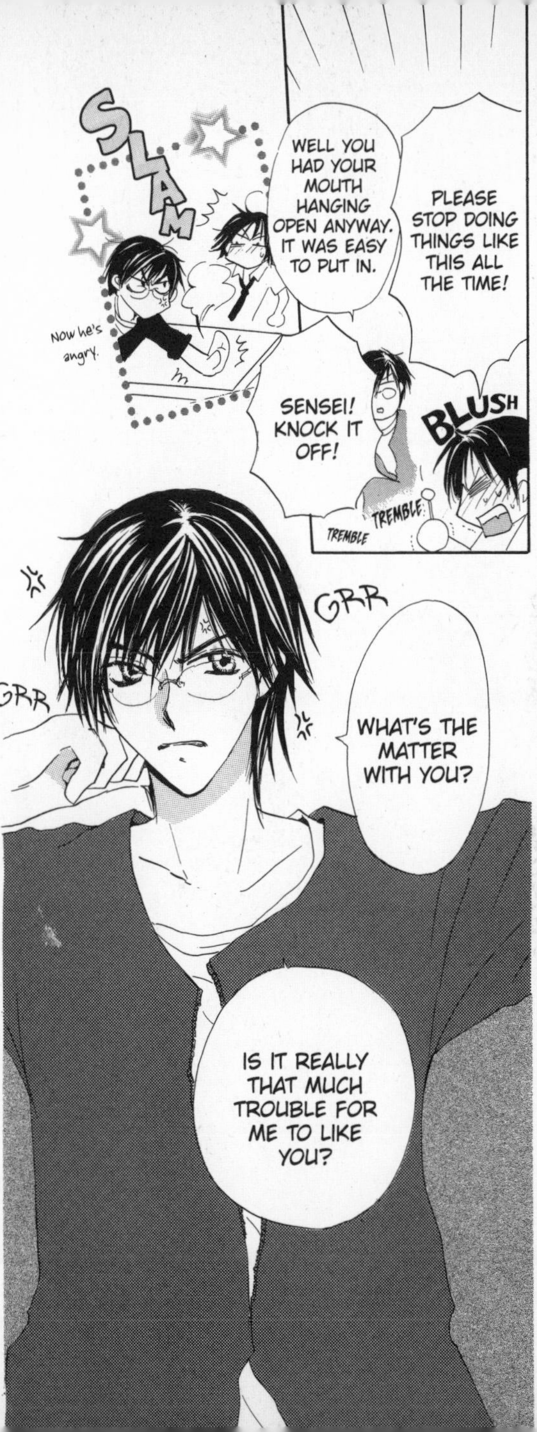
PLEASE STOP DOING THINGS LIKE THIS ALL THE TIME!
WELL YOU HAD YOUR MOUTH HANGING OPEN ANYWAY. IT WAS EASY TO PUT IN.
SLAM
Now he's angry.
SENSEI! KNOCK IT OFF!
BLUSH
TREMBLE
TREMBLE
GRR
GRR
WHAT'S THE MATTER WITH YOU?
IS IT REALLY THAT MUCH TROUBLE FOR ME TO LIKE YOU?

Tell us Crossroad!

"Natsu's Short-Sleeves"

Natsu has now started wearing short-sleeved shirts.

But his school uniform is still a collared shirt with longer sleeves.

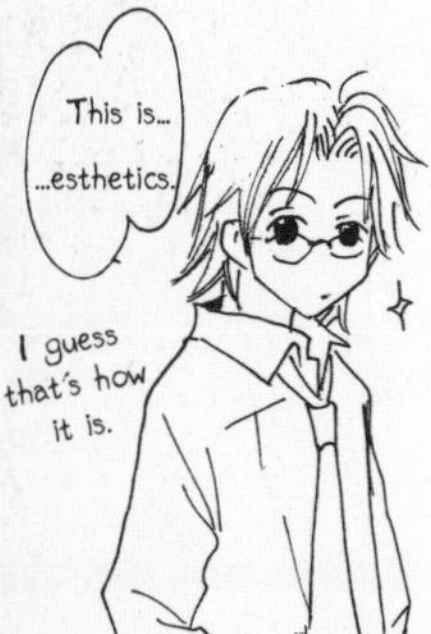
This is... ...esthetics.
I guess that's how it is.

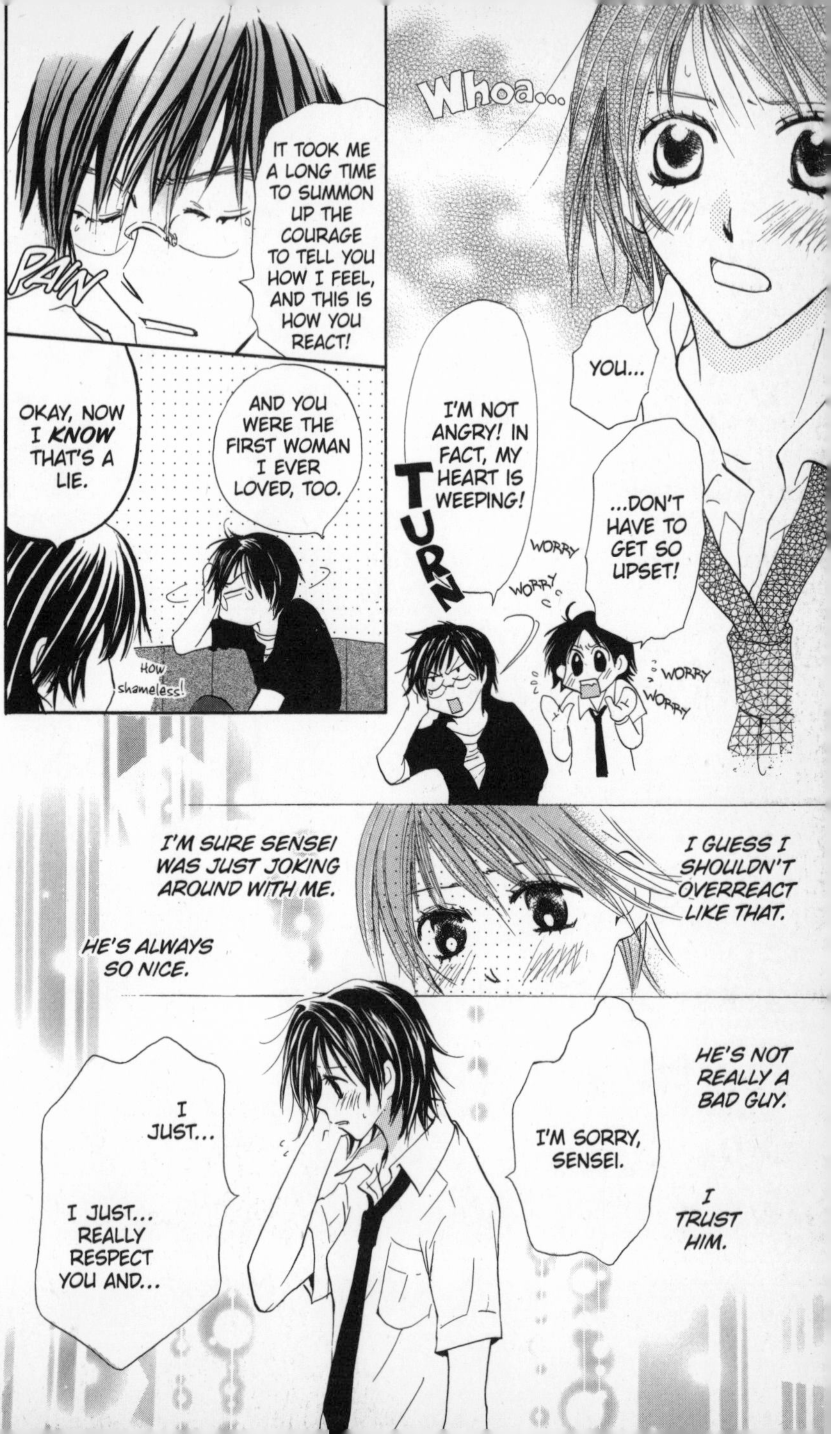
Whoa...
YOU...
...DON'T HAVE TO GET SO UPSET!
WORRY WORRY
I'M NOT ANGRY! IN FACT, MY HEART IS WEEPING!
TURN
WORRY WORRY
IT TOOK ME A LONG TIME TO SUMMON UP THE COURAGE TO TELL YOU HOW I FEEL, AND THIS IS HOW YOU REACT!
PAIN
AND YOU WERE THE FIRST WOMAN I EVER LOVED, TOO.
OKAY, NOW I ***KNOW*** THAT'S A LIE.
How shameless!
I GUESS I SHOULDN'T OVERREACT LIKE THAT.
I'M SURE SENSEI WAS JUST JOKING AROUND WITH ME.
HE'S ALWAYS SO NICE.
HE'S NOT REALLY A BAD GUY.
I TRUST HIM.
I'M SORRY, SENSEI.
I JUST...
I JUST... REALLY RESPECT YOU AND...

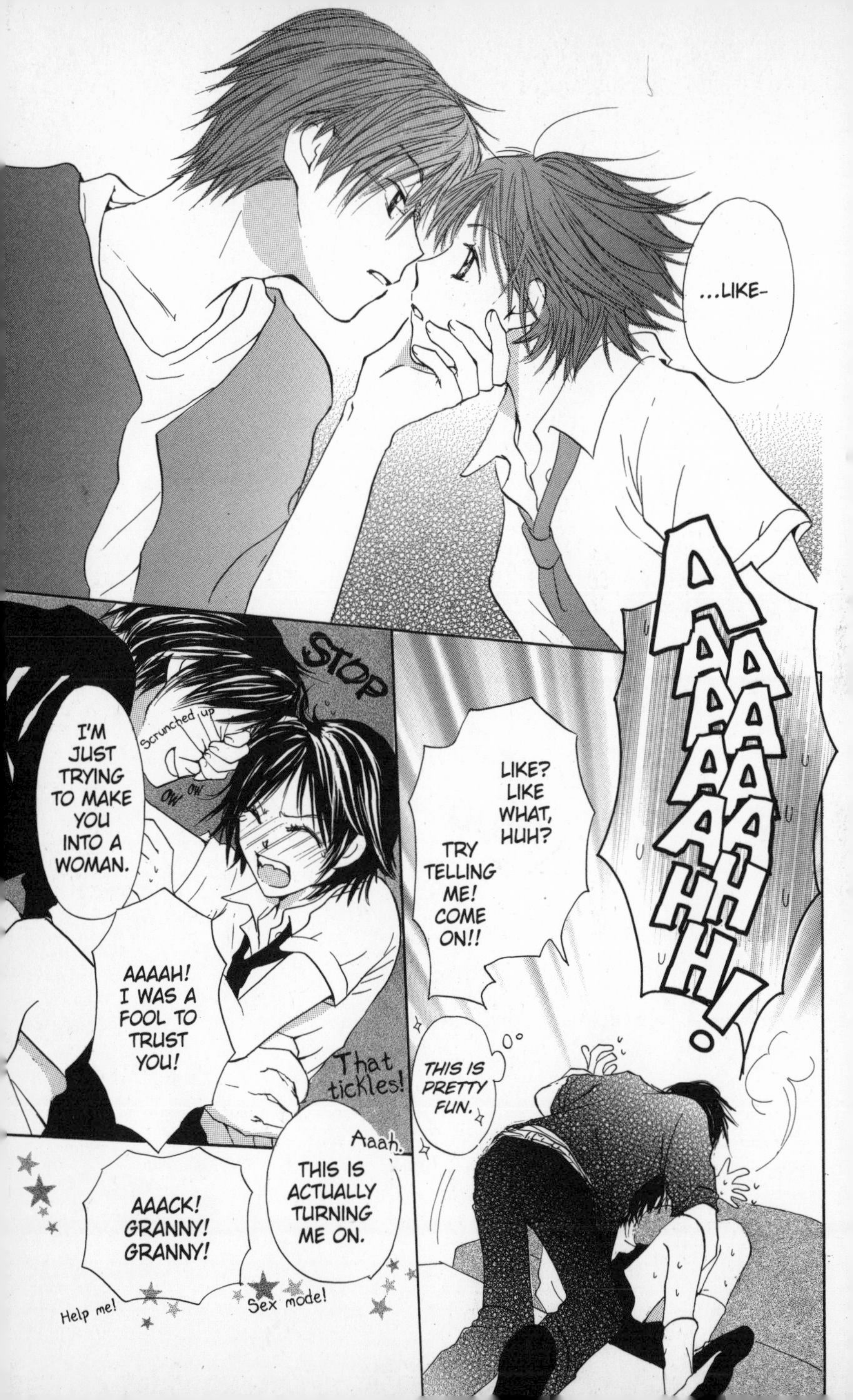
...LIKE-
AAAAAAAAAAHHHH!
LIKE? LIKE WHAT, HUH? TRY TELLING ME! COME ON!!
STOP
Scrunched up
OW OW
I'M JUST TRYING TO MAKE YOU INTO A WOMAN.
AAAAH! I WAS A FOOL TO TRUST YOU!
That tickles!
THIS IS PRETTY FUN.
Aaah.
THIS IS ACTUALLY TURNING ME ON.
Sex mode!
AAACK! GRANNY! GRANNY!
Help me!

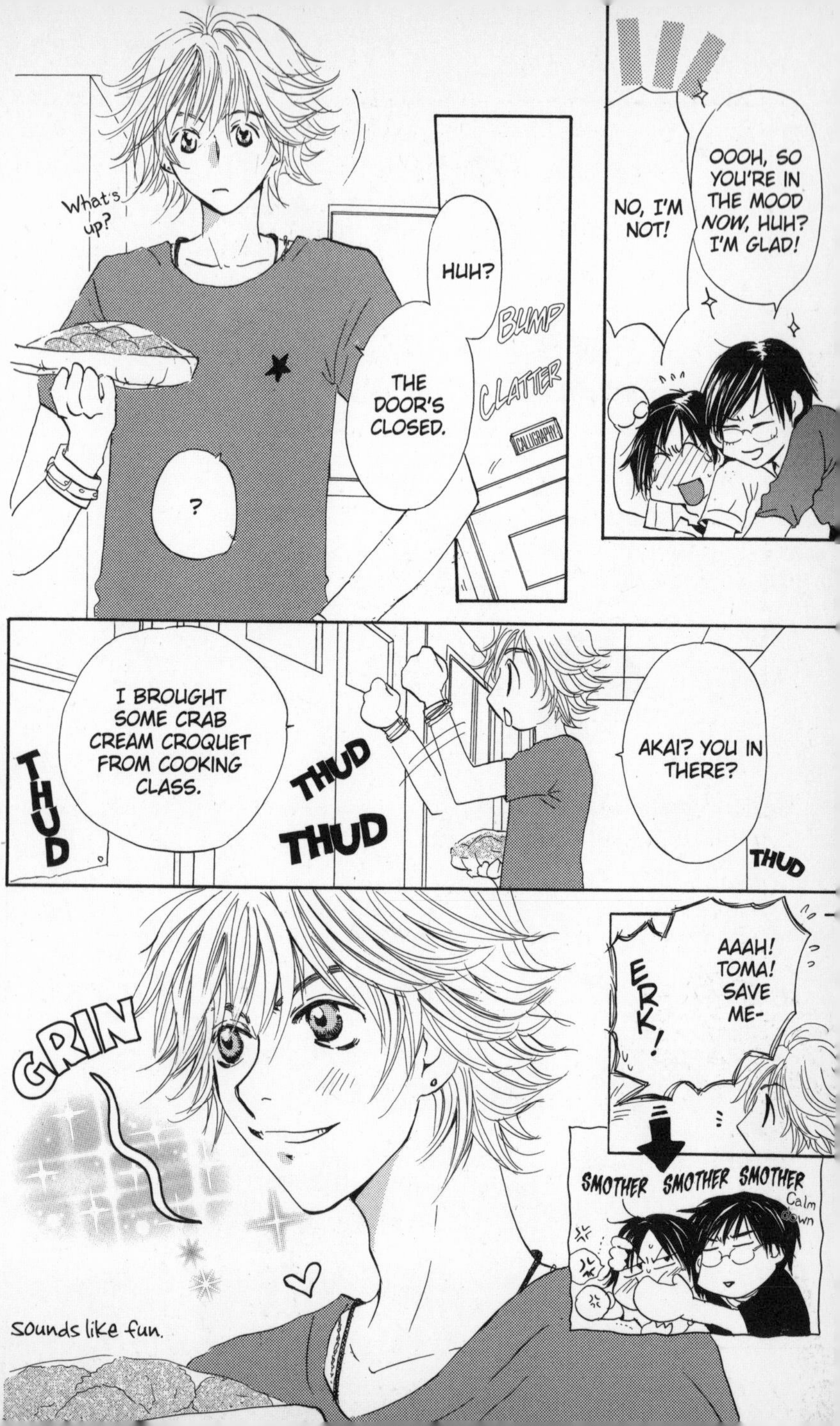
OOOH, SO YOU'RE IN THE MOOD NOW, HUH? I'M GLAD!
NO, I'M NOT!
HUH?
BUMP
CLATTER
THE DOOR'S CLOSED.
CALLIGRAPHY
What's up?
?
AKAI? YOU IN THERE?
THUD
THUD
THUD
I BROUGHT SOME CRAB CREAM CROQUET FROM COOKING CLASS.
THUD
AAAH! TOMA! SAVE ME-
ERK!
SMOTHER SMOTHER SMOTHER
Calm down
GRIN
Sounds like fun.

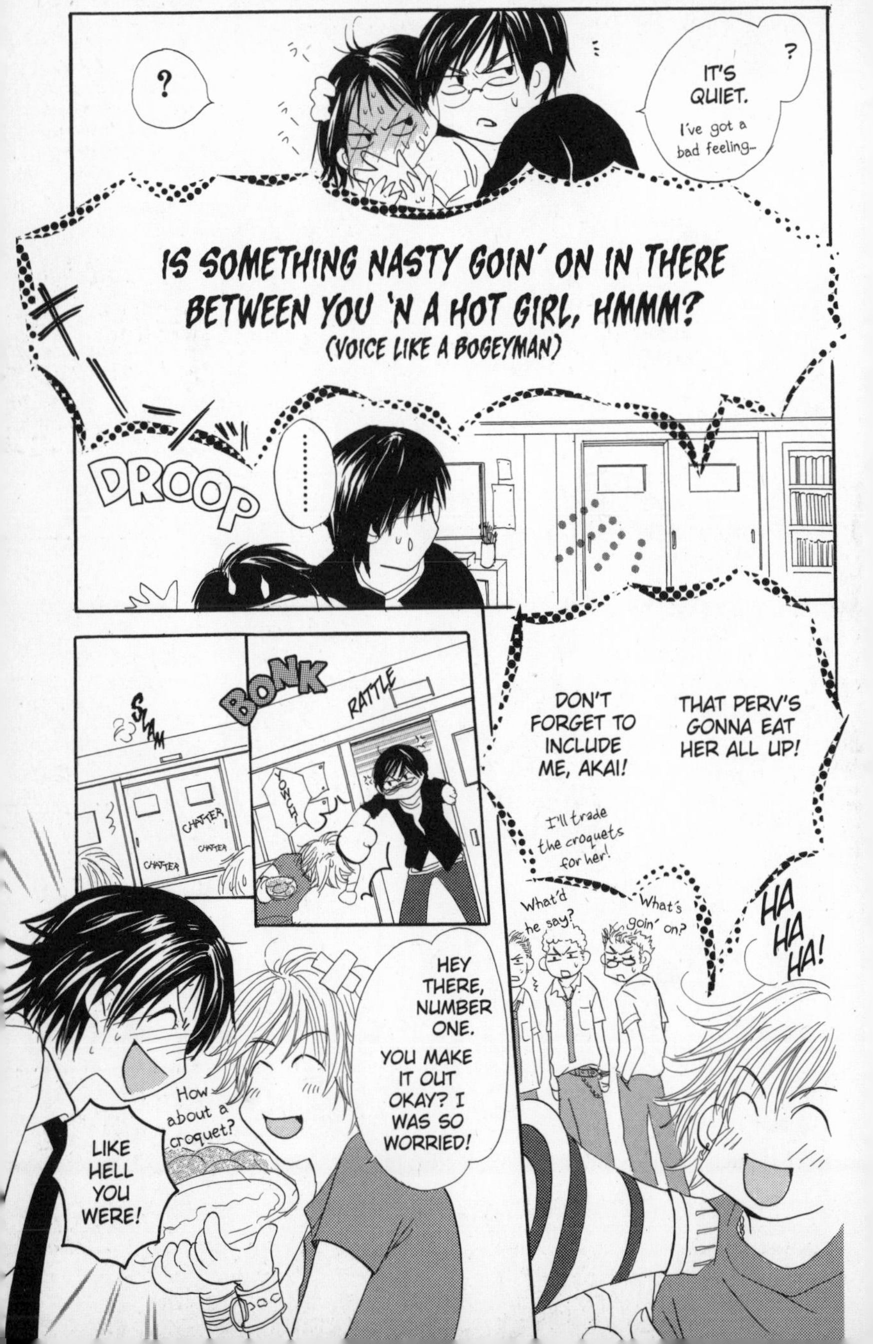
?
IT'S QUIET.
I've got a bad feeling...
?
IS SOMETHING NASTY GOIN' ON IN THERE BETWEEN YOU 'N A HOT GIRL, HMMM?
(VOICE LIKE A BOGEYMAN)
......
DROOP
THAT PERV'S GONNA EAT HER ALL UP!
DON'T FORGET TO INCLUDE ME, AKAI!
I'll trade the croquets for her!
BONK
RATTLE
YOWCH!
SLAM
CHATTER
CHATTER
CHATTER
HA HA HA!
What's goin' on?
What'd he say?
HEY THERE, NUMBER ONE.
YOU MAKE IT OUT OKAY? I WAS SO WORRIED!
How about a croquet?
LIKE HELL YOU WERE!

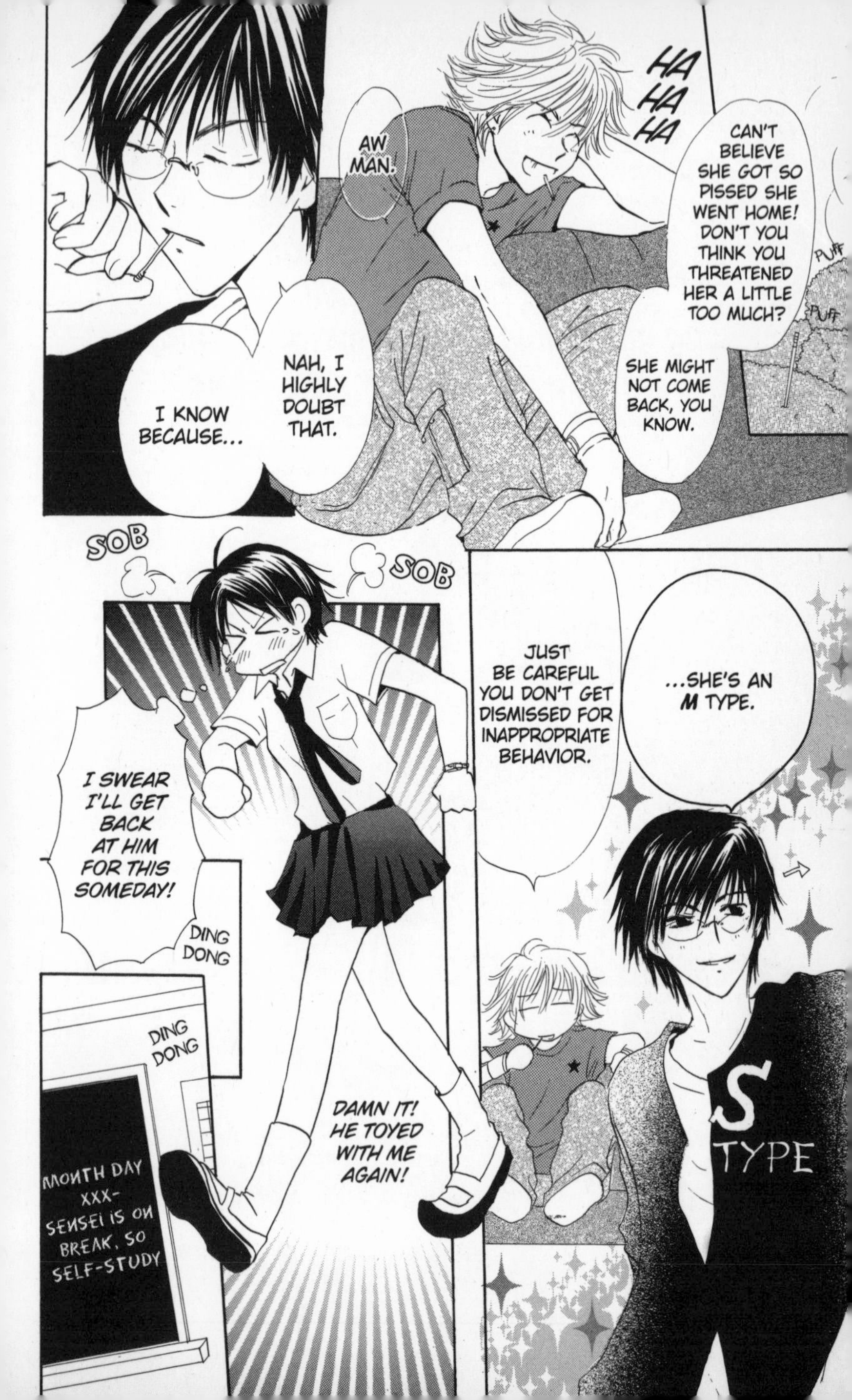
HA HA HA
CAN'T BELIEVE SHE GOT SO PISSED SHE WENT HOME! DON'T YOU THINK YOU THREATENED HER A LITTLE TOO MUCH?
PUFF
AW MAN.
PUFF
SHE MIGHT NOT COME BACK, YOU KNOW.
NAH, I HIGHLY DOUBT THAT.
I KNOW BECAUSE...
...SHE'S AN M TYPE.
JUST BE CAREFUL YOU DON'T GET DISMISSED FOR INAPPROPRIATE BEHAVIOR.
S TYPE
SOB SOB
I SWEAR I'LL GET BACK AT HIM FOR THIS SOMEDAY!
DING DONG
DING DONG
DAMN IT! HE TOYED WITH ME AGAIN!
MONTH DAY XXX-SENSEI IS ON BREAK, SO SELF-STUDY

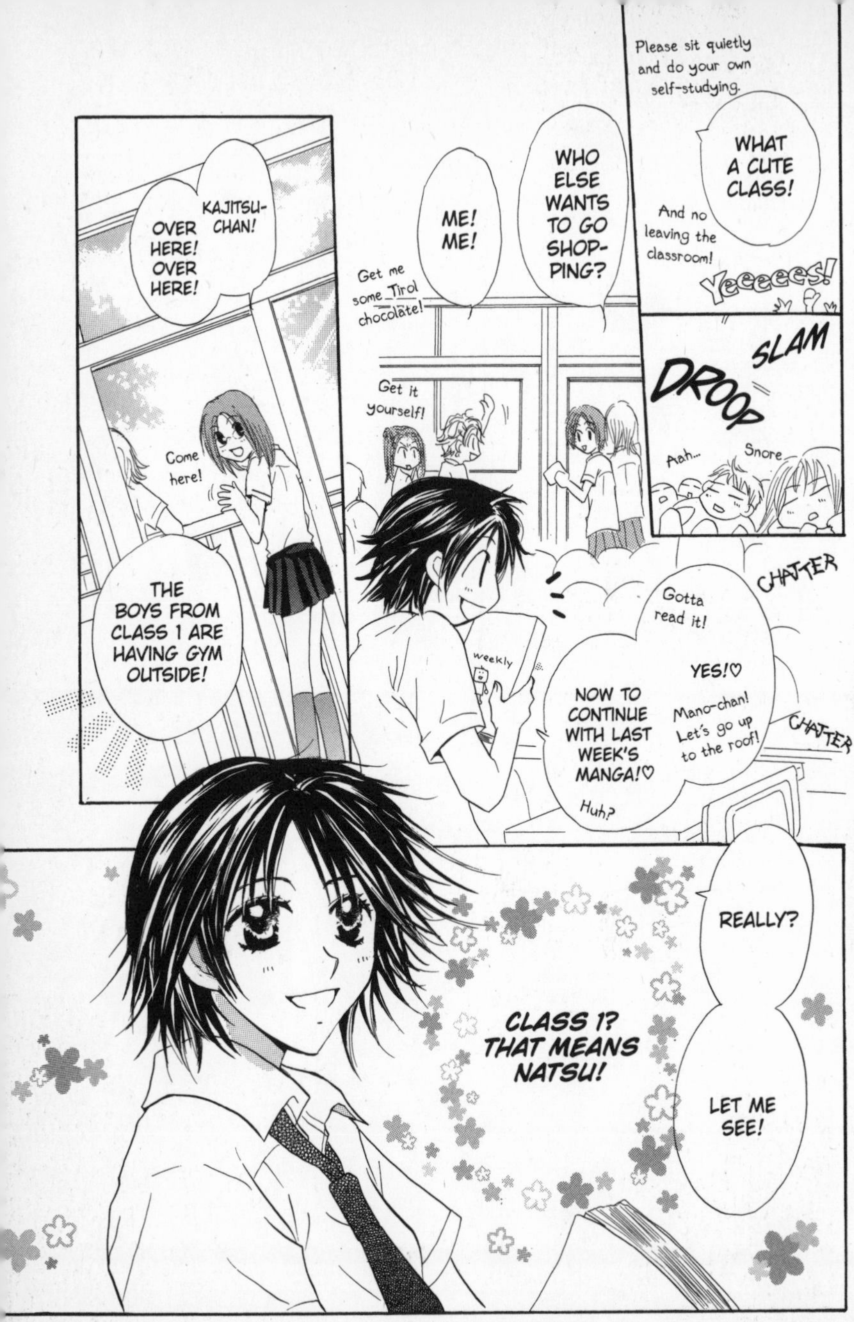
Please sit quietly and do your own self-studying.
WHAT A CUTE CLASS!
And no leaving the classroom!
Yeeeeees!
SLAM
DROOP
Aah...
Snore
WHO ELSE WANTS TO GO SHOPPING?
ME! ME!
Get me some Tirol chocolate!
Get it yourself!
CHATTER
Gotta read it!
YES!♡
Mano-chan! Let's go up to the roof!
CHATTER
NOW TO CONTINUE WITH LAST WEEK'S MANGA!♡
Huh?
weekly
KAJITSU-CHAN! OVER HERE! OVER HERE!
Come here!
THE BOYS FROM CLASS 1 ARE HAVING GYM OUTSIDE!
REALLY?
LET ME SEE!
CLASS 1? THAT MEANS NATSU!

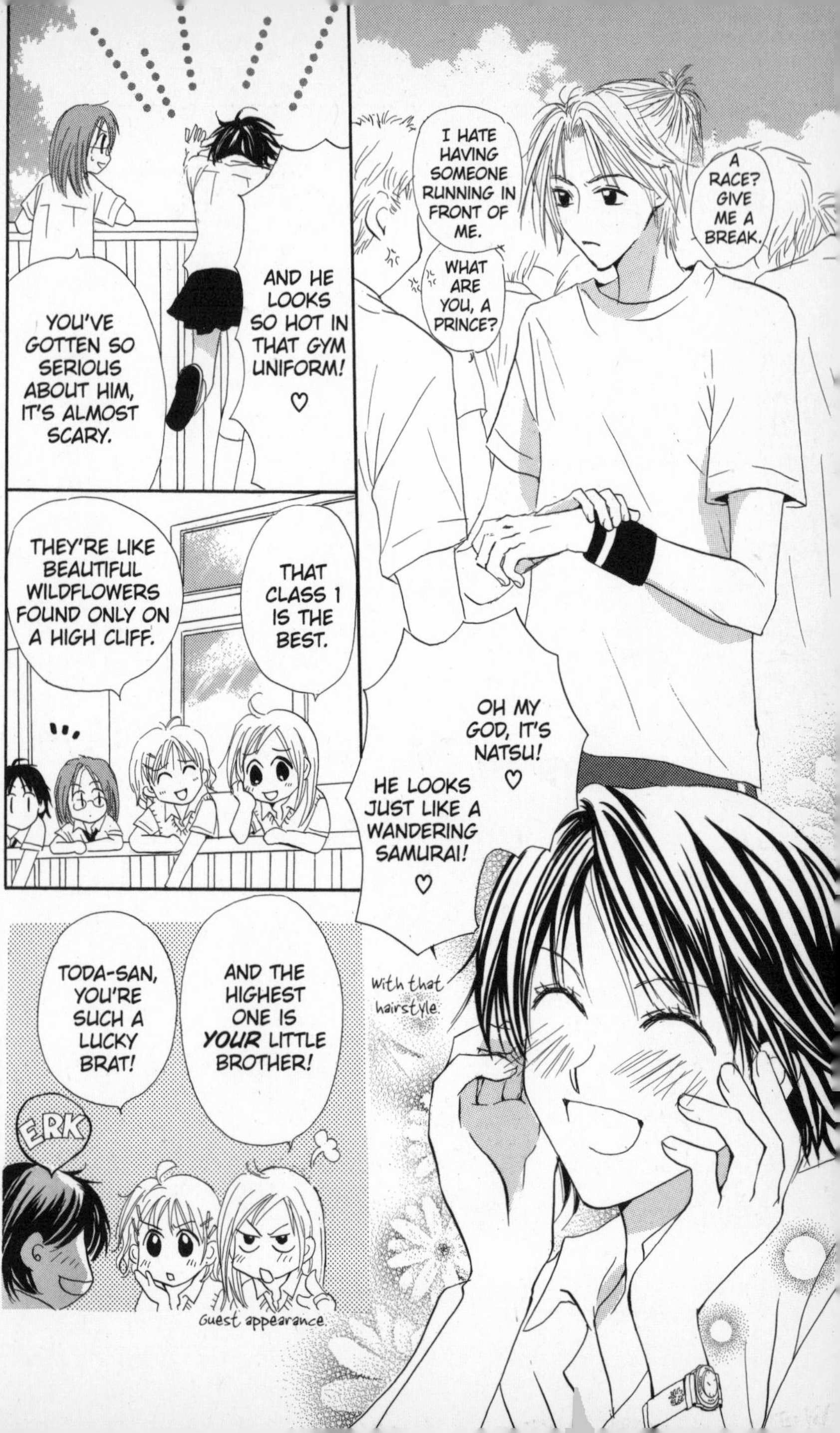
A RACE? GIVE ME A BREAK.
I HATE HAVING SOMEONE RUNNING IN FRONT OF ME.
WHAT ARE YOU, A PRINCE?
OH MY GOD, IT'S NATSU! ♡
HE LOOKS JUST LIKE A WANDERING SAMURAI! ♡
With that hairstyle.
AND HE LOOKS SO HOT IN THAT GYM UNIFORM! ♡
YOU'VE GOTTEN SO SERIOUS ABOUT HIM, IT'S ALMOST SCARY.
THAT CLASS 1 IS THE BEST.
THEY'RE LIKE BEAUTIFUL WILDFLOWERS FOUND ONLY ON A HIGH CLIFF.
AND THE HIGHEST ONE IS *YOUR* LITTLE BROTHER!
TODA-SAN, YOU'RE SUCH A LUCKY BRAT!
ERK
Guest appearance.

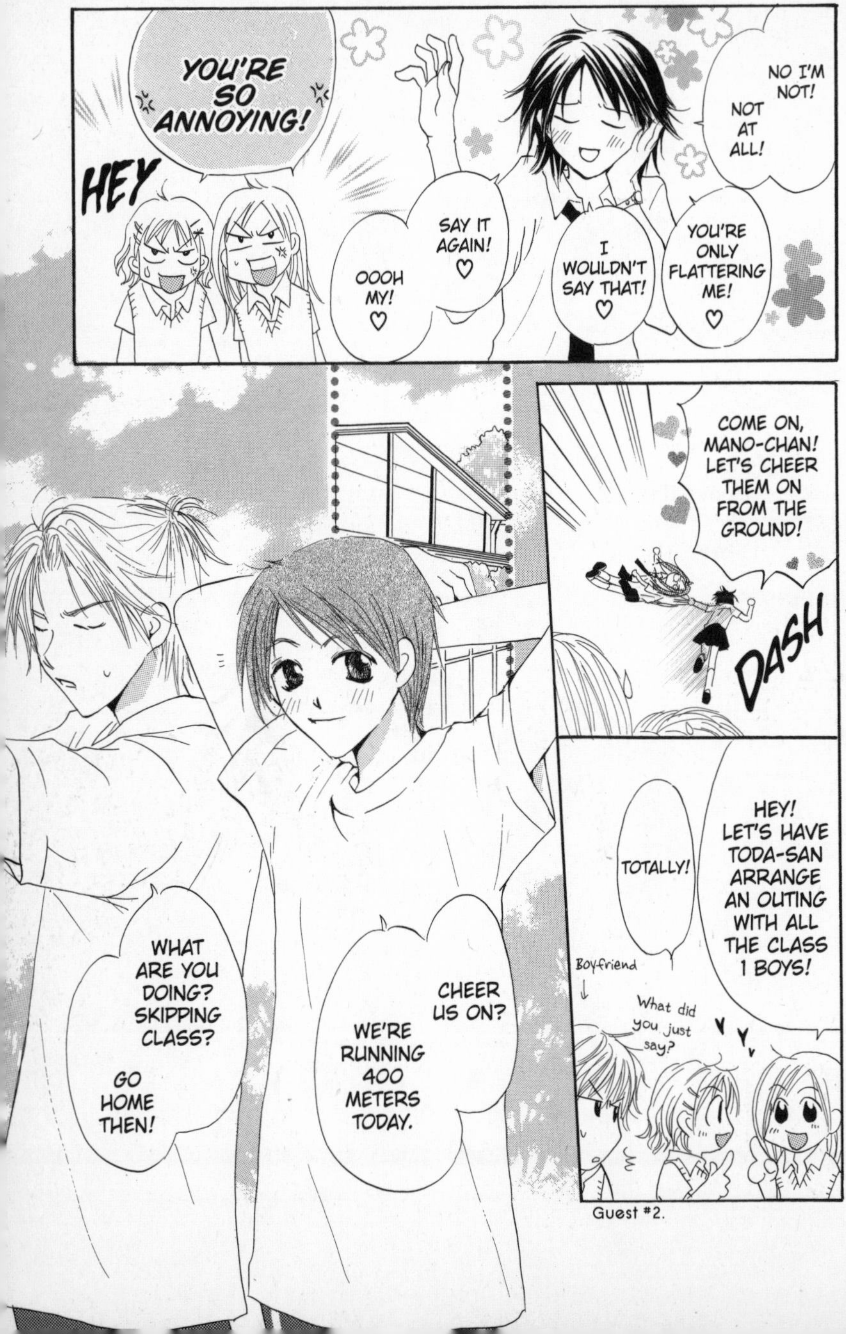
NO I'M NOT!
NOT AT ALL!
YOU'RE ONLY FLATTERING ME! ♡
I WOULDN'T SAY THAT! ♡
SAY IT AGAIN! ♡
OOOH MY! ♡
YOU'RE SO ANNOYING!
HEY
COME ON, MANO-CHAN! LET'S CHEER THEM ON FROM THE GROUND!
DASH
HEY! LET'S HAVE TODA-SAN ARRANGE AN OUTING WITH ALL THE CLASS 1 BOYS!
TOTALLY!
Boyfriend
What did you just say?
CHEER US ON?
WE'RE RUNNING 400 METERS TODAY.
WHAT ARE YOU DOING? SKIPPING CLASS?
GO HOME THEN!
Guest #2.

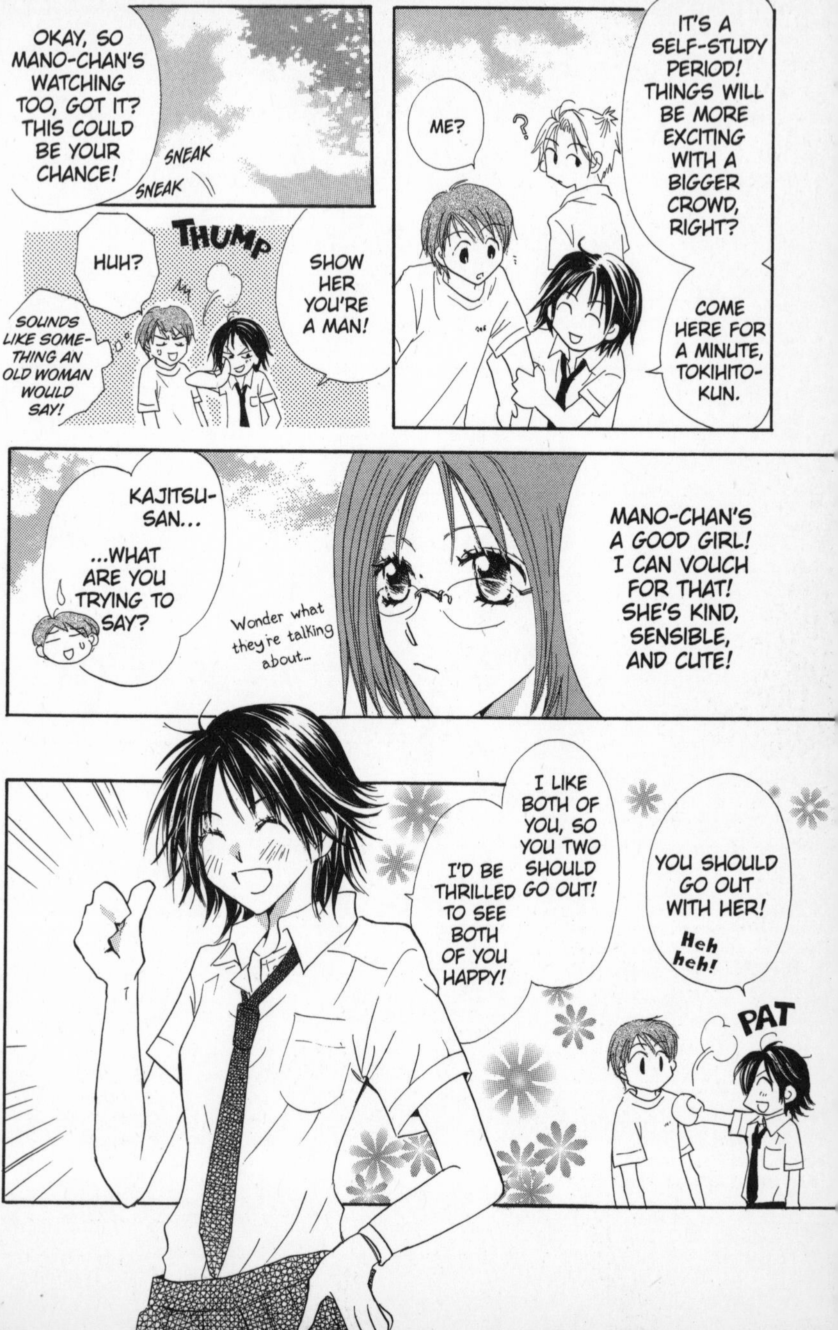
IT'S A SELF-STUDY PERIOD! THINGS WILL BE MORE EXCITING WITH A BIGGER CROWD, RIGHT?
ME?
COME HERE FOR A MINUTE, TOKIHITO-KUN.
OKAY, SO MANO-CHAN'S WATCHING TOO, GOT IT? THIS COULD BE YOUR CHANCE!
SNEAK
SNEAK
SHOW HER YOU'RE A MAN!
THUMP
HUH?
SOUNDS LIKE SOMETHING AN OLD WOMAN WOULD SAY!
MANO-CHAN'S A GOOD GIRL! I CAN VOUCH FOR THAT! SHE'S KIND, SENSIBLE, AND CUTE!
Wonder what they're talking about...
KAJITSU-SAN...
...WHAT ARE YOU TRYING TO SAY?
YOU SHOULD GO OUT WITH HER!
Heh heh!
PAT
I LIKE BOTH OF YOU, SO YOU TWO SHOULD GO OUT!
I'D BE THRILLED TO SEE BOTH OF YOU HAPPY!

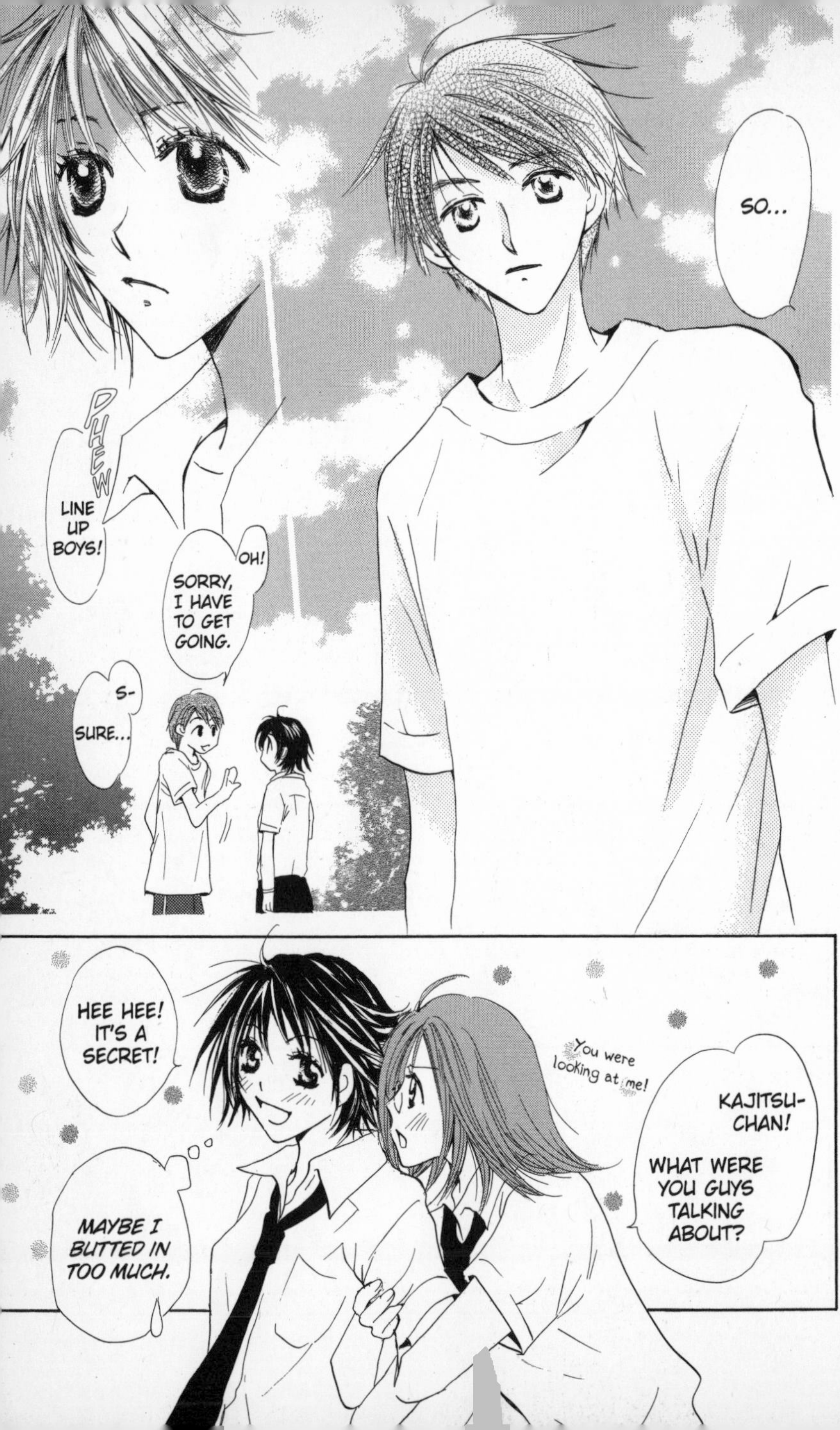
SO...
PHEW
LINE UP BOYS!
OH!
SORRY, I HAVE TO GET GOING.
S- SURE...
KAJITSU-CHAN!
WHAT WERE YOU GUYS TALKING ABOUT?
You were looking at me!
HEE HEE! IT'S A SECRET!
MAYBE I BUTTED IN TOO MUCH.

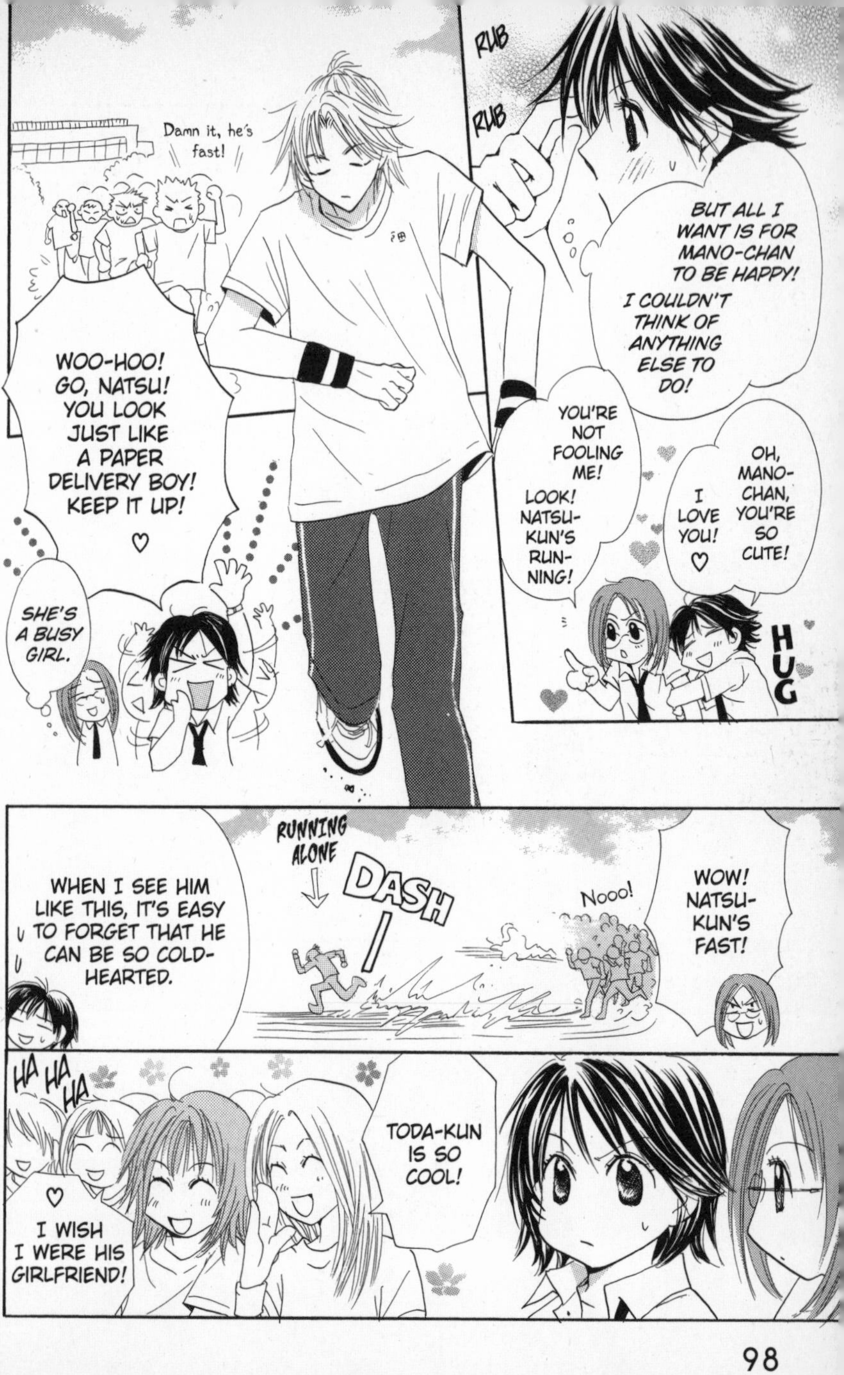

RUB
RUB
BUT ALL I WANT IS FOR MANO-CHAN TO BE HAPPY!
I COULDN'T THINK OF ANYTHING ELSE TO DO!
OH, MANO-CHAN, YOU'RE SO CUTE!
I LOVE YOU! ♡
YOU'RE NOT FOOLING ME!
LOOK! NATSU-KUN'S RUNNING!
HUG
Damn it, he's fast!
WOO-HOO! GO, NATSU! YOU LOOK JUST LIKE A PAPER DELIVERY BOY! KEEP IT UP! ♡
SHE'S A BUSY GIRL.
WOW! NATSU-KUN'S FAST!
Nooo!
DASH
RUNNING ALONE
WHEN I SEE HIM LIKE THIS, IT'S EASY TO FORGET THAT HE CAN BE SO COLD-HEARTED.
TODA-KUN IS SO COOL!
♡ I WISH I WERE HIS GIRLFRIEND!
HA HA HA

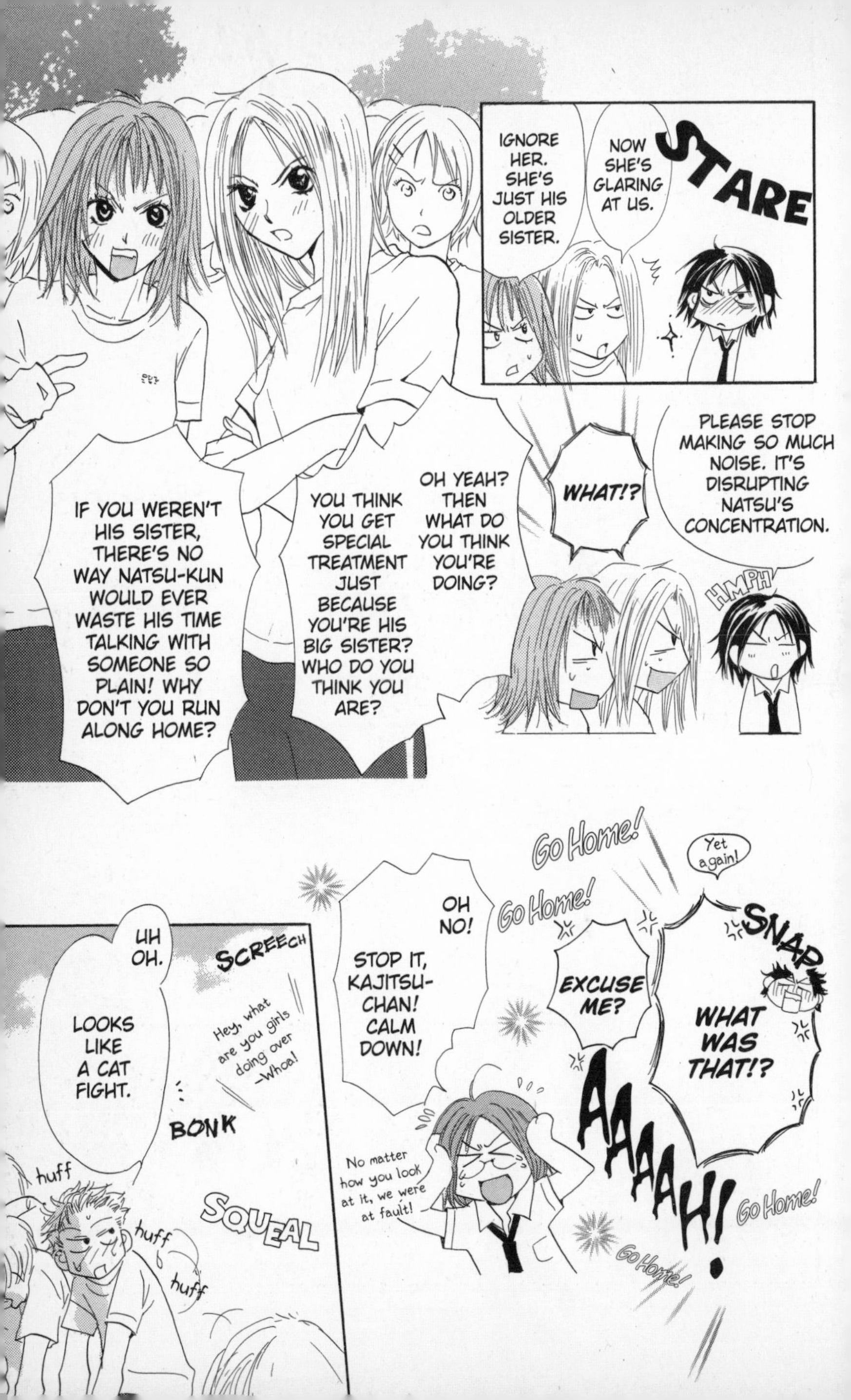
STARE
NOW SHE'S GLARING AT US.
IGNORE HER. SHE'S JUST HIS OLDER SISTER.
PLEASE STOP MAKING SO MUCH NOISE. IT'S DISRUPTING NATSU'S CONCENTRATION.
WHAT!?
HMPH
OH YEAH? THEN WHAT DO YOU THINK YOU'RE DOING?
YOU THINK YOU GET SPECIAL TREATMENT JUST BECAUSE YOU'RE HIS BIG SISTER? WHO DO YOU THINK YOU ARE?
IF YOU WEREN'T HIS SISTER, THERE'S NO WAY NATSU-KUN WOULD EVER WASTE HIS TIME TALKING WITH SOMEONE SO PLAIN! WHY DON'T YOU RUN ALONG HOME?
Yet again!
Go Home!
Go Home!
SNAP
WHAT WAS THAT!?
EXCUSE ME?
OH NO!
STOP IT, KAJITSU-CHAN! CALM DOWN!
AAAAAH!
No matter how you look at it, we were at fault!
Go Home!
Go Home!
UH OH.
SCREECH
LOOKS LIKE A CAT FIGHT.
Hey, what are you girls doing over —Whoa!
BONK
huff
huff
huff
SQUEAL

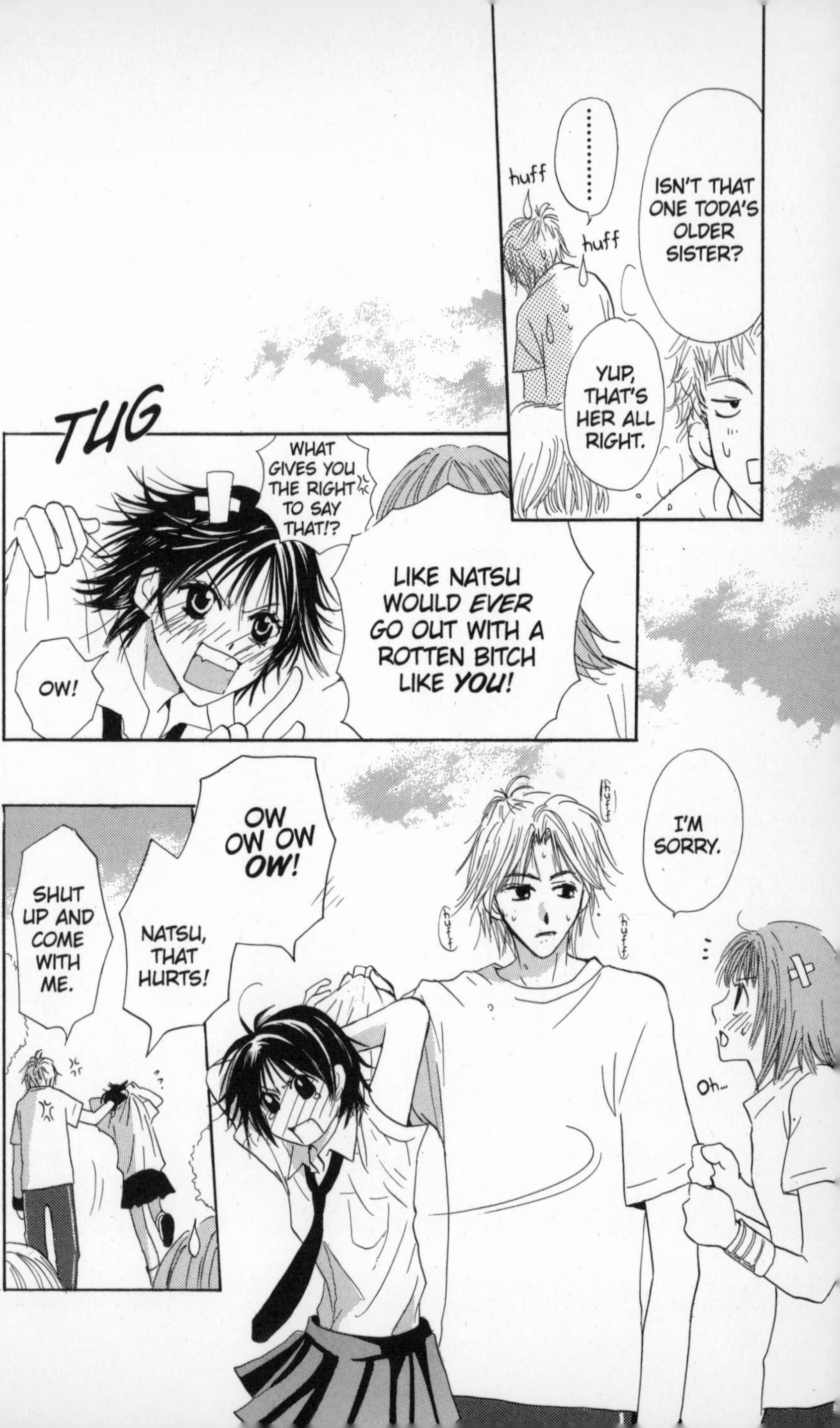
ISN'T THAT ONE TODA'S OLDER SISTER?
......
huff
huff
YUP, THAT'S HER ALL RIGHT.
TUG
WHAT GIVES YOU THE RIGHT TO SAY THAT!?
LIKE NATSU WOULD *EVER* GO OUT WITH A ROTTEN BITCH LIKE ***YOU***!
OW!
I'M SORRY.
OW OW OW ***OW***!
NATSU, THAT HURTS!
SHUT UP AND COME WITH ME.
Oh...

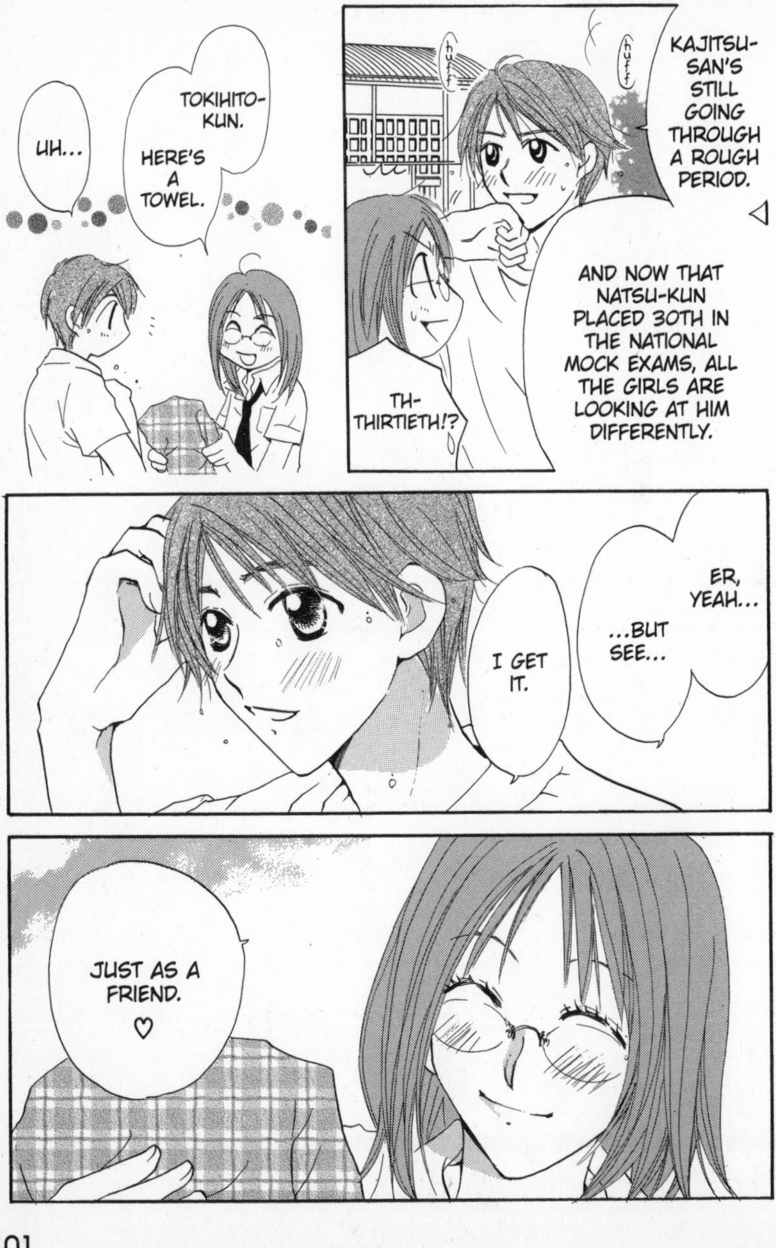
KAJITSU-SAN'S STILL GOING THROUGH A ROUGH PERIOD.
huff
huff
AND NOW THAT NATSU-KUN PLACED 30TH IN THE NATIONAL MOCK EXAMS, ALL THE GIRLS ARE LOOKING AT HIM DIFFERENTLY.
TH-THIRTIETH!?
TOKIHITO-KUN.
HERE'S A TOWEL.
UH...
ER, YEAH...
...BUT SEE...
I GET IT.
JUST AS A FRIEND. ♡

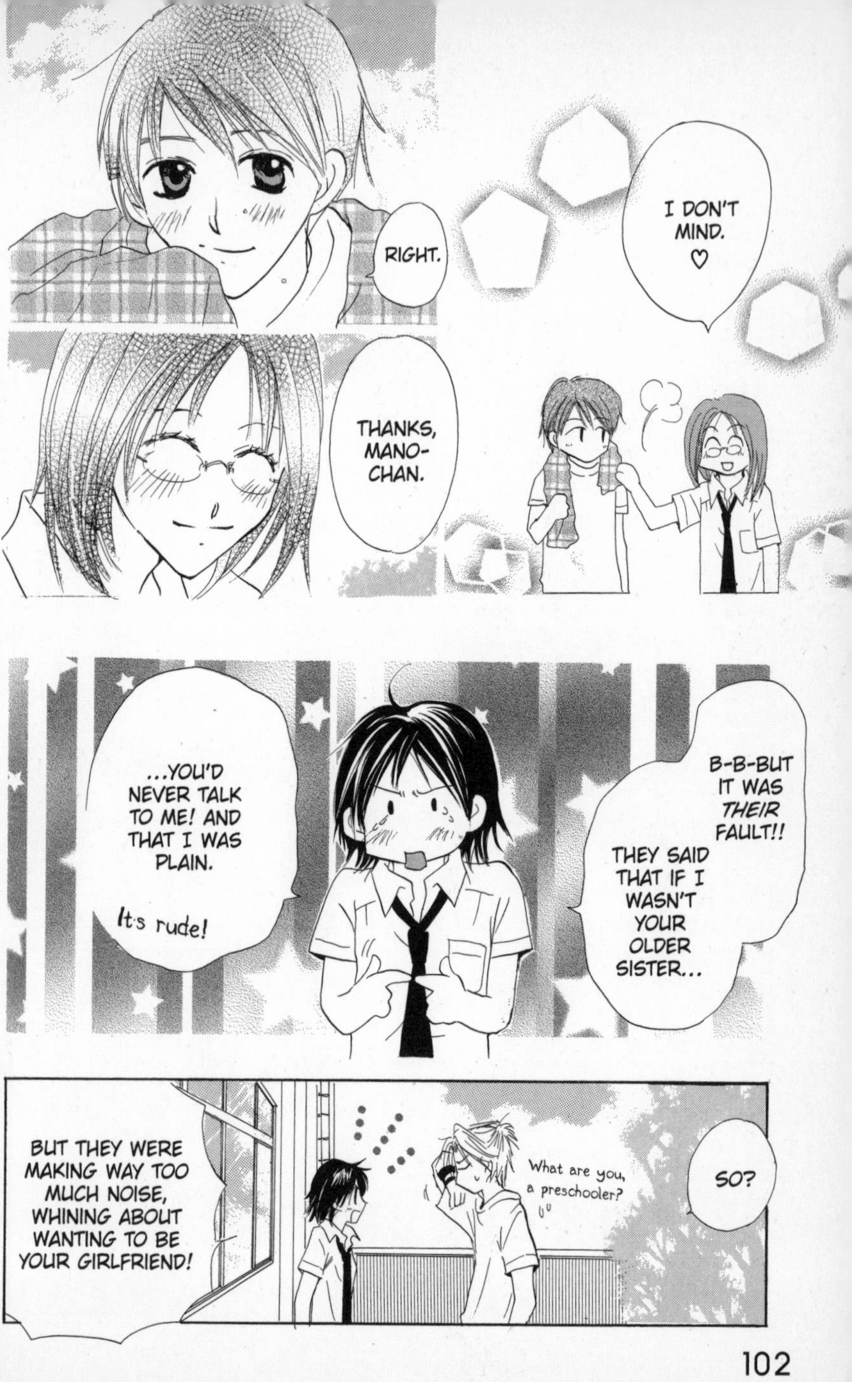
I DON'T MIND. ♡
RIGHT.
THANKS, MANO-CHAN.
B-B-BUT IT WAS *THEIR* FAULT!!
THEY SAID THAT IF I WASN'T YOUR OLDER SISTER...
...YOU'D NEVER TALK TO ME! AND THAT I WAS PLAIN.
It's rude!
SO?
What are you, a preschooler?
BUT THEY WERE MAKING WAY TOO MUCH NOISE, WHINING ABOUT WANTING TO BE YOUR GIRLFRIEND!

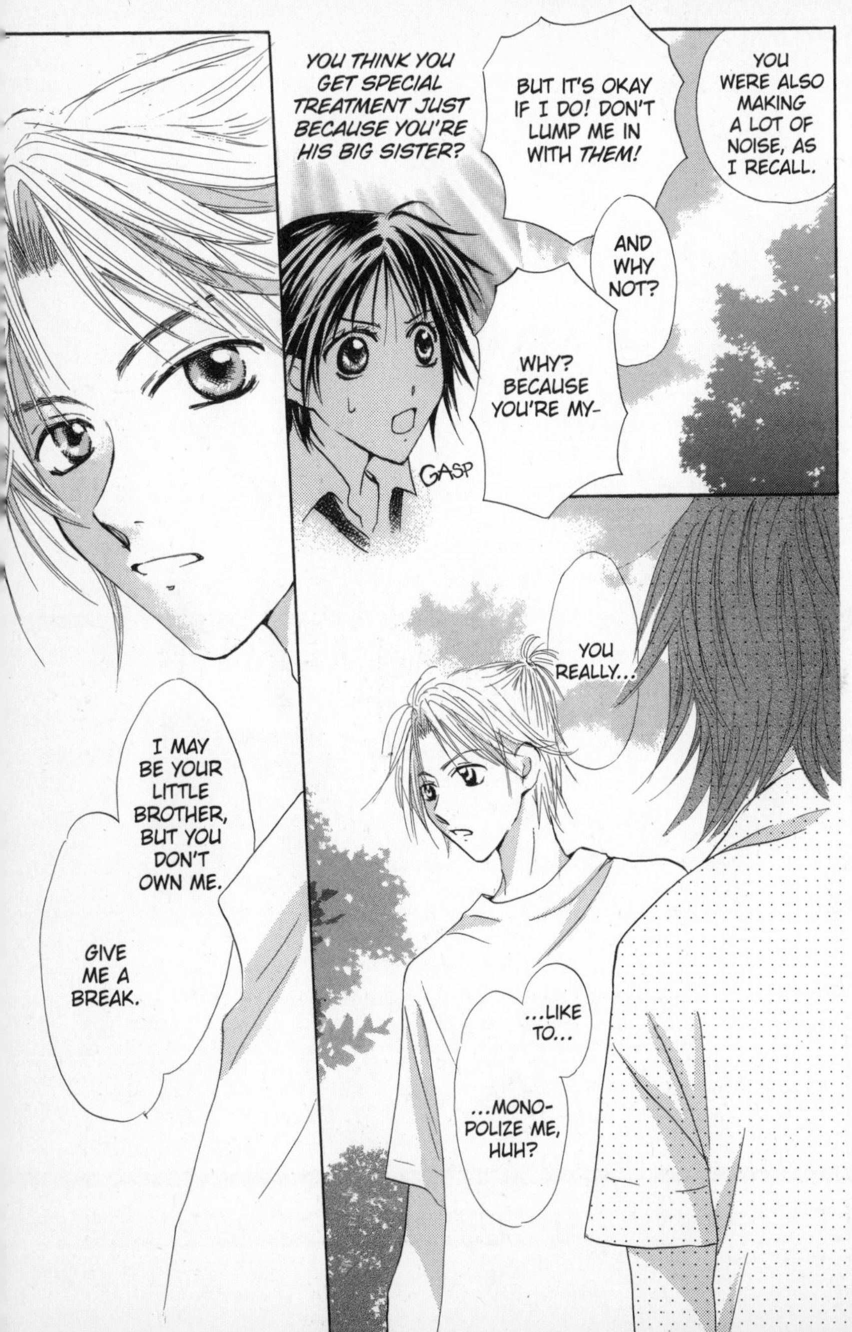

YOU WERE ALSO MAKING A LOT OF NOISE, AS I RECALL.
BUT IT'S OKAY IF I DO! DON'T LUMP ME IN WITH *THEM*!
AND WHY NOT?
WHY? BECAUSE YOU'RE MY-
GASP
YOU THINK YOU GET SPECIAL TREATMENT JUST BECAUSE YOU'RE HIS BIG SISTER?
YOU REALLY...
...LIKE TO...
...MONO-POLIZE ME, HUH?
I MAY BE YOUR LITTLE BROTHER, BUT YOU DON'T OWN ME.
GIVE ME A BREAK.

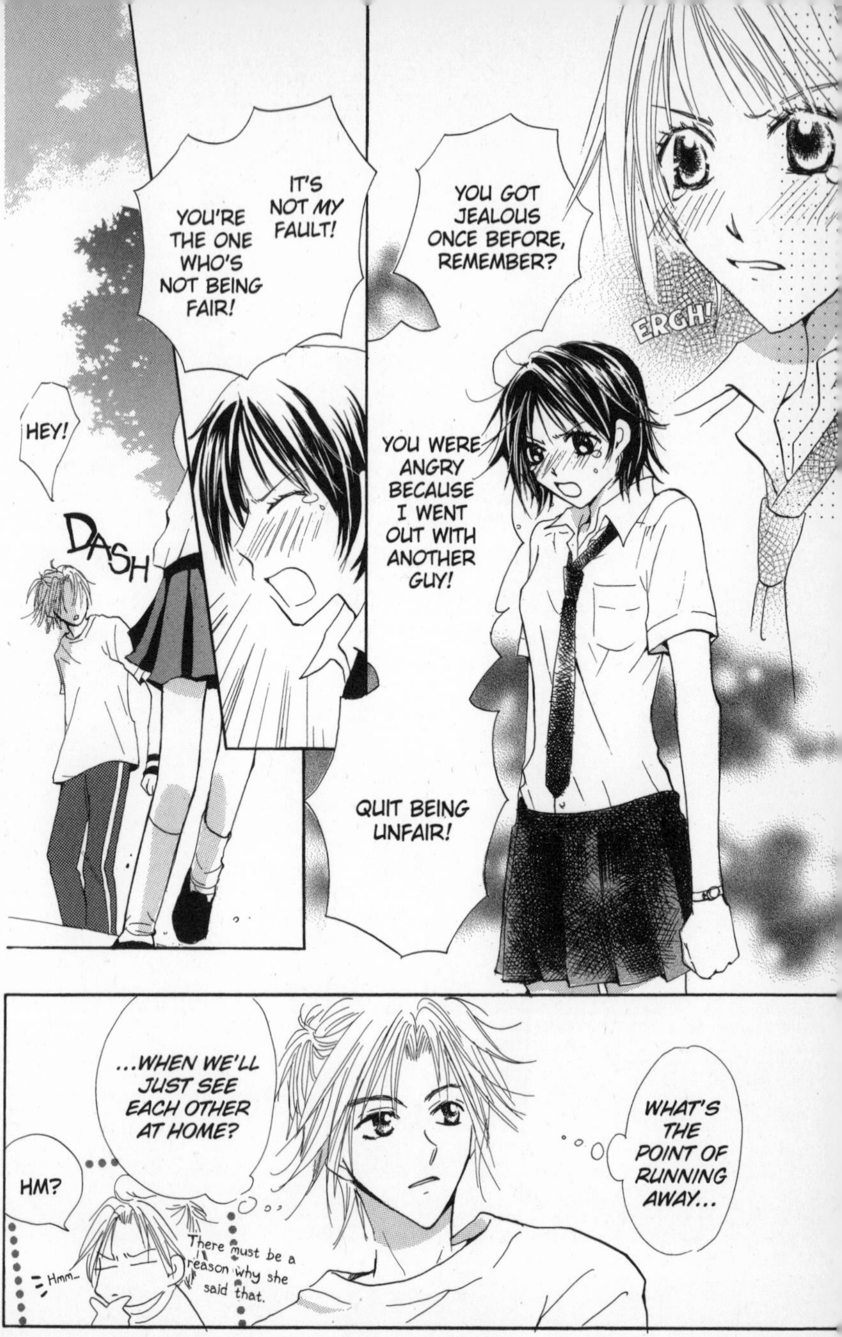
YOU GOT JEALOUS ONCE BEFORE, REMEMBER?
ERGH!
YOU WERE ANGRY BECAUSE I WENT OUT WITH ANOTHER GUY!
QUIT BEING UNFAIR!
IT'S NOT MY FAULT!
YOU'RE THE ONE WHO'S NOT BEING FAIR!
HEY!
DASH
WHAT'S THE POINT OF RUNNING AWAY...
...WHEN WE'LL JUST SEE EACH OTHER AT HOME?
HM?
There must be a reason why she said that.
Hmm..

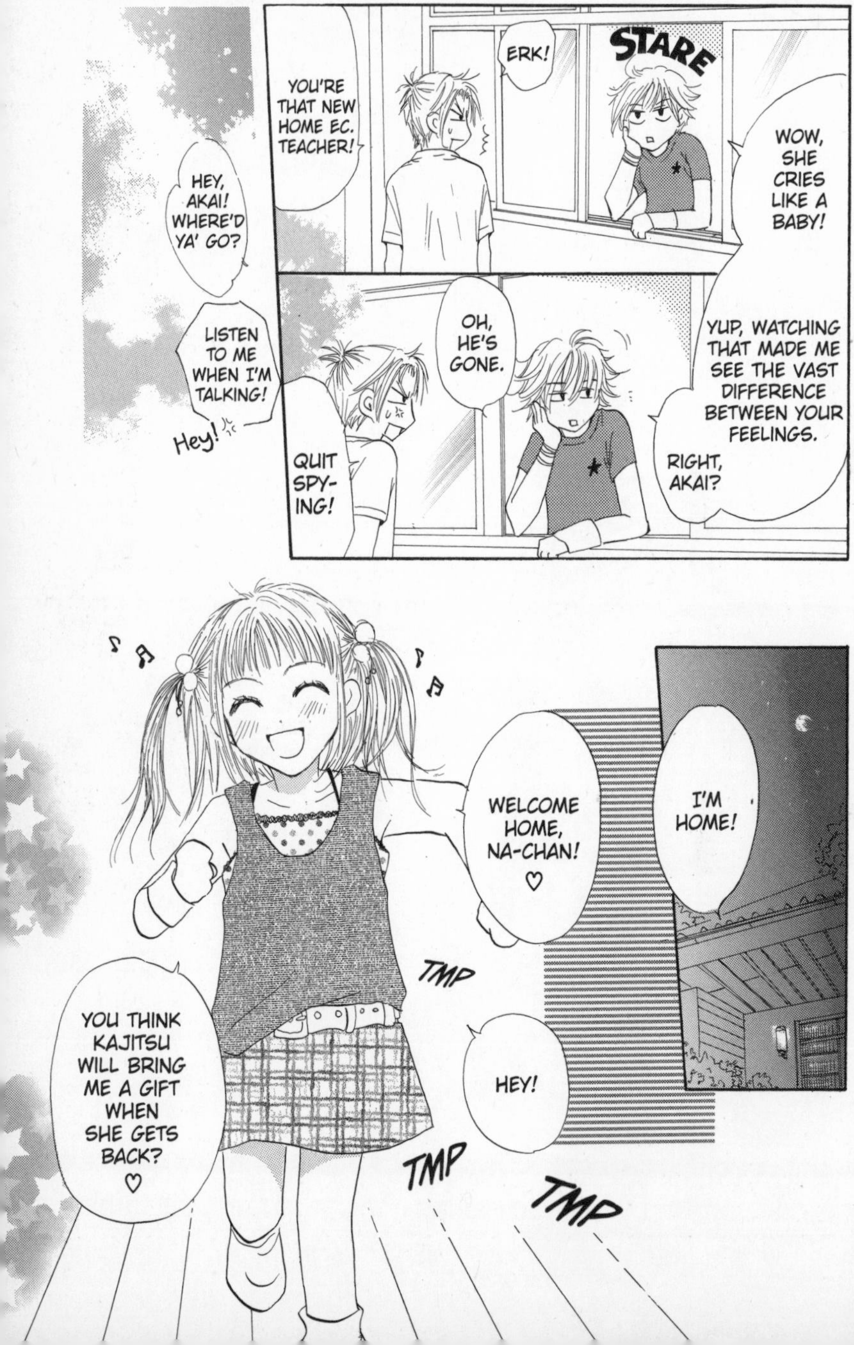
STARE
WOW, SHE CRIES LIKE A BABY!
ERK!
YOU'RE THAT NEW HOME EC. TEACHER!
YUP, WATCHING THAT MADE ME SEE THE VAST DIFFERENCE BETWEEN YOUR FEELINGS.
RIGHT, AKAI?
OH, HE'S GONE.
QUIT SPY-ING!
HEY, AKAI! WHERE'D YA' GO?
LISTEN TO ME WHEN I'M TALKING!
Hey!
I'M HOME!
WELCOME HOME, NA-CHAN! ♡
TMP
HEY!
TMP
TMP
YOU THINK KAJITSU WILL BRING ME A GIFT WHEN SHE GETS BACK? ♡

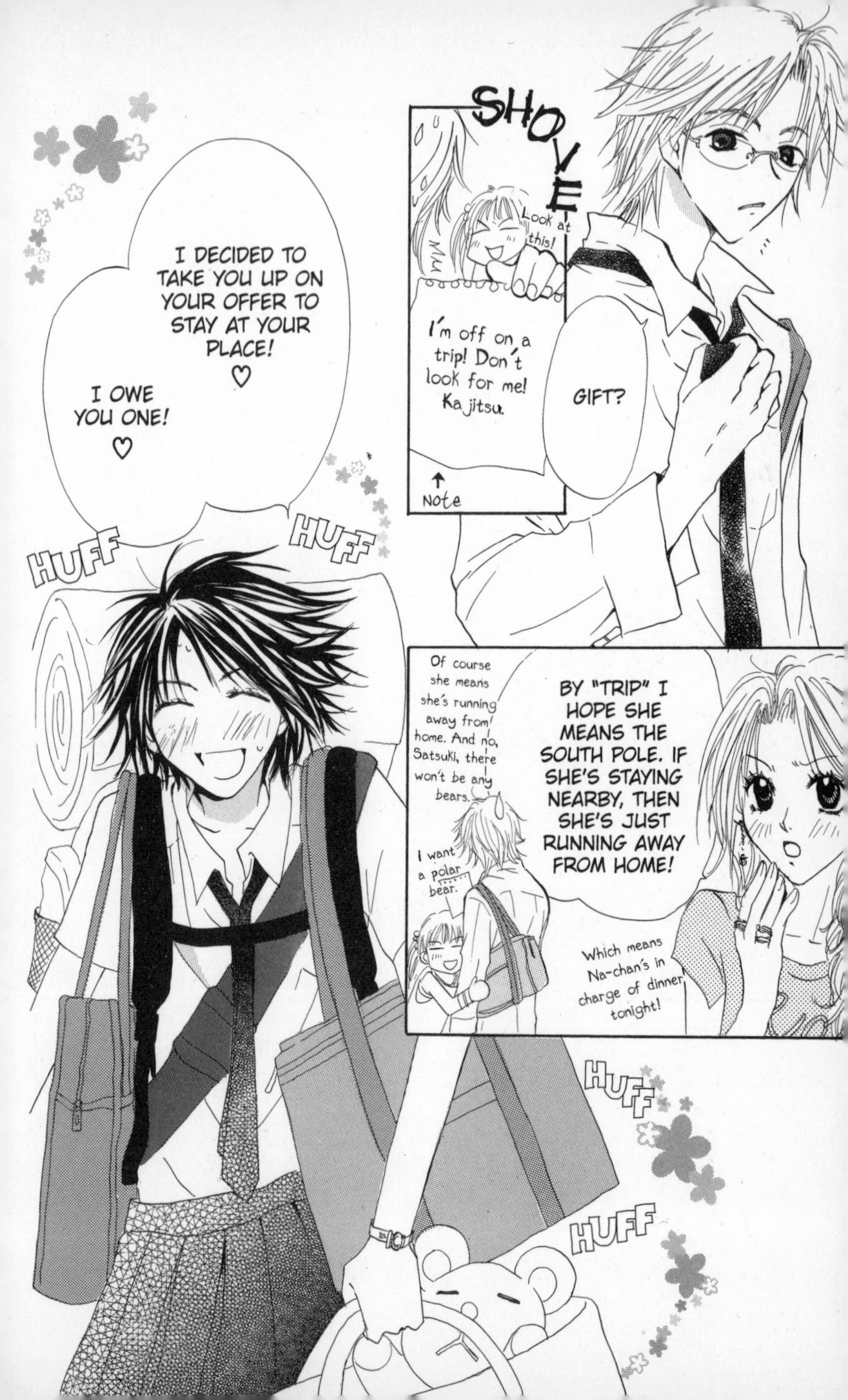
SHOVE
Look at this!
I'm off on a trip! Don't look for me! Kajitsu.
↑ Note
GIFT?
BY "TRIP" I HOPE SHE MEANS THE SOUTH POLE. IF SHE'S STAYING NEARBY, THEN SHE'S JUST RUNNING AWAY FROM HOME!
Of course she means she's running away from home. And no, Satsuki, there won't be any bears.
I want a polar bear.
Which means Na-chan's in charge of dinner tonight!
I DECIDED TO TAKE YOU UP ON YOUR OFFER TO STAY AT YOUR PLACE! ♡
I OWE YOU ONE! ♡
HUFF
HUFF
HUFF
HUFF

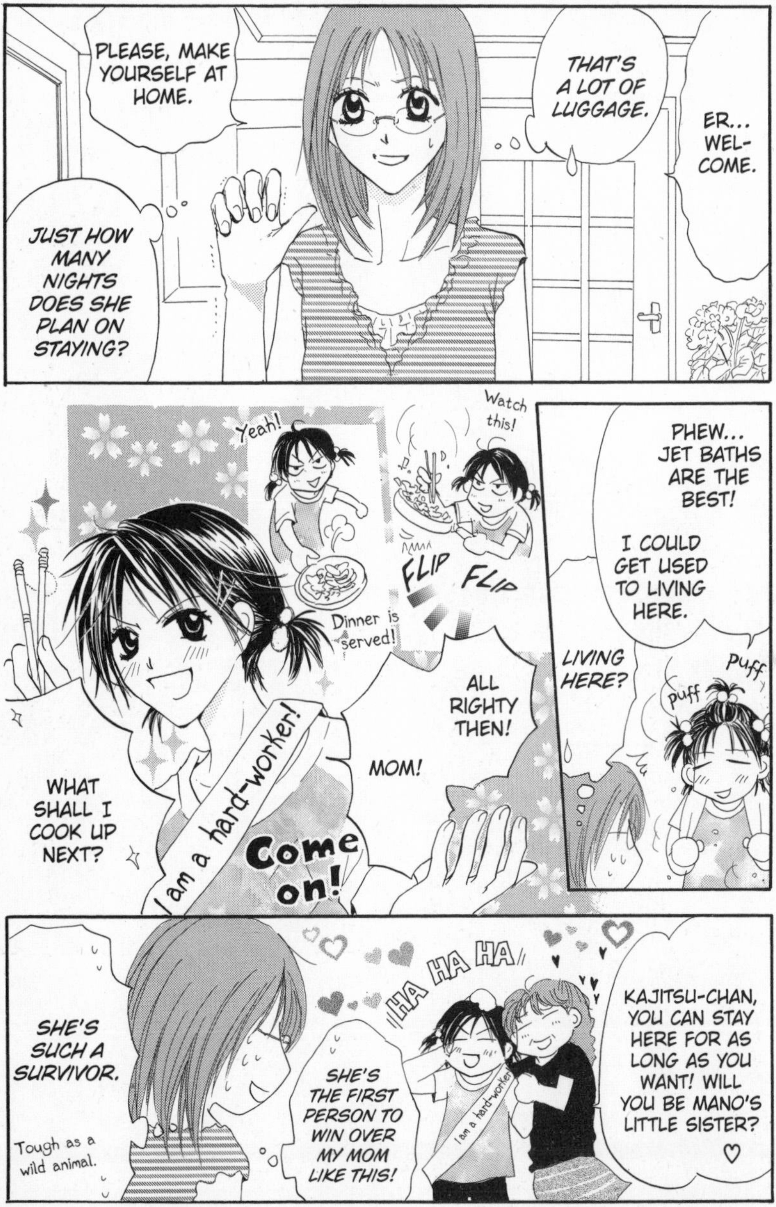
ER... WEL-COME.
THAT'S A LOT OF LUGGAGE.
PLEASE, MAKE YOURSELF AT HOME.
JUST HOW MANY NIGHTS DOES SHE PLAN ON STAYING?
PHEW... JET BATHS ARE THE BEST!
I COULD GET USED TO LIVING HERE.
puff
puff
LIVING HERE?
Watch this!
FLIP FLIP
Yeah!
Dinner is served!
ALL RIGHTY THEN!
MOM!
WHAT SHALL I COOK UP NEXT?
I am a hard-worker!
Come on!
KAJITSU-CHAN, YOU CAN STAY HERE FOR AS LONG AS YOU WANT! WILL YOU BE MANO'S LITTLE SISTER? ♡
HA HA HA
I am a hard-worker
SHE'S THE FIRST PERSON TO WIN OVER MY MOM LIKE THIS!
SHE'S SUCH A SURVIVOR.
Tough as a wild animal.

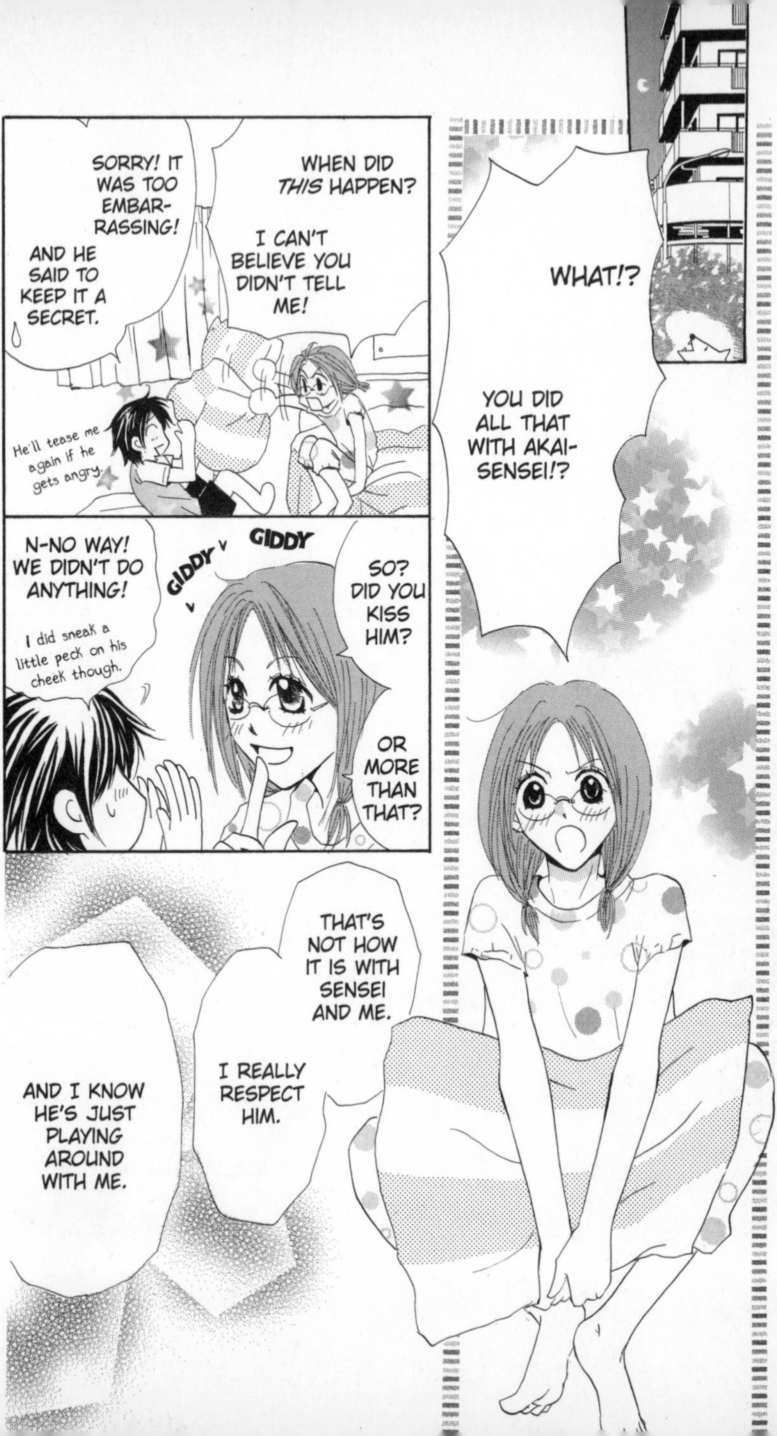
WHAT!?
YOU DID ALL THAT WITH AKAI-SENSEI!?
WHEN DID THIS HAPPEN?
I CAN'T BELIEVE YOU DIDN'T TELL ME!
SORRY! IT WAS TOO EMBAR-RASSING!
AND HE SAID TO KEEP IT A SECRET.
He'll tease me again if he gets angry.
GIDDY
GIDDY
SO? DID YOU KISS HIM?
OR MORE THAN THAT?
N-NO WAY! WE DIDN'T DO ANYTHING!
I did sneak a little peck on his cheek though.
THAT'S NOT HOW IT IS WITH SENSEI AND ME.
I REALLY RESPECT HIM.
AND I KNOW HE'S JUST PLAYING AROUND WITH ME.

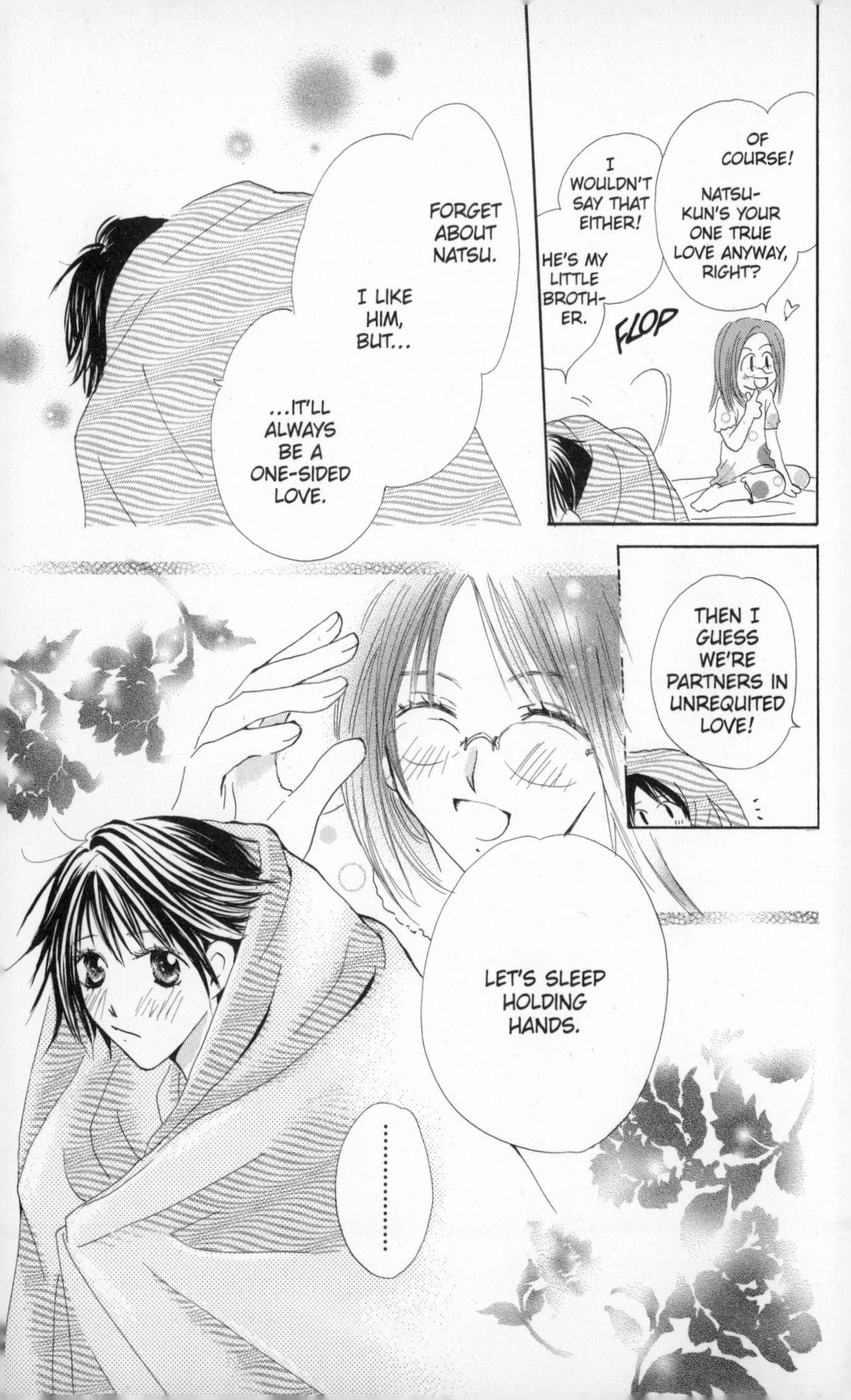
OF COURSE!
NATSU-KUN'S YOUR ONE TRUE LOVE ANYWAY, RIGHT?
I WOULDN'T SAY THAT EITHER!
HE'S MY LITTLE BROTHER.
FLOP
FORGET ABOUT NATSU.
I LIKE HIM, BUT...
...IT'LL ALWAYS BE A ONE-SIDED LOVE.
THEN I GUESS WE'RE PARTNERS IN UNREQUITED LOVE!
LET'S SLEEP HOLDING HANDS.
....

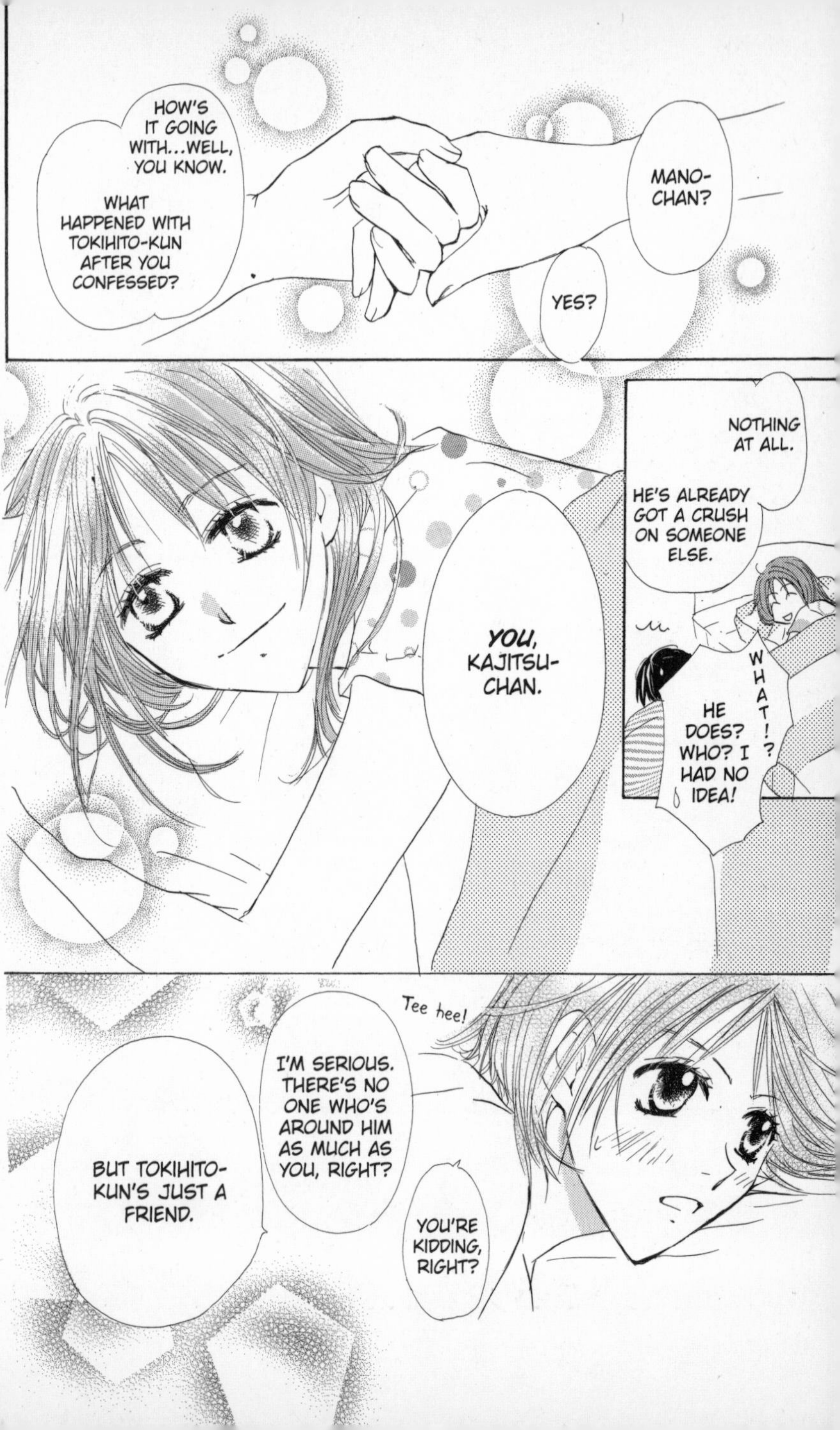

MANO-CHAN?
YES?
HOW'S IT GOING WITH...WELL, YOU KNOW.
WHAT HAPPENED WITH TOKIHITO-KUN AFTER YOU CONFESSED?
NOTHING AT ALL.
HE'S ALREADY GOT A CRUSH ON SOMEONE ELSE.
WHAT!?
HE DOES? WHO? I HAD NO IDEA!
YOU, KAJITSU-CHAN.
YOU'RE KIDDING, RIGHT?
Tee hee!
I'M SERIOUS. THERE'S NO ONE WHO'S AROUND HIM AS MUCH AS YOU, RIGHT?
BUT TOKIHITO-KUN'S JUST A FRIEND.

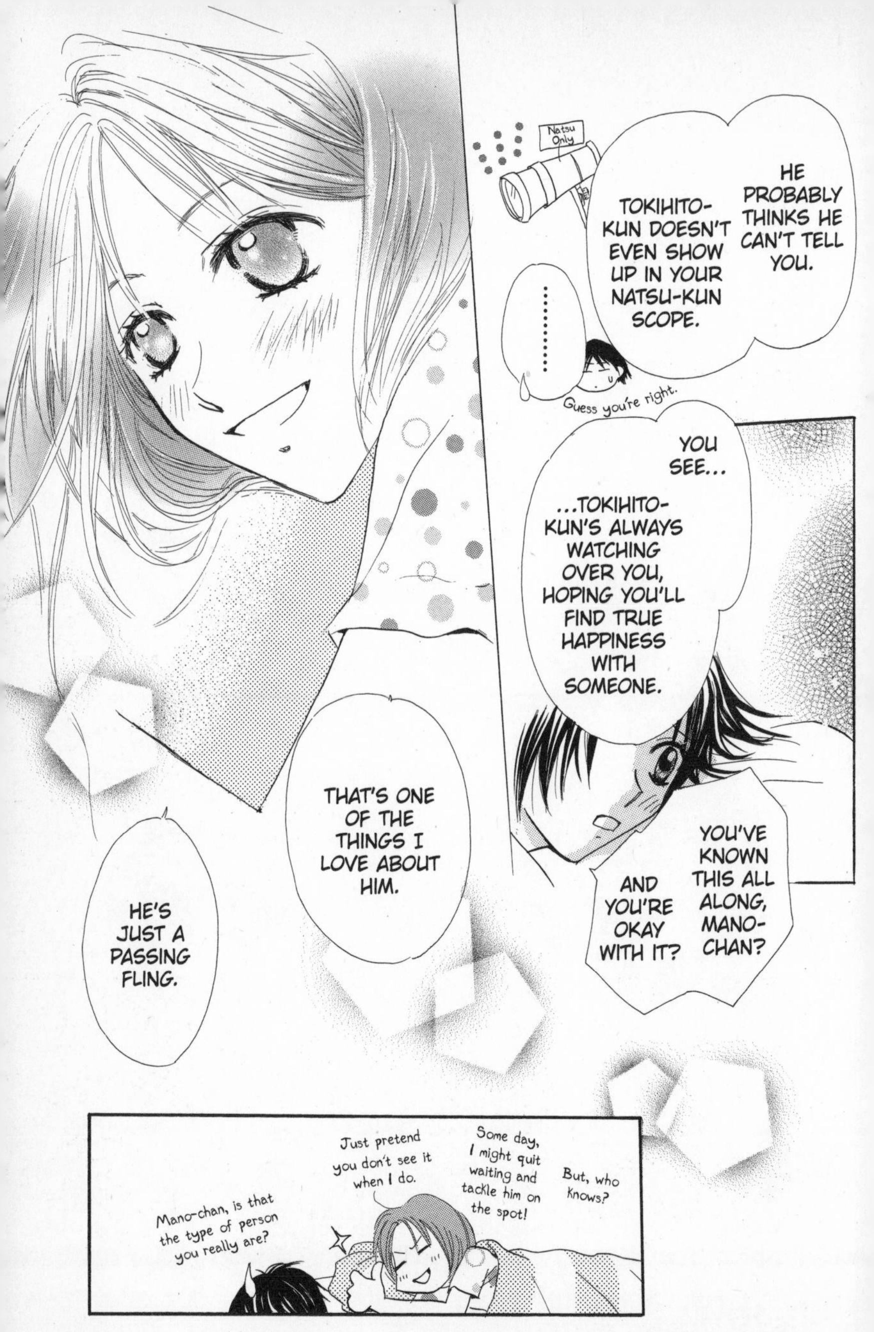
Natsu Only
HE PROBABLY THINKS HE CAN'T TELL YOU.
TOKIHITO-KUN DOESN'T EVEN SHOW UP IN YOUR NATSU-KUN SCOPE.
......
Guess you're right.
YOU SEE...
...TOKIHITO-KUN'S ALWAYS WATCHING OVER YOU, HOPING YOU'LL FIND TRUE HAPPINESS WITH SOMEONE.
YOU'VE KNOWN THIS ALL ALONG, MANO-CHAN?
AND YOU'RE OKAY WITH IT?
THAT'S ONE OF THE THINGS I LOVE ABOUT HIM.
HE'S JUST A PASSING FLING.
But, who knows?
Some day, I might quit waiting and tackle him on the spot!
Just pretend you don't see it when I do.
Mano-chan, is that the type of person you really are?

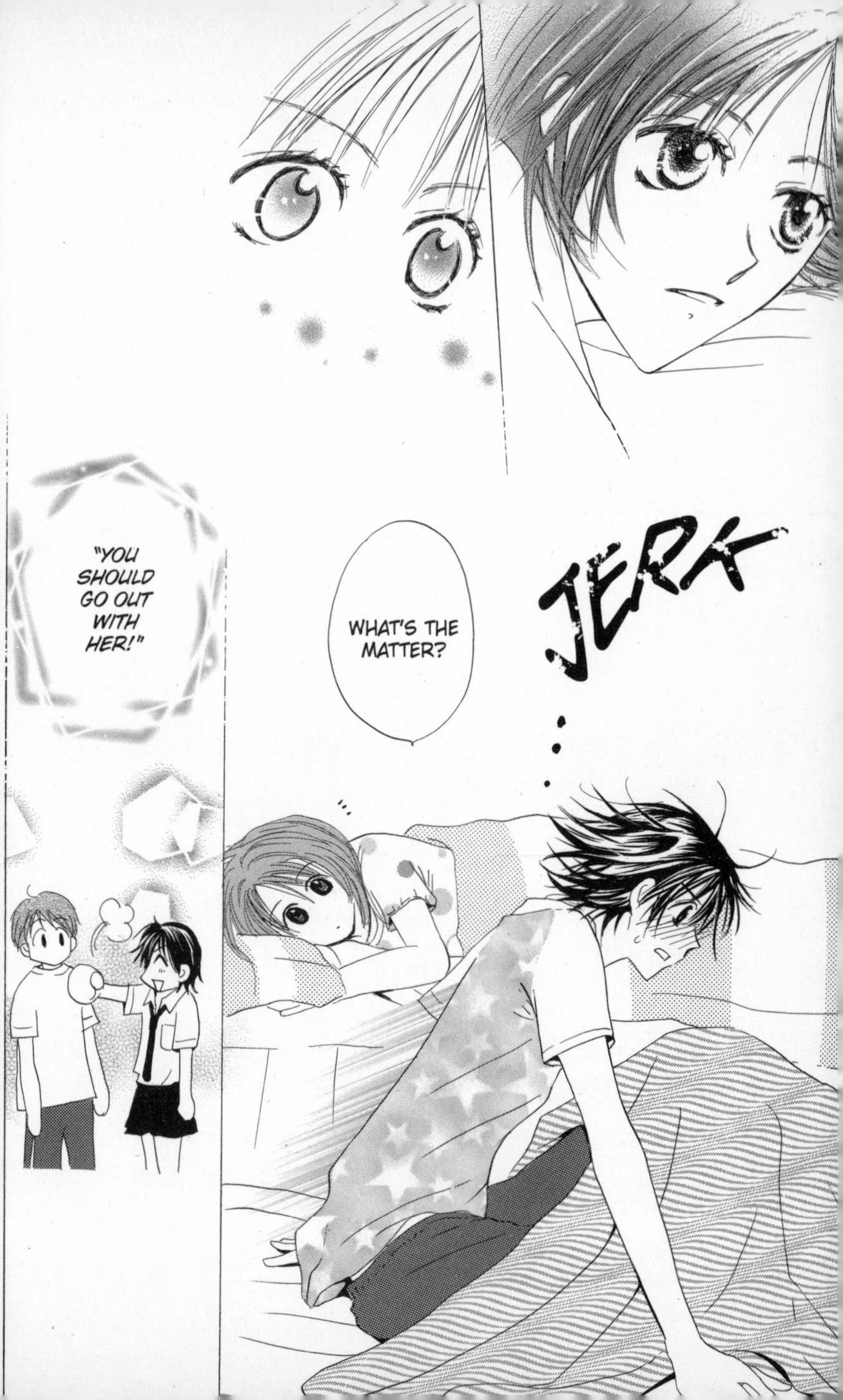
JERK
WHAT'S THE MATTER?
"YOU SHOULD GO OUT WITH HER!"

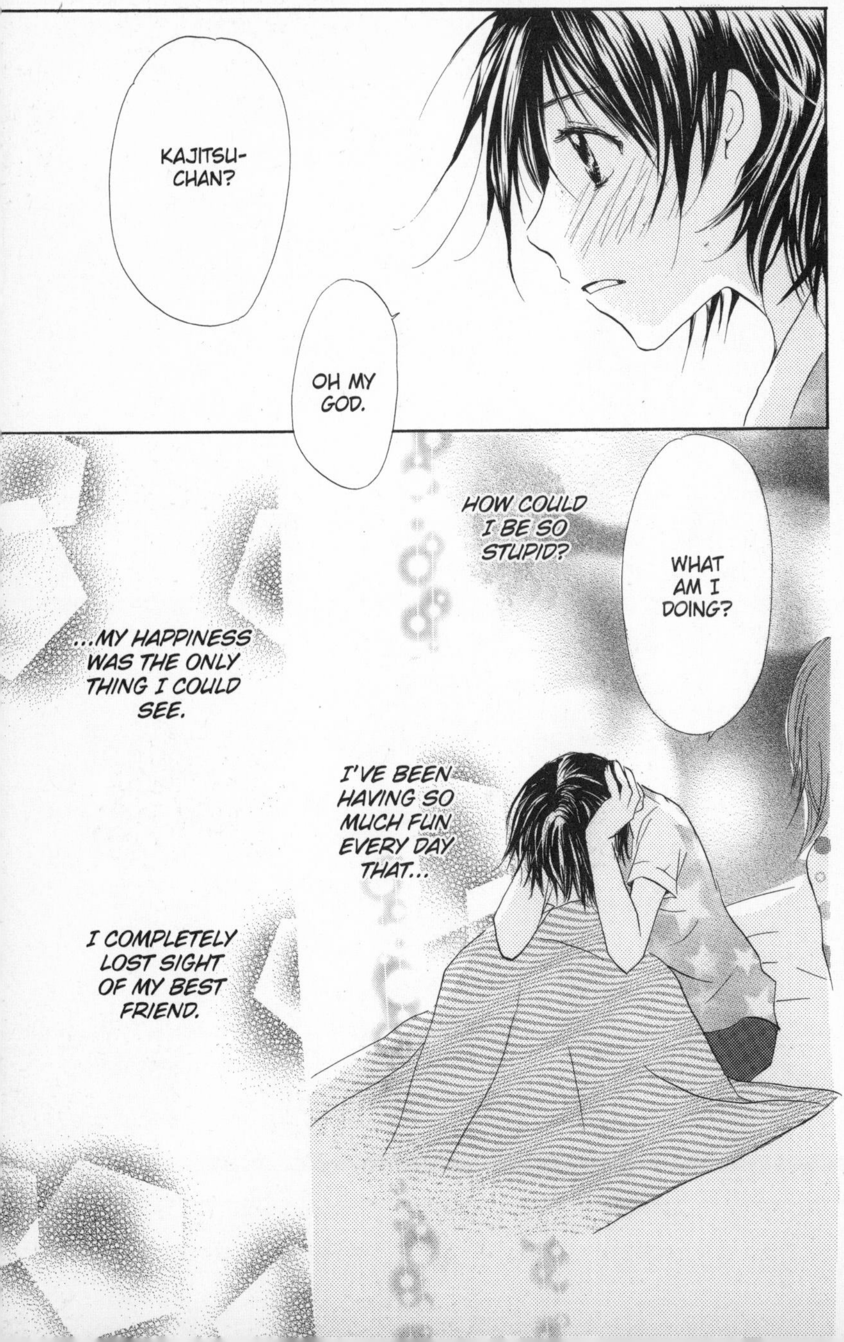
KAJITSU-CHAN?
OH MY GOD.
WHAT AM I DOING?
HOW COULD I BE SO STUPID?
I'VE BEEN HAVING SO MUCH FUN EVERY DAY THAT...
...MY HAPPINESS WAS THE ONLY THING I COULD SEE.
I COMPLETELY LOST SIGHT OF MY BEST FRIEND.

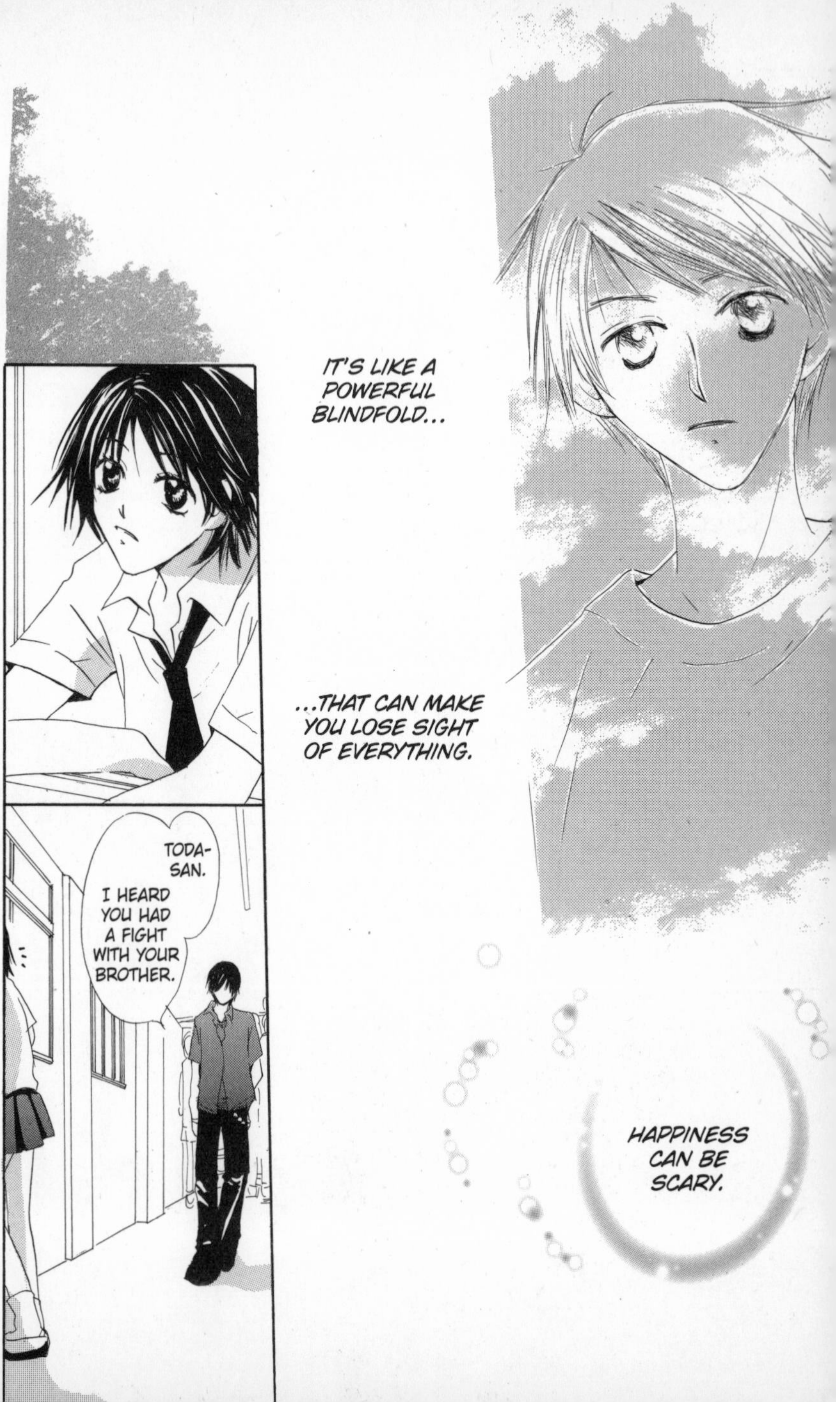
HAPPINESS CAN BE SCARY.
IT'S LIKE A POWERFUL BLINDFOLD...
...THAT CAN MAKE YOU LOSE SIGHT OF EVERYTHING.
TODA-SAN. I HEARD YOU HAD A FIGHT WITH YOUR BROTHER.
...

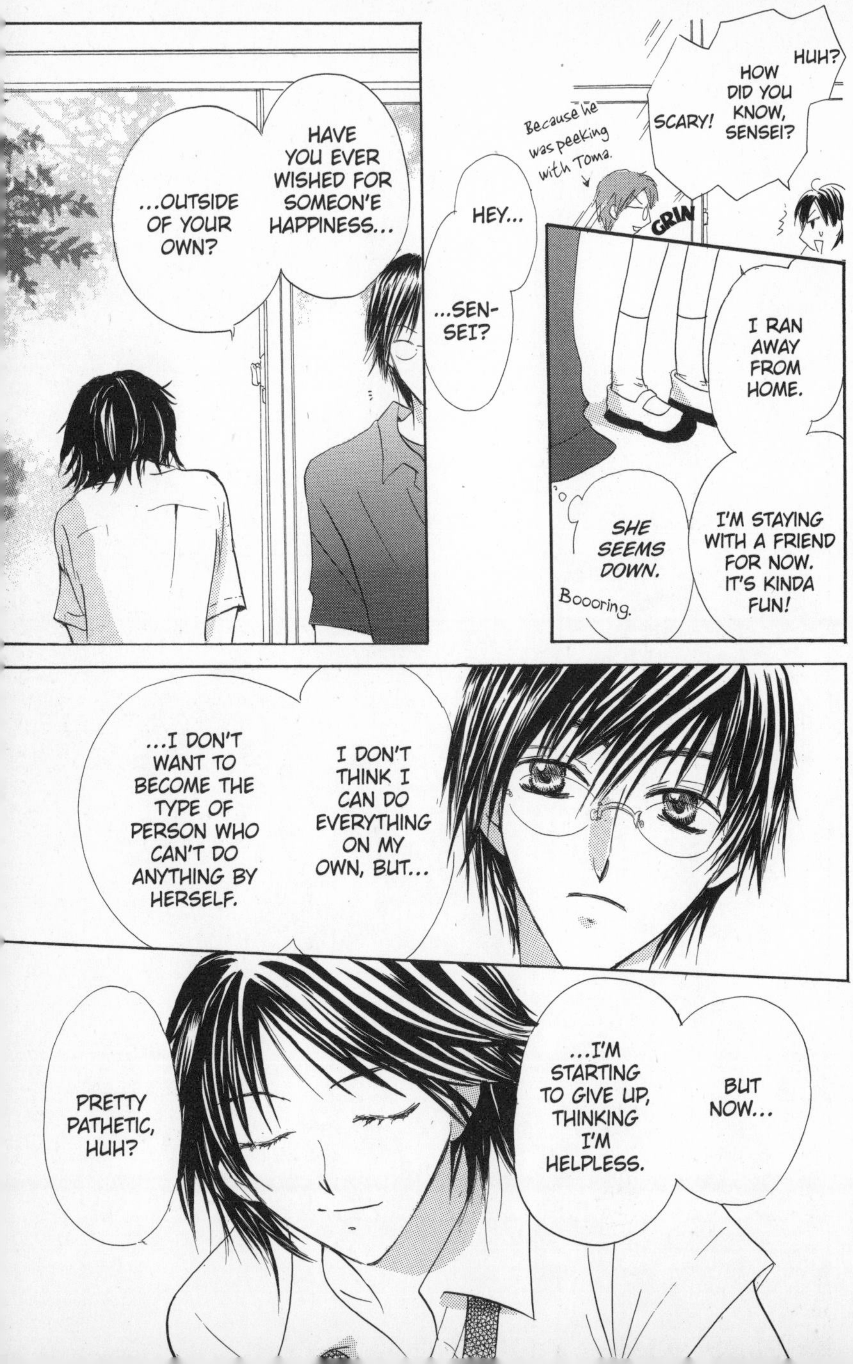
HUH?
HOW DID YOU KNOW, SENSEI?
SCARY!
Because he was peeking with Toma.
GRIN
I RAN AWAY FROM HOME.
I'M STAYING WITH A FRIEND FOR NOW. IT'S KINDA FUN!
SHE SEEMS DOWN.
Boooring.
HEY...
...SEN-SEI?
HAVE YOU EVER WISHED FOR SOMEON'E HAPPINESS...
...OUTSIDE OF YOUR OWN?
I DON'T THINK I CAN DO EVERYTHING ON MY OWN, BUT...
...I DON'T WANT TO BECOME THE TYPE OF PERSON WHO CAN'T DO ANYTHING BY HERSELF.
BUT NOW...
...I'M STARTING TO GIVE UP, THINKING I'M HELPLESS.
PRETTY PATHETIC, HUH?

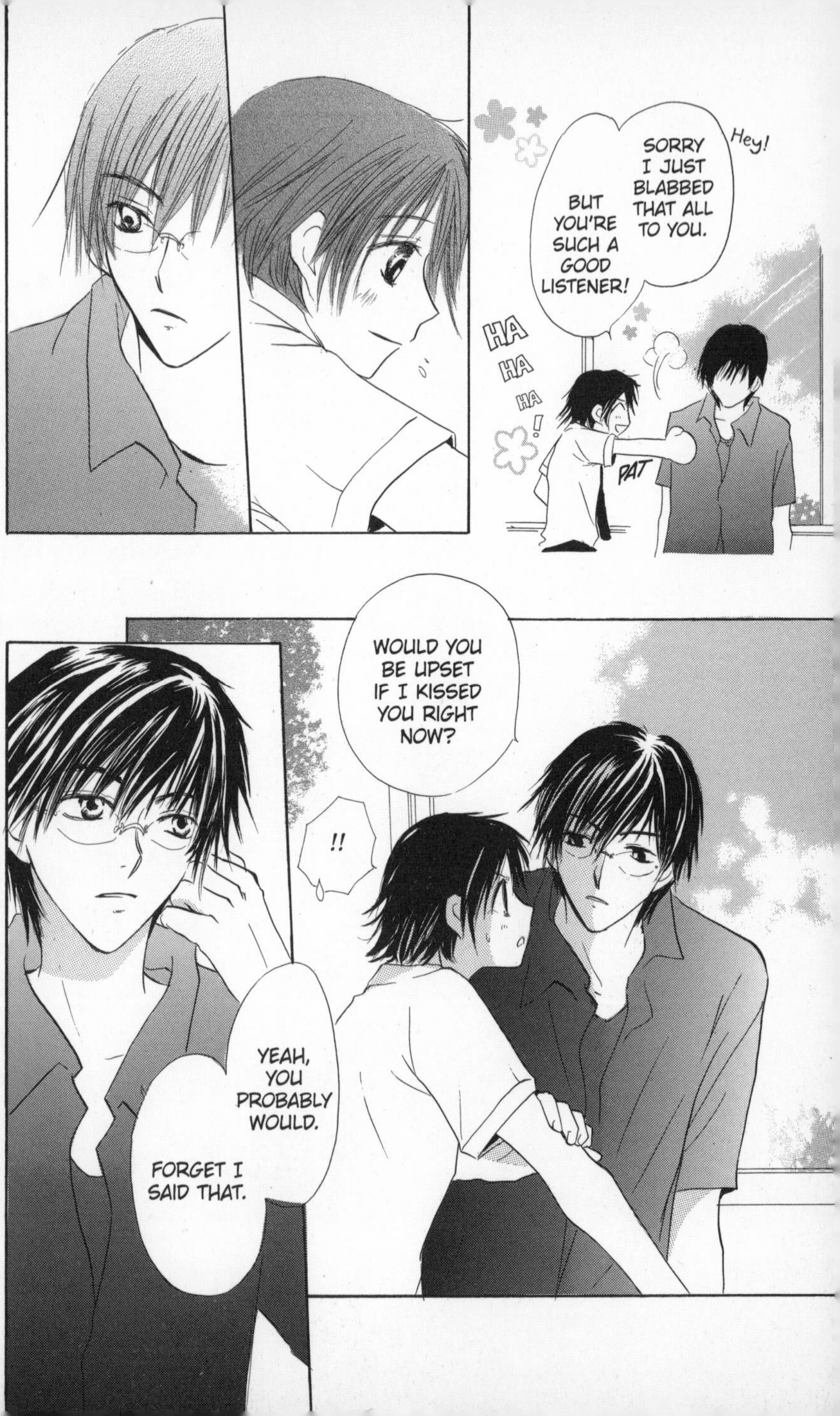
Hey!
SORRY I JUST BLABBED THAT ALL TO YOU.
BUT YOU'RE SUCH A GOOD LISTENER!
HA HA HA!
PAT
WOULD YOU BE UPSET IF I KISSED YOU RIGHT NOW?
!!
YEAH, YOU PROBABLY WOULD.
FORGET I SAID THAT.

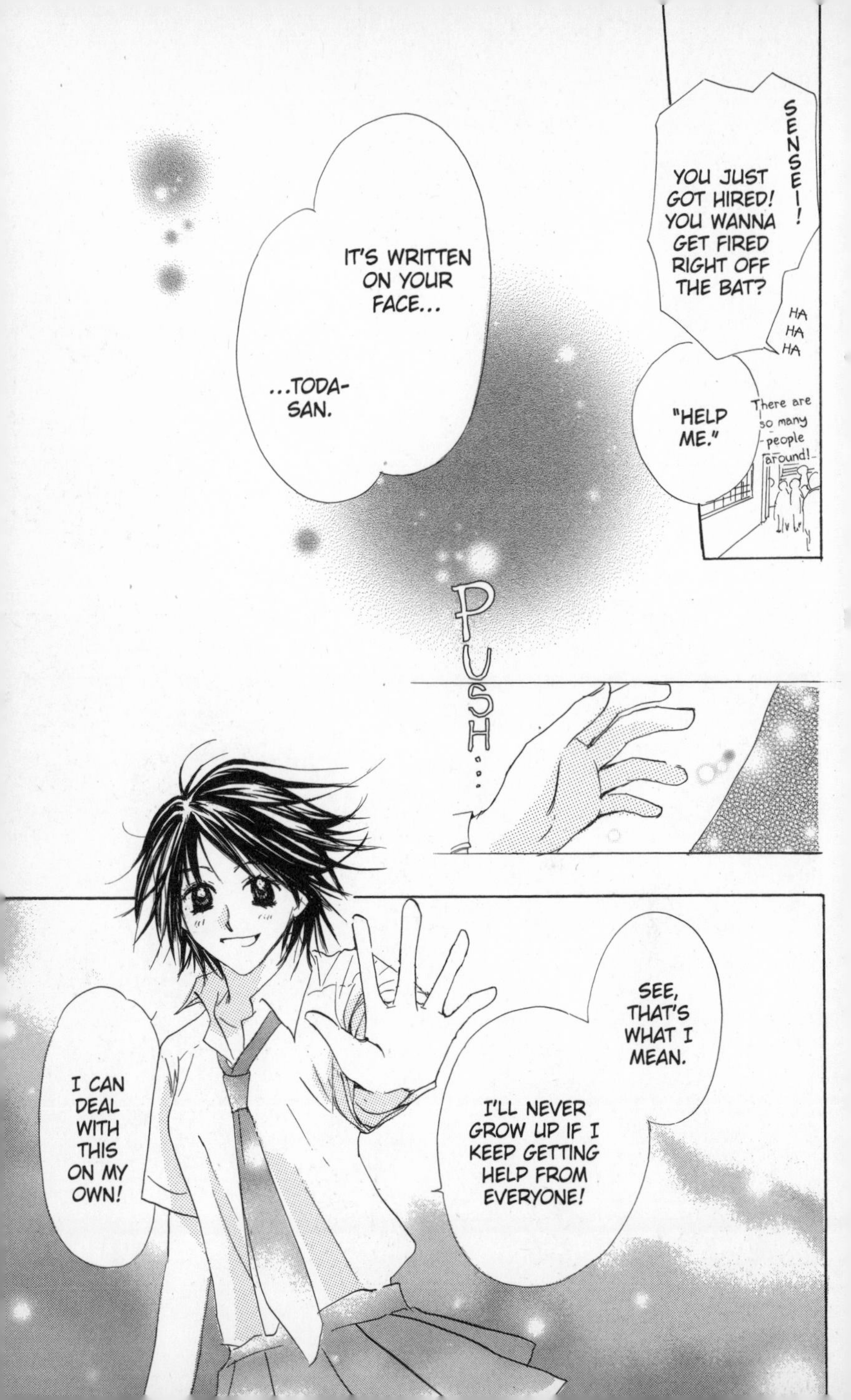
SENSEI!
YOU JUST GOT HIRED! YOU WANNA GET FIRED RIGHT OFF THE BAT?
HA HA HA
"HELP ME."
There are so many people around!
IT'S WRITTEN ON YOUR FACE...
...TODA-SAN.
PUSH..
SEE, THAT'S WHAT I MEAN.
I'LL NEVER GROW UP IF I KEEP GETTING HELP FROM EVERYONE!
I CAN DEAL WITH THIS ON MY OWN!

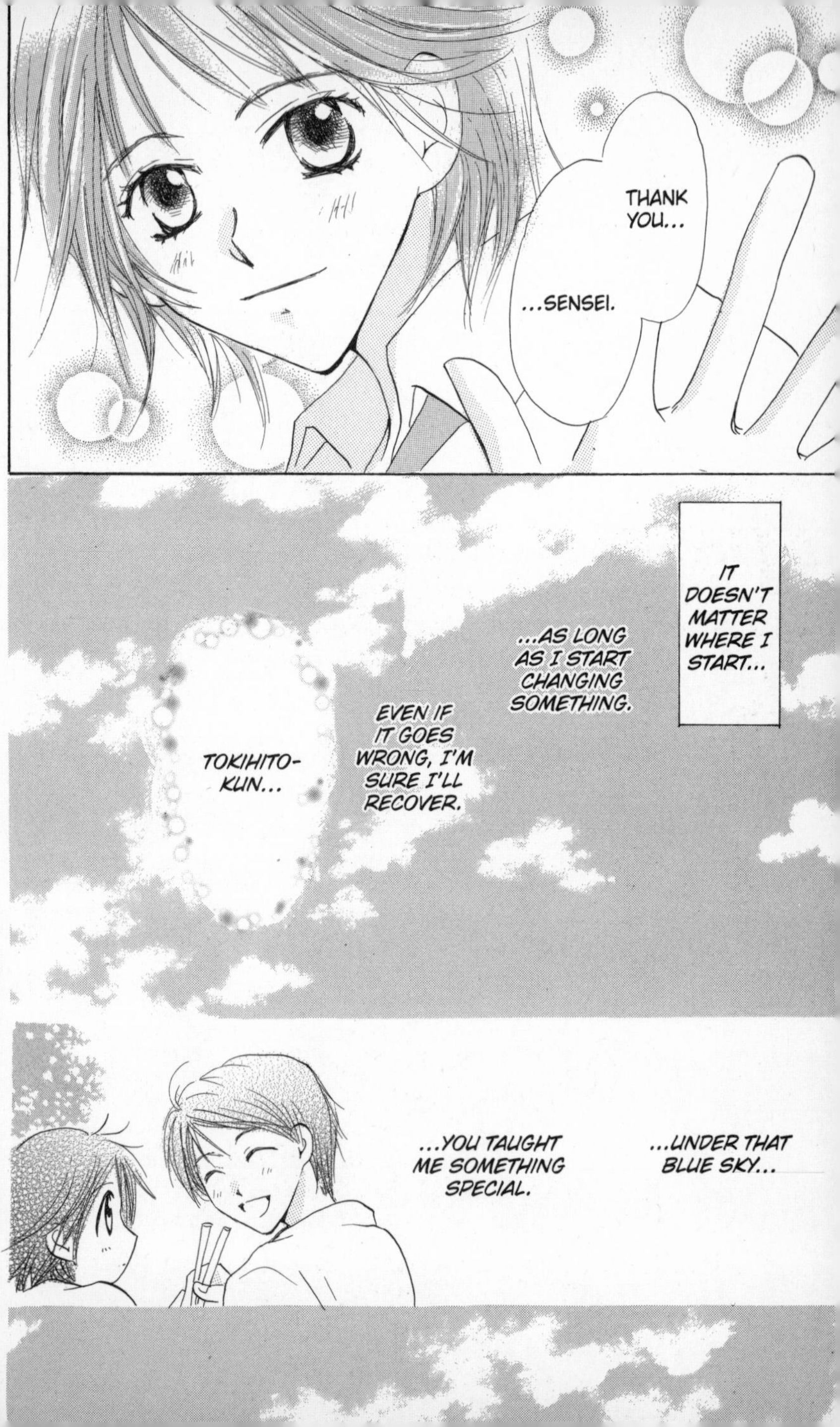
THANK YOU...
...SENSEI.
IT DOESN'T MATTER WHERE I START...
...AS LONG AS I START CHANGING SOMETHING.
EVEN IF IT GOES WRONG, I'M SURE I'LL RECOVER.
TOKIHITO-KUN...
...UNDER THAT BLUE SKY...
...YOU TAUGHT ME SOMETHING SPECIAL.

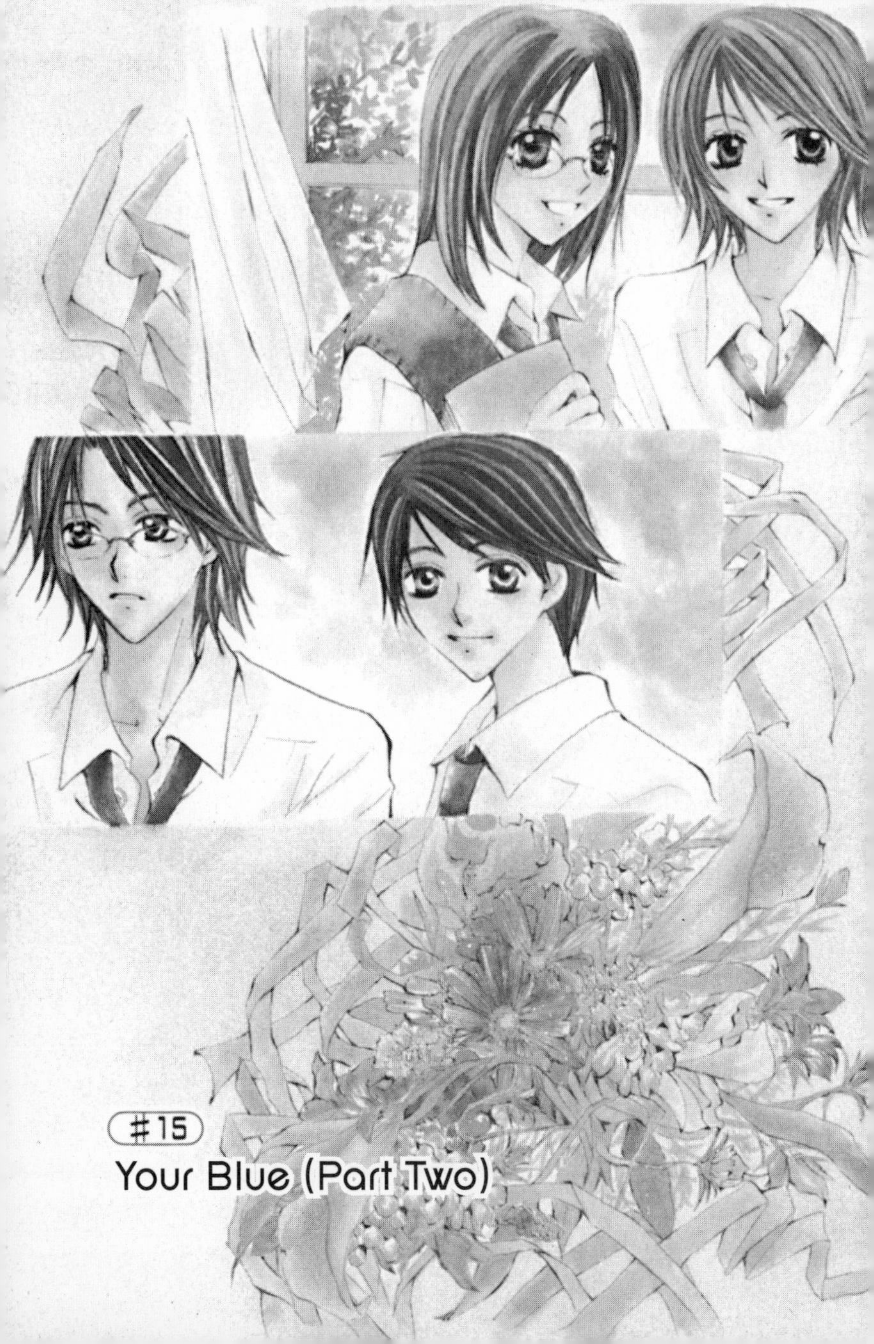

#15 Your Blue (Part Two)

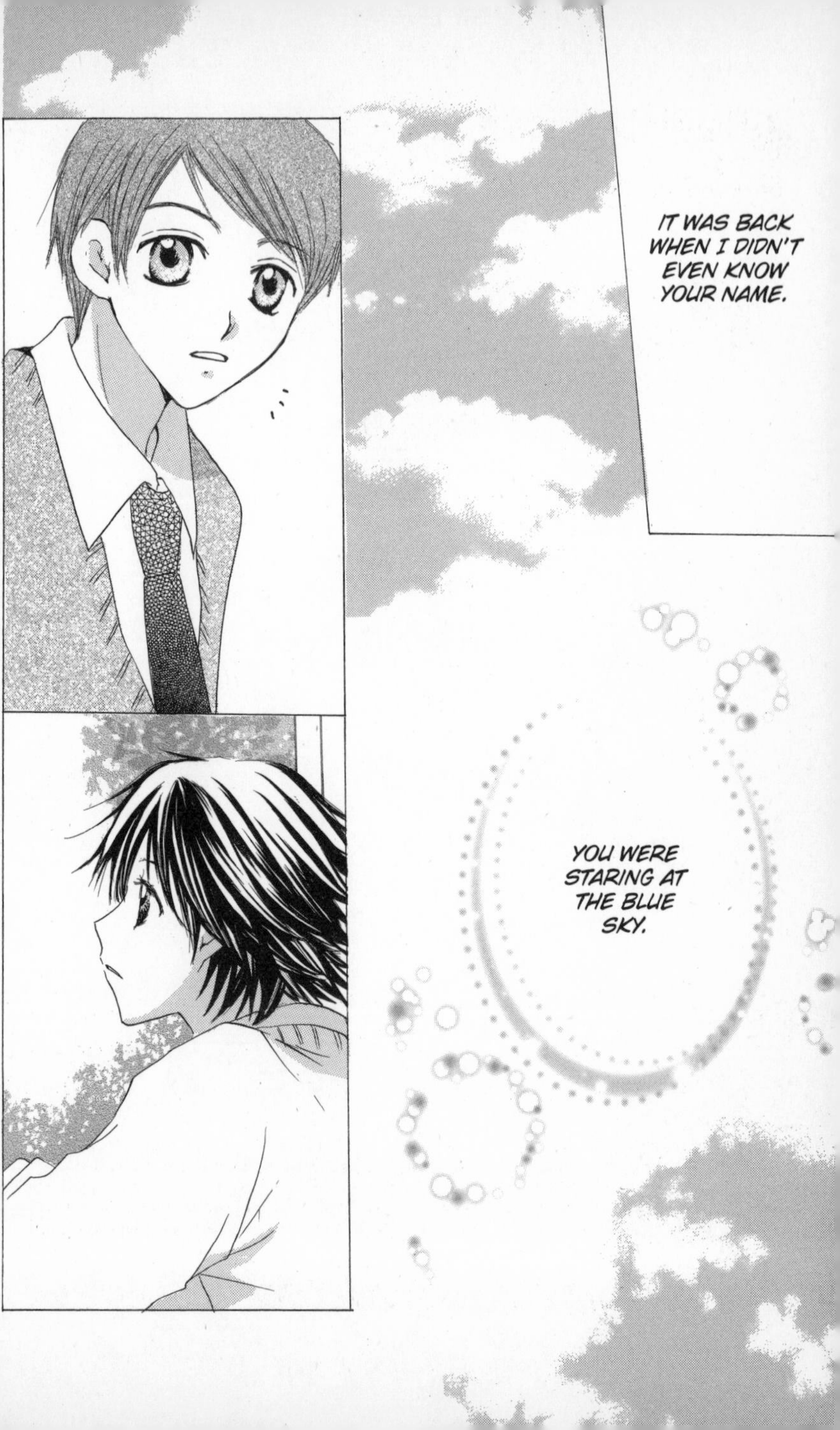
IT WAS BACK WHEN I DIDN'T EVEN KNOW YOUR NAME.
YOU WERE STARING AT THE BLUE SKY.

crossroad Chapter 15: Your Blue (Part Two)

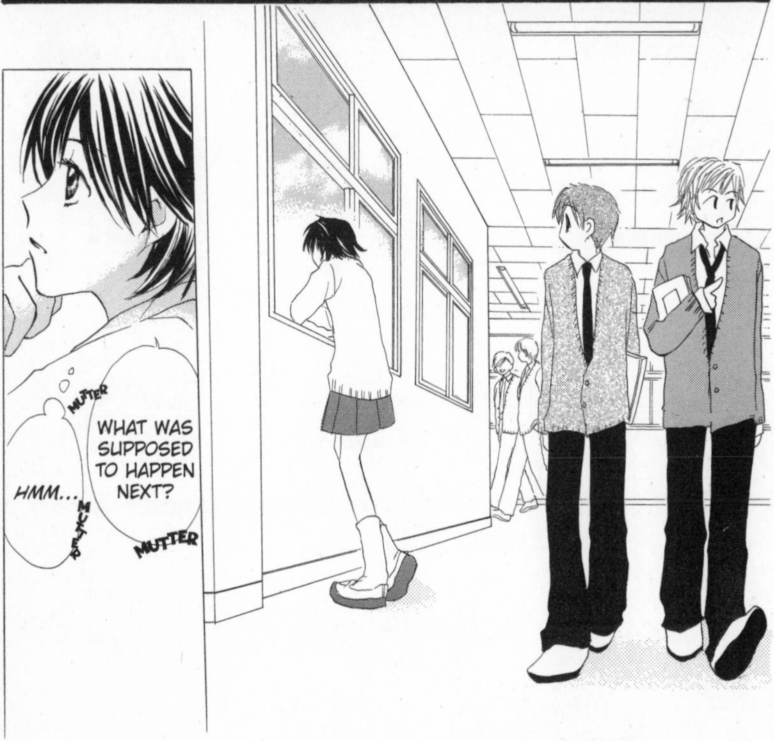
MUTTER
WHAT WAS SUPPOSED TO HAPPEN NEXT?
MUTTER
HMM...
MUTTER

Author's Story

When I redecorated my workplace, I also decided to buy myself a new bike. My last one was pretty run-down, and only slightly faster than walking. I couldn't stand it any longer, so I exchanged it for a glittering orange baby! Not only is my new baby fast, but comfortable! I can just zip along on it. Gaze upon my beautiful bike! Isn't its orange body just brilliant? I want to show it off to the world, so I use it all over town. The other day, though, when I put it in the bike lot at my apartment, there was a sparkly orange bike sitting right next to it. I smiled sadly to myself.

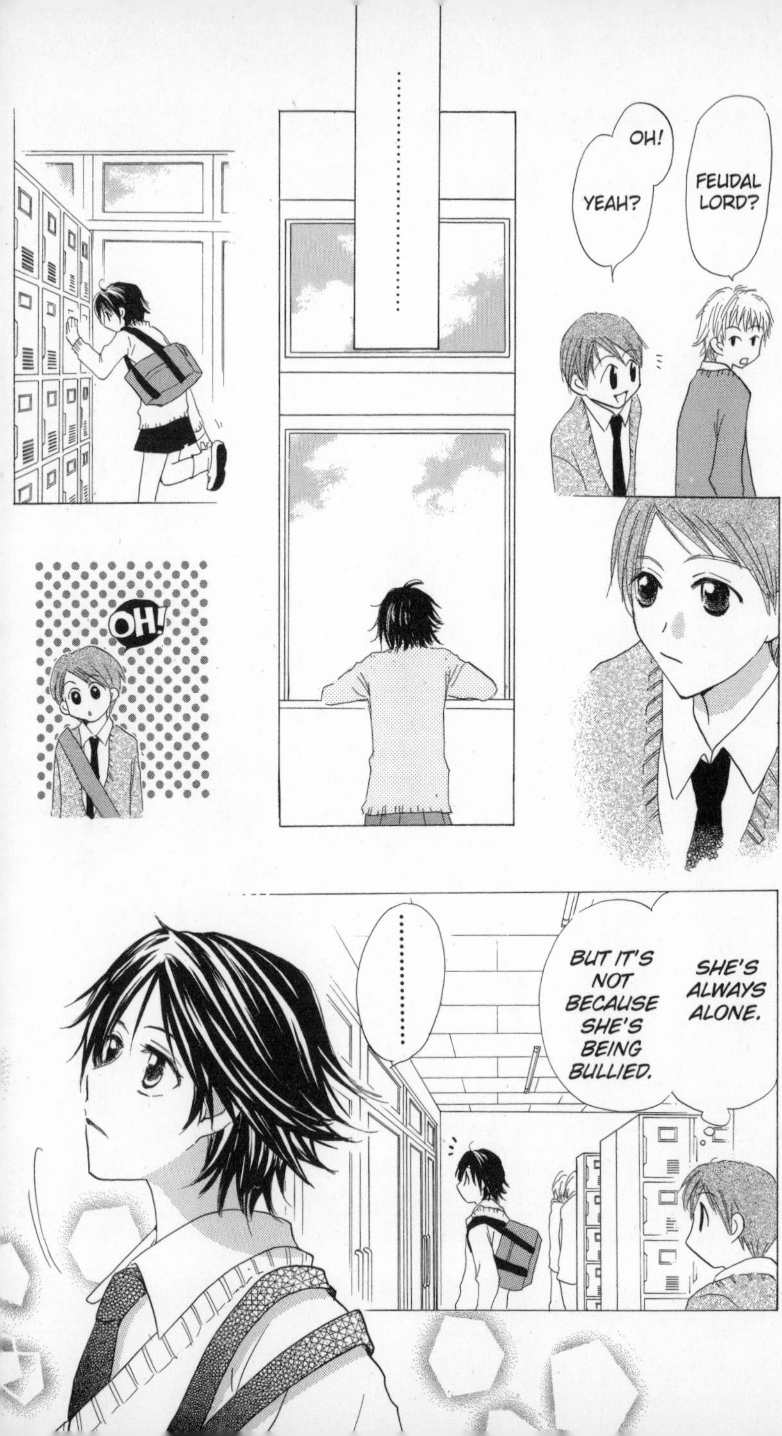
FEUDAL LORD?
OH! YEAH?
……
OH!
SHE'S ALWAYS ALONE.
BUT IT'S NOT BECAUSE SHE'S BEING BULLIED.
……

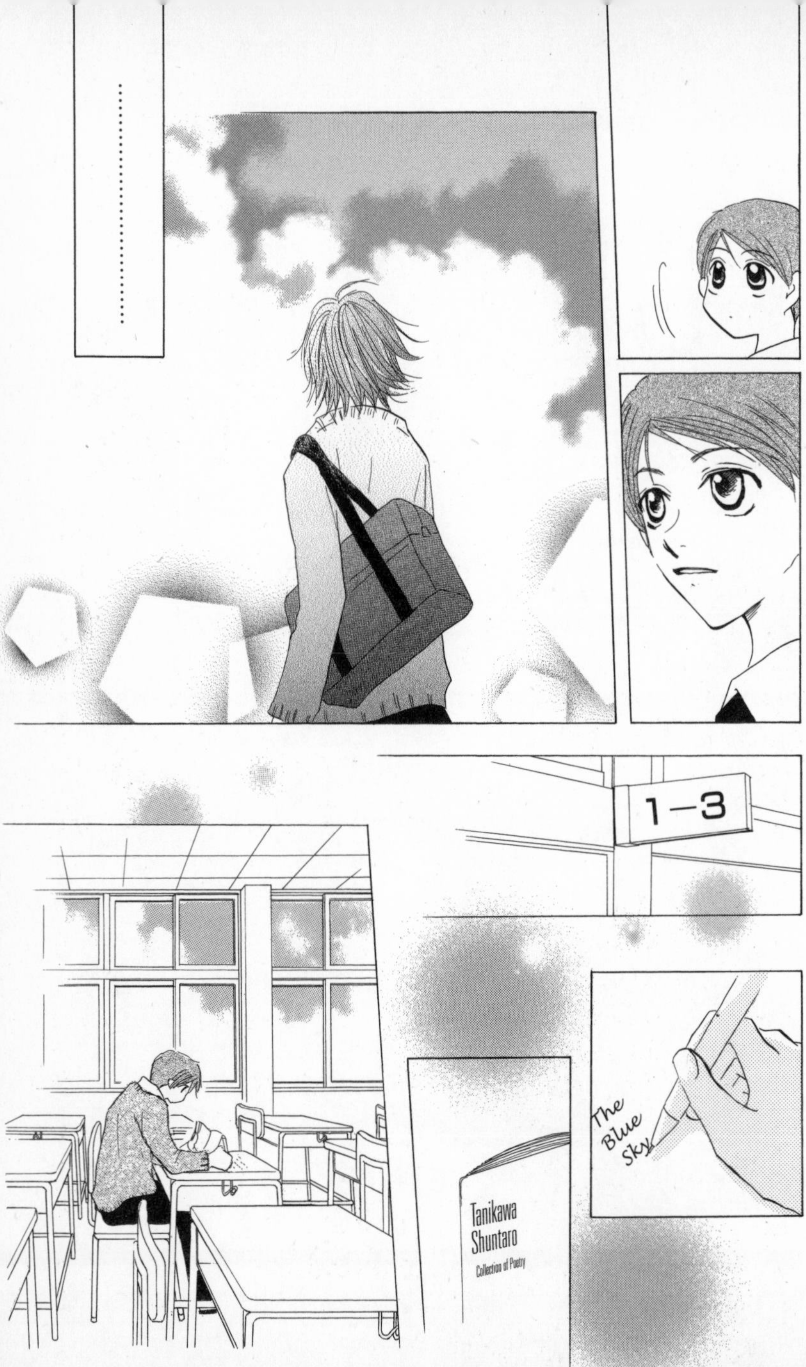
……………
1—3
The Blue Sky
Tanikawa Shuntaro
Collection of Poetry

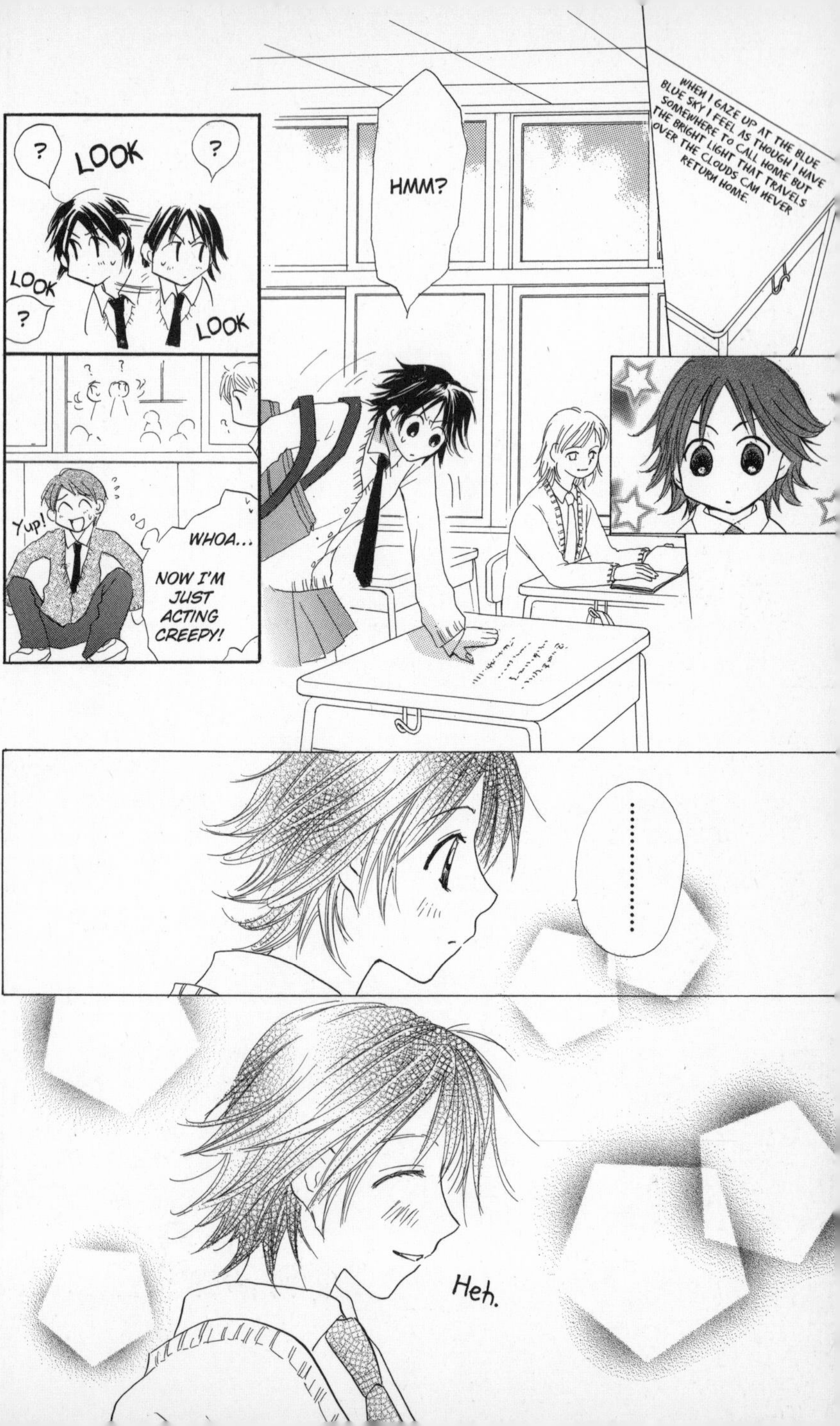
WHEN I GAZE UP AT THE BLUE BLUE SKY I FEEL AS THOUGH I HAVE SOMEWHERE TO CALL HOME BUT THE BRIGHT LIGHT THAT TRAVELS OVER THE CLOUDS CAN NEVER RETURN HOME.
HMM?
?
LOOK
?
LOOK
?
LOOK
?
?
Yup!
WHOA...
NOW I'M JUST ACTING CREEPY!
......
Heh.

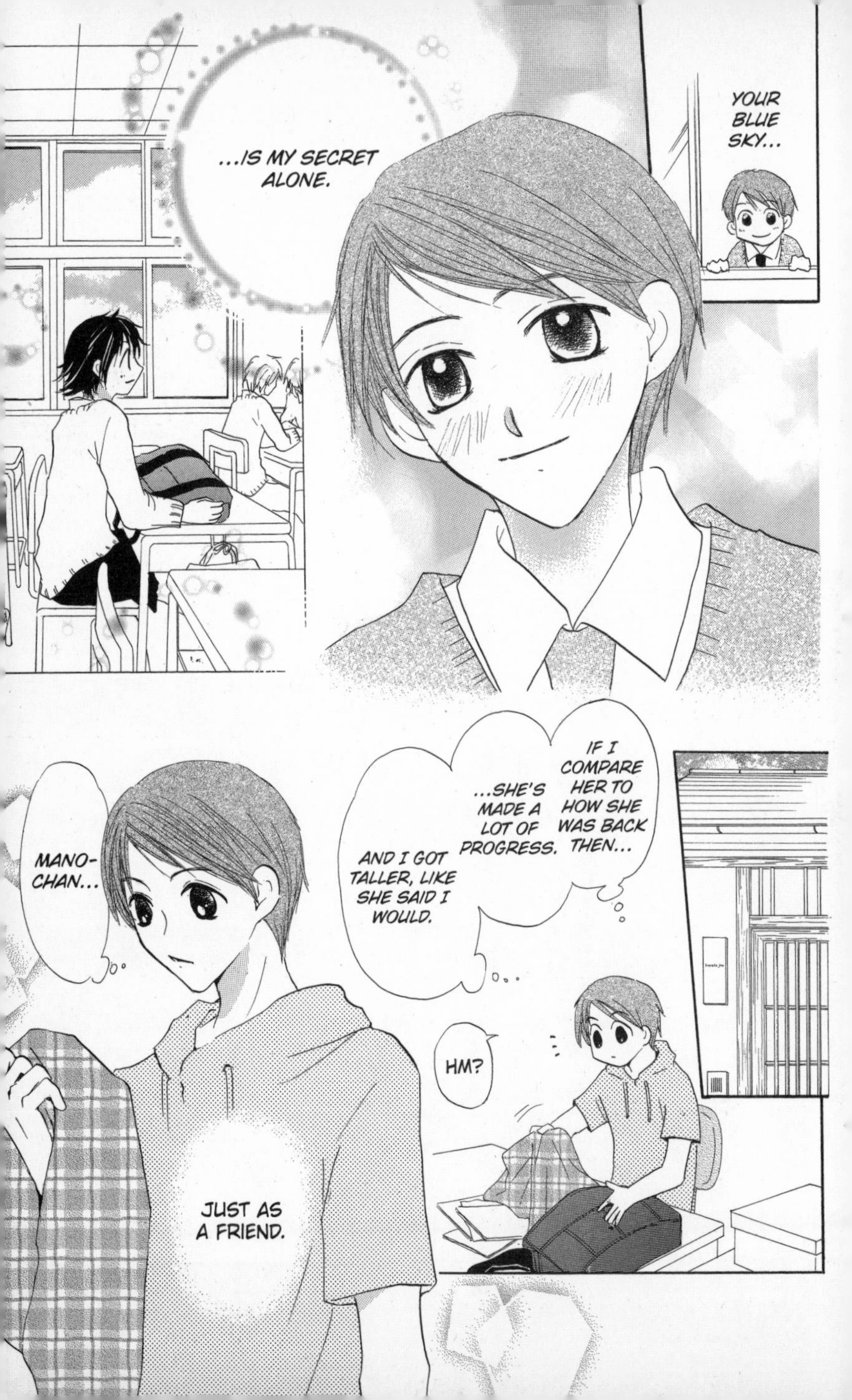
YOUR BLUE SKY...
...IS MY SECRET ALONE.
IF I COMPARE HER TO HOW SHE WAS BACK THEN...
...SHE'S MADE A LOT OF PROGRESS.
AND I GOT TALLER, LIKE SHE SAID I WOULD.
HM?
MANO-CHAN...
JUST AS A FRIEND.

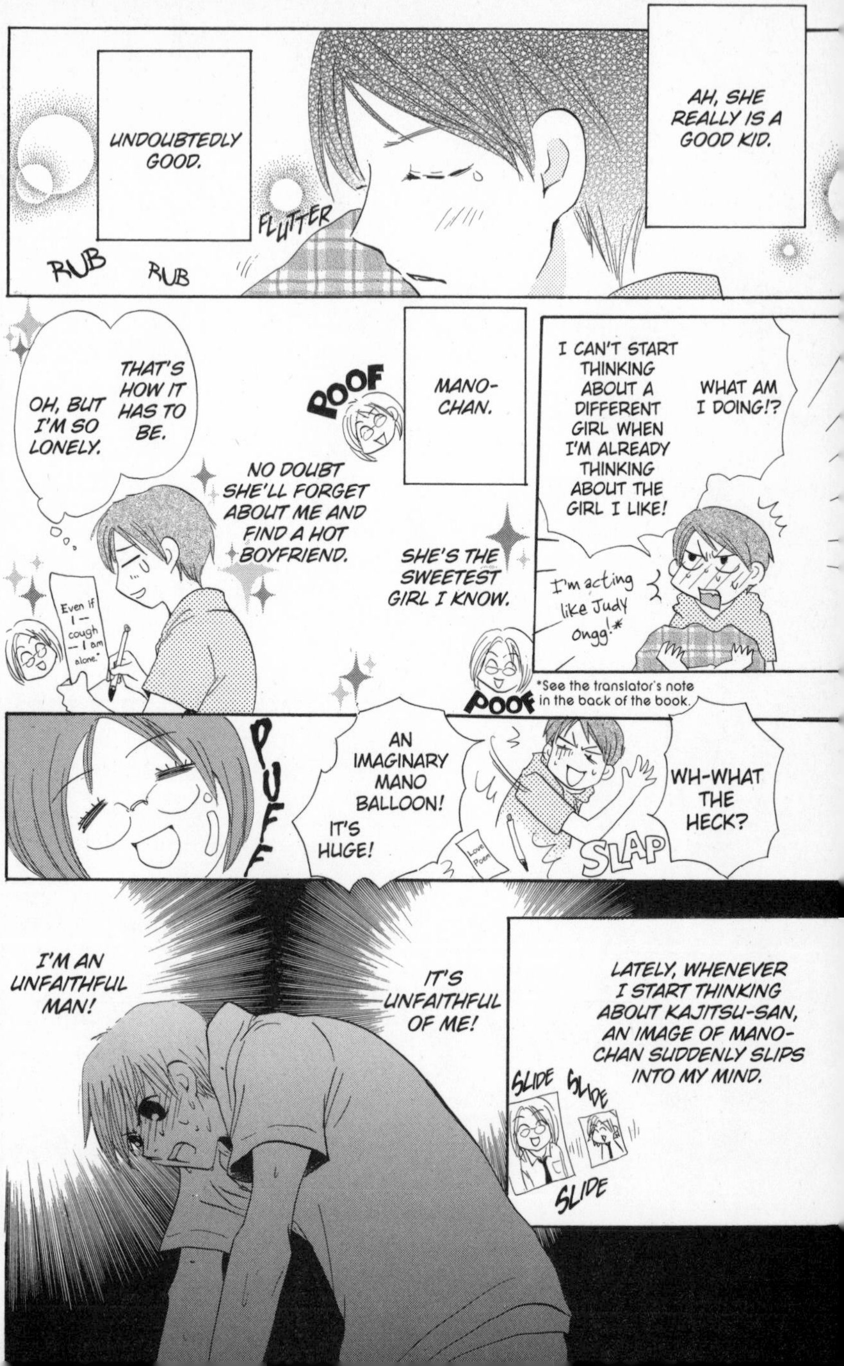
AH, SHE REALLY IS A GOOD KID.
UNDOUBTEDLY GOOD.
FLUTTER
RUB
RUB
WHAT AM I DOING!?
I CAN'T START THINKING ABOUT A DIFFERENT GIRL WHEN I'M ALREADY THINKING ABOUT THE GIRL I LIKE!
I'm acting like Judy Ongg!*
MANO-CHAN.
POOF
SHE'S THE SWEETEST GIRL I KNOW.
POOF
THAT'S HOW IT HAS TO BE.
OH, BUT I'M SO LONELY.
NO DOUBT SHE'LL FORGET ABOUT ME AND FIND A HOT BOYFRIEND.
Even if I -- cough -- I am alone."
WH-WHAT THE HECK?
SLAP
AN IMAGINARY MANO BALLOON!
IT'S HUGE!
Love Poem
PUFF
PUFF
LATELY, WHENEVER I START THINKING ABOUT KAJITSU-SAN, AN IMAGE OF MANO-CHAN SUDDENLY SLIPS INTO MY MIND.
SLIDE
SLIDE
SLIDE
IT'S UNFAITHFUL OF ME!
I'M AN UNFAITHFUL MAN!

*See the translator's note in the back of the book.

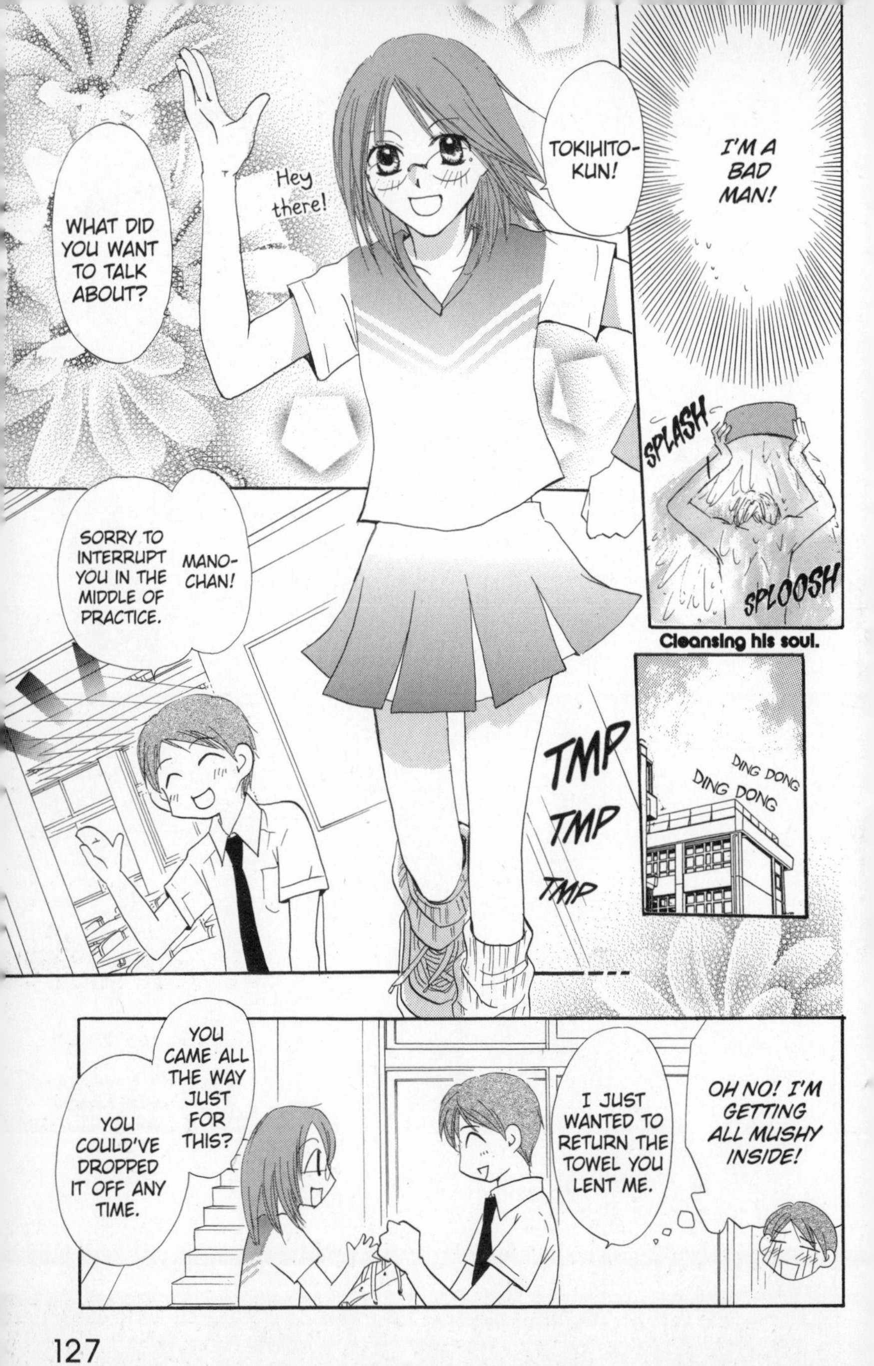
I'M A BAD MAN!
SPLASH
SPLOOSH
Cleansing his soul.
DING DONG
DING DONG
TMP
TMP
TMP
TOKIHITO-KUN!
Hey there!
WHAT DID YOU WANT TO TALK ABOUT?
MANO-CHAN!
SORRY TO INTERRUPT YOU IN THE MIDDLE OF PRACTICE.
OH NO! I'M GETTING ALL MUSHY INSIDE!
I JUST WANTED TO RETURN THE TOWEL YOU LENT ME.
YOU CAME ALL THE WAY JUST FOR THIS?
YOU COULD'VE DROPPED IT OFF ANY TIME.

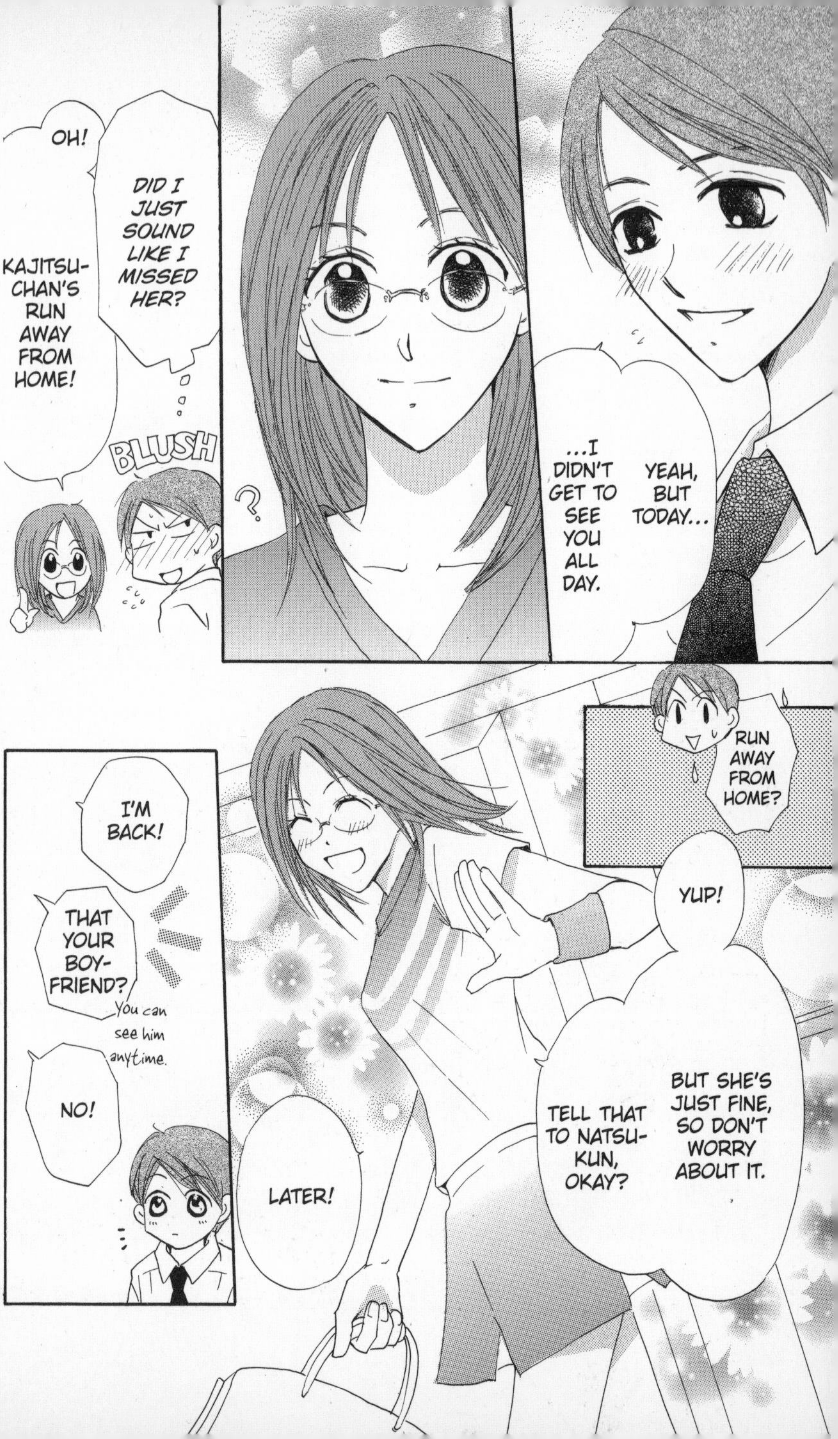
YEAH, BUT TODAY...
...I DIDN'T GET TO SEE YOU ALL DAY.
?
DID I JUST SOUND LIKE I MISSED HER?
BLUSH
OH! KAJITSU-CHAN'S RUN AWAY FROM HOME!
RUN AWAY FROM HOME?
YUP!
BUT SHE'S JUST FINE, SO DON'T WORRY ABOUT IT.
TELL THAT TO NATSU-KUN, OKAY?
LATER!
I'M BACK!
THAT YOUR BOY-FRIEND?
You can see him anytime.
NO!

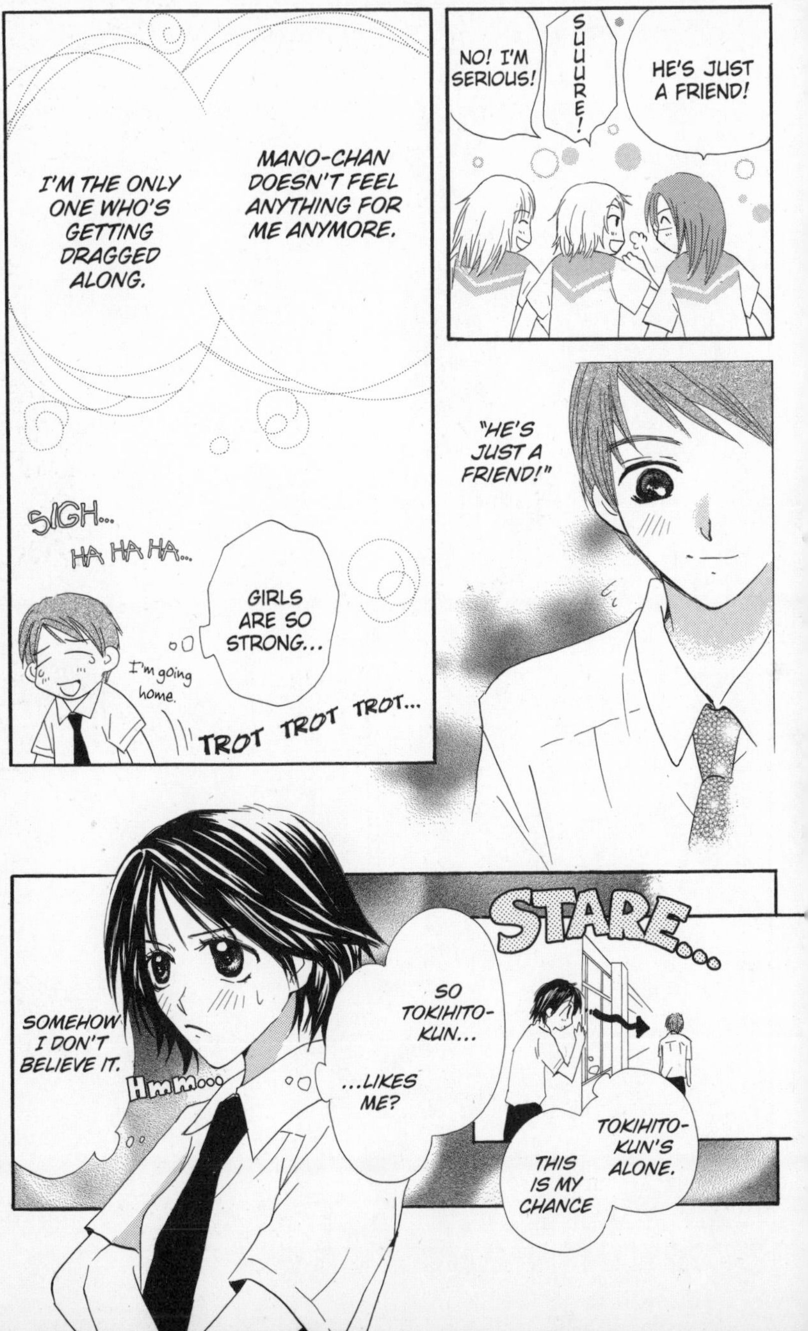
HE'S JUST A FRIEND!
SUUURE!
NO! I'M SERIOUS!
"HE'S JUST A FRIEND!"
MANO-CHAN DOESN'T FEEL ANYTHING FOR ME ANYMORE.
I'M THE ONLY ONE WHO'S GETTING DRAGGED ALONG.
GIRLS ARE SO STRONG...
SIGH...
HA HA HA...
I'm going home.
TROT TROT TROT...
STARE...
TOKIHITO-KUN'S ALONE.
THIS IS MY CHANCE
SO TOKIHITO-KUN...
...LIKES ME?
SOMEHOW I DON'T BELIEVE IT.
Hmm...

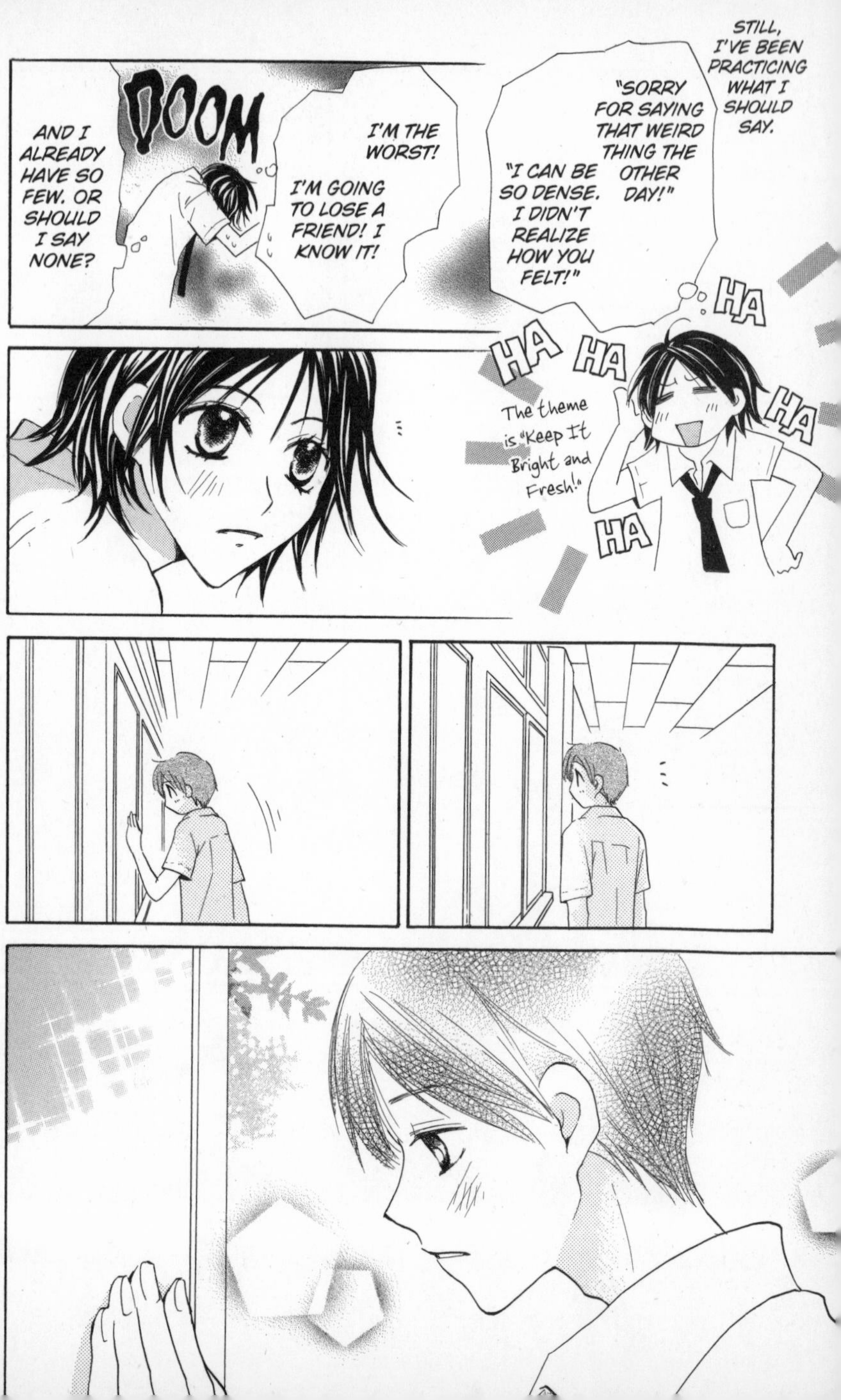
STILL, I'VE BEEN PRACTICING WHAT I SHOULD SAY.
"SORRY FOR SAYING THAT WEIRD THING THE OTHER DAY!"
"I CAN BE SO DENSE. I DIDN'T REALIZE HOW YOU FELT!"
HA
HA
HA
HA
HA
The theme is "Keep It Bright and Fresh!"
DOOM
I'M THE WORST!
I'M GOING TO LOSE A FRIEND! I KNOW IT!
AND I ALREADY HAVE SO FEW. OR SHOULD I SAY NONE?

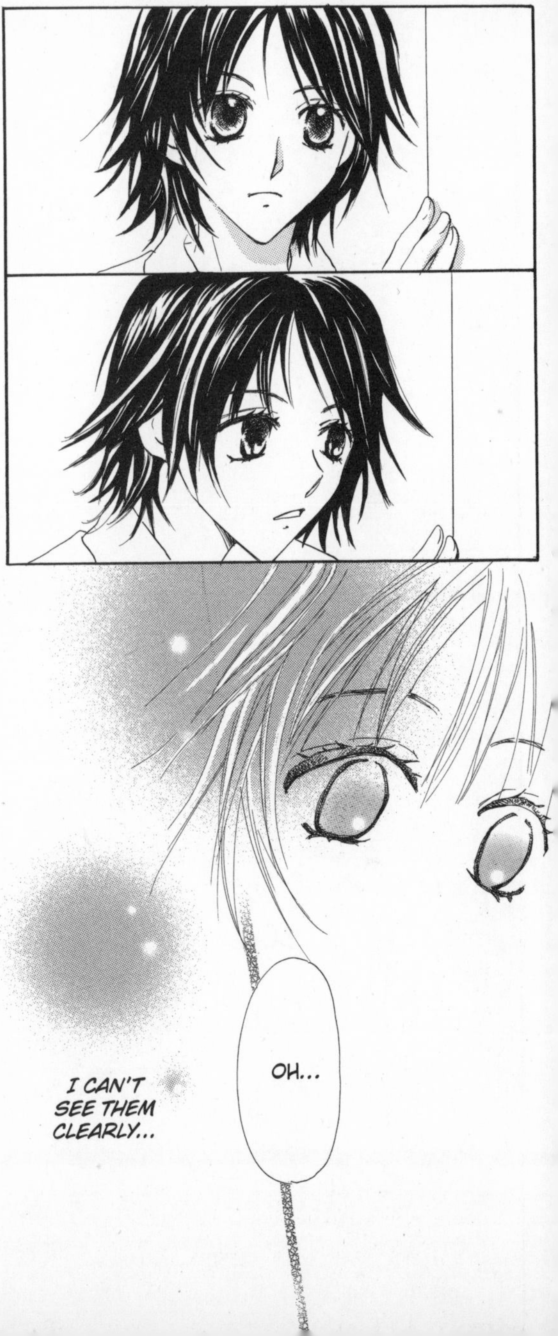
OH...
I CAN'T SEE THEM CLEARLY...

Happy Things.

I've been getting a lot of letters these days saying, "I'm so glad Kajitsu's gotten cuter!"

Kajitsu still has a lot more changing to do, so I'm looking forward to it.

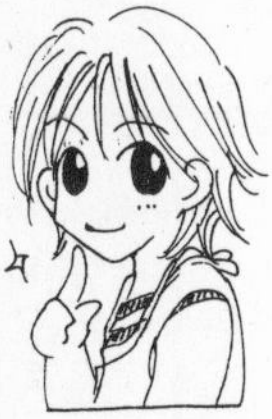

Screams

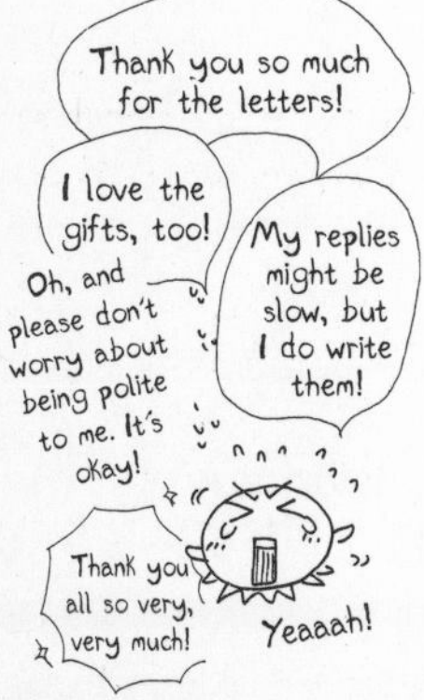
Thank you so much for the letters!
I love the gifts, too!
My replies might be slow, but I do write them!
Oh, and please don't worry about being polite to me. It's okay!
Thank you all so very, very much!
Yeaaah!

To send fan mail to Mizuki-san, mail it to:
5737 Kanan Rd. #591
Agoura Hills, CA 91301

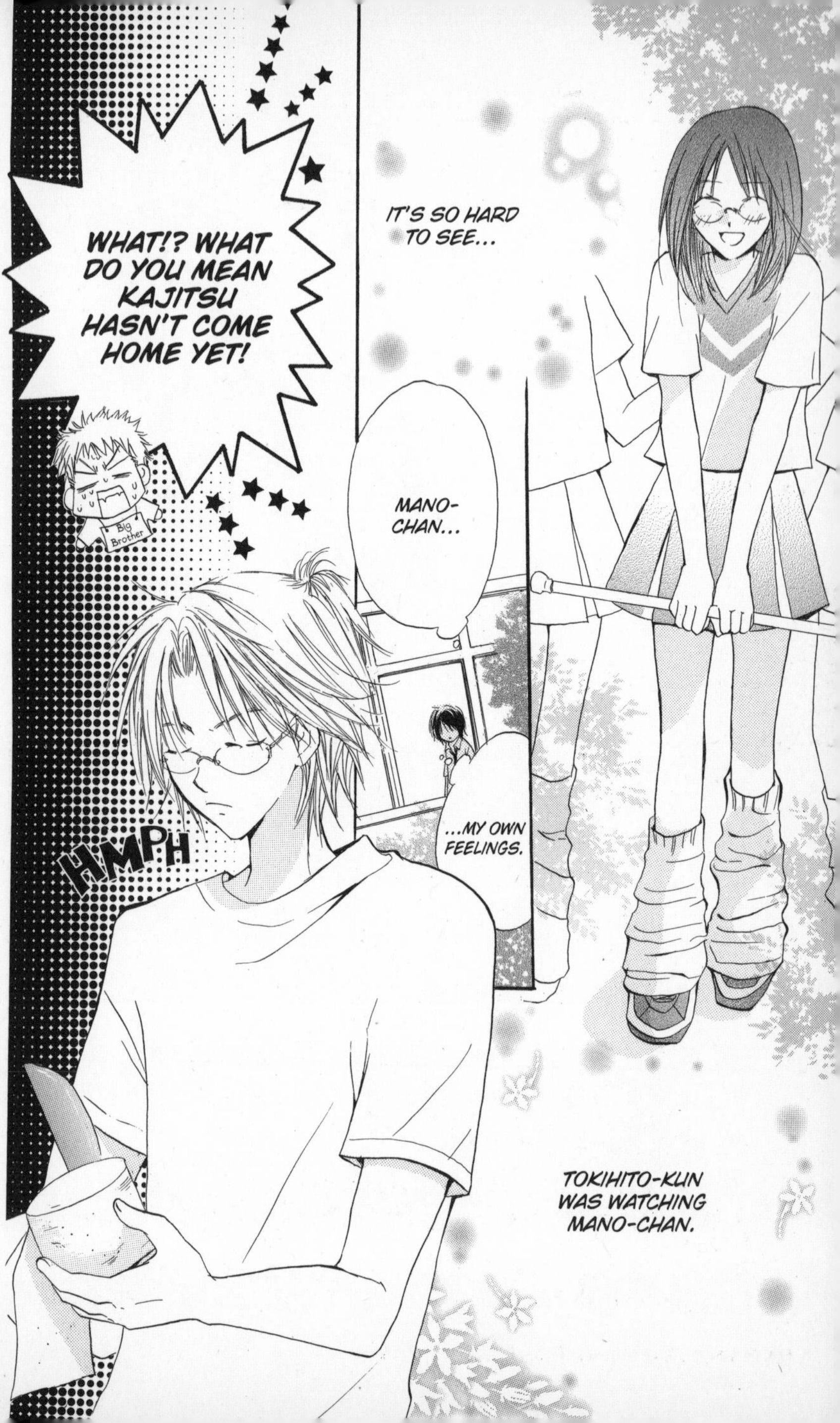
IT'S SO HARD TO SEE…
MANO-CHAN…
…MY OWN FEELINGS.
TOKIHITO-KUN WAS WATCHING MANO-CHAN.
WHAT!? WHAT DO YOU MEAN KAJITSU HASN'T COME HOME YET!
Big Brother
HMPH

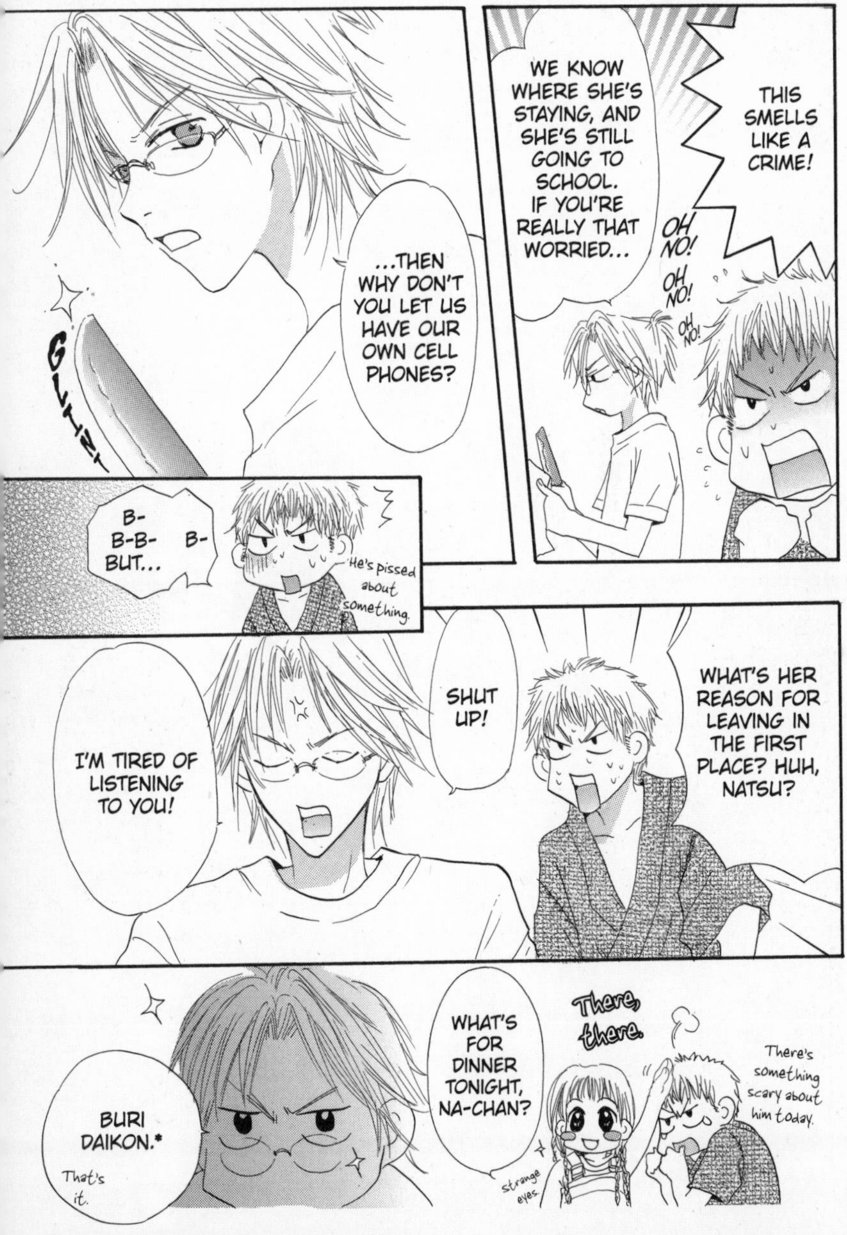
WE KNOW WHERE SHE'S STAYING, AND SHE'S STILL GOING TO SCHOOL. IF YOU'RE REALLY THAT WORRIED...
THIS SMELLS LIKE A CRIME!
OH NO! OH NO! OH NO!
...THEN WHY DON'T YOU LET US HAVE OUR OWN CELL PHONES?
GLINT
B- B-B- B- BUT...
He's pissed about something.
WHAT'S HER REASON FOR LEAVING IN THE FIRST PLACE? HUH, NATSU?
SHUT UP!
I'M TIRED OF LISTENING TO YOU!
There's something scary about him today.
There, there.
WHAT'S FOR DINNER TONIGHT, NA-CHAN?
strange eyes.
BURI DAIKON.*
That's it.

*Simmered daikon with a yellowtail collar.

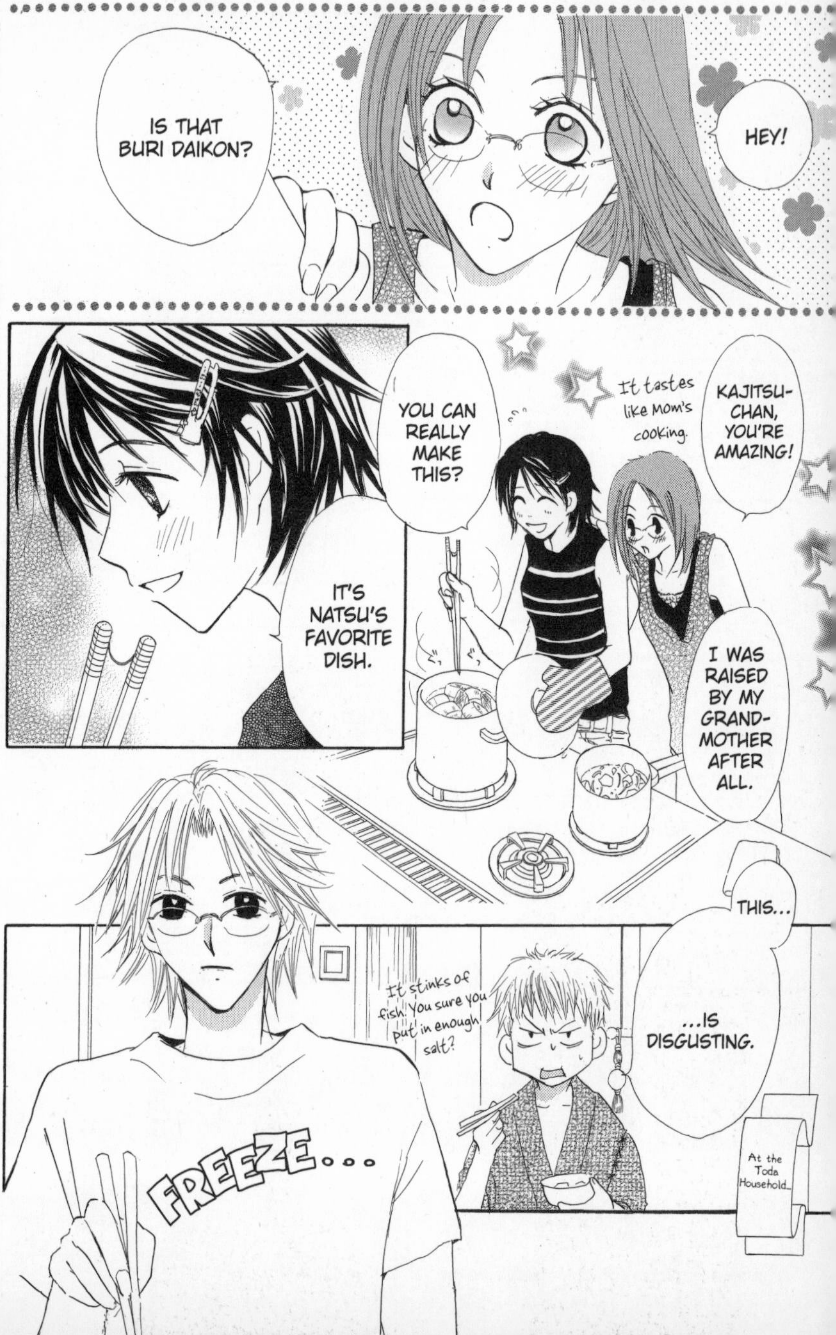
HEY!
IS THAT BURI DAIKON?
KAJITSU-CHAN, YOU'RE AMAZING!
It tastes like Mom's cooking.
YOU CAN REALLY MAKE THIS?
I WAS RAISED BY MY GRANDMOTHER AFTER ALL.
IT'S NATSU'S FAVORITE DISH.
At the Toda Household...
THIS...
...IS DISGUSTING.
It stinks of fish. You sure you put in enough salt?
FREEZE...

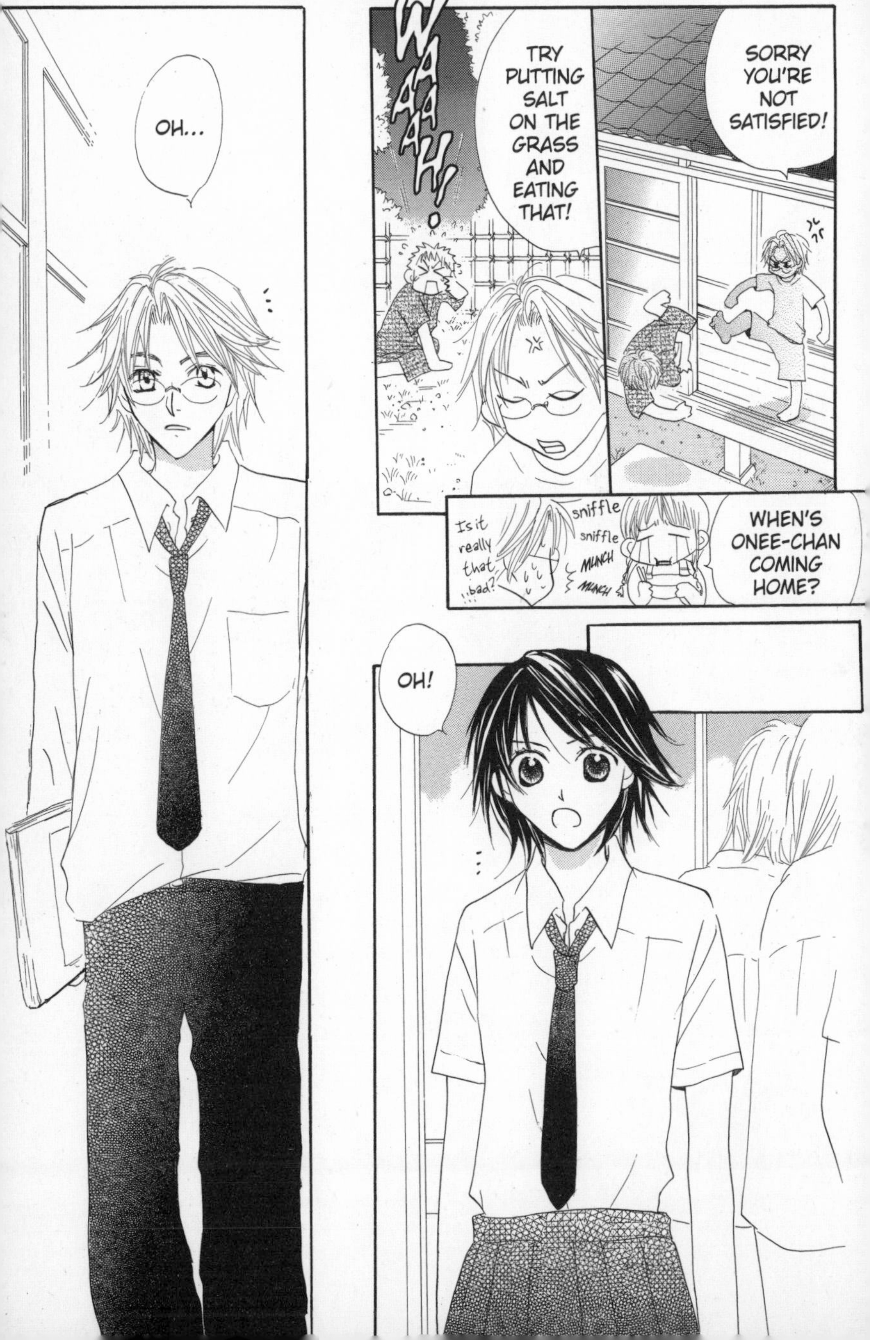
SORRY YOU'RE NOT SATISFIED!
TRY PUTTING SALT ON THE GRASS AND EATING THAT!
WAAAH!
WHEN'S ONEE-CHAN COMING HOME?
sniffle sniffle
MUNCH MUNCH
Is it really that bad?
OH!
OH...

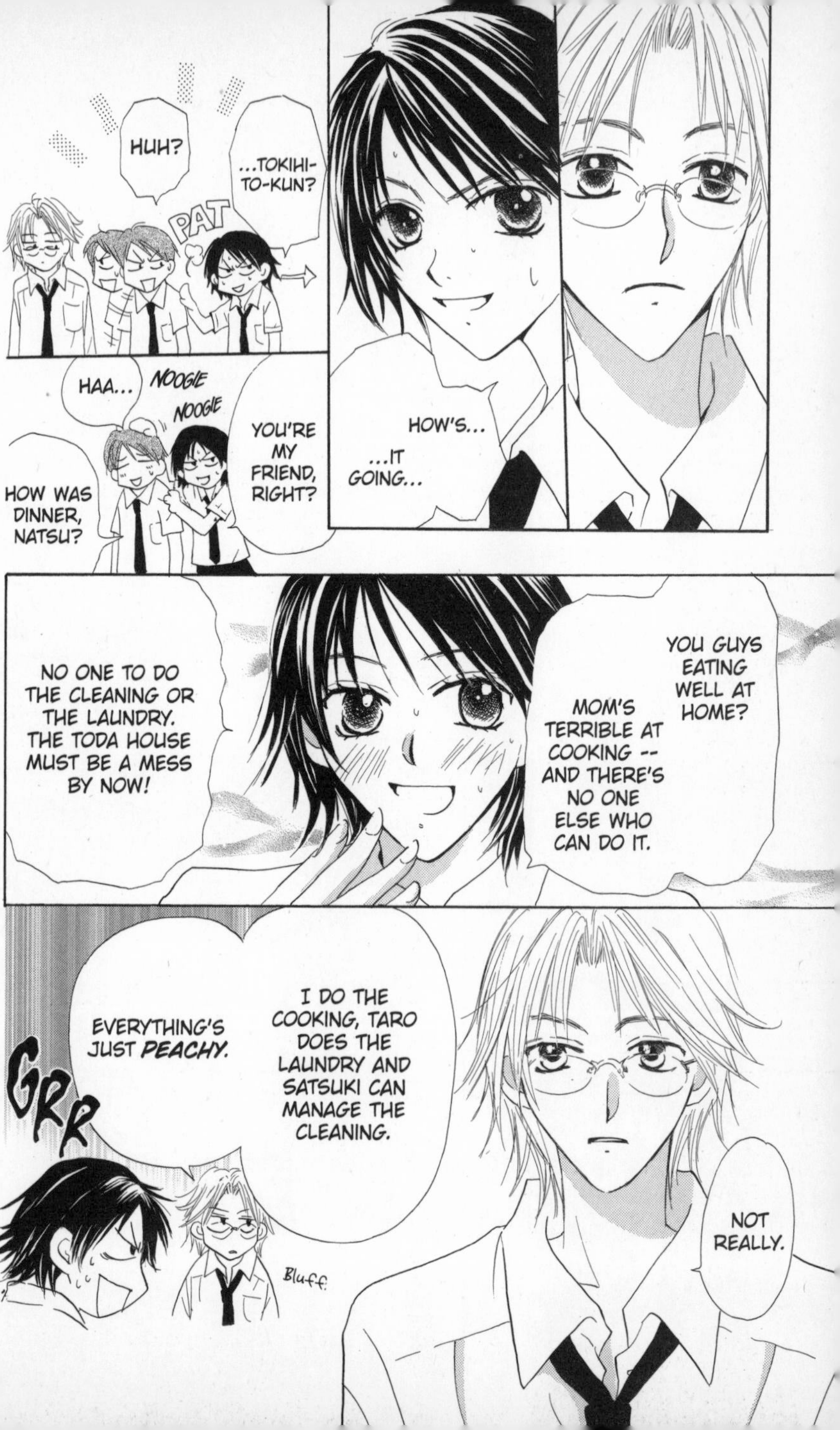
HOW'S...
...IT GOING...
...TOKIHITO-KUN?
HUH?
PAT
YOU'RE MY FRIEND, RIGHT?
NOOGIE NOOGIE
HAA...
HOW WAS DINNER, NATSU?
YOU GUYS EATING WELL AT HOME?
MOM'S TERRIBLE AT COOKING -- AND THERE'S NO ONE ELSE WHO CAN DO IT.
NO ONE TO DO THE CLEANING OR THE LAUNDRY. THE TODA HOUSE MUST BE A MESS BY NOW!
NOT REALLY.
I DO THE COOKING, TARO DOES THE LAUNDRY AND SATSUKI CAN MANAGE THE CLEANING.
EVERYTHING'S JUST PEACHY.
GRR
Bluff.

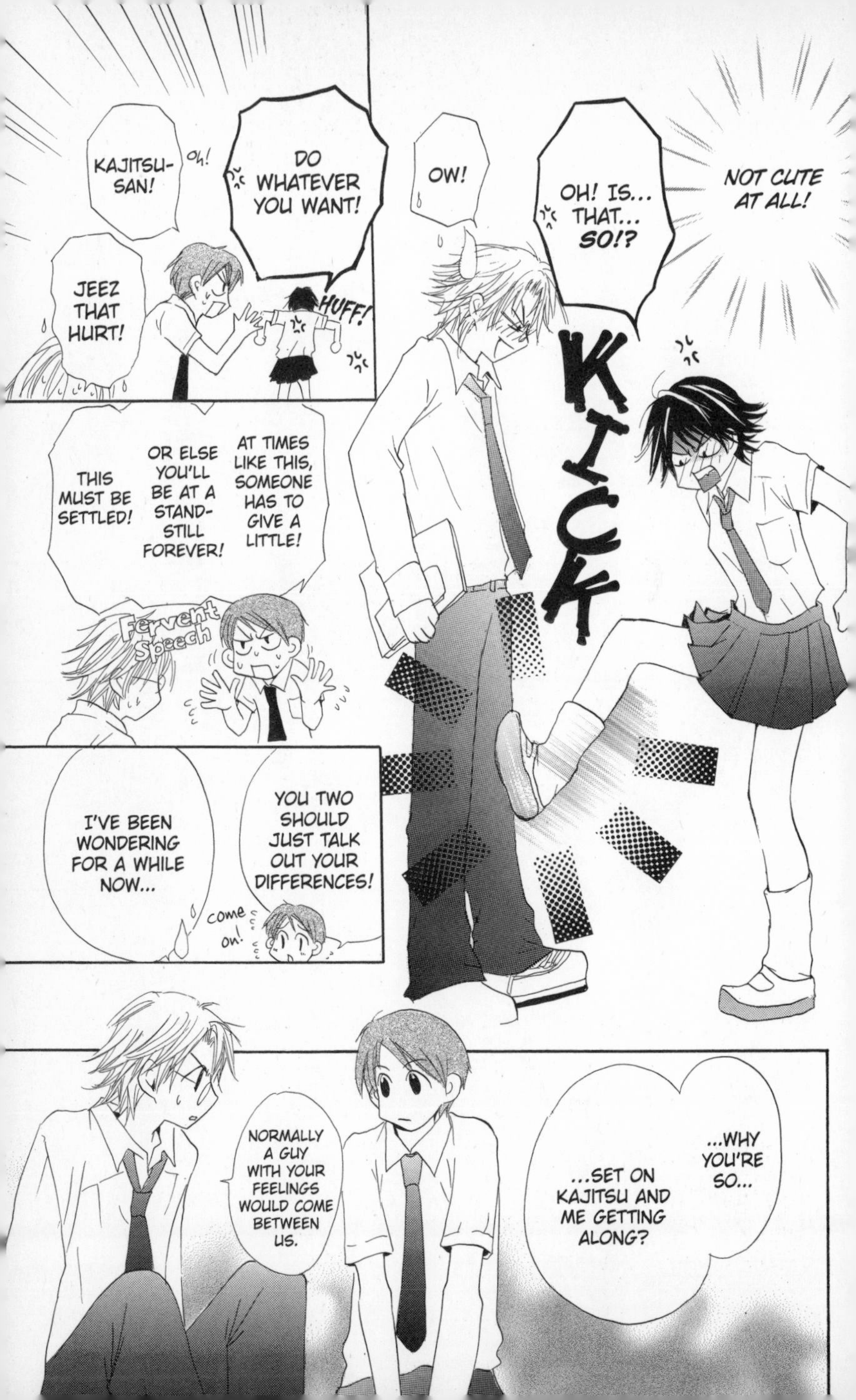
NOT CUTE AT ALL!
OH! IS... THAT... SO!?
KICK
OW!
DO WHATEVER YOU WANT!
Oh!
KAJITSU-SAN!
HUFF!
JEEZ THAT HURT!
AT TIMES LIKE THIS, SOMEONE HAS TO GIVE A LITTLE!
OR ELSE YOU'LL BE AT A STAND-STILL FOREVER!
THIS MUST BE SETTLED!
Fervent Speech
YOU TWO SHOULD JUST TALK OUT YOUR DIFFERENCES!
come on!
I'VE BEEN WONDERING FOR A WHILE NOW...
...WHY YOU'RE SO...
...SET ON KAJITSU AND ME GETTING ALONG?
NORMALLY A GUY WITH YOUR FEELINGS WOULD COME BETWEEN US.

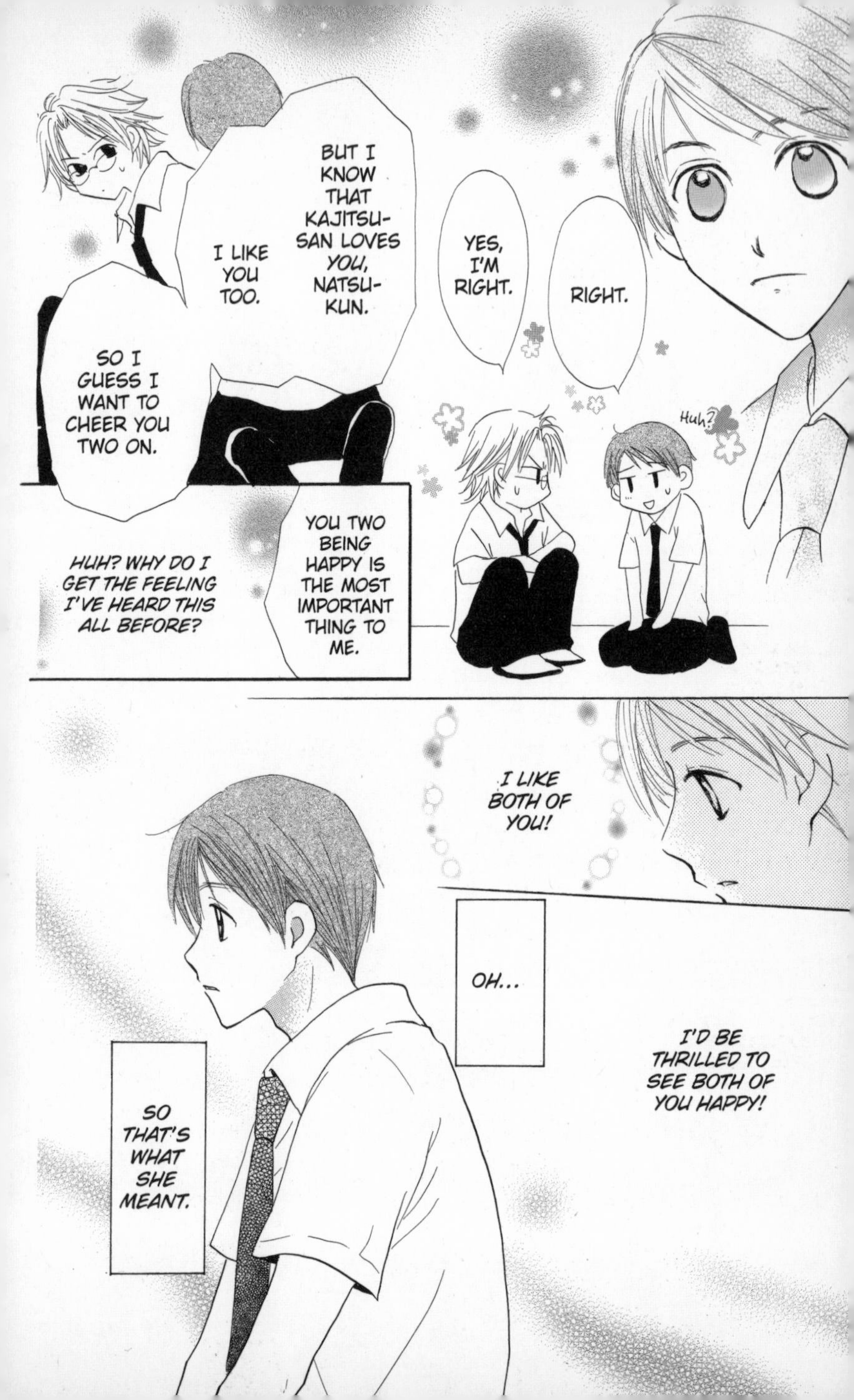
RIGHT.
YES, I'M RIGHT.
Huh?
BUT I KNOW THAT KAJITSU-SAN LOVES *YOU*, NATSU-KUN.
I LIKE YOU TOO.
SO I GUESS I WANT TO CHEER YOU TWO ON.
YOU TWO BEING HAPPY IS THE MOST IMPORTANT THING TO ME.
HUH? WHY DO I GET THE FEELING I'VE HEARD THIS ALL BEFORE?
I LIKE BOTH OF YOU!
I'D BE THRILLED TO SEE BOTH OF YOU HAPPY!
OH...
SO THAT'S WHAT SHE MEANT.

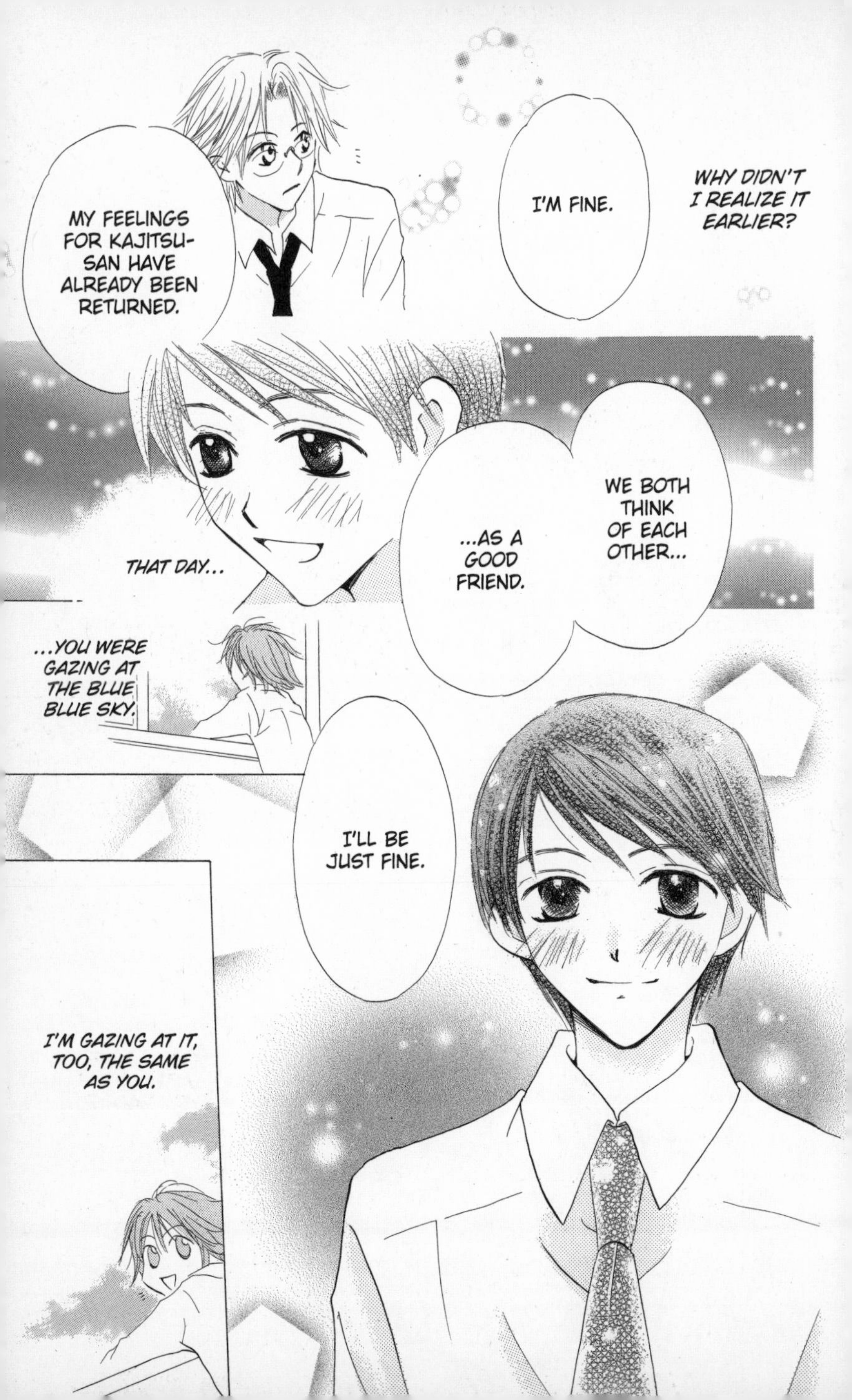
WHY DIDN'T I REALIZE IT EARLIER?
I'M FINE.
MY FEELINGS FOR KAJITSU-SAN HAVE ALREADY BEEN RETURNED.
WE BOTH THINK OF EACH OTHER...
...AS A GOOD FRIEND.
THAT DAY...
...YOU WERE GAZING AT THE BLUE BLUE SKY.
I'LL BE JUST FINE.
I'M GAZING AT IT, TOO, THE SAME AS YOU.

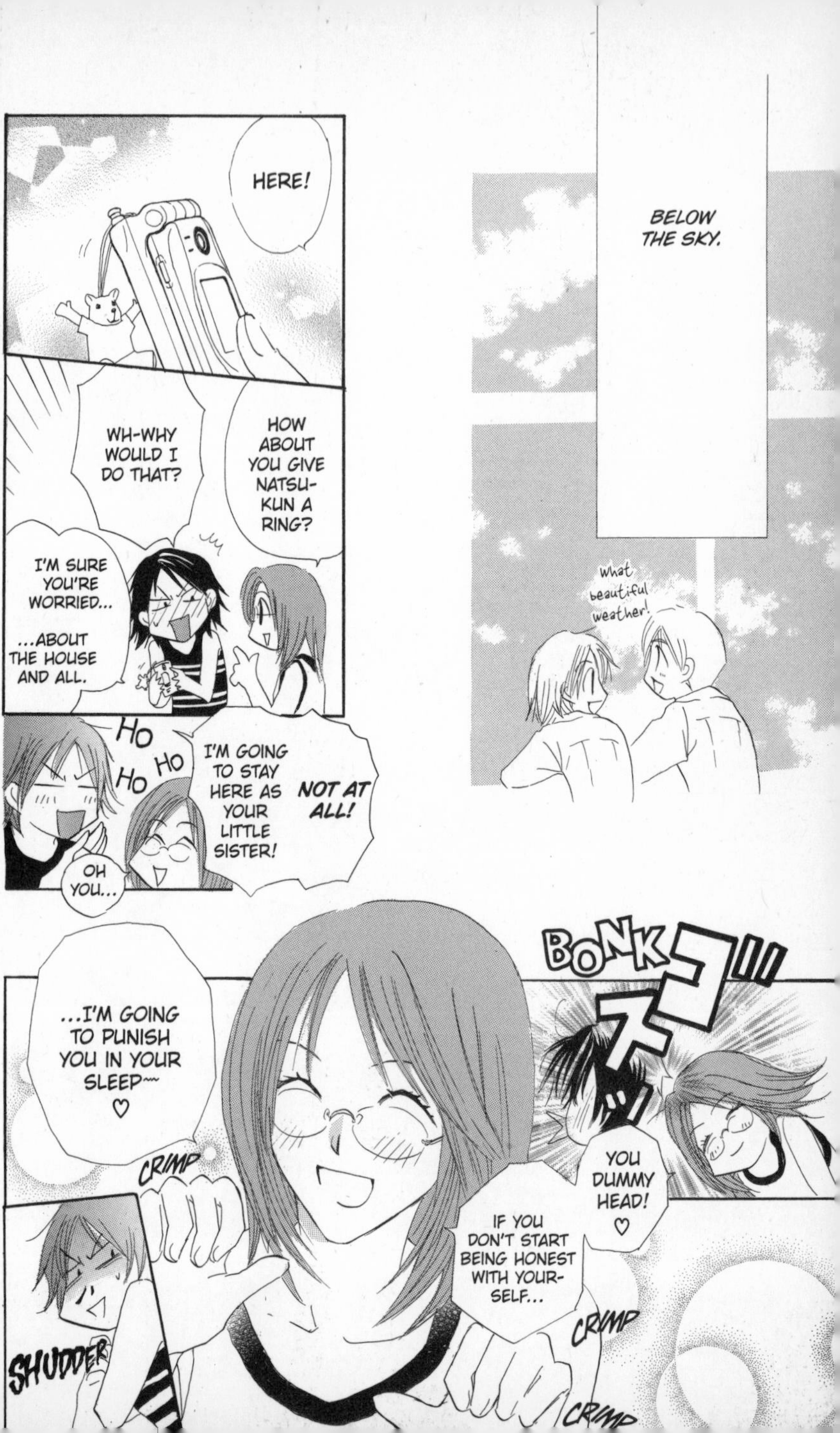
BELOW THE SKY.
What beautiful weather!
HERE!
HOW ABOUT YOU GIVE NATSU-KUN A RING?
WH-WHY WOULD I DO THAT?
I'M SURE YOU'RE WORRIED...
...ABOUT THE HOUSE AND ALL.
NOT AT ALL!
I'M GOING TO STAY HERE AS YOUR LITTLE SISTER!
HO HO HO
OH YOU...
BONK
YOU DUMMY HEAD! ♡
IF YOU DON'T START BEING HONEST WITH YOUR-SELF...
...I'M GOING TO PUNISH YOU IN YOUR SLEEP~~ ♡
CRIMP
CRIMP
CRIMP
SHUDDER

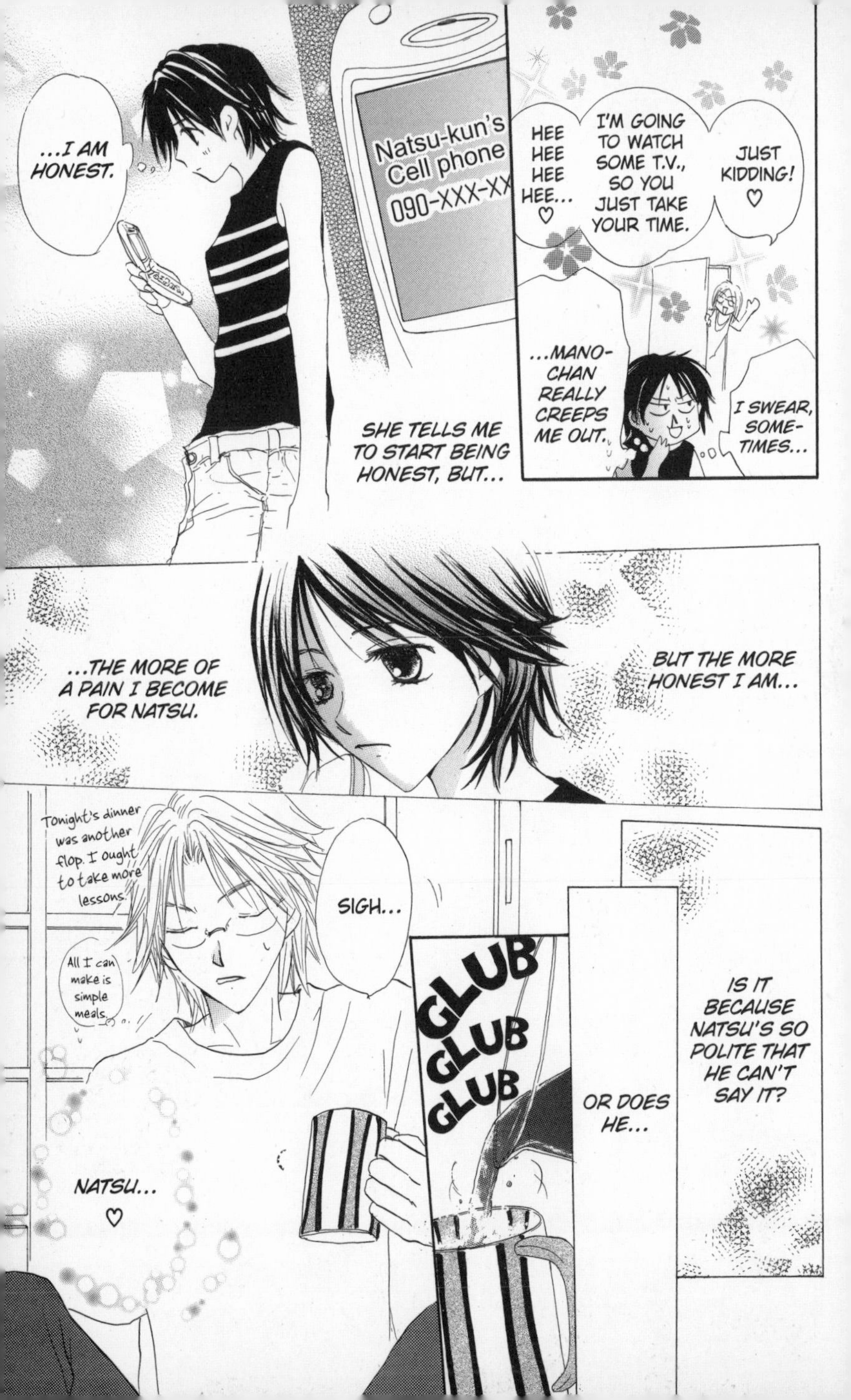
JUST KIDDING! ♡
I'M GOING TO WATCH SOME T.V., SO YOU JUST TAKE YOUR TIME.
HEE HEE HEE HEE... ♡
I SWEAR, SOME-TIMES...
...MANO-CHAN REALLY CREEPS ME OUT.
Natsu-kun's Cell phone 090-XXX-XX
SHE TELLS ME TO START BEING HONEST, BUT...
...I AM HONEST.
BUT THE MORE HONEST I AM...
...THE MORE OF A PAIN I BECOME FOR NATSU.
IS IT BECAUSE NATSU'S SO POLITE THAT HE CAN'T SAY IT?
OR DOES HE...
GLUB GLUB GLUB
SIGH...
Tonight's dinner was another flop. I ought to take more lessons.
All I can make is simple meals.
NATSU... ♡

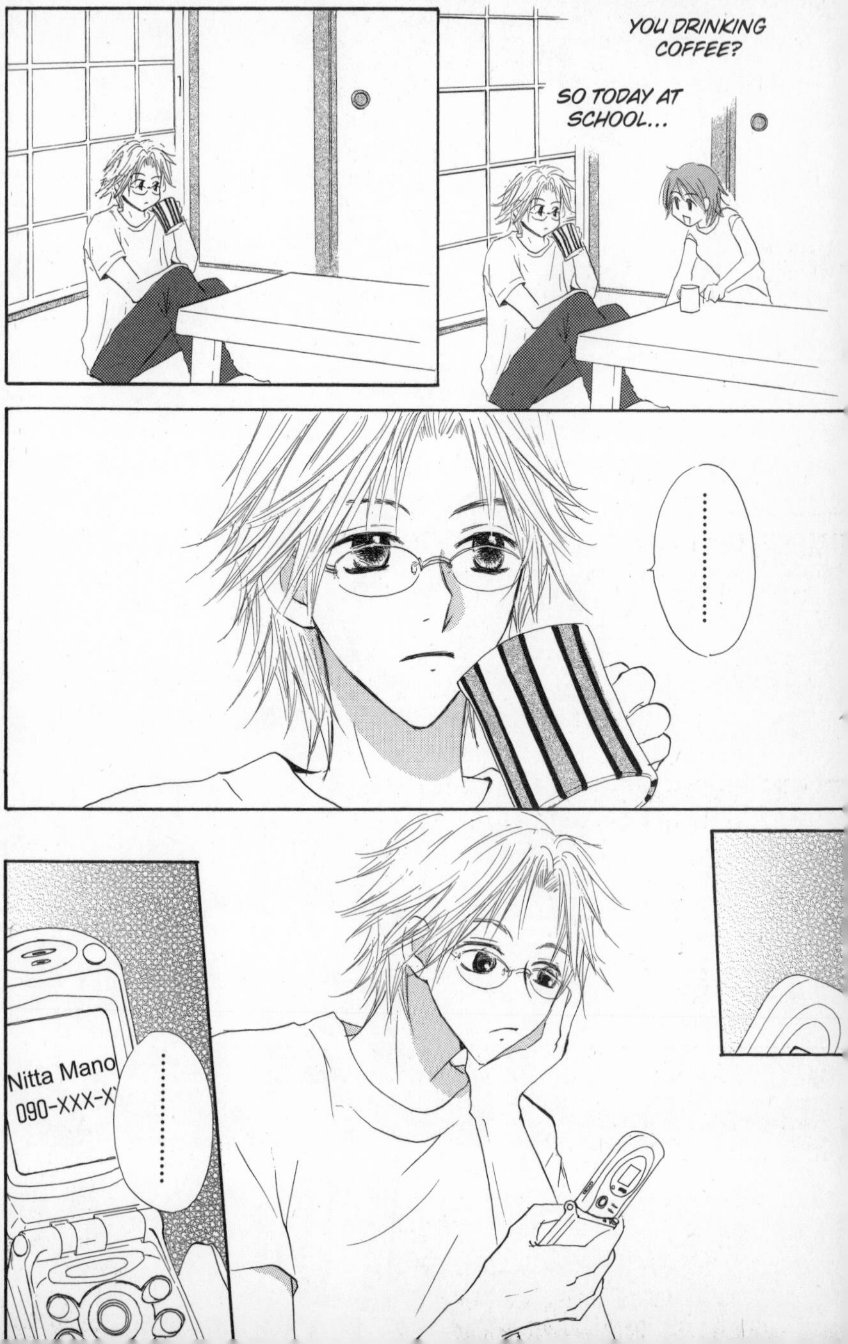
YOU DRINKING COFFEE?
SO TODAY AT SCHOOL...
......
......
Nitta Mano
090-XXX-X

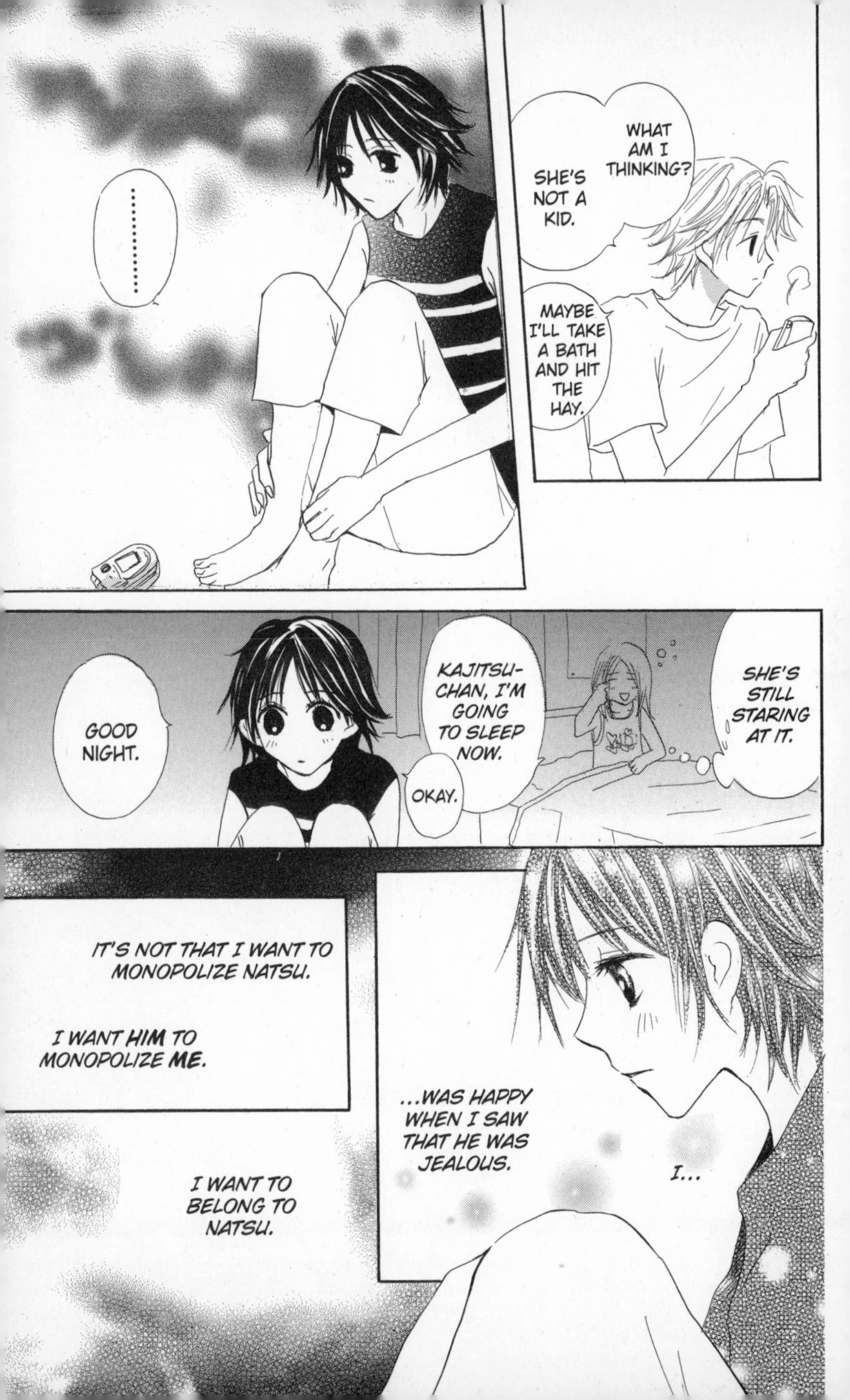
WHAT AM I THINKING?
SHE'S NOT A KID.
MAYBE I'LL TAKE A BATH AND HIT THE HAY.
......
SHE'S STILL STARING AT IT.
KAJITSU-CHAN, I'M GOING TO SLEEP NOW.
OKAY.
GOOD NIGHT.
I...
...WAS HAPPY WHEN I SAW THAT HE WAS JEALOUS.
IT'S NOT THAT I WANT TO MONOPOLIZE NATSU.
I WANT HIM TO MONOPOLIZE ME.
I WANT TO BELONG TO NATSU.

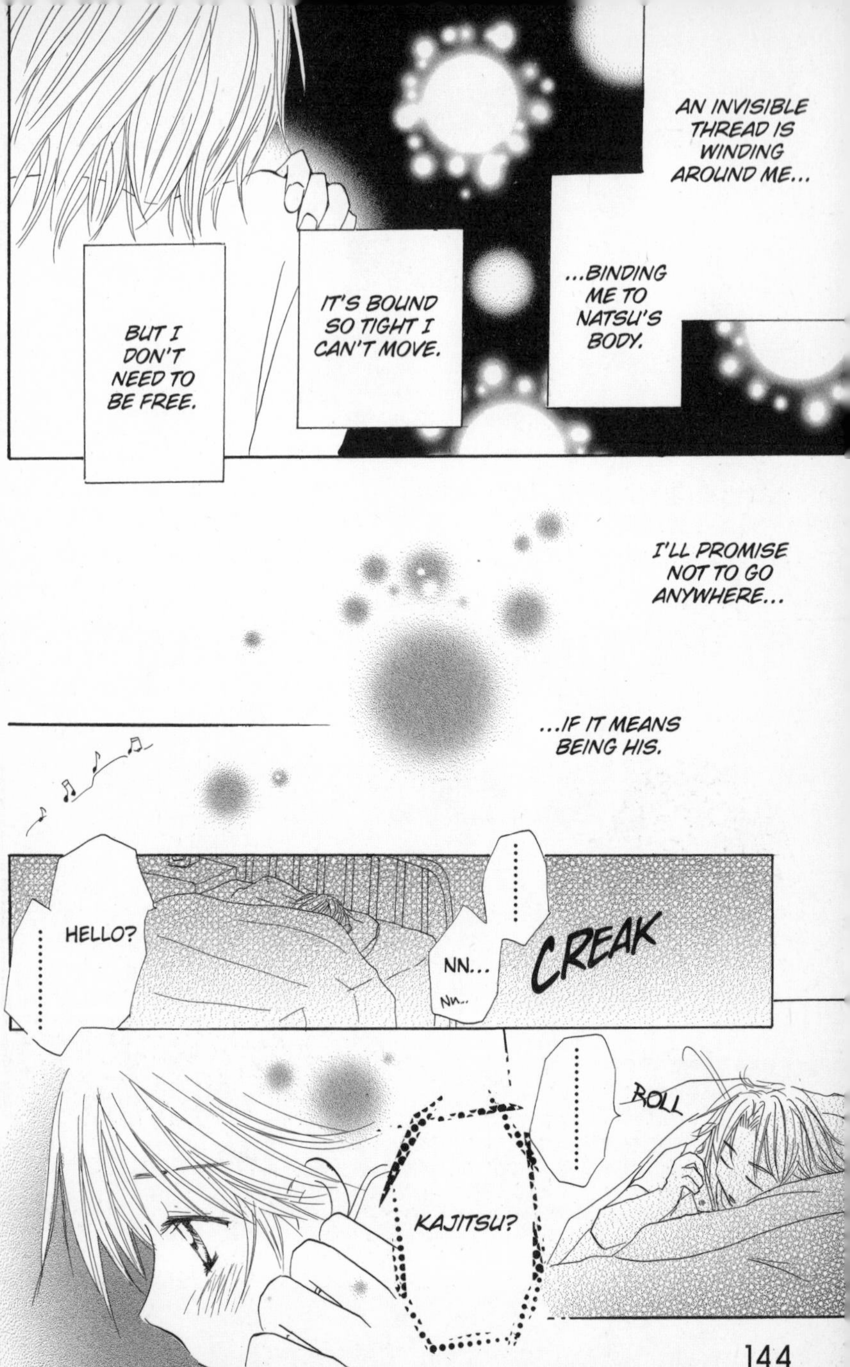
AN INVISIBLE THREAD IS WINDING AROUND ME...
...BINDING ME TO NATSU'S BODY.
IT'S BOUND SO TIGHT I CAN'T MOVE.
BUT I DON'T NEED TO BE FREE.
I'LL PROMISE NOT TO GO ANYWHERE...
...IF IT MEANS BEING HIS.
......
CREAK
NN... Nn..
HELLO? ......
......
ROLL
KAJITSU?

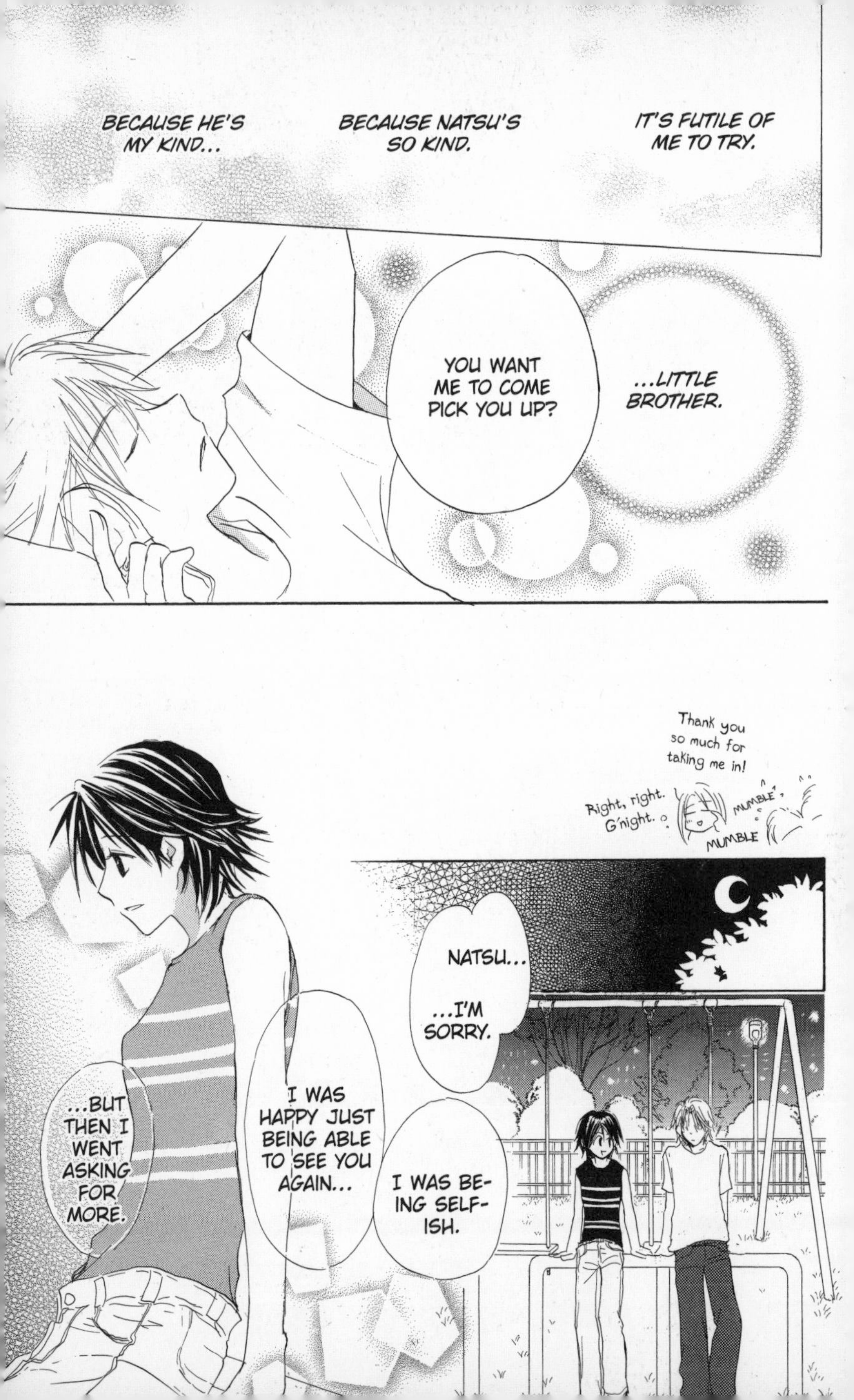
IT'S FUTILE OF ME TO TRY.
BECAUSE NATSU'S SO KIND.
BECAUSE HE'S MY KIND...
...LITTLE BROTHER.
YOU WANT ME TO COME PICK YOU UP?
Thank you so much for taking me in!
MUMBLE
MUMBLE
Right, right. G'night.
NATSU...
...I'M SORRY.
I WAS BE-ING SELF-ISH.
I WAS HAPPY JUST BEING ABLE TO SEE YOU AGAIN...
...BUT THEN I WENT ASKING FOR MORE.

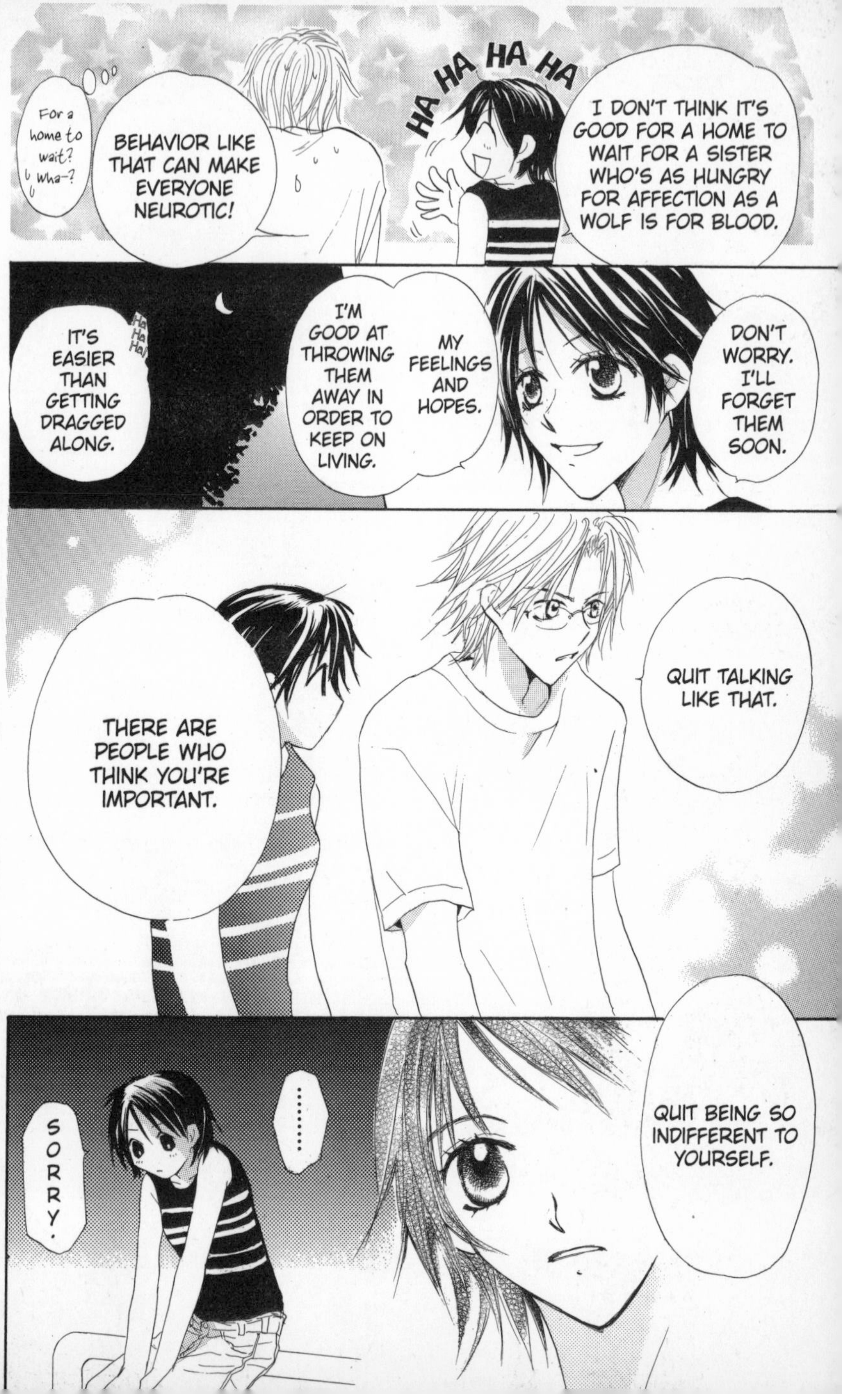
I DON'T THINK IT'S GOOD FOR A HOME TO WAIT FOR A SISTER WHO'S AS HUNGRY FOR AFFECTION AS A WOLF IS FOR BLOOD.
HA HA HA HA
BEHAVIOR LIKE THAT CAN MAKE EVERYONE NEUROTIC!
For a home to wait? Wha-?
DON'T WORRY. I'LL FORGET THEM SOON.
MY FEELINGS AND HOPES.
I'M GOOD AT THROWING THEM AWAY IN ORDER TO KEEP ON LIVING.
Ha Ha Ha!
IT'S EASIER THAN GETTING DRAGGED ALONG.
QUIT TALKING LIKE THAT.
THERE ARE PEOPLE WHO THINK YOU'RE IMPORTANT.
QUIT BEING SO INDIFFERENT TO YOURSELF.
......
SORRY.

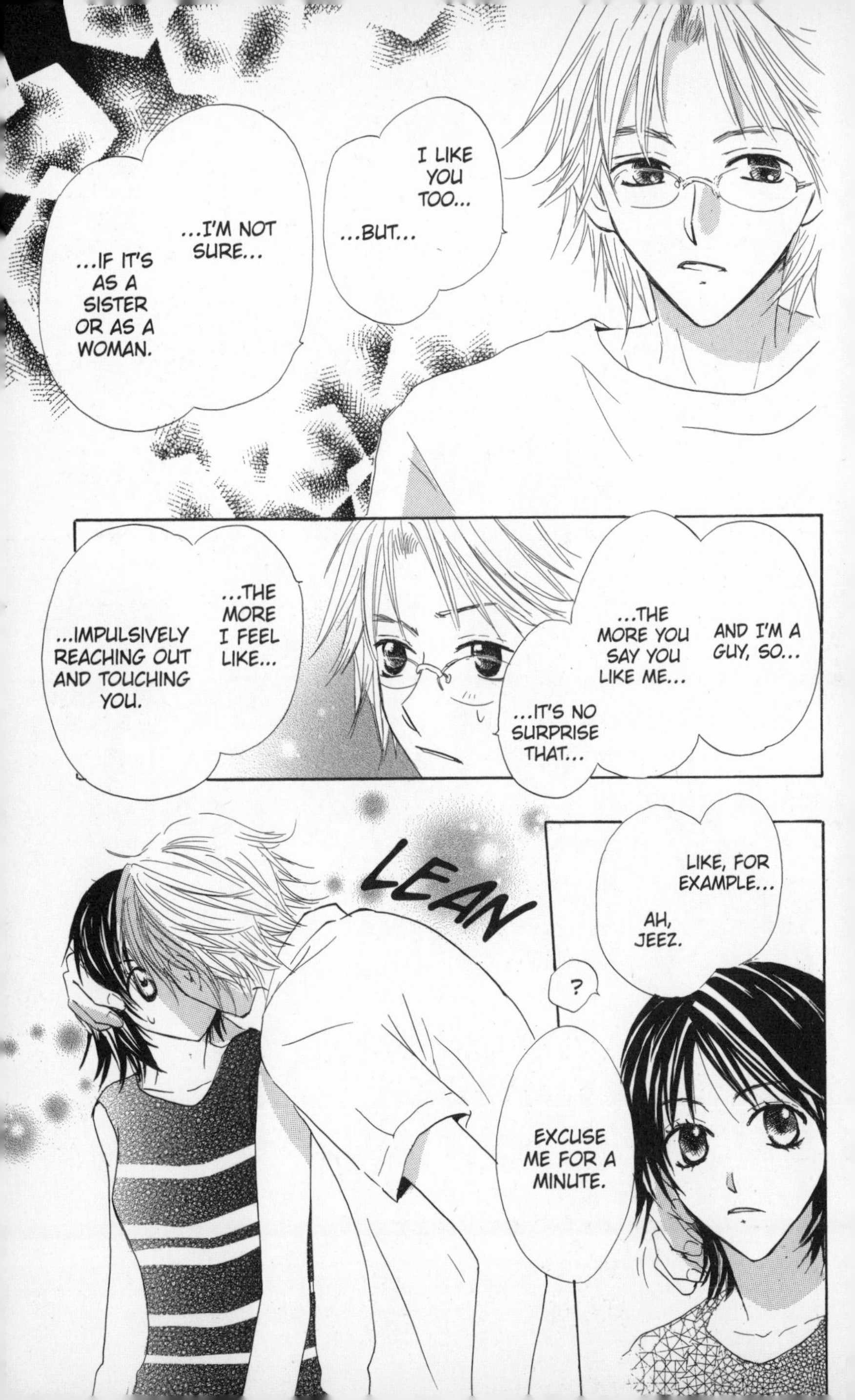
I LIKE YOU TOO... ...BUT...
...I'M NOT SURE... ...IF IT'S AS A SISTER OR AS A WOMAN.
AND I'M A GUY, SO... ...THE MORE YOU SAY YOU LIKE ME...
...IT'S NO SURPRISE THAT...
...THE MORE I FEEL LIKE... ...IMPULSIVELY REACHING OUT AND TOUCHING YOU.
LIKE, FOR EXAMPLE... AH, JEEZ.
?
EXCUSE ME FOR A MINUTE.
LEAN

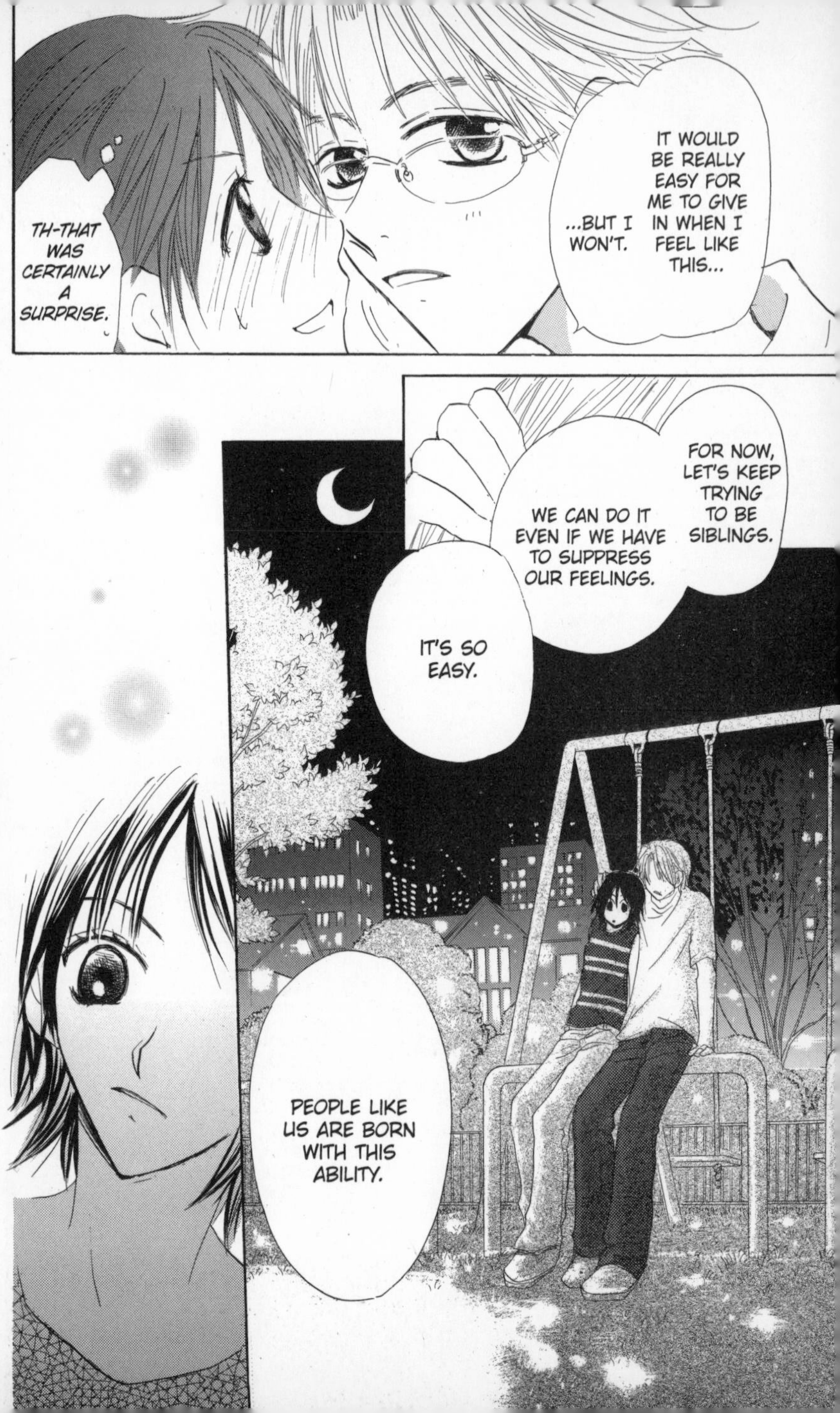
IT WOULD BE REALLY EASY FOR ME TO GIVE IN WHEN I FEEL LIKE THIS...
...BUT I WON'T.
TH-THAT WAS CERTAINLY A SURPRISE.
FOR NOW, LET'S KEEP TRYING TO BE SIBLINGS.
WE CAN DO IT EVEN IF WE HAVE TO SUPPRESS OUR FEELINGS.
IT'S SO EASY.
PEOPLE LIKE US ARE BORN WITH THIS ABILITY.

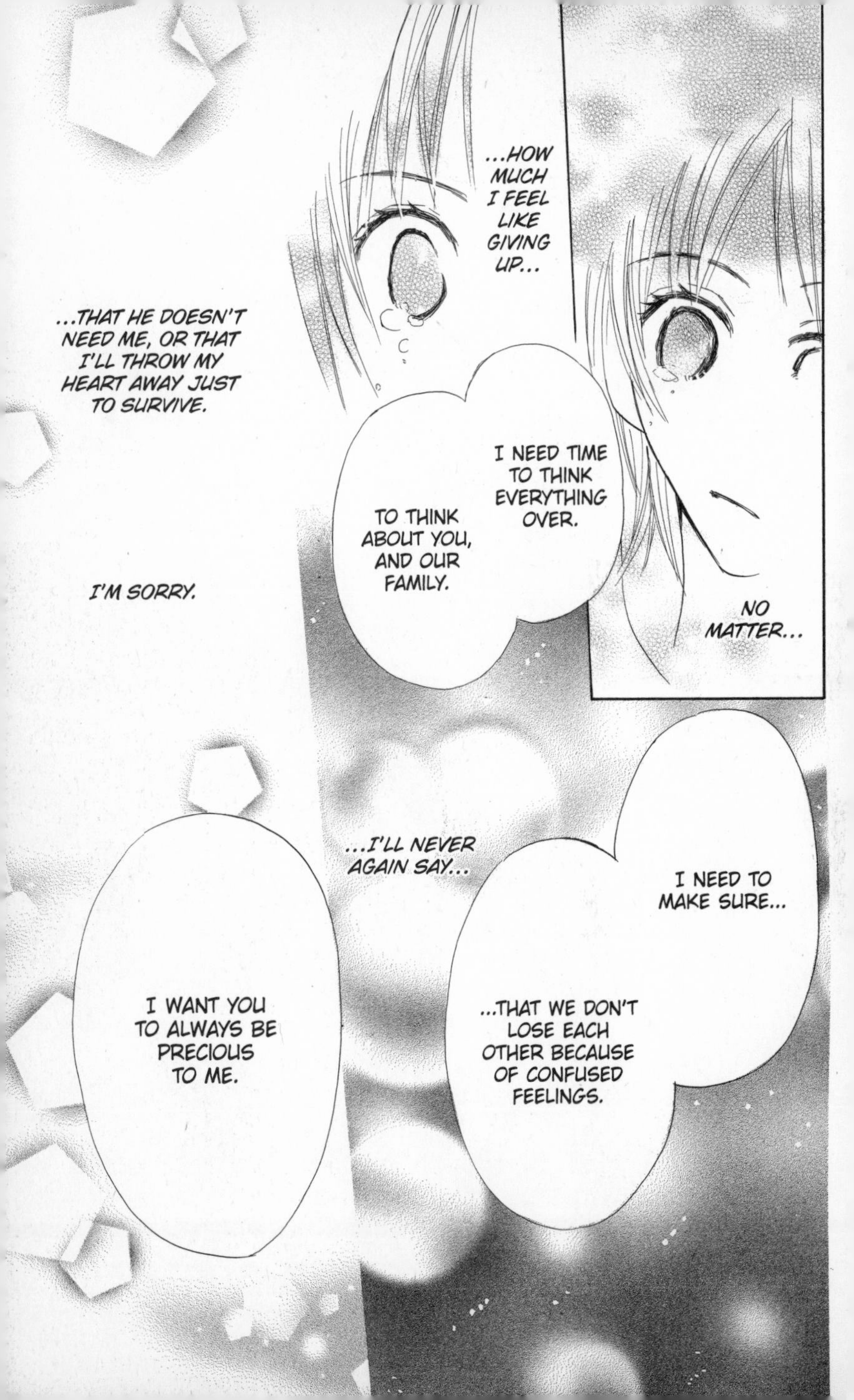
NO MATTER...
...HOW MUCH I FEEL LIKE GIVING UP...
I NEED TIME TO THINK EVERYTHING OVER.
TO THINK ABOUT YOU, AND OUR FAMILY.
...THAT HE DOESN'T NEED ME, OR THAT I'LL THROW MY HEART AWAY JUST TO SURVIVE.
I'M SORRY.
I NEED TO MAKE SURE...
...THAT WE DON'T LOSE EACH OTHER BECAUSE OF CONFUSED FEELINGS.
...I'LL NEVER AGAIN SAY...
I WANT YOU TO ALWAYS BE PRECIOUS TO ME.

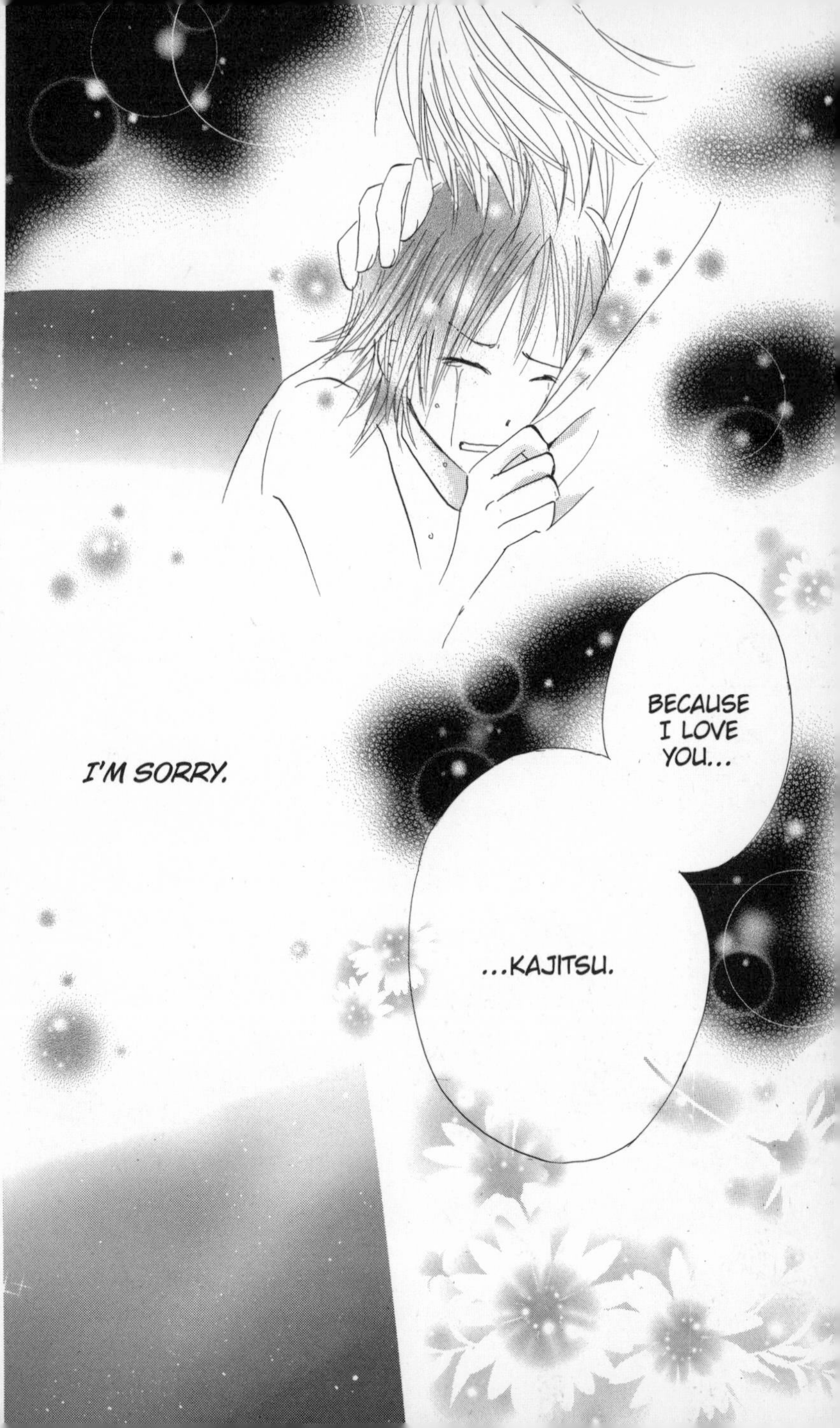
BECAUSE I LOVE YOU...
...KAJITSU.
I'M SORRY.

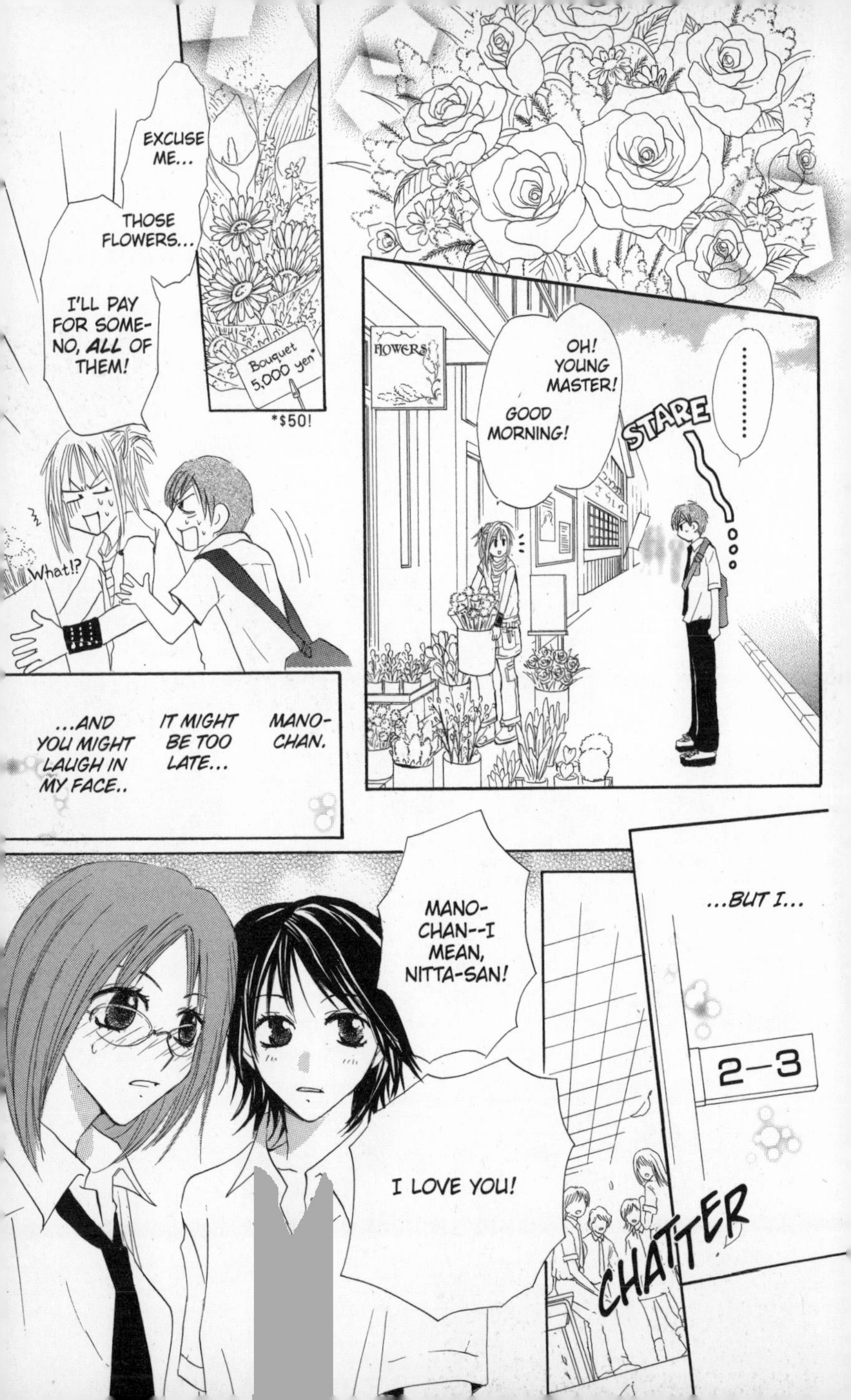
......
STARE
OH! YOUNG MASTER!
GOOD MORNING!
EXCUSE ME...
THOSE FLOWERS...
I'LL PAY FOR SOME-NO, ***ALL*** OF THEM!
Bouquet 5,000 yen*
*$50!
What!?
MANO-CHAN.
IT MIGHT BE TOO LATE...
...AND YOU MIGHT LAUGH IN MY FACE..
...BUT I...
2–3
CHATTER
MANO-CHAN--I MEAN, NITTA-SAN!
I LOVE YOU!

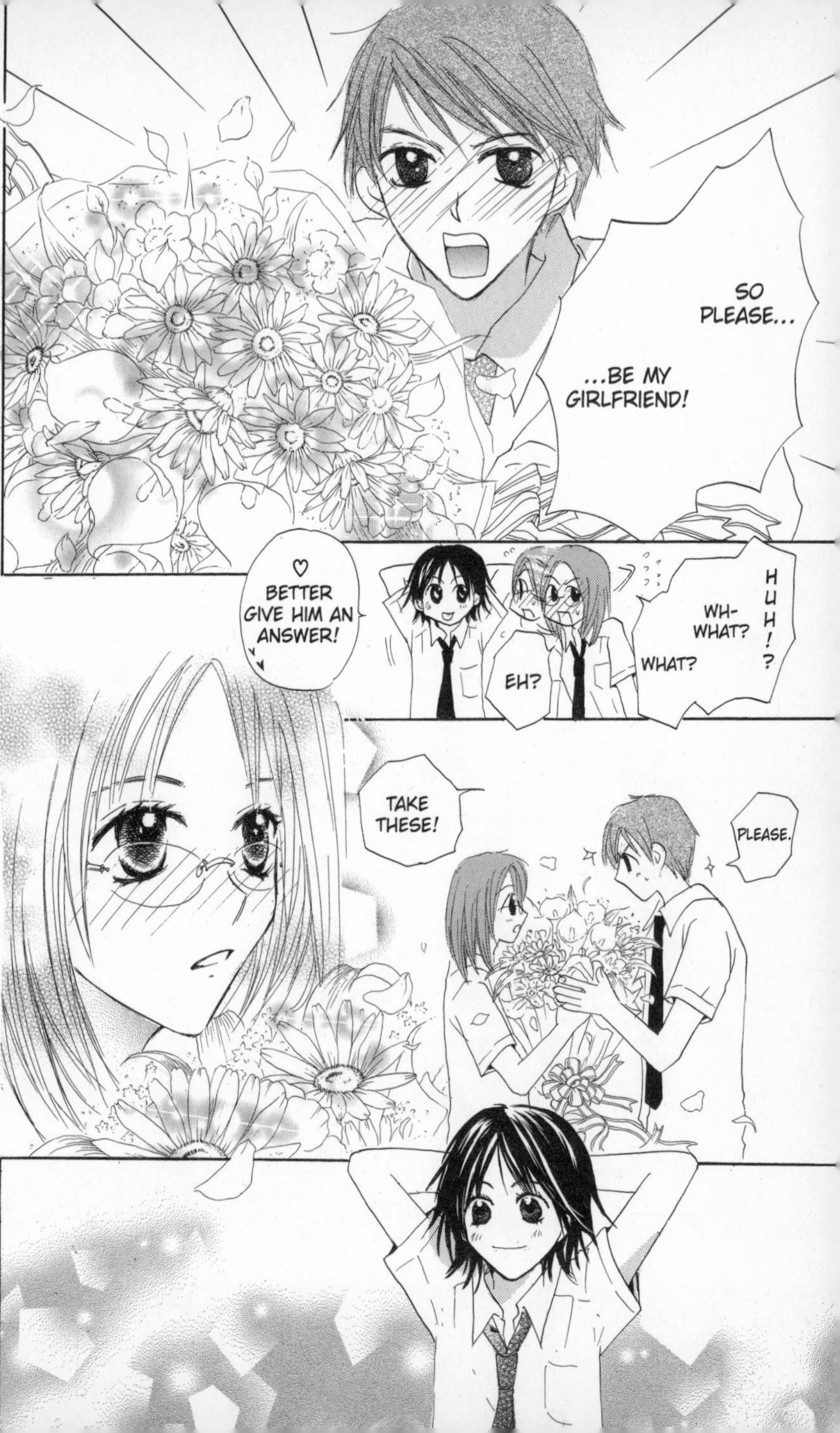
SO PLEASE...
...BE MY GIRLFRIEND!
HUH!?
WH-WHAT?
WHAT?
EH?
♡ BETTER GIVE HIM AN ANSWER!
PLEASE.
TAKE THESE!

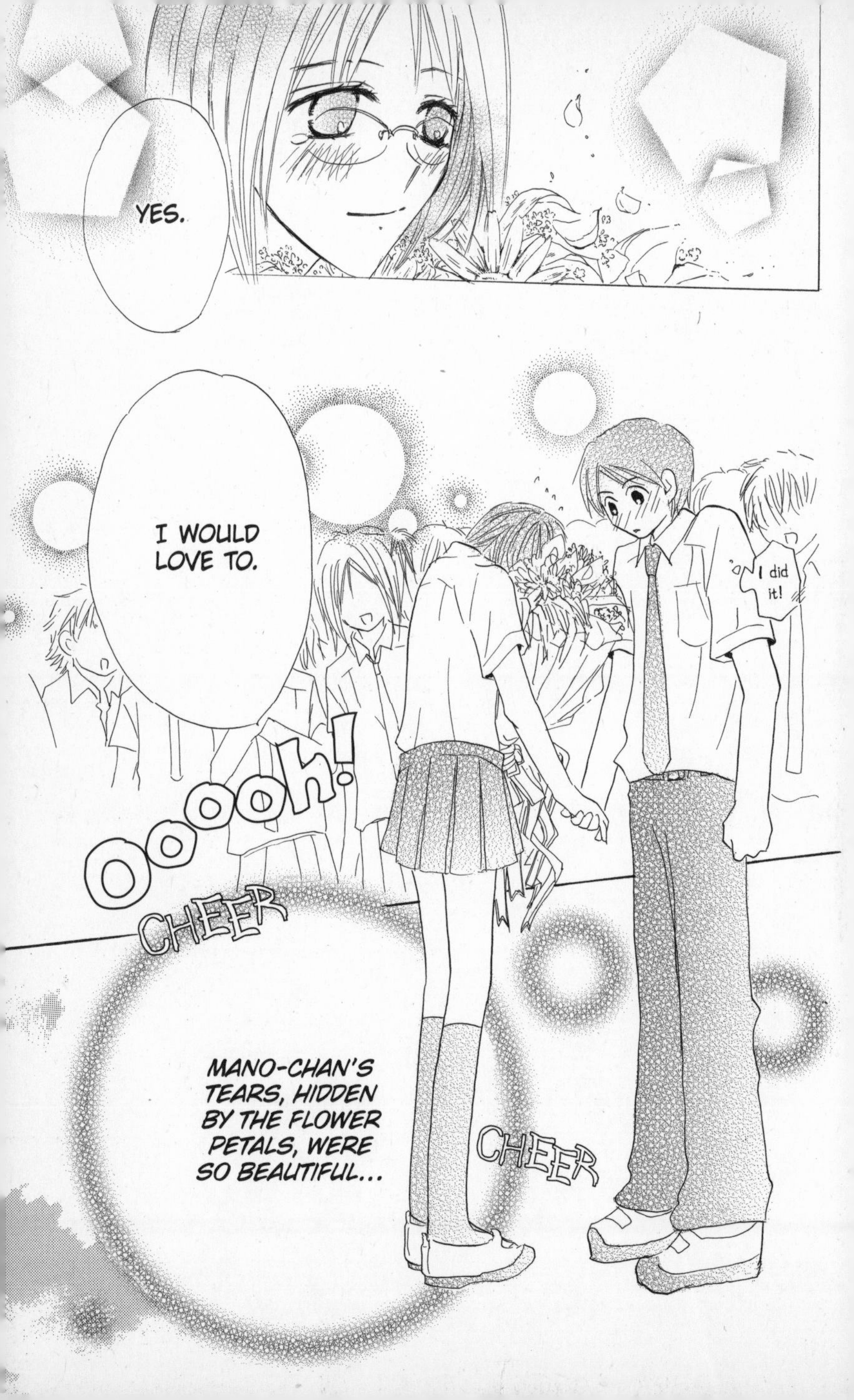
YES.
I did it!
I WOULD LOVE TO.
Oooooh!
CHEER
MANO-CHAN'S TEARS, HIDDEN BY THE FLOWER PETALS, WERE SO BEAUTIFUL...
CHEER

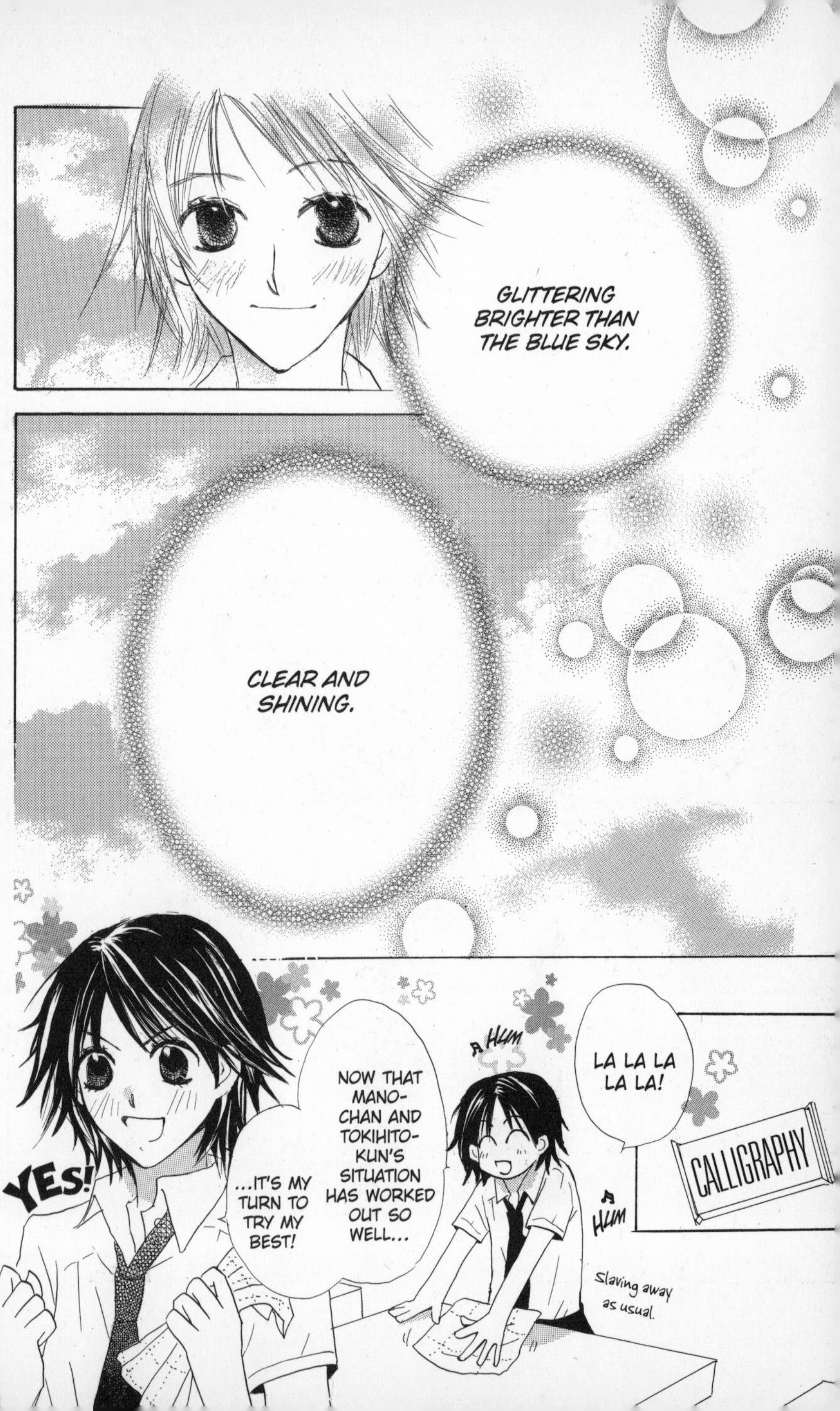
GLITTERING BRIGHTER THAN THE BLUE SKY.
CLEAR AND SHINING.
LA LA LA LA LA!
HUM
HUM
CALLIGRAPHY
Slaving away as usual.
NOW THAT MANO-CHAN AND TOKIHITO-KUN'S SITUATION HAS WORKED OUT SO WELL...
...IT'S MY TURN TO TRY MY BEST!
YES!

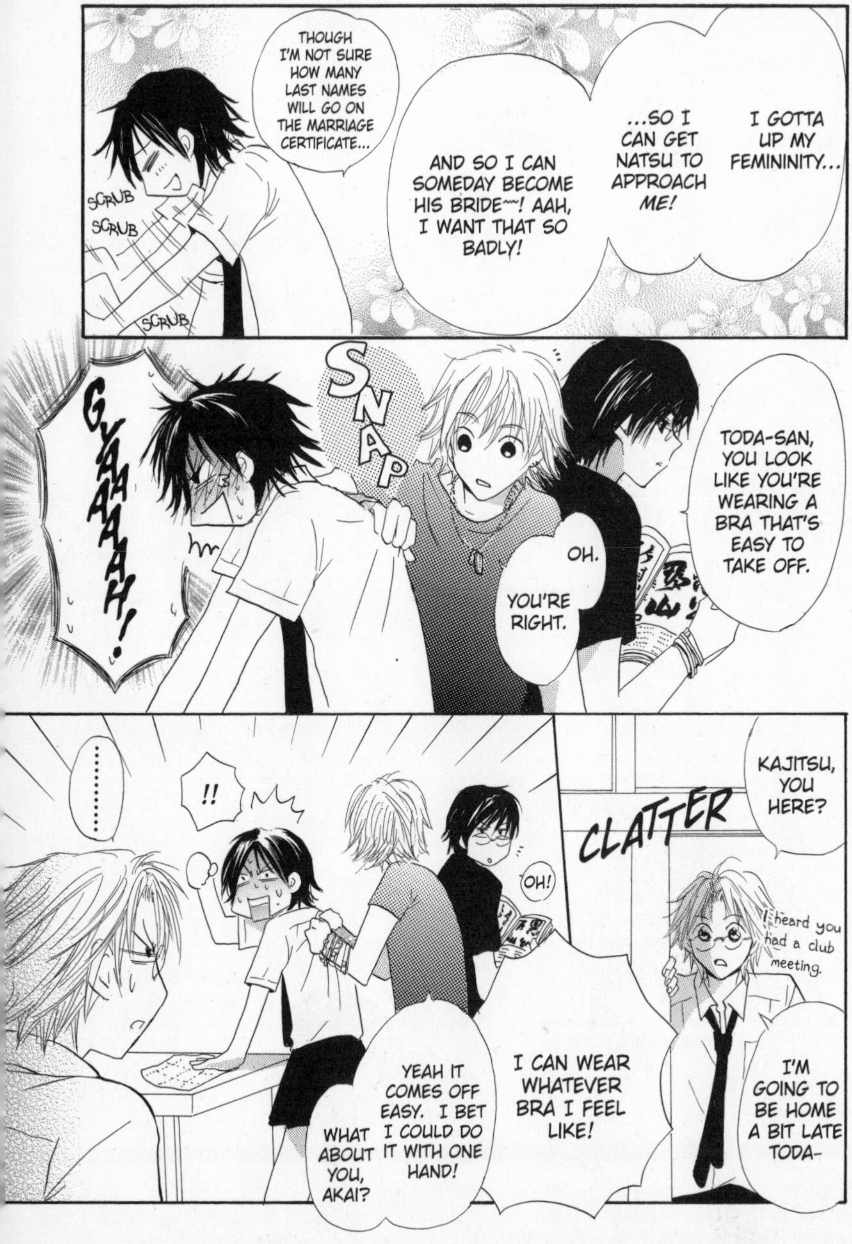
I GOTTA UP MY FEMININITY...
...SO I CAN GET NATSU TO APPROACH ME!
AND SO I CAN SOMEDAY BECOME HIS BRIDE~~! AAH, I WANT THAT SO BADLY!
THOUGH I'M NOT SURE HOW MANY LAST NAMES WILL GO ON THE MARRIAGE CERTIFICATE...
SCRUB
SCRUB
SCRUB
TODA-SAN, YOU LOOK LIKE YOU'RE WEARING A BRA THAT'S EASY TO TAKE OFF.
OH.
YOU'RE RIGHT.
SNAP
GYAAAAAAH!
KAJITSU, YOU HERE?
CLATTER
I heard you had a club meeting.
I'M GOING TO BE HOME A BIT LATE TODA-
OH!
I CAN WEAR WHATEVER BRA I FEEL LIKE!
YEAH IT COMES OFF EASY. I BET I COULD DO IT WITH ONE HAND!
WHAT ABOUT YOU, AKAI?
!!
......

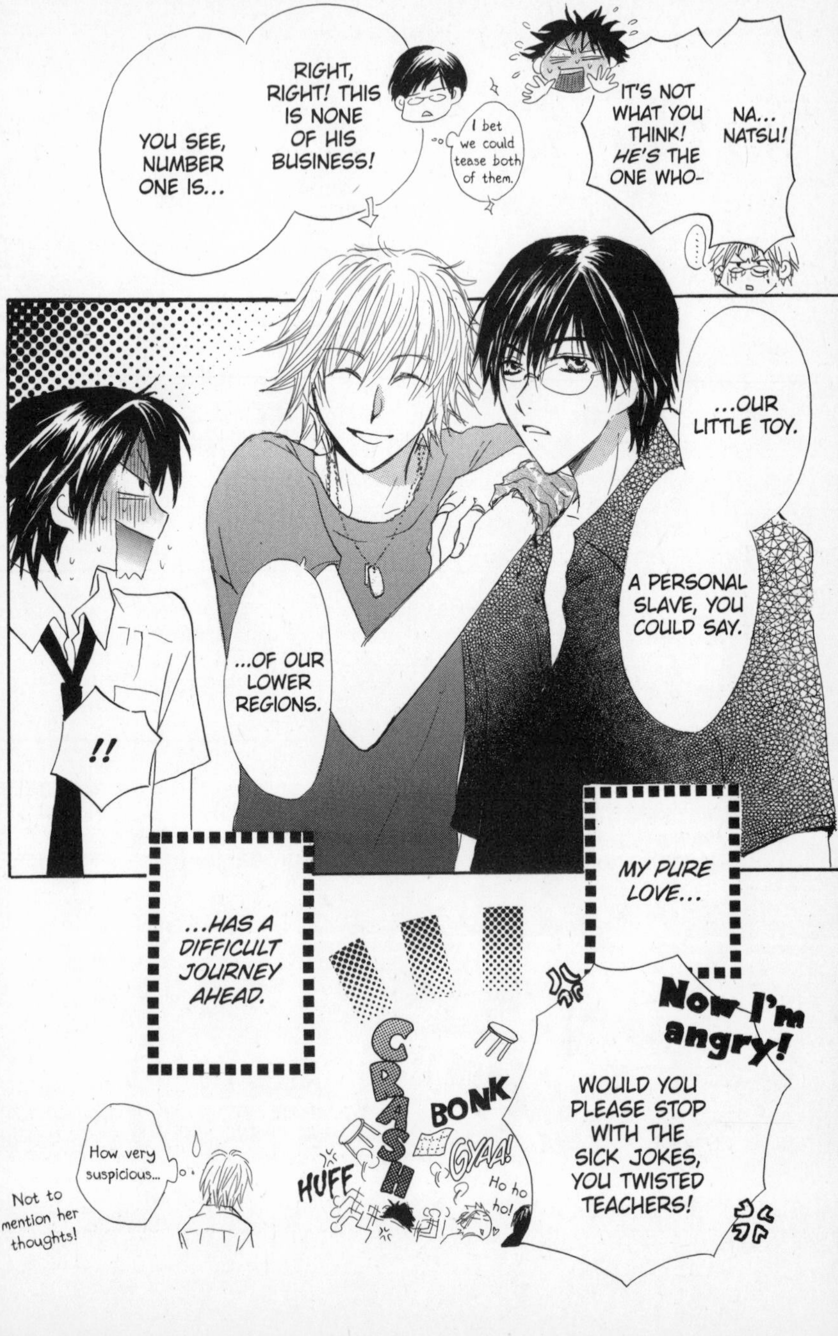
NA... NATSU!
IT'S NOT WHAT YOU THINK! HE'S THE ONE WHO-
...
I bet we could tease both of them.
RIGHT, RIGHT! THIS IS NONE OF HIS BUSINESS!
YOU SEE, NUMBER ONE IS...
...OUR LITTLE TOY.
A PERSONAL SLAVE, YOU COULD SAY.
...OF OUR LOWER REGIONS.
!!
MY PURE LOVE...
...HAS A DIFFICULT JOURNEY AHEAD.
Now I'm angry!
WOULD YOU PLEASE STOP WITH THE SICK JOKES, YOU TWISTED TEACHERS!
BONK
CRASH
GYAA!
Ho ho ho!
HUFF
How very suspicious...
Not to mention her thoughts!

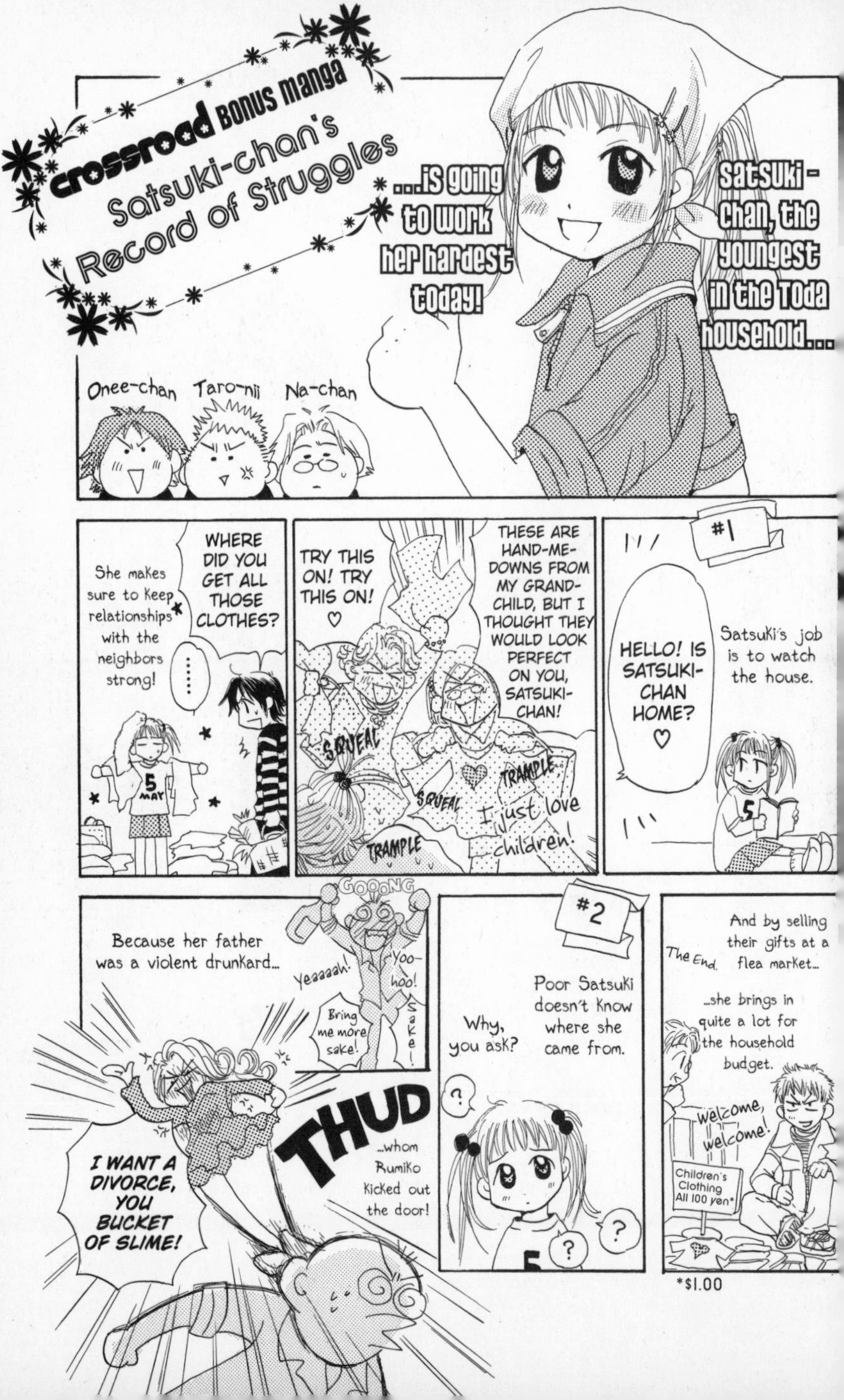
Crossroad BONUS MANGA
Satsuki-chan's Record of Struggles
Satsuki-chan, the youngest in the Toda household...
...is going to work her hardest today!
Onee-chan
Taro-nii
Na-chan
#1
Satsuki's job is to watch the house.
HELLO! IS SATSUKI-CHAN HOME? ♡
THESE ARE HAND-ME-DOWNS FROM MY GRAND-CHILD, BUT I THOUGHT THEY WOULD LOOK PERFECT ON YOU, SATSUKI-CHAN!
TRY THIS ON! TRY THIS ON! ♡
SQUEAL
TRAMPLE
SQUEAL
TRAMPLE
I just love children!
WHERE DID YOU GET ALL THOSE CLOTHES?
......
She makes sure to keep relationships with the neighbors strong!
And by selling their gifts at a flea market...
The End.
...she brings in quite a lot for the household budget.
Welcome, welcome!
Children's Clothing All 100 yen*
#2
Poor Satsuki doesn't know where she came from.
Why, you ask?
?
?
?
Because her father was a violent drunkard...
GOOONG
Yoo-hoo!
Yeaaaah!
Bring me more sake!
Sake!
THUD
...whom Rumiko kicked out the door!
I WANT A DIVORCE, YOU BUCKET OF SLIME!
*$1.00

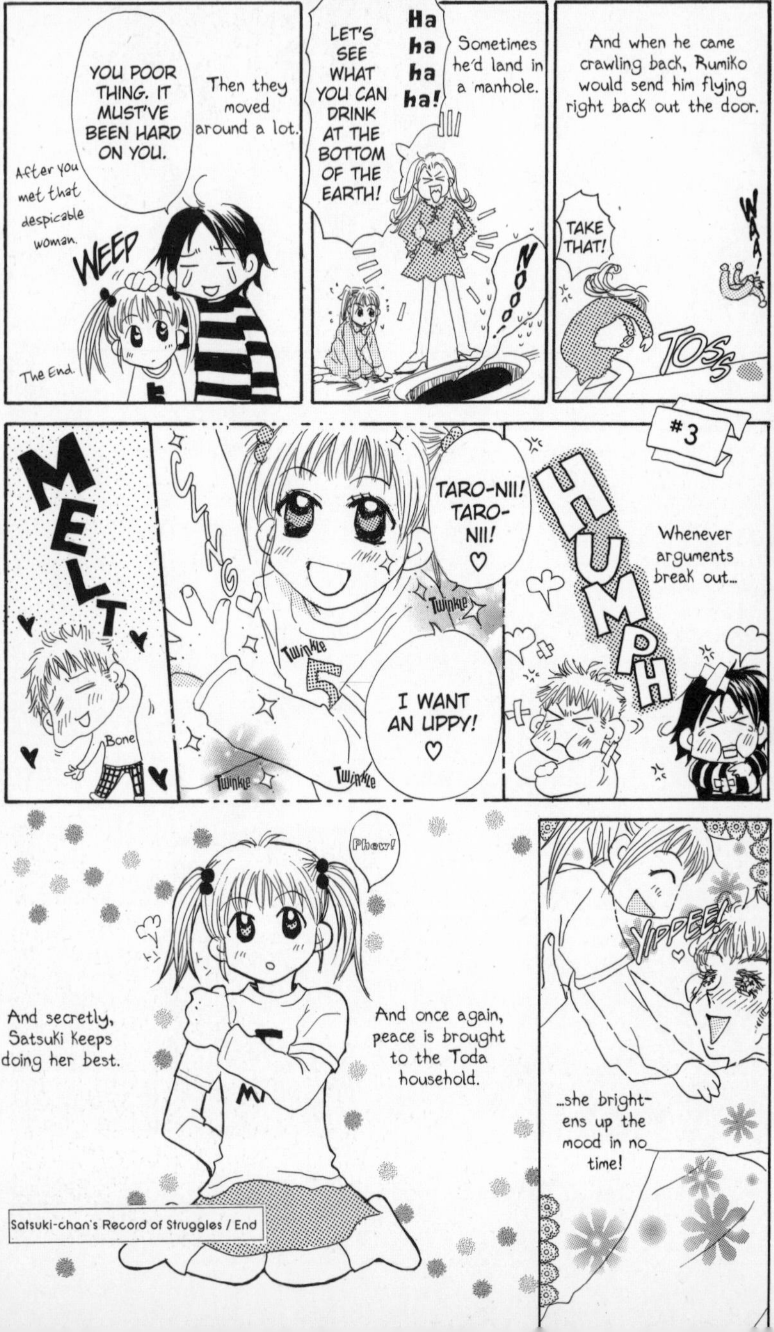
And when he came crawling back, Rumiko would send him flying right back out the door.
TAKE THAT!
WAAA!
TOSS
Sometimes he'd land in a manhole.
Ha ha ha ha!
LET'S SEE WHAT YOU CAN DRINK AT THE BOTTOM OF THE EARTH!
NOOOO!
Then they moved around a lot.
YOU POOR THING. IT MUST'VE BEEN HARD ON YOU.
After you met that despicable woman.
WEEP
The End.
#3
Whenever arguments break out...
HUMPH
TARO-NII! TARO-NII! ♡
CLING
I WANT AN UPPY! ♡
Twinkle
Twinkle
Twinkle
Twinkle
MELT
Bone
YIPPEE! ♡
...she brightens up the mood in no time!
And once again, peace is brought to the Toda household.
Phew!
And secretly, Satsuki keeps doing her best.
Satsuki-chan's Record of Struggles / End

*This is the "cramped" version of Satsuki-chan's activities.

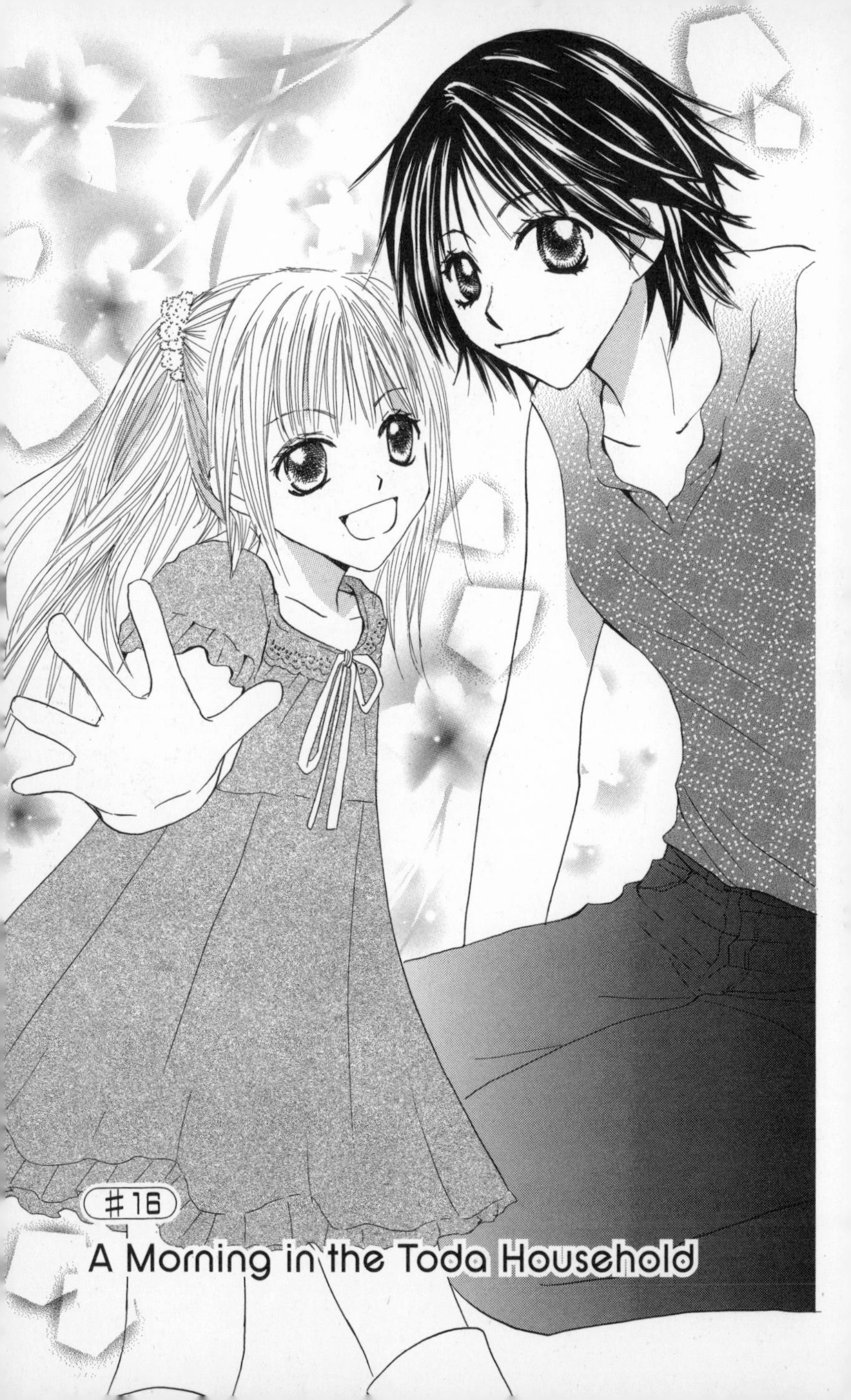
#16
A Morning in the Toda Household

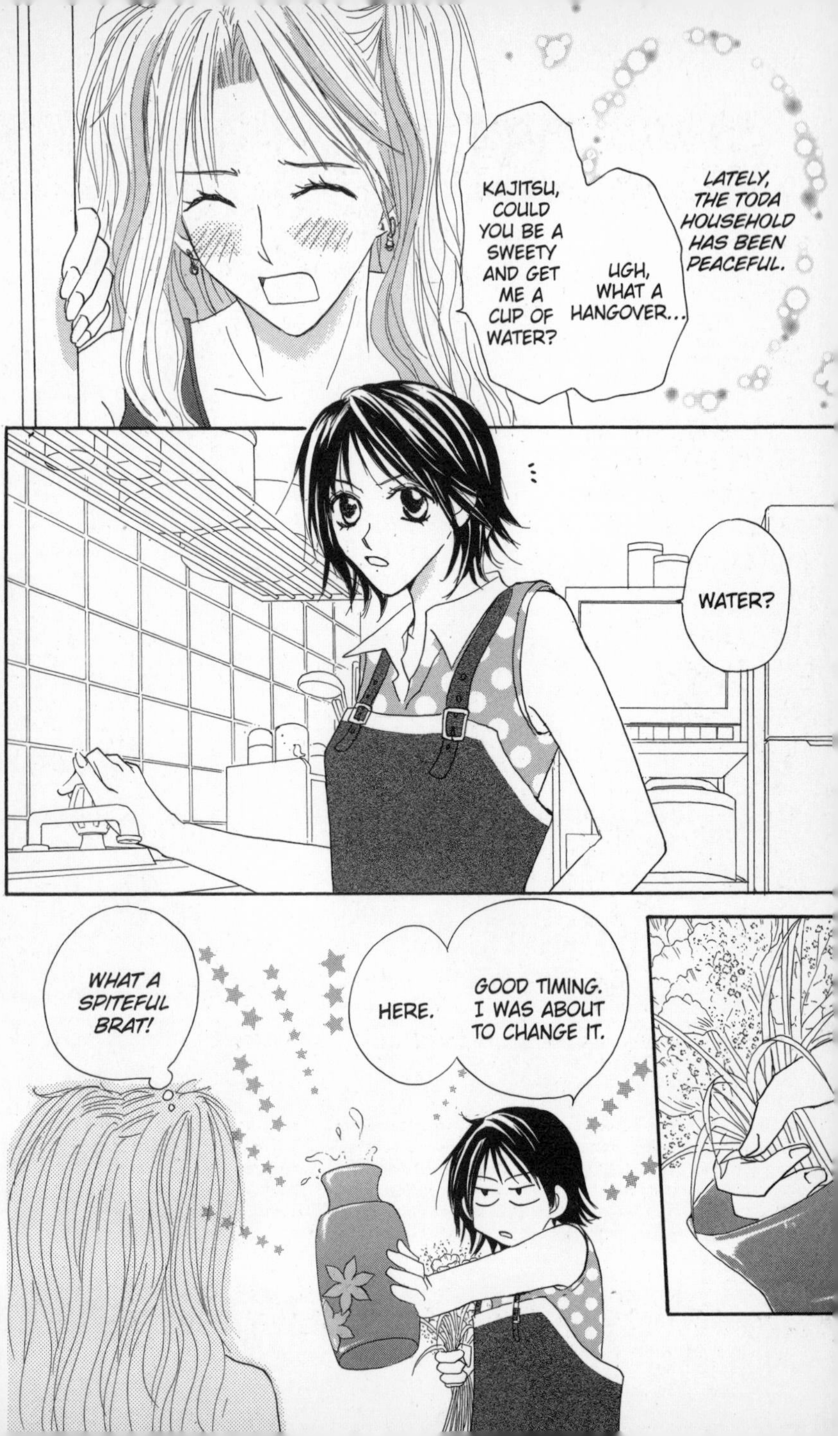
LATELY, THE TODA HOUSEHOLD HAS BEEN PEACEFUL.
UGH, WHAT A HANGOVER...
KAJITSU, COULD YOU BE A SWEETY AND GET ME A CUP OF WATER?
WATER?
GOOD TIMING. I WAS ABOUT TO CHANGE IT.
HERE.
WHAT A SPITEFUL BRAT!

crossroad Chapter 16: A Morning in the Toda Household

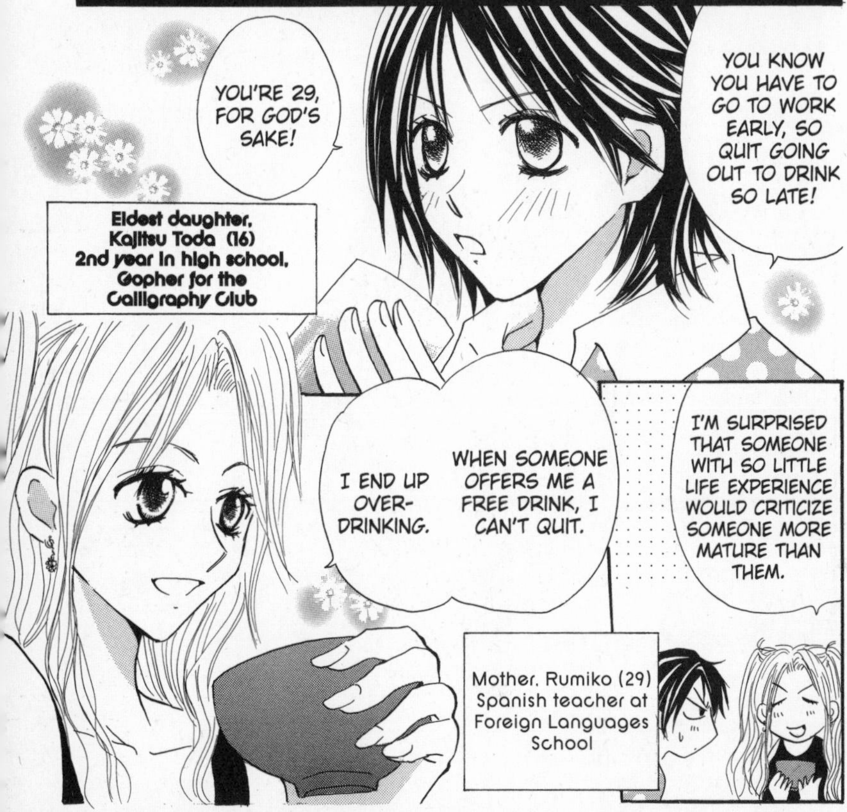
YOU KNOW YOU HAVE TO GO TO WORK EARLY, SO QUIT GOING OUT TO DRINK SO LATE!
YOU'RE 29, FOR GOD'S SAKE!
Eldest daughter, Kajitsu Toda (16) 2nd year in high school, Gopher for the Calligraphy Club
I'M SURPRISED THAT SOMEONE WITH SO LITTLE LIFE EXPERIENCE WOULD CRITICIZE SOMEONE MORE MATURE THAN THEM.
Mother, Rumiko (29) Spanish teacher at Foreign Languages School
WHEN SOMEONE OFFERS ME A FREE DRINK, I CAN'T QUIT.
I END UP OVER-DRINKING.

Feelings of Nostalgia 5

Satsuki is in grade school, but she doesn't wear a Knapsack. That's because I already detested Knapsacks by second grade. I thought they were sooo childish. The school-regulated jersey was also considered "lame" so I didn't wear it and would get yelled at by the teachers...and that is how I grew up into an adult (laugh). I'd like to draw Satsuki's grade school life, too. Someday, I'll write it. I really have too many, "Oh, I'll write that someday," stories. Like Crossroad...

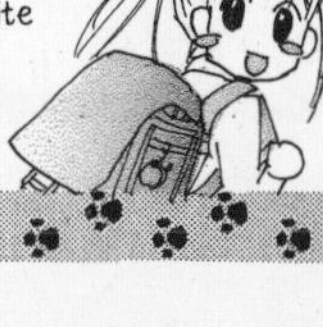

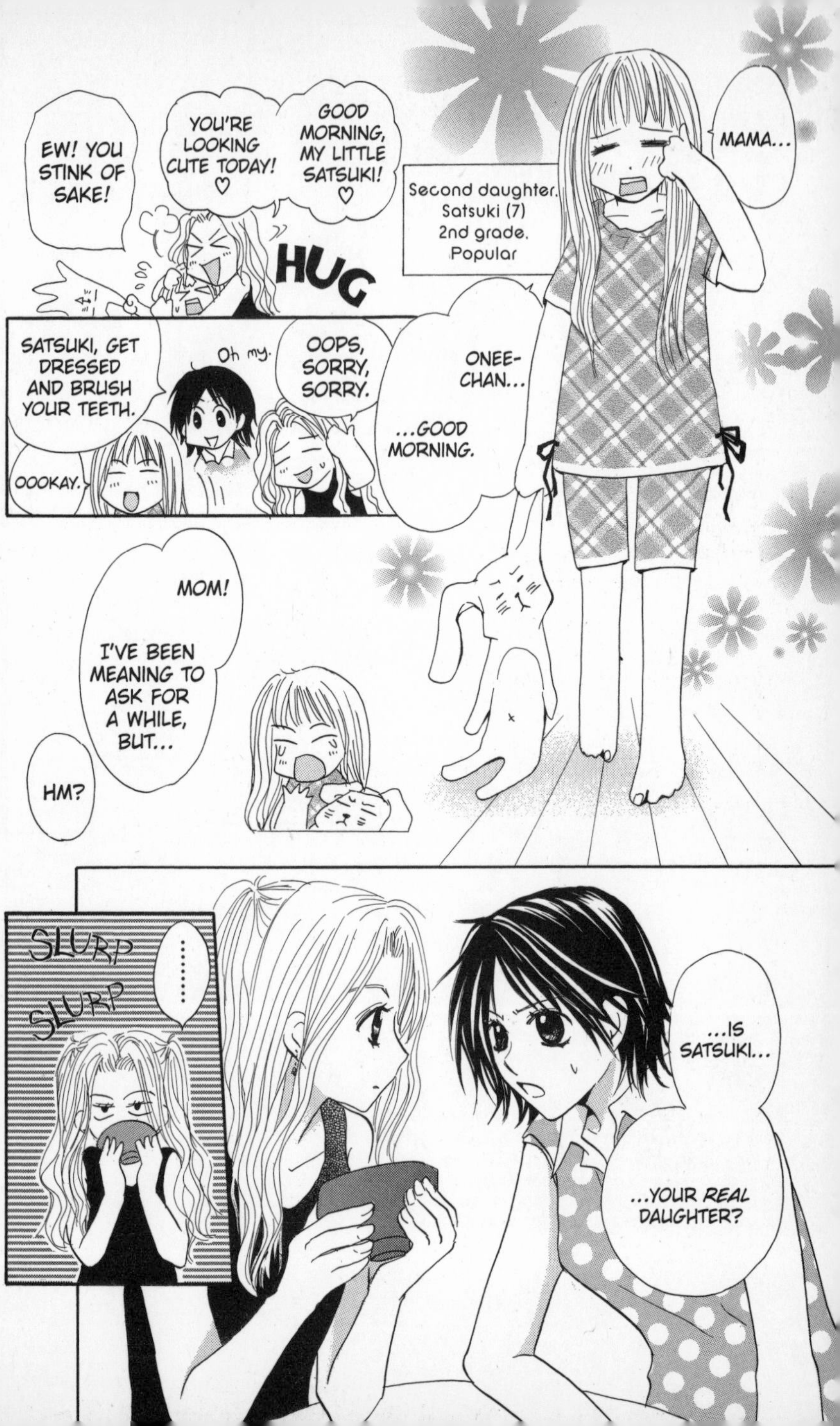
MAMA...
Second daughter. Satsuki (7) 2nd grade. Popular
ONEE-CHAN...
...GOOD MORNING.
GOOD MORNING, MY LITTLE SATSUKI! ♡
YOU'RE LOOKING CUTE TODAY! ♡
HUG
EW! YOU STINK OF SAKE!
OOPS, SORRY, SORRY.
Oh my.
SATSUKI, GET DRESSED AND BRUSH YOUR TEETH.
OOOKAY.
MOM!
I'VE BEEN MEANING TO ASK FOR A WHILE, BUT...
HM?
...IS SATSUKI...
...YOUR *REAL* DAUGHTER?
......
SLURP
SLURP

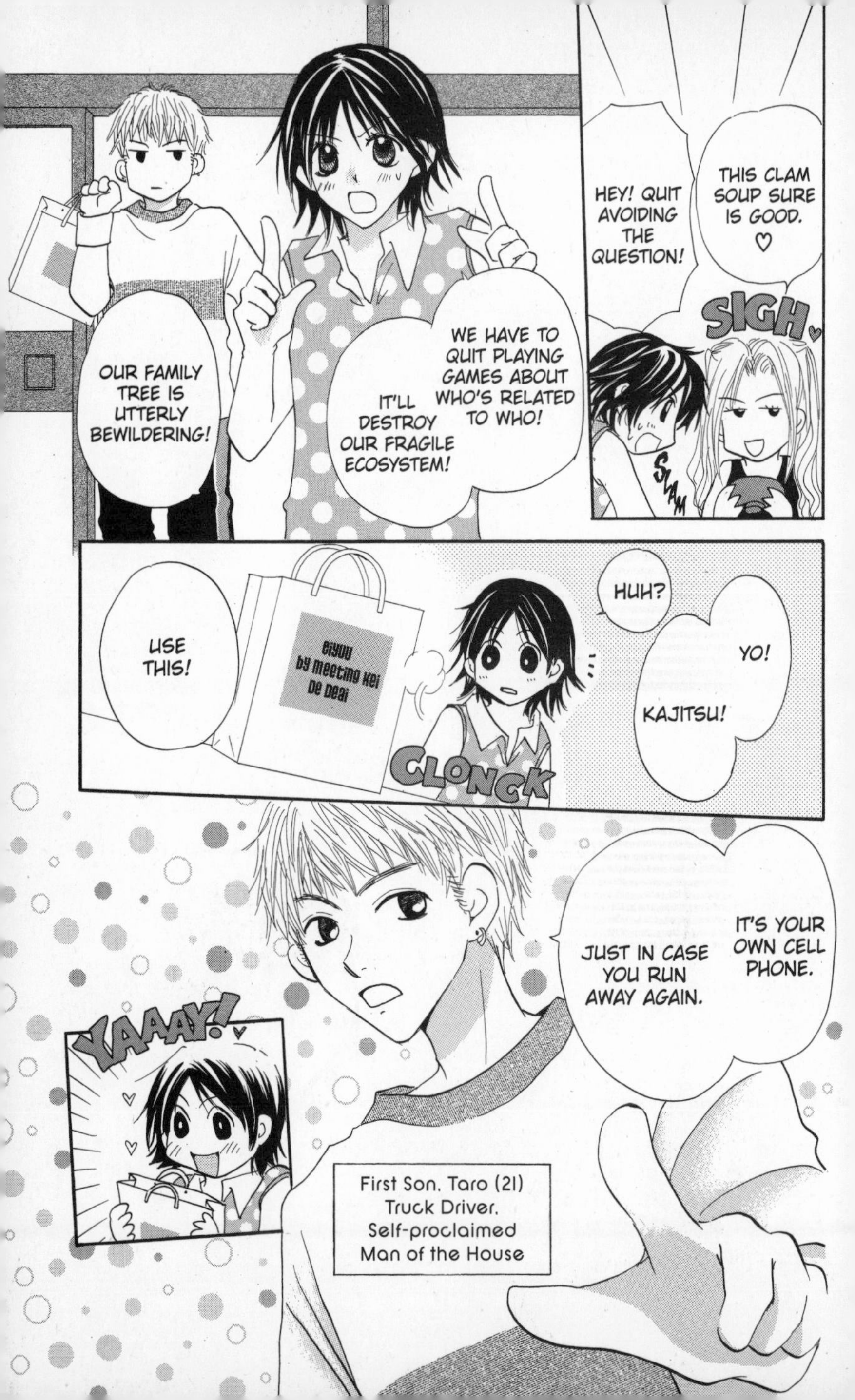
THIS CLAM SOUP SURE IS GOOD. ♡
HEY! QUIT AVOIDING THE QUESTION!
SIGH
SLAM
WE HAVE TO QUIT PLAYING GAMES ABOUT WHO'S RELATED TO WHO!
IT'LL DESTROY OUR FRAGILE ECOSYSTEM!
OUR FAMILY TREE IS UTTERLY BEWILDERING!
YO! KAJITSU!
HUH?
eiyuu by meeting kei de deai
CLONCK
USE THIS!
IT'S YOUR OWN CELL PHONE.
JUST IN CASE YOU RUN AWAY AGAIN.
First Son, Taro (21) Truck Driver. Self-proclaimed Man of the House
YAAAY!

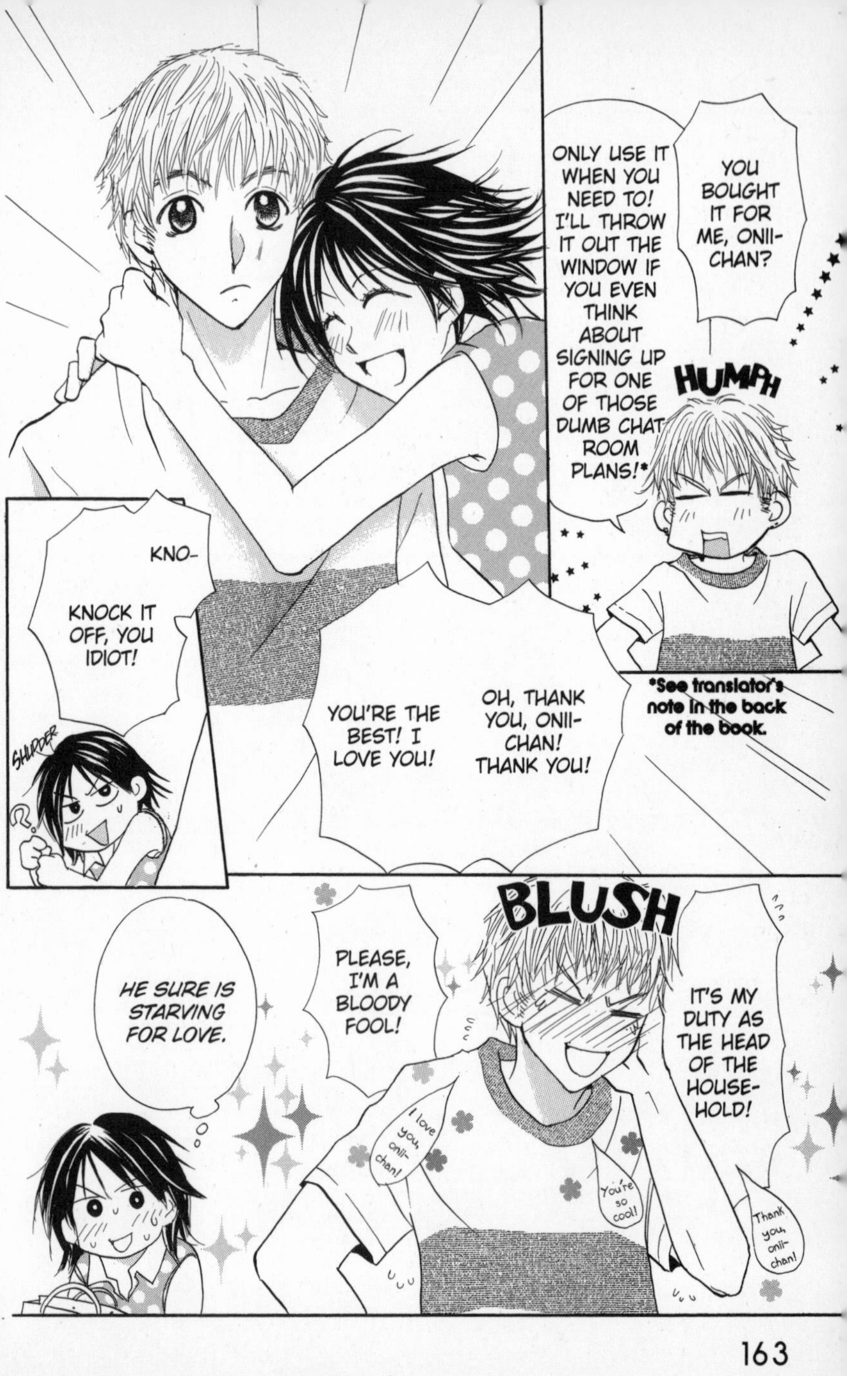
YOU BOUGHT IT FOR ME, ONII-CHAN?
ONLY USE IT WHEN YOU NEED TO! I'LL THROW IT OUT THE WINDOW IF YOU EVEN THINK ABOUT SIGNING UP FOR ONE OF THOSE DUMB CHAT ROOM PLANS!*
HUMPH
*See translator's note in the back of the book.
OH, THANK YOU, ONII-CHAN! THANK YOU!
YOU'RE THE BEST! I LOVE YOU!
KNO-
KNOCK IT OFF, YOU IDIOT!
SHUDDER
BLUSH
IT'S MY DUTY AS THE HEAD OF THE HOUSE-HOLD!
Thank you, onii-chan!
You're so cool!
I love you, onii-chan!
PLEASE, I'M A BLOODY FOOL!
HE SURE IS STARVING FOR LOVE.

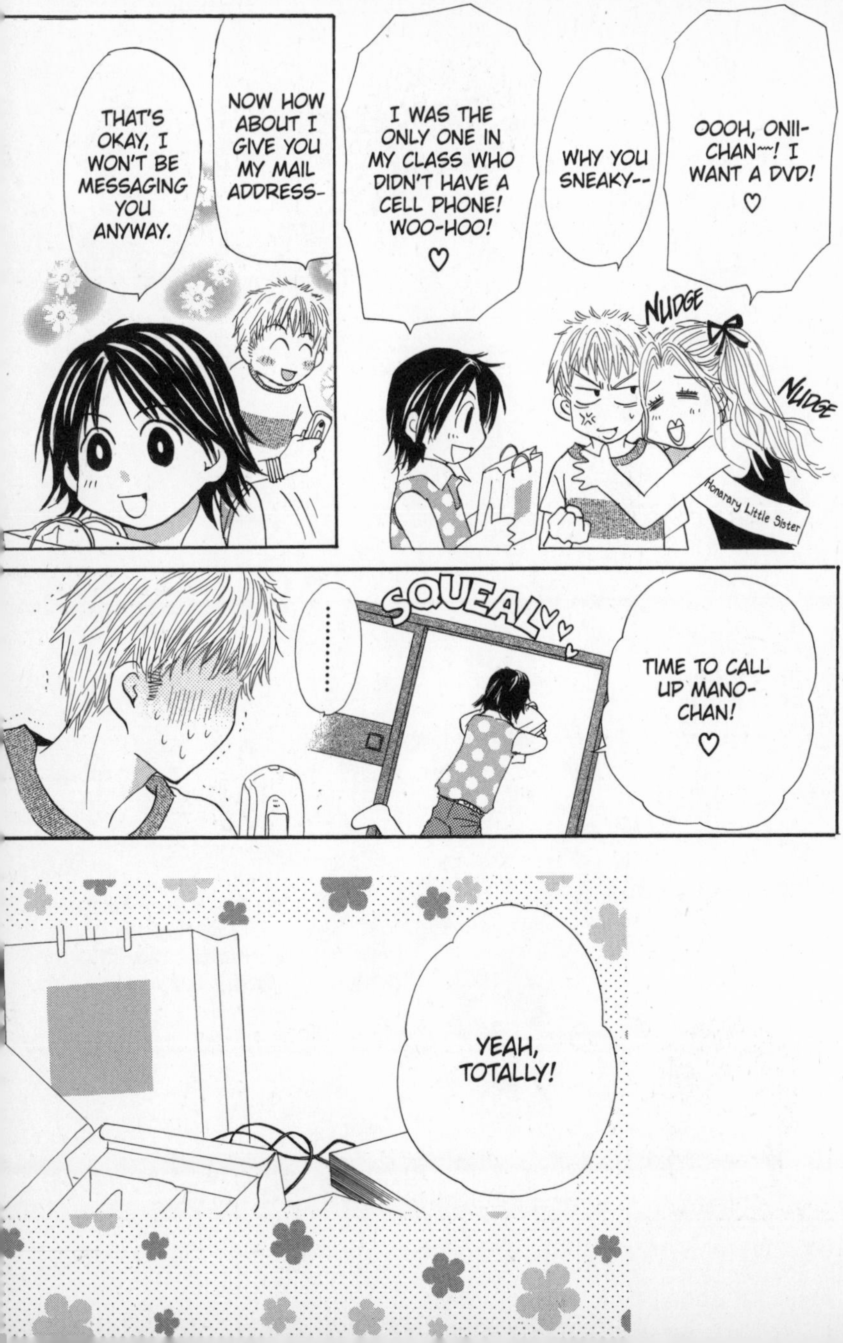
OOOH, ONII-CHAN~~! I WANT A DVD! ♡
WHY YOU SNEAKY--
NUDGE
NUDGE
Honarary Little Sister
I WAS THE ONLY ONE IN MY CLASS WHO DIDN'T HAVE A CELL PHONE! WOO-HOO! ♡
NOW HOW ABOUT I GIVE YOU MY MAIL ADDRESS-
THAT'S OKAY, I WON'T BE MESSAGING YOU ANYWAY.
TIME TO CALL UP MANO-CHAN! ♡
SQUEAL♡
....
YEAH, TOTALLY!

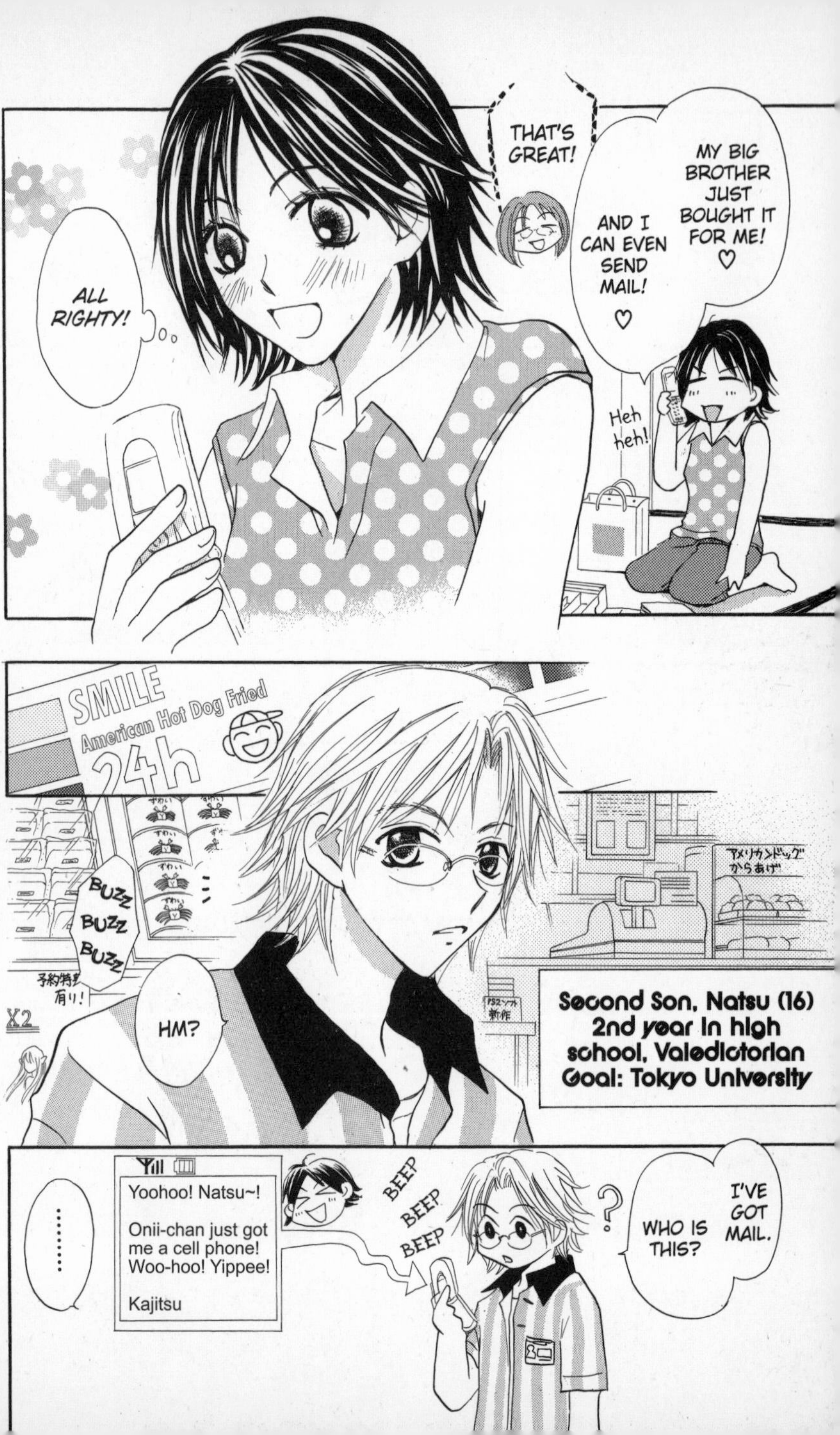

MY BIG BROTHER JUST BOUGHT IT FOR ME! ♡
AND I CAN EVEN SEND MAIL! ♡
THAT'S GREAT!
Heh heh!
ALL RIGHTY!
アメリカンドッグ からあげ
SMILE
American Hot Dog Fried
24h
Second Son, Natsu (16) 2nd year in high school, Valedictorian Goal: Tokyo University
PS2ソフト 新作
HM?
BUZZ BUZZ BUZZ
予約特典有り!
X2
I'VE GOT MAIL.
WHO IS THIS?
?
BEEP BEEP BEEP
Yoohoo! Natsu~!
Onii-chan just got me a cell phone! Woo-hoo! Yippee!
Kajitsu
....

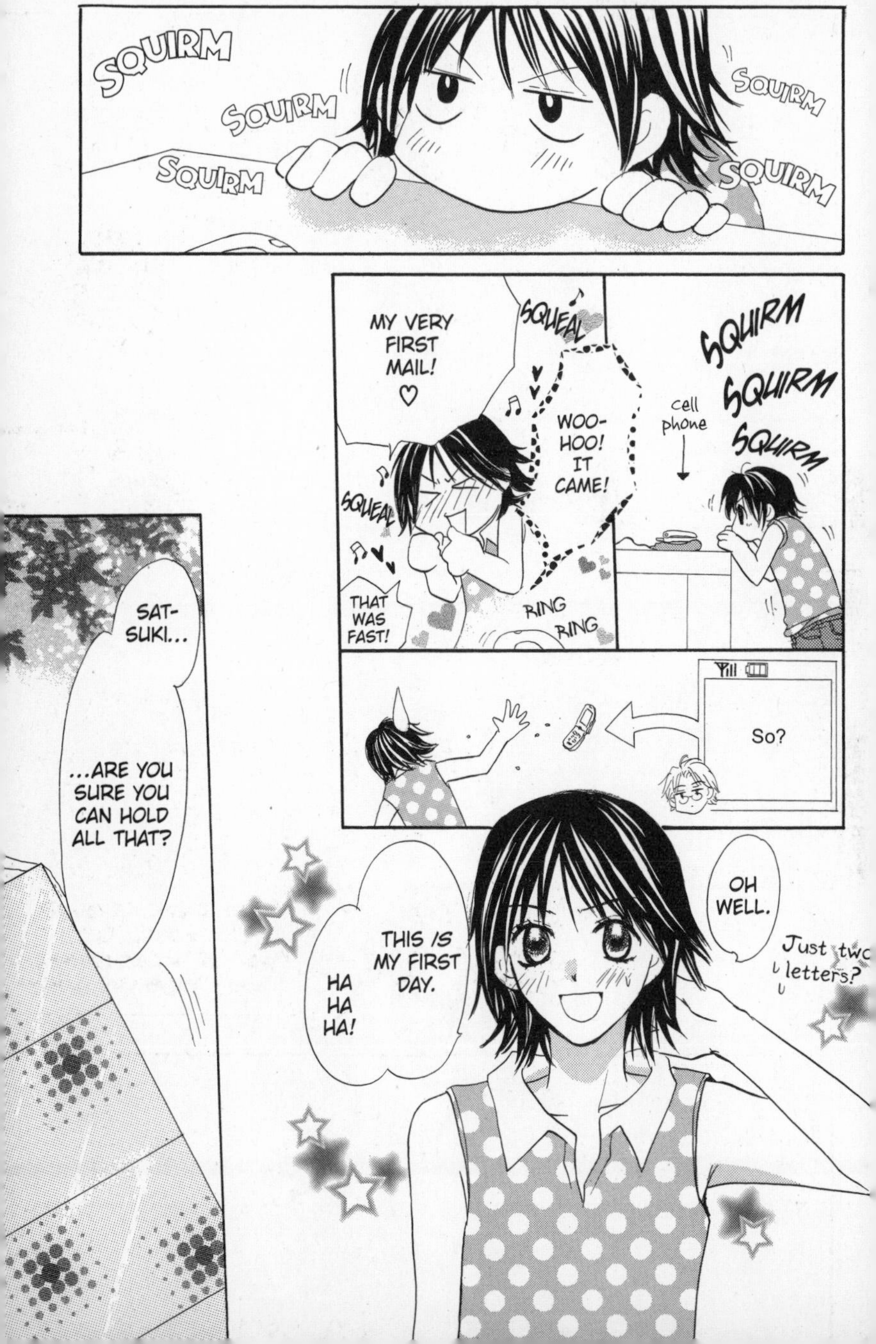
SQUIRM
SQUIRM
SQUIRM
SQUIRM
SQUIRM
SQUIRM
SQUIRM
SQUIRM
Cell phone
RING
RING
MY VERY FIRST MAIL! ♡
SQUEAL
WOO-HOO! IT CAME!
SQUEAL
THAT WAS FAST!
So?
OH WELL.
Just two letters?
THIS IS MY FIRST DAY.
HA HA HA!
SAT-SUKI...
...ARE YOU SURE YOU CAN HOLD ALL THAT?

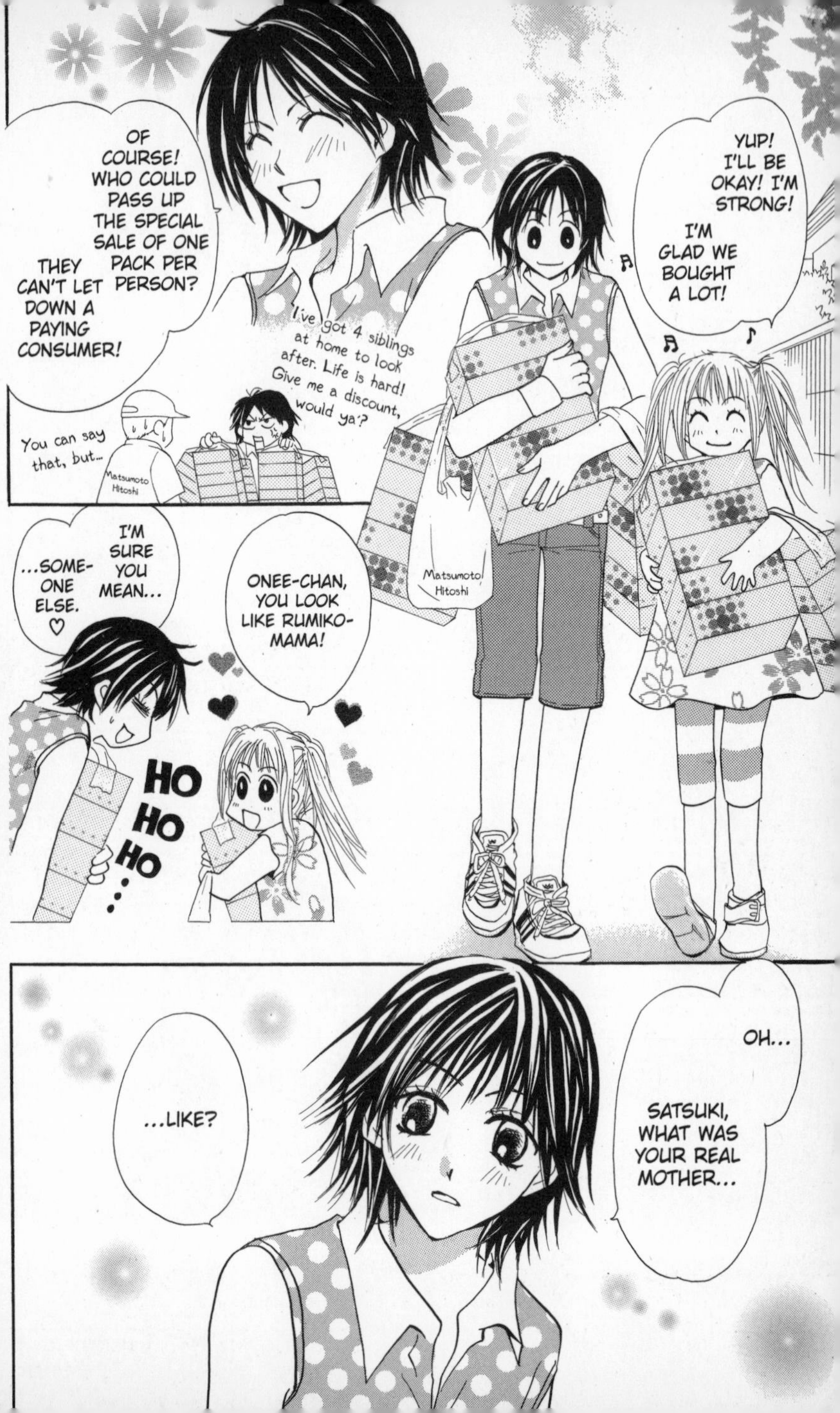
YUP! I'LL BE OKAY! I'M STRONG!
I'M GLAD WE BOUGHT A LOT!
Matsumoto Hitoshi
OF COURSE! WHO COULD PASS UP THE SPECIAL SALE OF ONE PACK PER PERSON?
THEY CAN'T LET DOWN A PAYING CONSUMER!
I've got 4 siblings at home to look after. Life is hard! Give me a discount, would ya'?
You can say that, but...
Matsumoto Hitoshi
ONEE-CHAN, YOU LOOK LIKE RUMIKO-MAMA!
I'M SURE YOU MEAN...
...SOME-ONE ELSE. ♡
HO HO HO...
OH...
SATSUKI, WHAT WAS YOUR REAL MOTHER...
...LIKE?

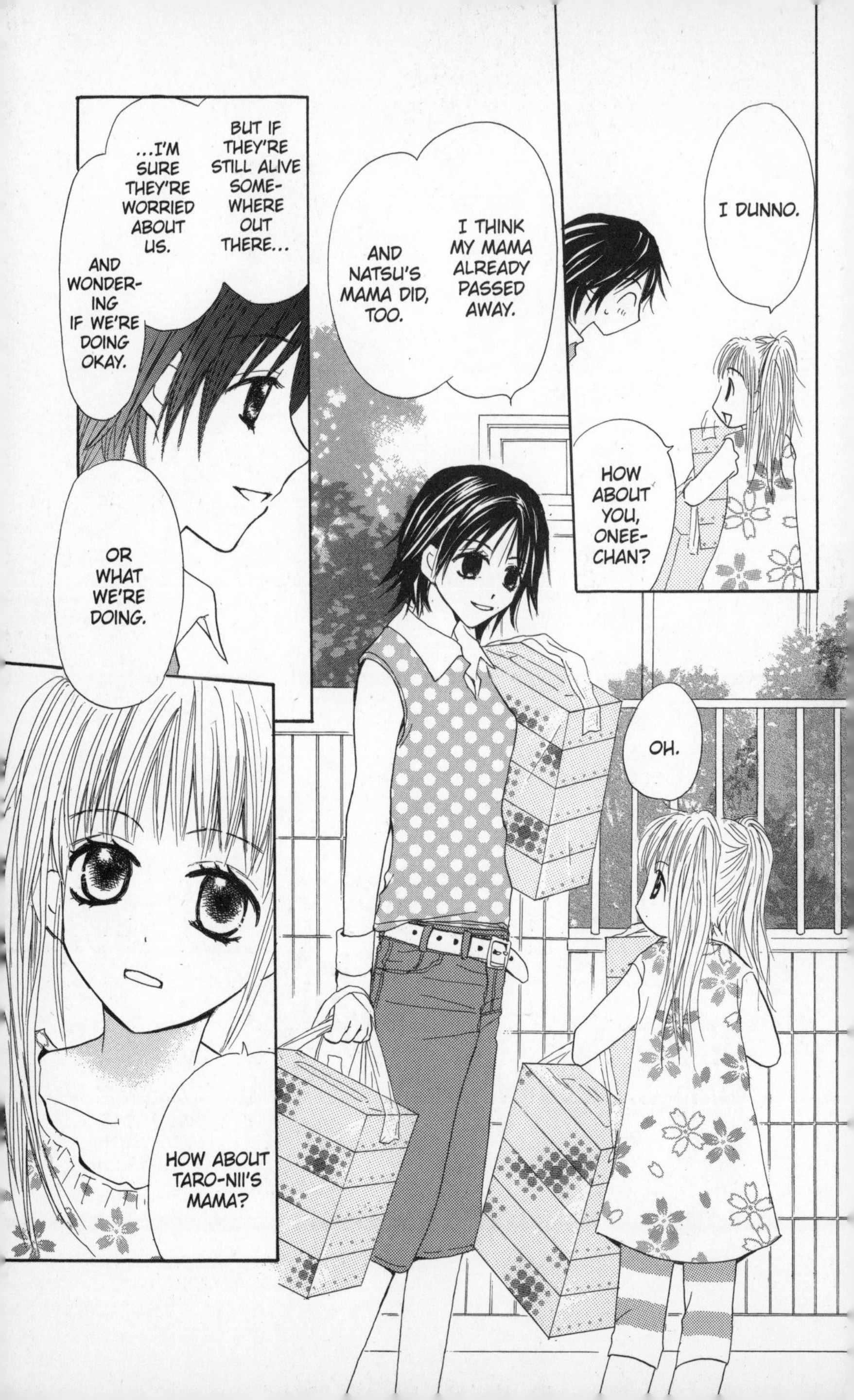
I DUNNO.
HOW ABOUT YOU, ONEE-CHAN?
I THINK MY MAMA ALREADY PASSED AWAY.
AND NATSU'S MAMA DID, TOO.
OH.
BUT IF THEY'RE STILL ALIVE SOME-WHERE OUT THERE...
...I'M SURE THEY'RE WORRIED ABOUT US.
AND WONDER-ING IF WE'RE DOING OKAY.
OR WHAT WE'RE DOING.
HOW ABOUT TARO-NII'S MAMA?

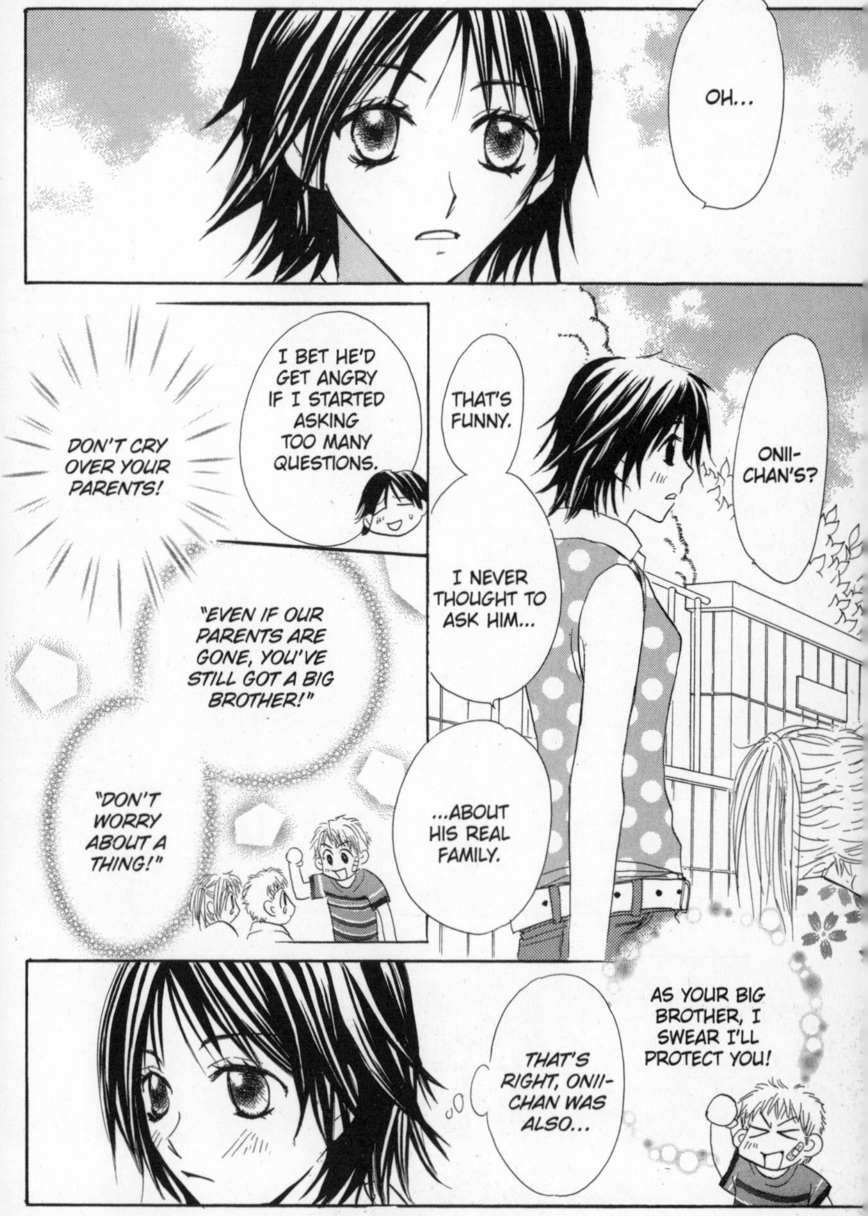
OH...
ONII-CHAN'S?
THAT'S FUNNY.
I NEVER THOUGHT TO ASK HIM...
...ABOUT HIS REAL FAMILY.
I BET HE'D GET ANGRY IF I STARTED ASKING TOO MANY QUESTIONS.
DON'T CRY OVER YOUR PARENTS!
"EVEN IF OUR PARENTS ARE GONE, YOU'VE STILL GOT A BIG BROTHER!"
"DON'T WORRY ABOUT A THING!"
AS YOUR BIG BROTHER, I SWEAR I'LL PROTECT YOU!
THAT'S RIGHT, ONII-CHAN WAS ALSO...

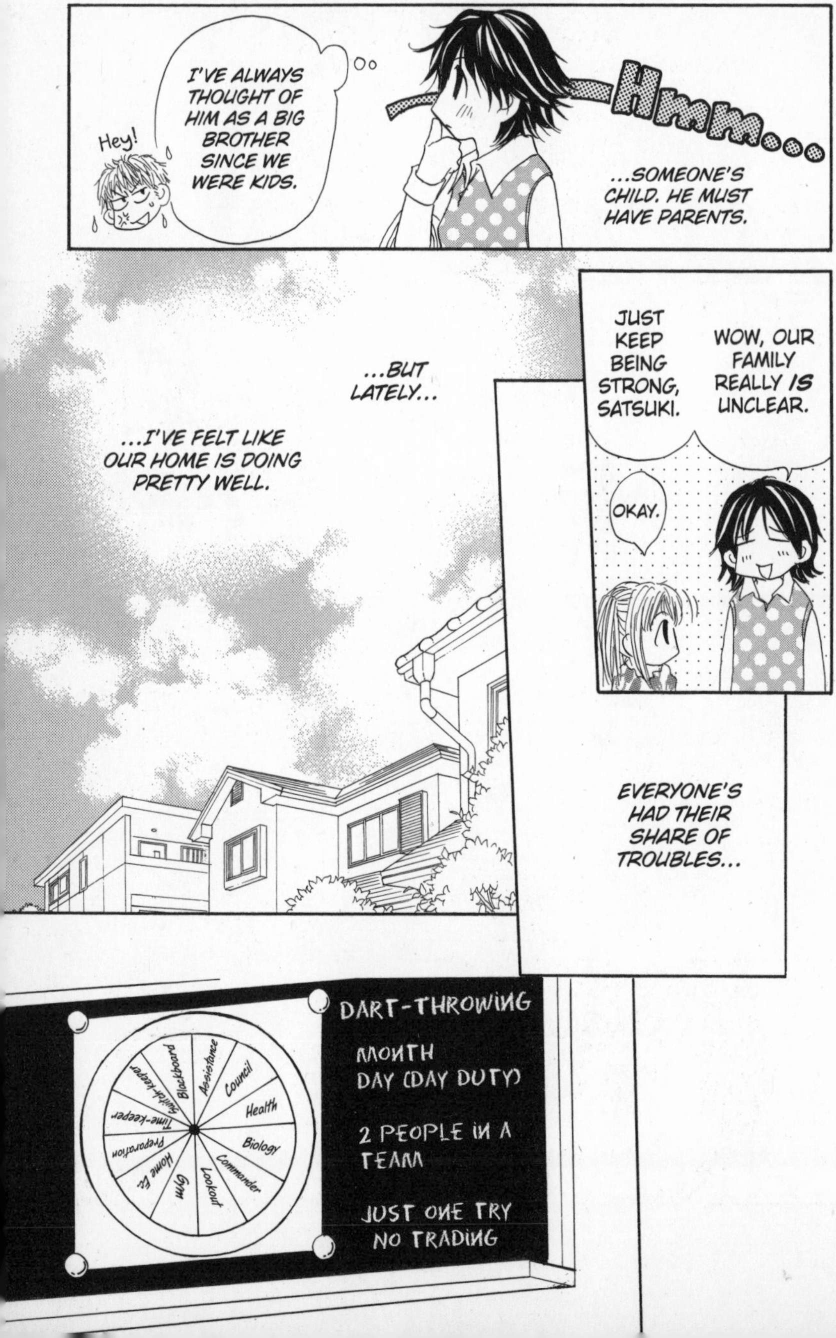
Hmmm...
...SOMEONE'S CHILD. HE MUST HAVE PARENTS.
I'VE ALWAYS THOUGHT OF HIM AS A BIG BROTHER SINCE WE WERE KIDS.
Hey!
WOW, OUR FAMILY REALLY IS UNCLEAR.
JUST KEEP BEING STRONG, SATSUKI.
OKAY.
EVERYONE'S HAD THEIR SHARE OF TROUBLES...
...BUT LATELY...
...I'VE FELT LIKE OUR HOME IS DOING PRETTY WELL.
DART-THROWING
MONTH
DAY (DAY DUTY)
2 PEOPLE IN A TEAM
JUST ONE TRY
NO TRADING
Blackboard
Assistance
Council
Health
Biology
Commander
Lookout
Gym
Home Ec
Preparation
Time-keeper
Switch-keeper

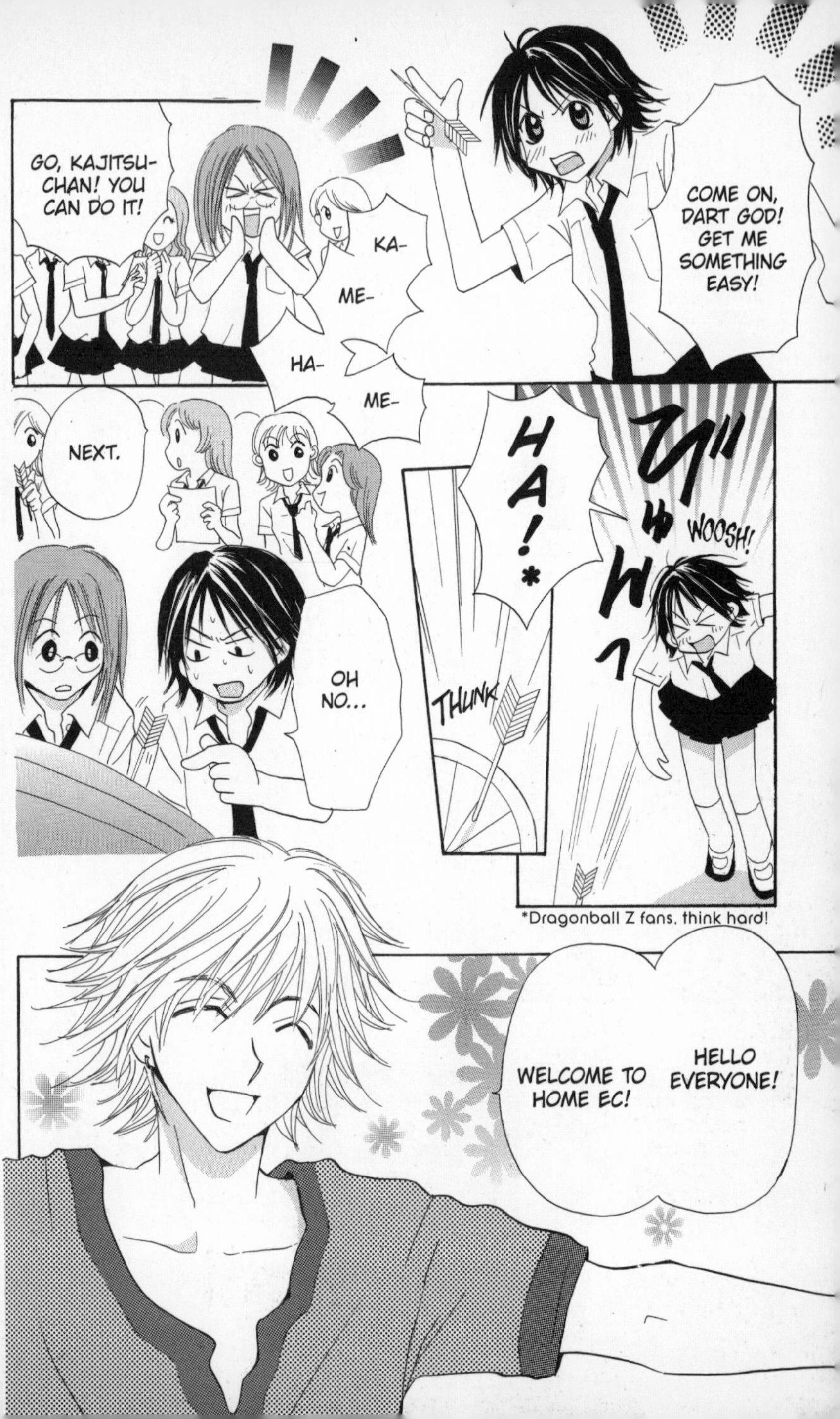
COME ON, DART GOD! GET ME SOMETHING EASY!
GO, KAJITSU-CHAN! YOU CAN DO IT!
KA-
ME-
HA-
ME-
HA!*
びゅん
WOOSH!
THUNK
NEXT.
OH NO...
HELLO EVERYONE!
WELCOME TO HOME EC!

*Dragonball Z fans, think hard!

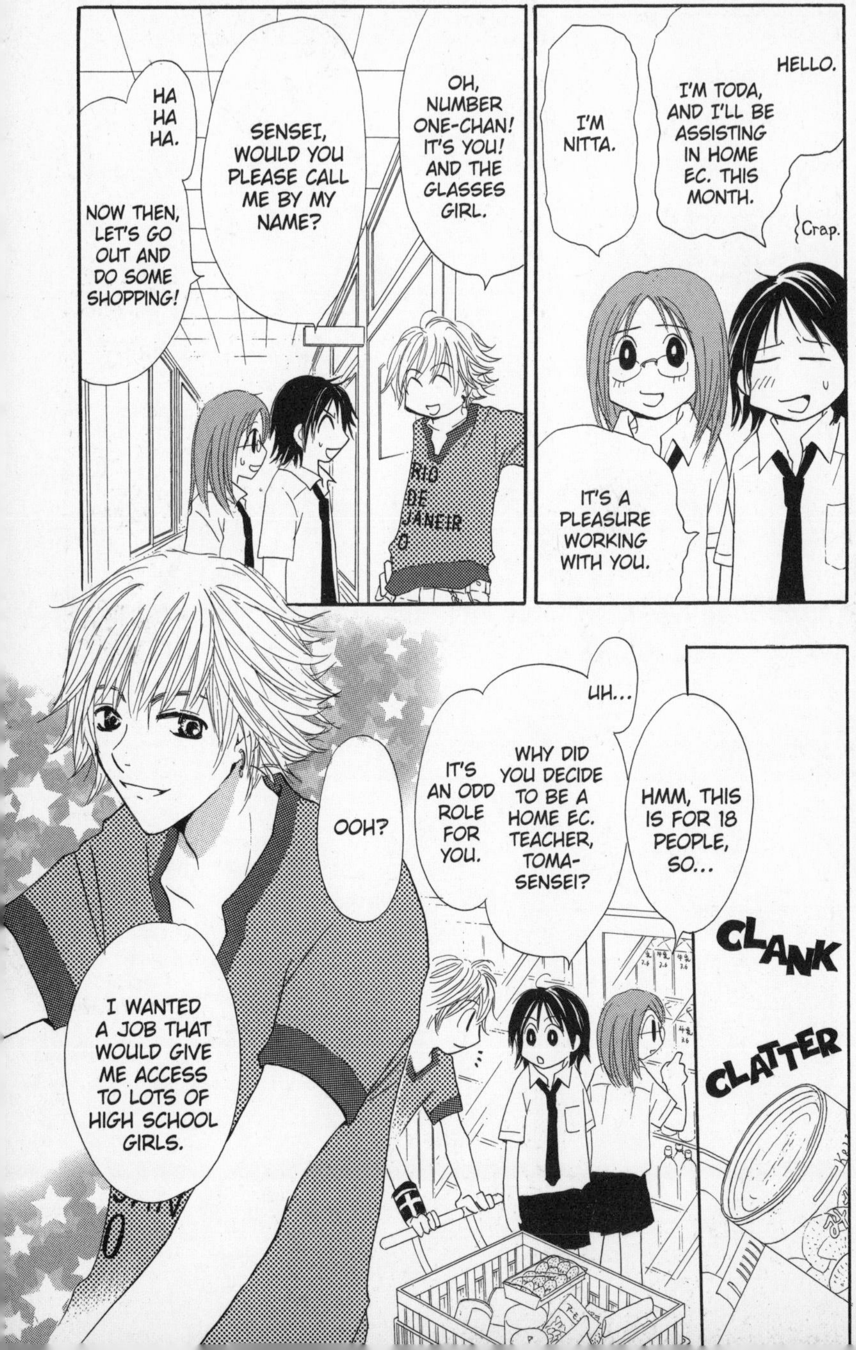
HELLO.
I'M TODA, AND I'LL BE ASSISTING IN HOME EC. THIS MONTH.
Crap.
I'M NITTA.
IT'S A PLEASURE WORKING WITH YOU.
OH, NUMBER ONE-CHAN! IT'S YOU! AND THE GLASSES GIRL.
SENSEI, WOULD YOU PLEASE CALL ME BY MY NAME?
HA HA HA.
NOW THEN, LET'S GO OUT AND DO SOME SHOPPING!
HMM, THIS IS FOR 18 PEOPLE, SO...
CLANK
CLATTER
UH...
WHY DID YOU DECIDE TO BE A HOME EC. TEACHER, TOMA-SENSEI?
IT'S AN ODD ROLE FOR YOU.
OOH?
I WANTED A JOB THAT WOULD GIVE ME ACCESS TO LOTS OF HIGH SCHOOL GIRLS.

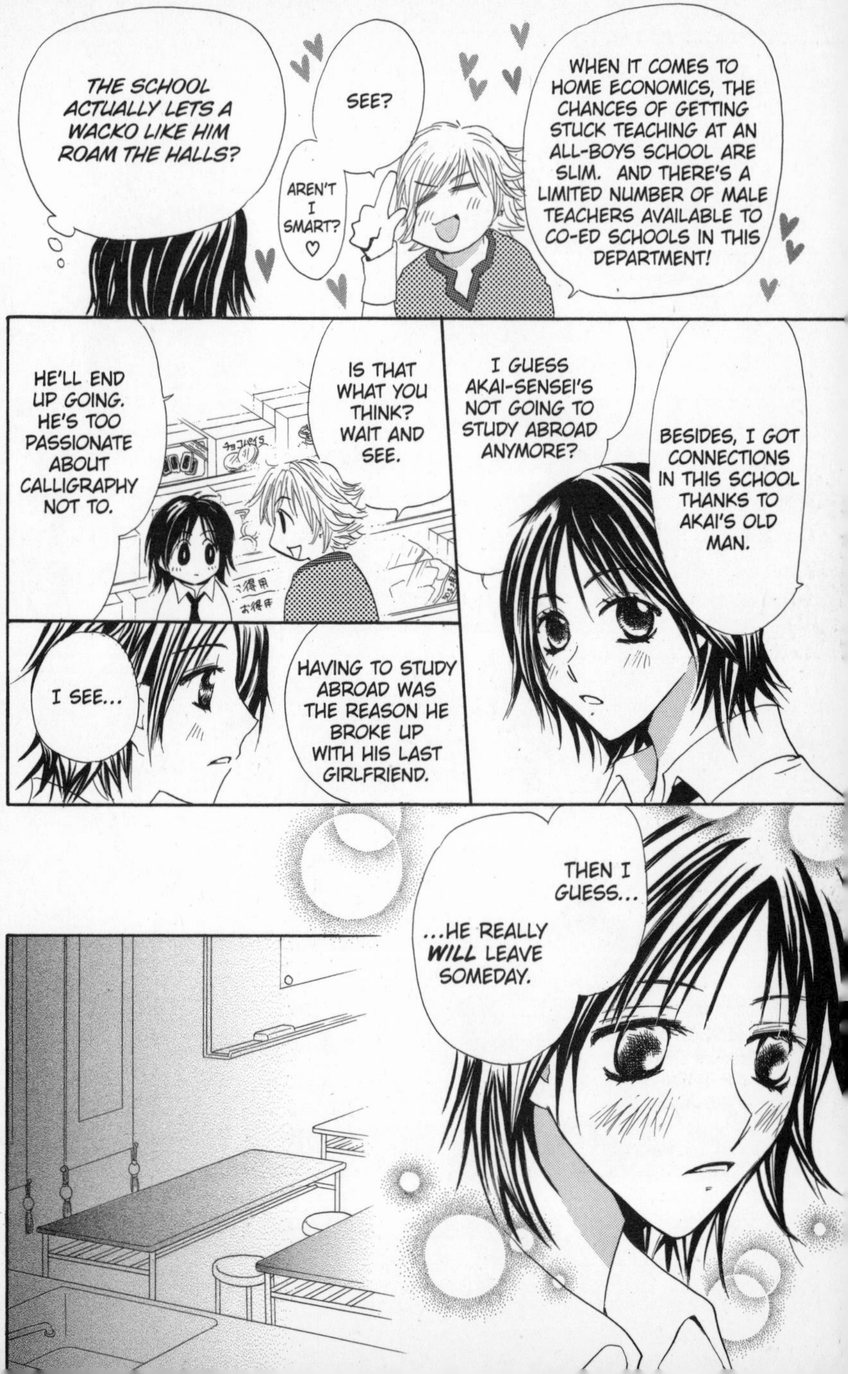
WHEN IT COMES TO HOME ECONOMICS, THE CHANCES OF GETTING STUCK TEACHING AT AN ALL-BOYS SCHOOL ARE SLIM. AND THERE'S A LIMITED NUMBER OF MALE TEACHERS AVAILABLE TO CO-ED SCHOOLS IN THIS DEPARTMENT!
SEE?
AREN'T I SMART? ♡
THE SCHOOL ACTUALLY LETS A WACKO LIKE HIM ROAM THE HALLS?
BESIDES, I GOT CONNECTIONS IN THIS SCHOOL THANKS TO AKAI'S OLD MAN.
I GUESS AKAI-SENSEI'S NOT GOING TO STUDY ABROAD ANYMORE?
IS THAT WHAT YOU THINK? WAIT AND SEE.
HE'LL END UP GOING. HE'S TOO PASSIONATE ABOUT CALLIGRAPHY NOT TO.
HAVING TO STUDY ABROAD WAS THE REASON HE BROKE UP WITH HIS LAST GIRLFRIEND.
I SEE...
THEN I GUESS...
...HE REALLY *WILL* LEAVE SOMEDAY.

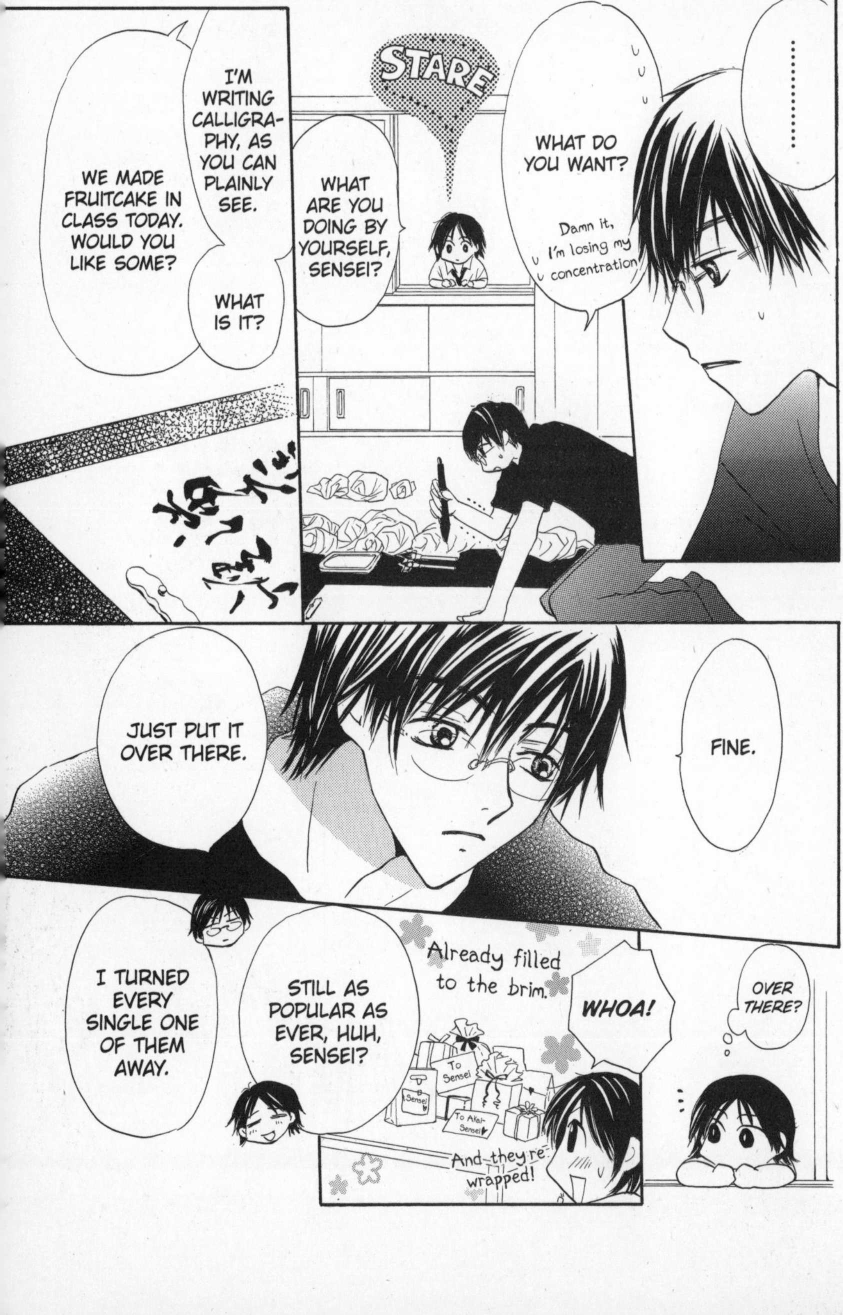
......
WHAT DO YOU WANT?
Damn it, I'm losing my concentration
STARE
WHAT ARE YOU DOING BY YOURSELF, SENSEI?
I'M WRITING CALLIGRAPHY, AS YOU CAN PLAINLY SEE.
WHAT IS IT?
WE MADE FRUITCAKE IN CLASS TODAY. WOULD YOU LIKE SOME?
FINE.
JUST PUT IT OVER THERE.
OVER THERE?
WHOA!
Already filled to the brim.
To Sensei
Sensei
To Akai-Sensei
And they're wrapped!
STILL AS POPULAR AS EVER, HUH, SENSEI?
I TURNED EVERY SINGLE ONE OF THEM AWAY.

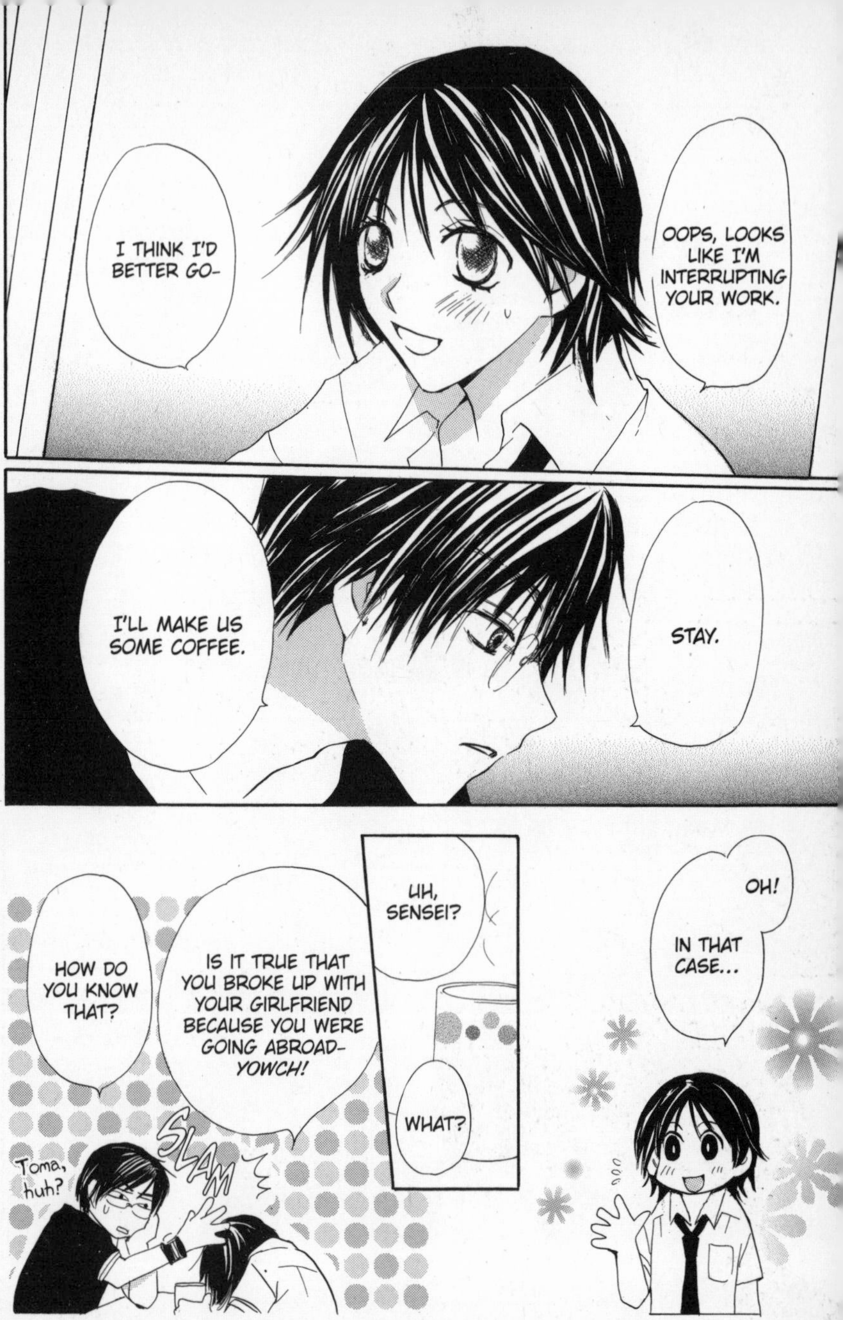
OOPS, LOOKS LIKE I'M INTERRUPTING YOUR WORK.
I THINK I'D BETTER GO-
STAY.
I'LL MAKE US SOME COFFEE.
OH!
IN THAT CASE...
UH, SENSEI?
WHAT?
IS IT TRUE THAT YOU BROKE UP WITH YOUR GIRLFRIEND BECAUSE YOU WERE GOING ABROAD-YOWCH!
SLAM
HOW DO YOU KNOW THAT?
Toma, huh?

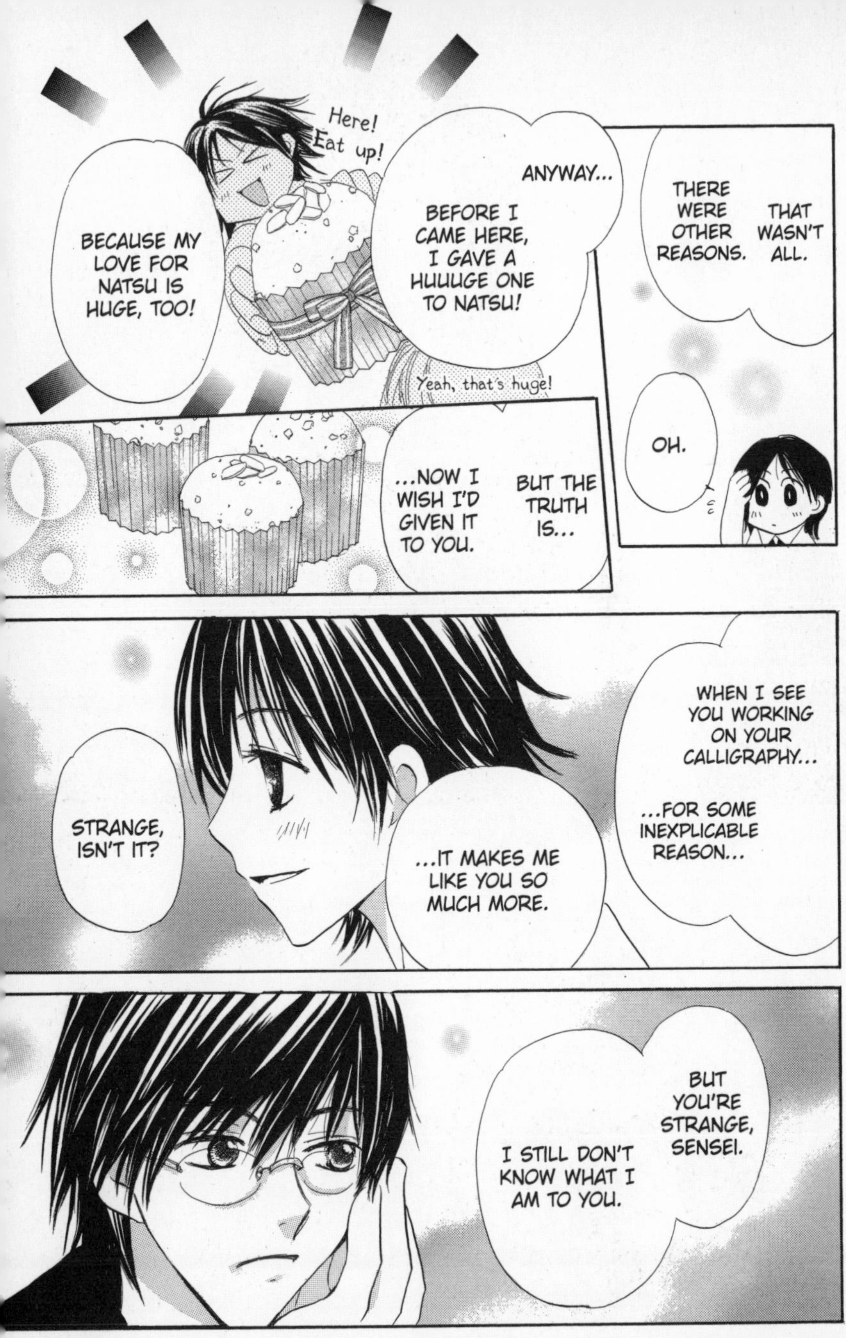
THAT WASN'T ALL.
THERE WERE OTHER REASONS.
OH.
ANYWAY...
BEFORE I CAME HERE, I GAVE A HUUUGE ONE TO NATSU!
Here! Eat up!
BECAUSE MY LOVE FOR NATSU IS HUGE, TOO!
Yeah, that's huge!
BUT THE TRUTH IS...
...NOW I WISH I'D GIVEN IT TO YOU.
WHEN I SEE YOU WORKING ON YOUR CALLIGRAPHY...
...FOR SOME INEXPLICABLE REASON...
...IT MAKES ME LIKE YOU SO MUCH MORE.
STRANGE, ISN'T IT?
BUT YOU'RE STRANGE, SENSEI.
I STILL DON'T KNOW WHAT I AM TO YOU.

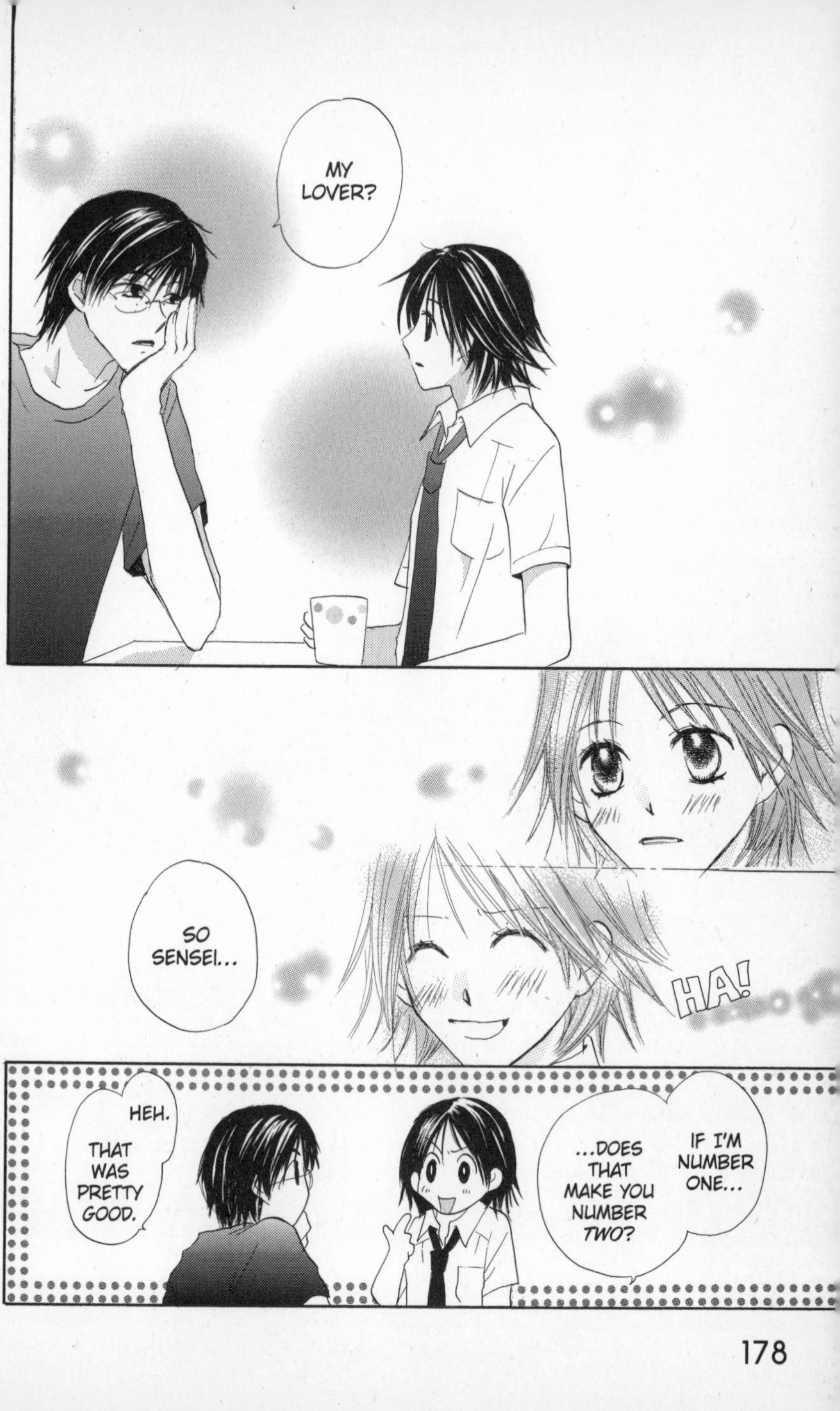
MY LOVER?
HA!
SO SENSEI...
IF I'M NUMBER ONE...
...DOES THAT MAKE YOU NUMBER *TWO*?
HEH.
THAT WAS PRETTY GOOD.

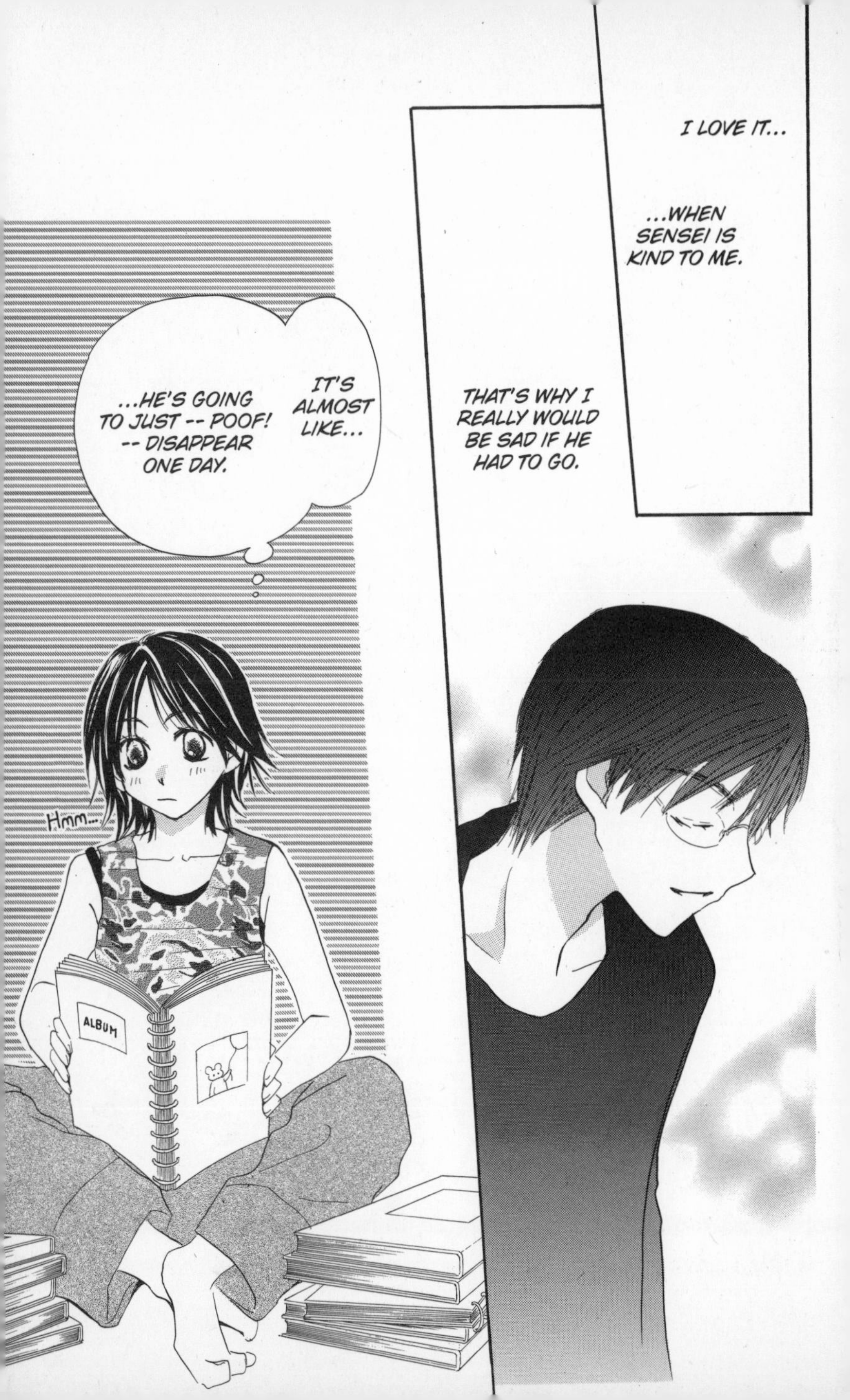
I LOVE IT...
...WHEN SENSEI IS KIND TO ME.
THAT'S WHY I REALLY WOULD BE SAD IF HE HAD TO GO.
IT'S ALMOST LIKE...
...HE'S GOING TO JUST -- POOF! -- DISAPPEAR ONE DAY.
Hmm...
ALBUM

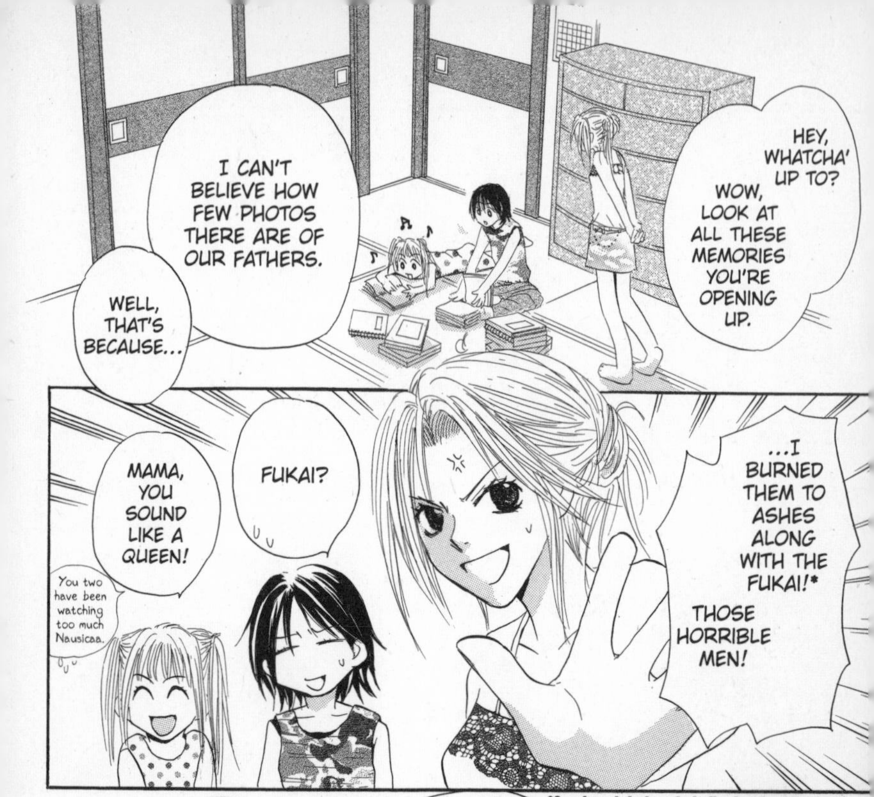
HEY, WHATCHA' UP TO?
WOW, LOOK AT ALL THESE MEMORIES YOU'RE OPENING UP.
I CAN'T BELIEVE HOW FEW PHOTOS THERE ARE OF OUR FATHERS.
WELL, THAT'S BECAUSE...
...I BURNED THEM TO ASHES ALONG WITH THE FUKAI!*
THOSE HORRIBLE MEN!
FUKAI?
MAMA, YOU SOUND LIKE A QUEEN!
You two have been watching too much Nausicaa.

*See translator's note in the back of the book.

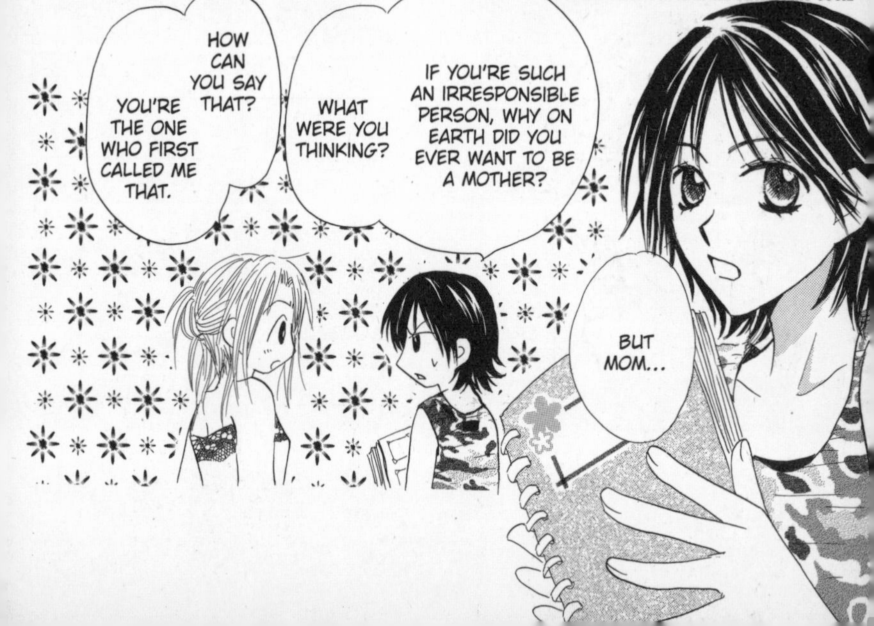
BUT MOM...
IF YOU'RE SUCH AN IRRESPONSIBLE PERSON, WHY ON EARTH DID YOU EVER WANT TO BE A MOTHER?
WHAT WERE YOU THINKING?
HOW CAN YOU SAY THAT?
YOU'RE THE ONE WHO FIRST CALLED ME THAT.

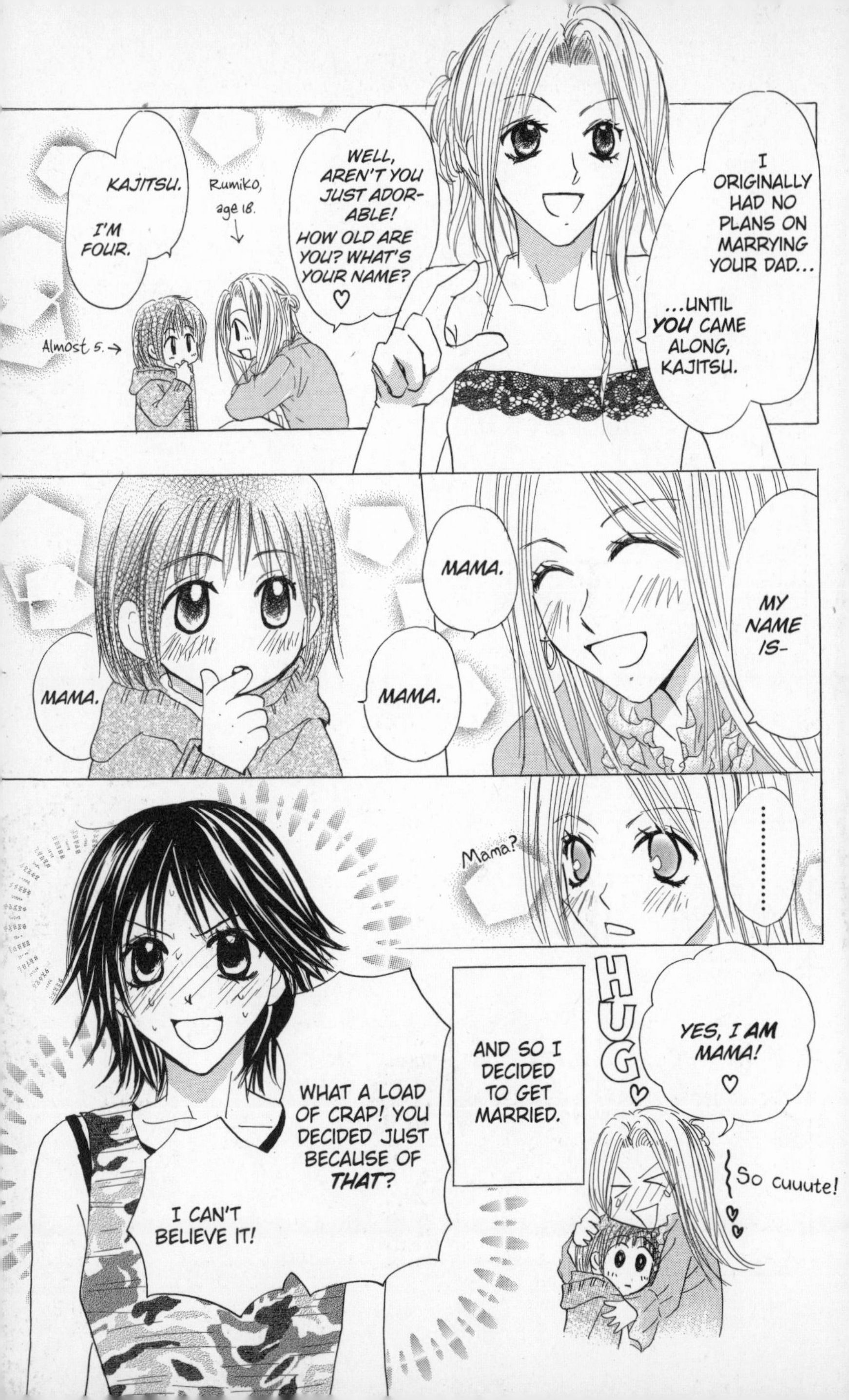

I ORIGINALLY HAD NO PLANS ON MARRYING YOUR DAD...
...UNTIL YOU CAME ALONG, KAJITSU.
WELL, AREN'T YOU JUST ADORABLE! HOW OLD ARE YOU? WHAT'S YOUR NAME? ♡
Rumiko, age 18.
KAJITSU.
I'M FOUR.
Almost 5.
MY NAME IS-
MAMA.
MAMA.
MAMA.
......
Mama?
HUG ♡
YES, I AM MAMA! ♡
So cuuute! ♡
AND SO I DECIDED TO GET MARRIED.
WHAT A LOAD OF CRAP! YOU DECIDED JUST BECAUSE OF THAT?
I CAN'T BELIEVE IT!

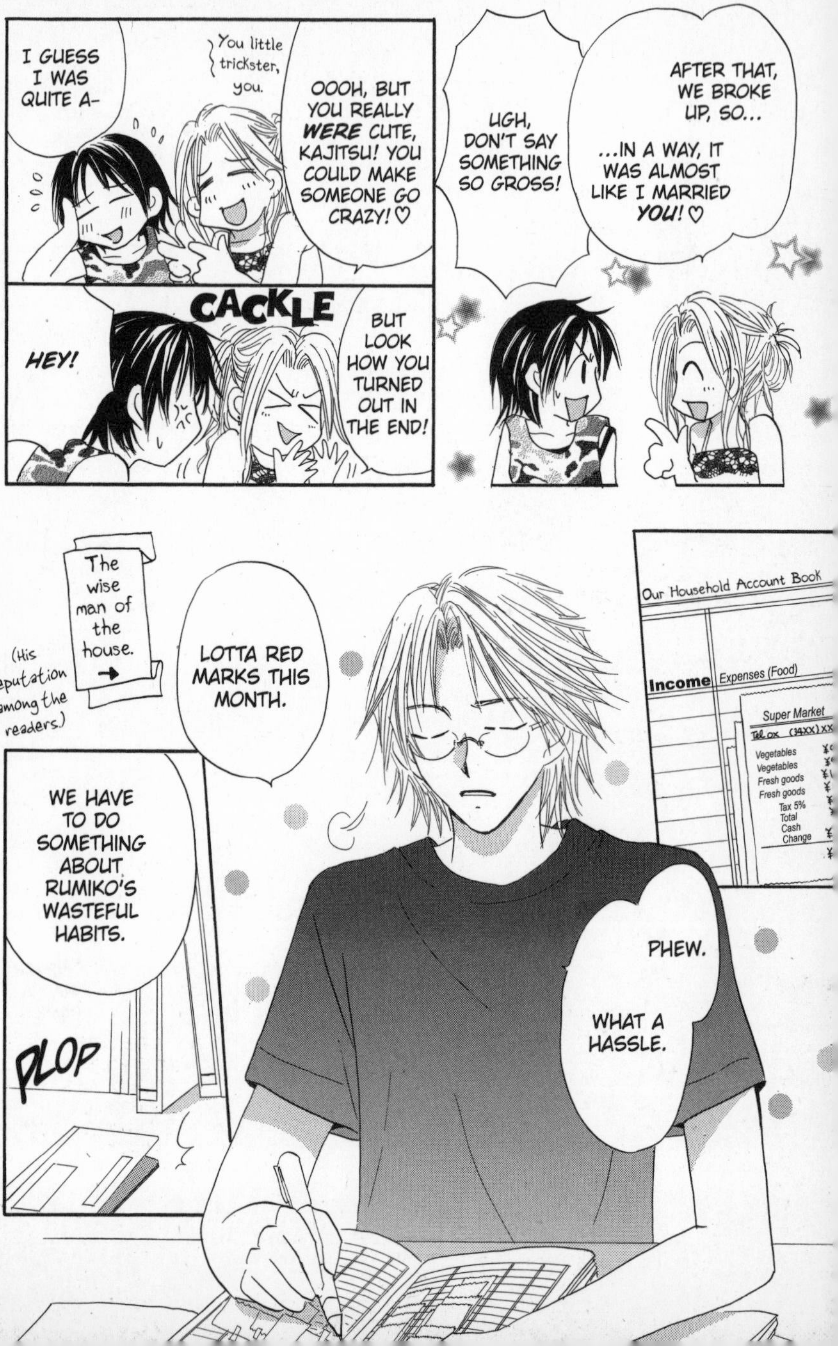
AFTER THAT, WE BROKE UP, SO...
...IN A WAY, IT WAS ALMOST LIKE I MARRIED *YOU!* ♡
UGH, DON'T SAY SOMETHING SO GROSS!
I GUESS I WAS QUITE A-
OOOH, BUT YOU REALLY *WERE* CUTE, KAJITSU! YOU COULD MAKE SOMEONE GO CRAZY! ♡
You little trickster, you.
BUT LOOK HOW YOU TURNED OUT IN THE END!
CACKLE
HEY!
Our Household Account Book
Income
Expenses (Food)
Super Market
Vegetables
Vegetables
Fresh goods
Fresh goods
Tax 5%
Total
Cash
Change
LOTTA RED MARKS THIS MONTH.
The wise man of the house.
(His reputation among the readers.)
PHEW.
WHAT A HASSLE.
WE HAVE TO DO SOMETHING ABOUT RUMIKO'S WASTEFUL HABITS.
PLOP

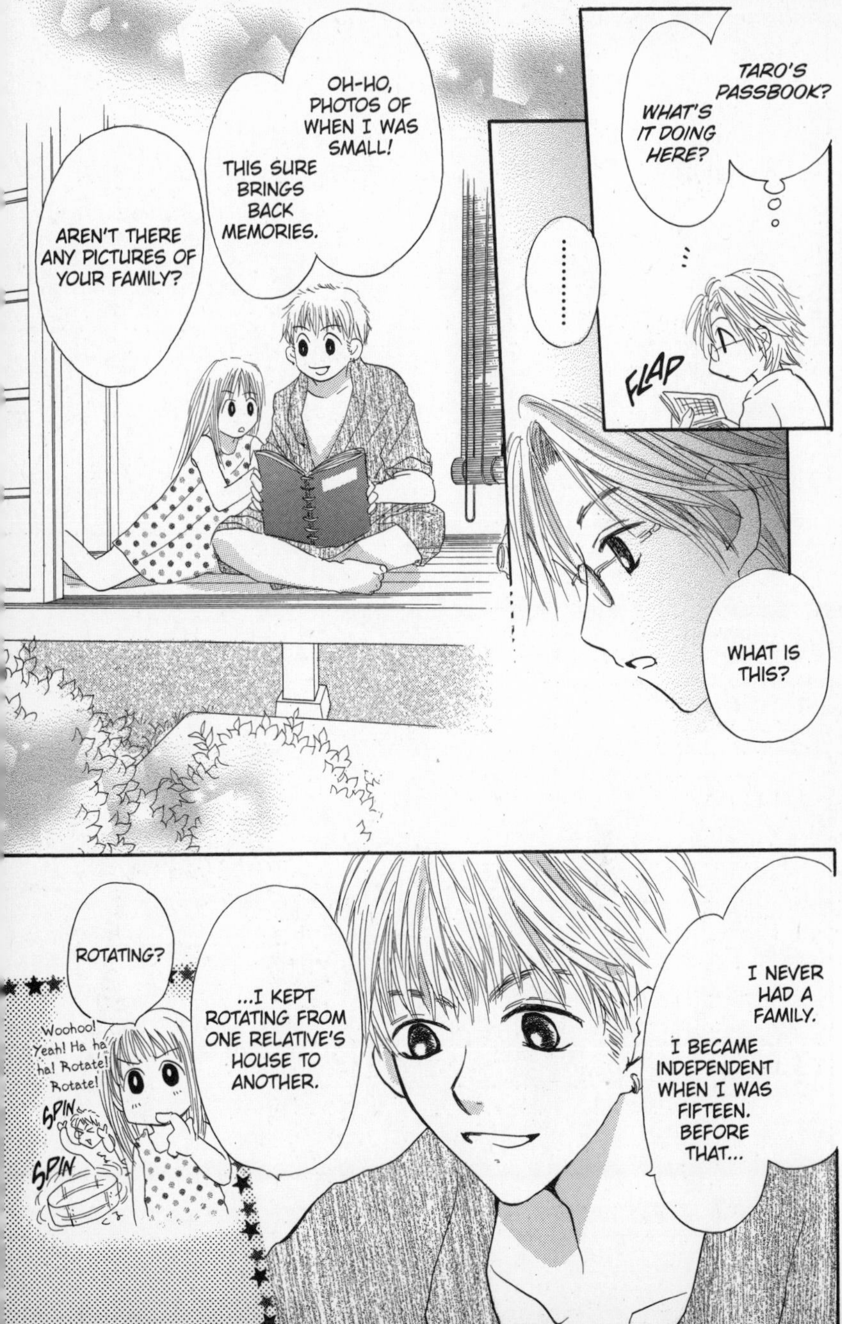
TARO'S PASSBOOK? WHAT'S IT DOING HERE?
...
FLAP
......
WHAT IS THIS?
OH-HO, PHOTOS OF WHEN I WAS SMALL!
THIS SURE BRINGS BACK MEMORIES.
AREN'T THERE ANY PICTURES OF YOUR FAMILY?
I NEVER HAD A FAMILY.
I BECAME INDEPENDENT WHEN I WAS FIFTEEN. BEFORE THAT...
...I KEPT ROTATING FROM ONE RELATIVE'S HOUSE TO ANOTHER.
ROTATING?
Woohoo! Yeah! Ha ha ha! Rotate! Rotate!
SPIN
SPIN

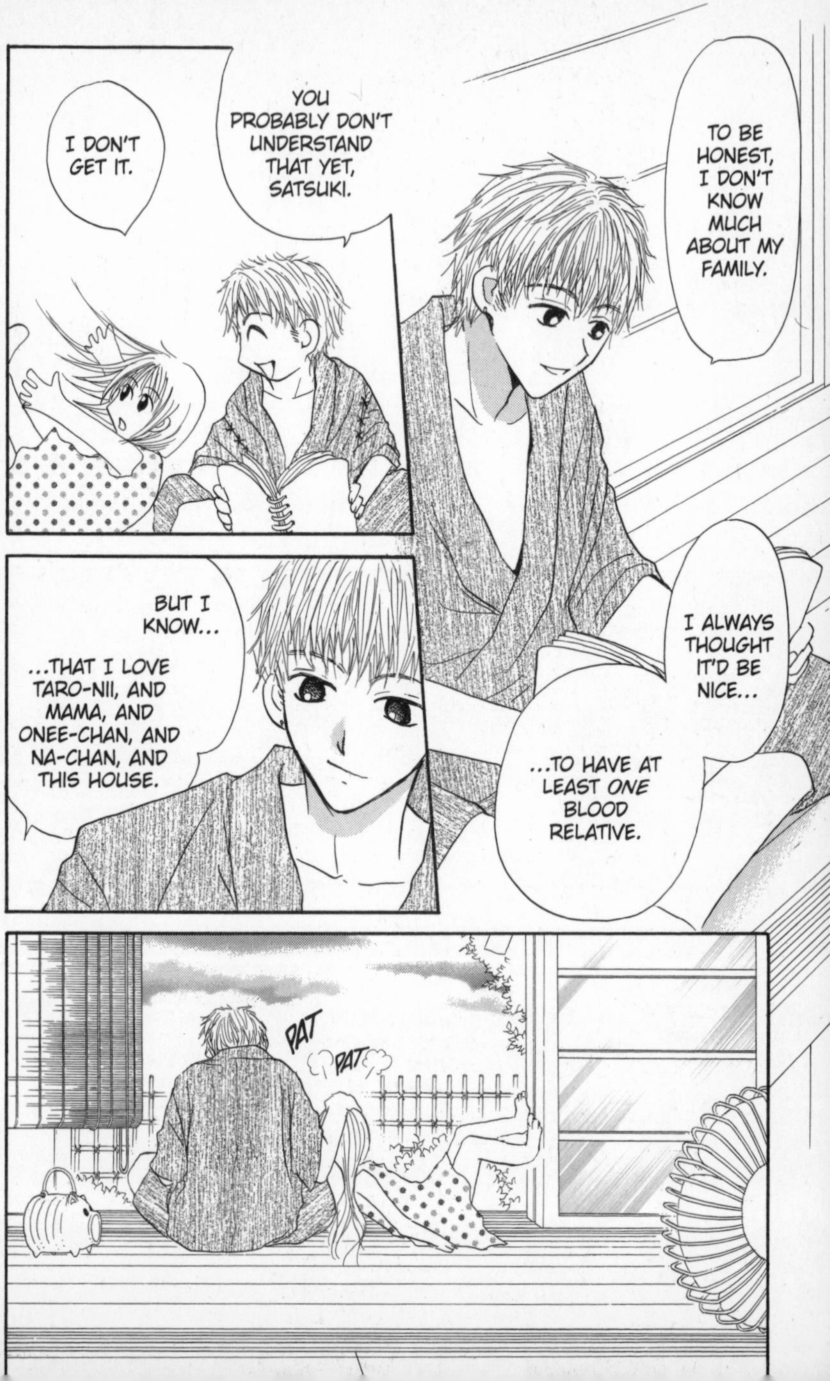

TO BE HONEST, I DON'T KNOW MUCH ABOUT MY FAMILY.
I ALWAYS THOUGHT IT'D BE NICE...
...TO HAVE AT LEAST *ONE* BLOOD RELATIVE.
YOU PROBABLY DON'T UNDERSTAND THAT YET, SATSUKI.
I DON'T GET IT.
BUT I KNOW...
...THAT I LOVE TARO-NII, AND MAMA, AND ONEE-CHAN, AND NA-CHAN, AND THIS HOUSE.
PAT
PAT

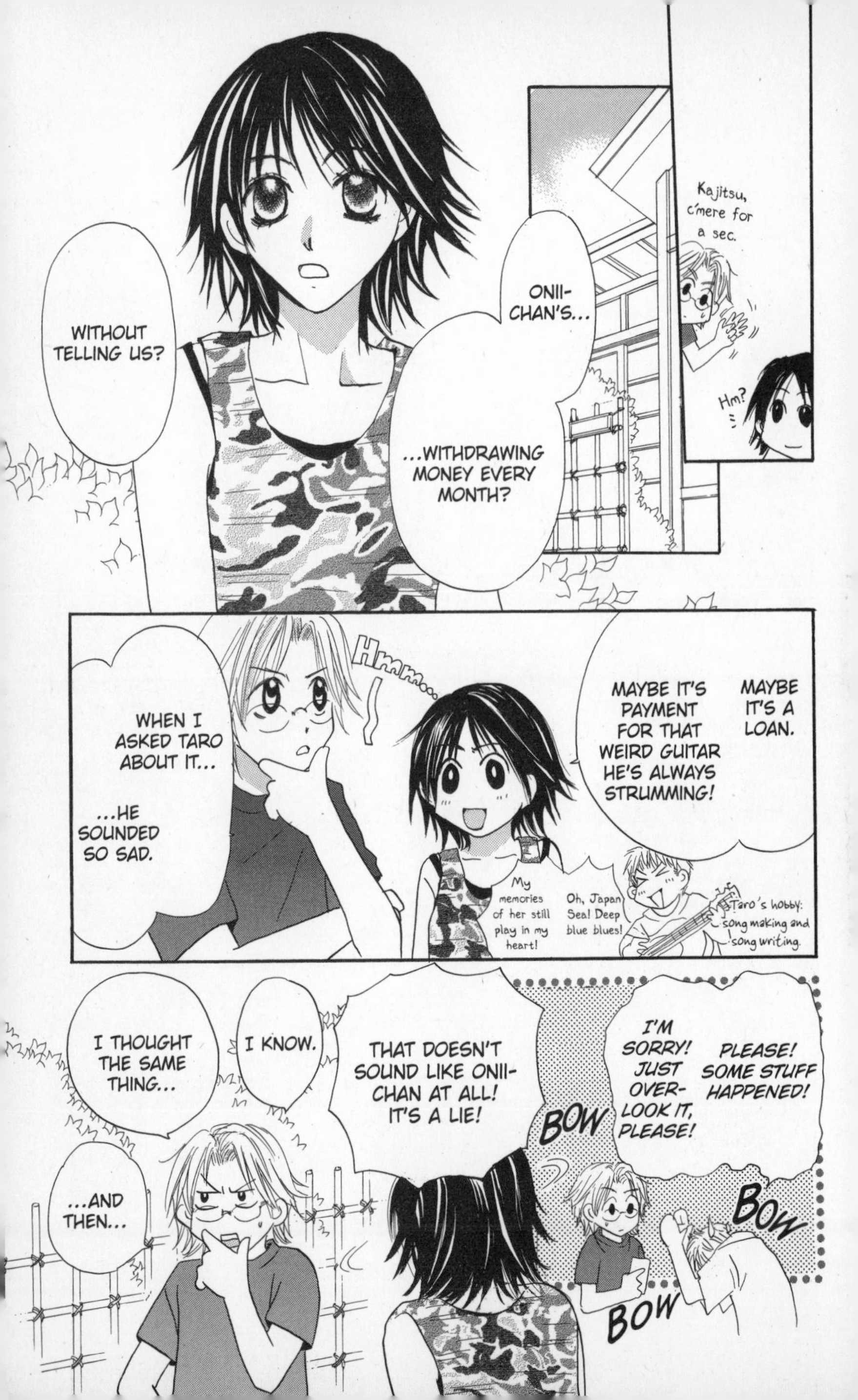
Kajitsu, c'mere for a sec.
Hm?
ONII-CHAN'S...
...WITHDRAWING MONEY EVERY MONTH?
WITHOUT TELLING US?
MAYBE IT'S A LOAN.
MAYBE IT'S PAYMENT FOR THAT WEIRD GUITAR HE'S ALWAYS STRUMMING!
Hmm...
WHEN I ASKED TARO ABOUT IT...
...HE SOUNDED SO SAD.
Taro's hobby: song making and song writing.
Oh, Japan Sea! Deep blue blues!
My memories of her still play in my heart!
PLEASE! SOME STUFF HAPPENED!
I'M SORRY! JUST OVER-LOOK IT, PLEASE!
BOW
BOW
BOW
THAT DOESN'T SOUND LIKE ONII-CHAN AT ALL! IT'S A LIE!
I KNOW.
I THOUGHT THE SAME THING...
...AND THEN...

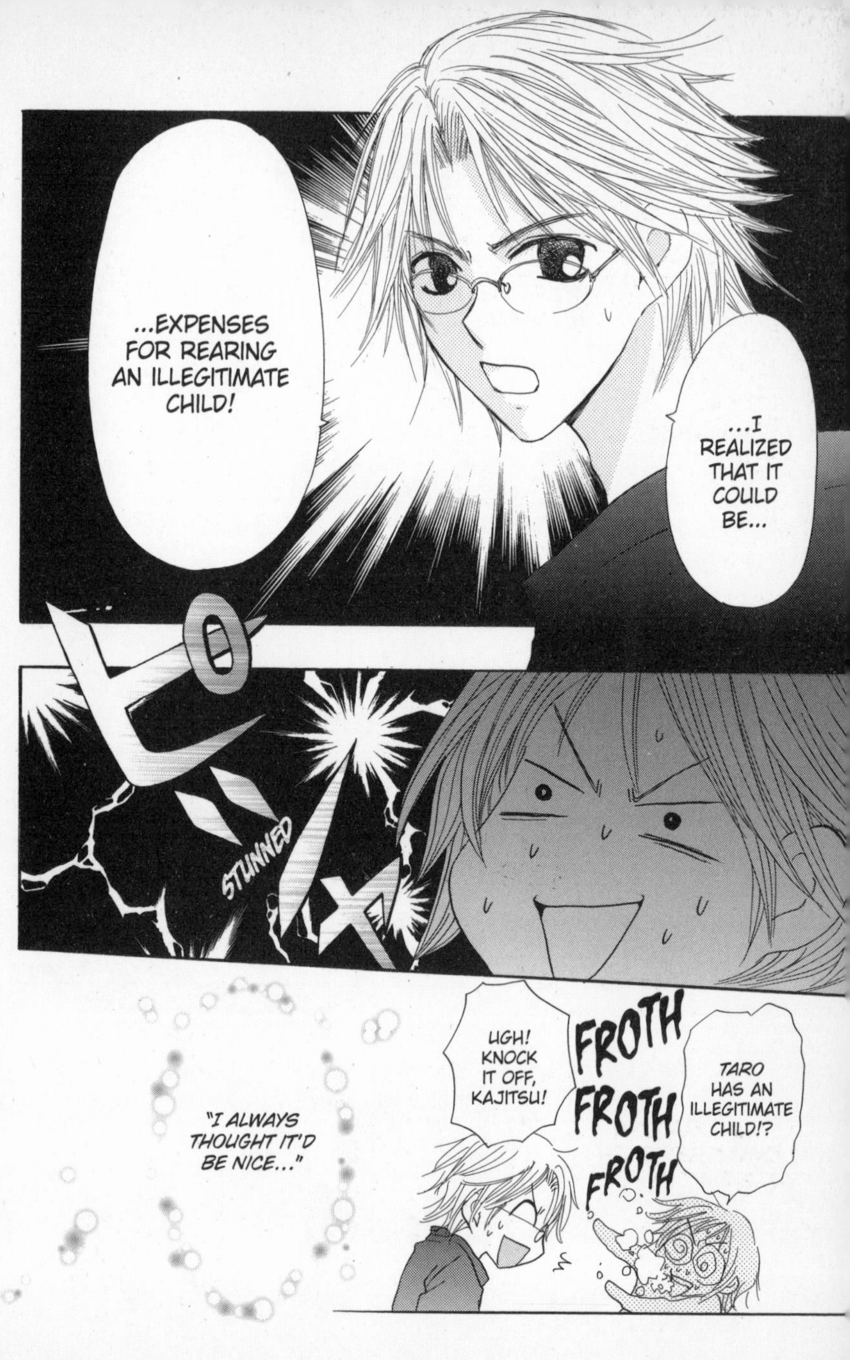
...I REALIZED THAT IT COULD BE...
...EXPENSES FOR REARING AN ILLEGITIMATE CHILD!
STUNNED
TARO HAS AN ILLEGITIMATE CHILD!?
FROTH FROTH FROTH
UGH! KNOCK IT OFF, KAJITSU!
"I ALWAYS THOUGHT IT'D BE NICE..."

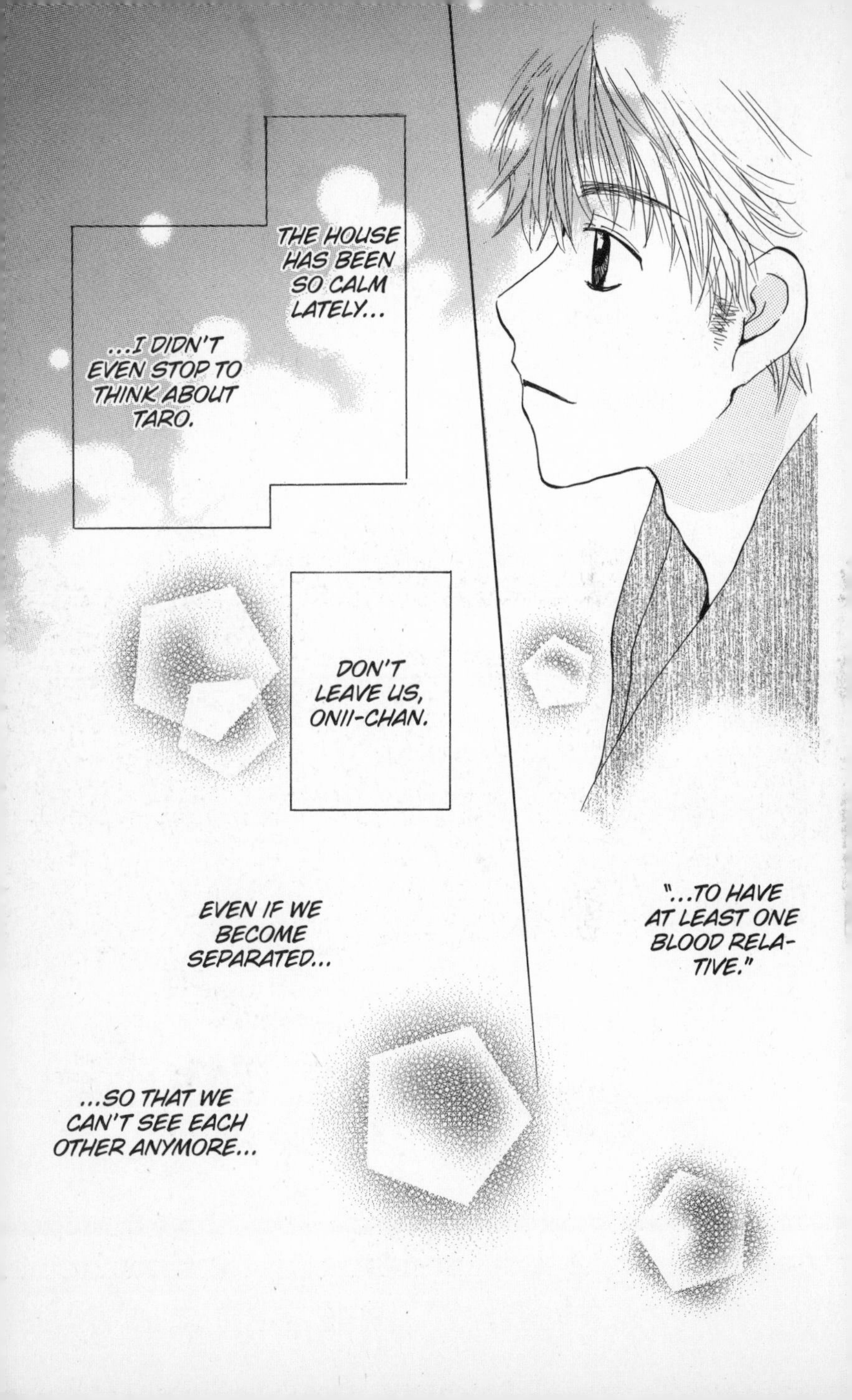
"...TO HAVE AT LEAST ONE BLOOD RELA-TIVE."
THE HOUSE HAS BEEN SO CALM LATELY...
...I DIDN'T EVEN STOP TO THINK ABOUT TARO.
DON'T LEAVE US, ONII-CHAN.
EVEN IF WE BECOME SEPARATED...
...SO THAT WE CAN'T SEE EACH OTHER ANYMORE...

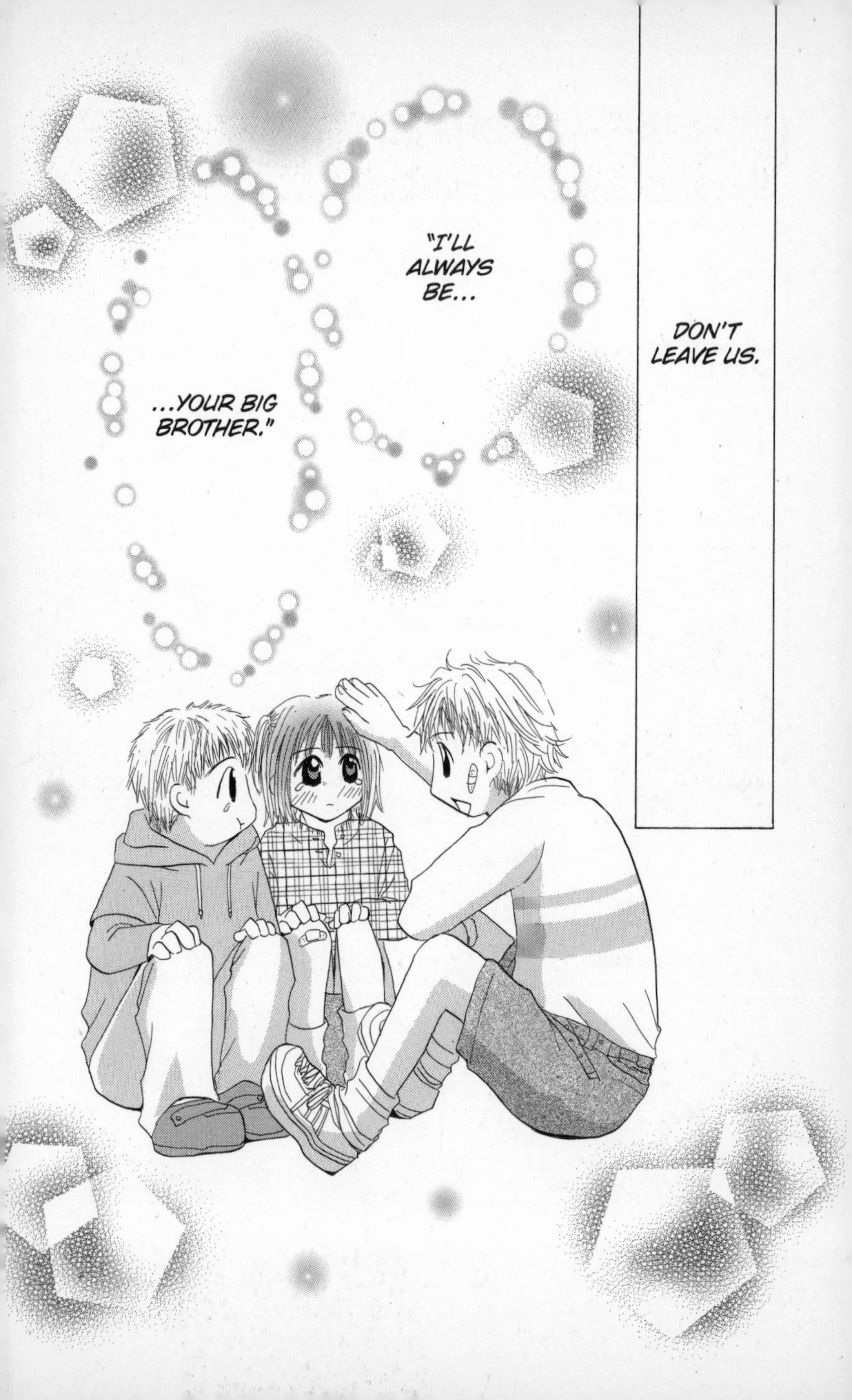
DON'T LEAVE US.
"I'LL ALWAYS BE...
...YOUR BIG BROTHER."

Satsuki-chan's Record of Struggles 2

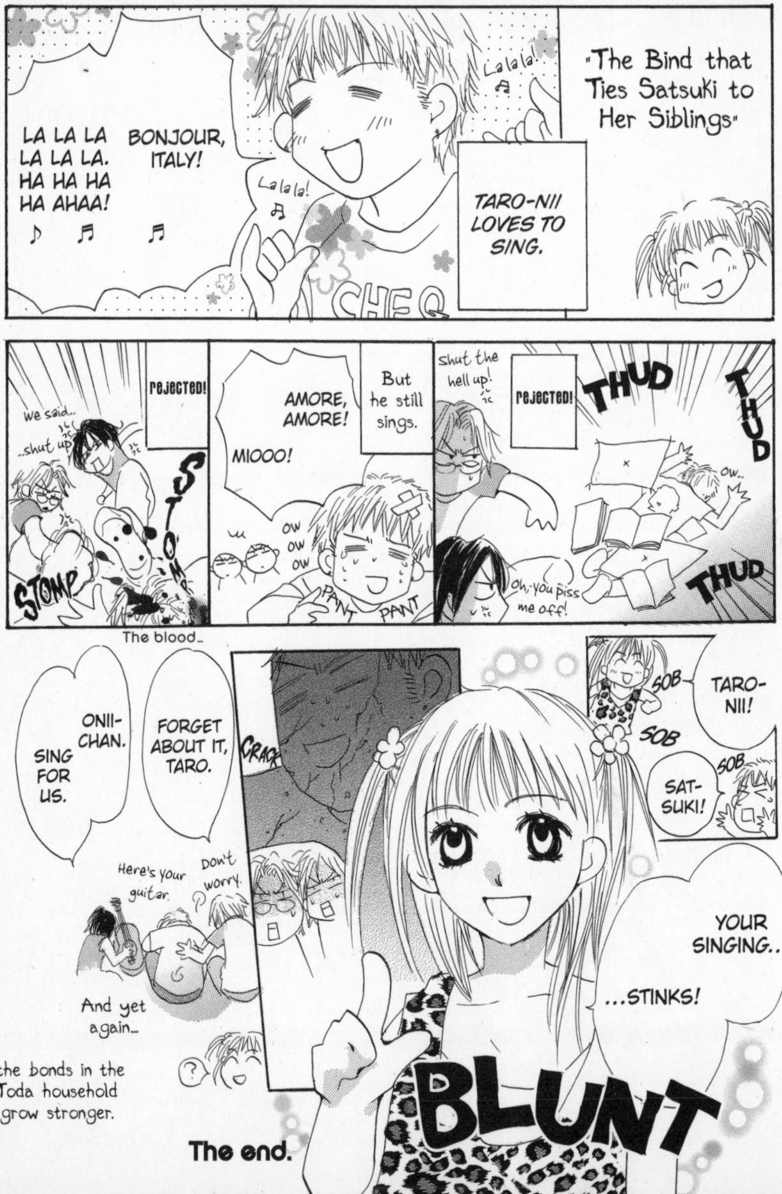
"The Bind that Ties Satsuki to Her Siblings"
La la la!
TARO-NII LOVES TO SING.
BONJOUR, ITALY!
LA LA LA LA LA LA. HA HA HA HA AHAA!
La la la!
CHEQ
rejected!
THUD
THUD
shut the hell up!
ow..
THUD
Oh, you piss me off!
But he still sings.
AMORE, AMORE!
MIOOO!
OW OW OW
PANT PANT
rejected!
STOMP
We said..
..shut up
STOMP
TARO-NII!
SOB
SOB
SAT-SUKI!
SOB
YOUR SINGING...
...STINKS!
BLUNT
The blood..
FORGET ABOUT IT, TARO.
ONII-CHAN.
SING FOR US.
CRACK
Don't worry.
Here's your guitar.
And yet again...
...the bonds in the Toda household grow stronger.
The end.

Cha-cha-cha and Shake it Shake it

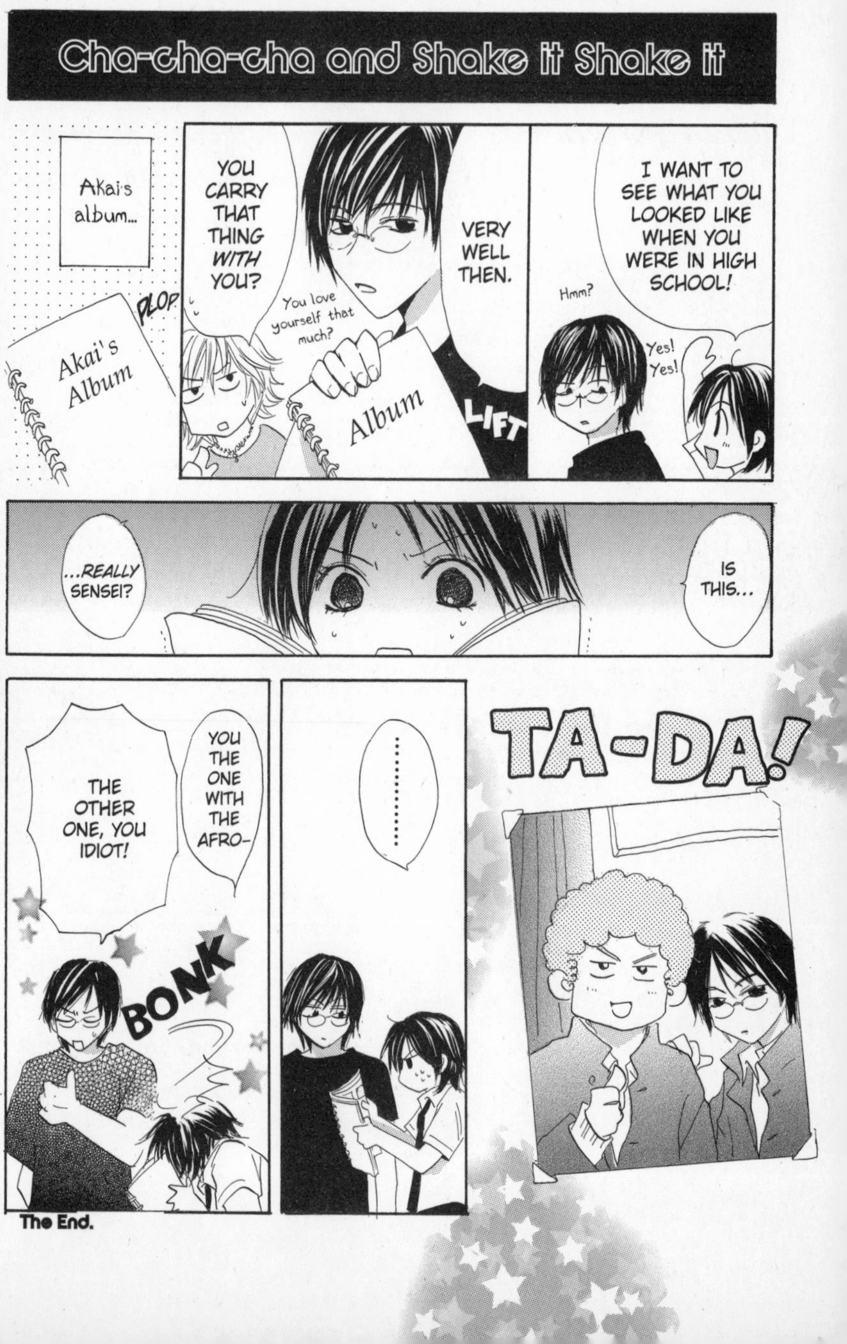
I WANT TO SEE WHAT YOU LOOKED LIKE WHEN YOU WERE IN HIGH SCHOOL!
Hmm?
Yes! Yes!
VERY WELL THEN.
YOU CARRY THAT THING WITH YOU?
You love yourself that much?
Album
LIFT
Akai's album...
PLOP
Akai's Album
IS THIS...
...REALLY SENSEI?
TA-DA!
....
YOU THE ONE WITH THE AFRO-
THE OTHER ONE, YOU IDIOT!
BONK

The End.

Shioko's Afterword.

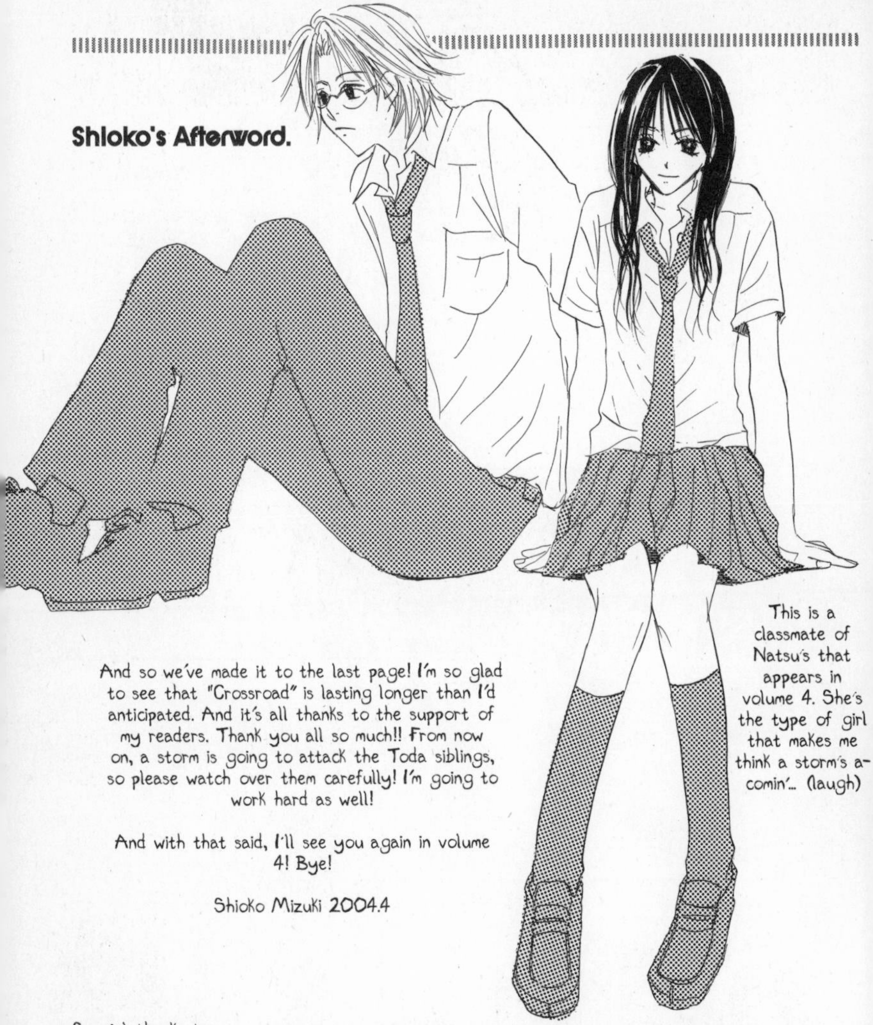

This is a classmate of Natsu's that appears in volume 4. She's the type of girl that makes me think a storm's a-comin'... (laugh)

And so we've made it to the last page! I'm so glad to see that "Crossroad" is lasting longer than I'd anticipated. And it's all thanks to the support of my readers. Thank you all so much!! From now on, a storm is going to attack the Toda siblings, so please watch over them carefully! I'm going to work hard as well!

And with that said, I'll see you again in volume 4! Bye!

Shioko Mizuki 2004.4

Special thanks to:
Kise-san, Akane-chan, Ari-chan, Hou-chan, Megumi-chan, Miho-chan, Kozawa-san, and my editor.
Thank you so much!!!

Crossroad volume 3 / end

Shioko Mizuki c/o Audry Taylor
5737 Kanan Rd. #591
Agoura Hills, CA 91301

Please send something if you like.

In the next steamy volume of *Crossroad*... ♡

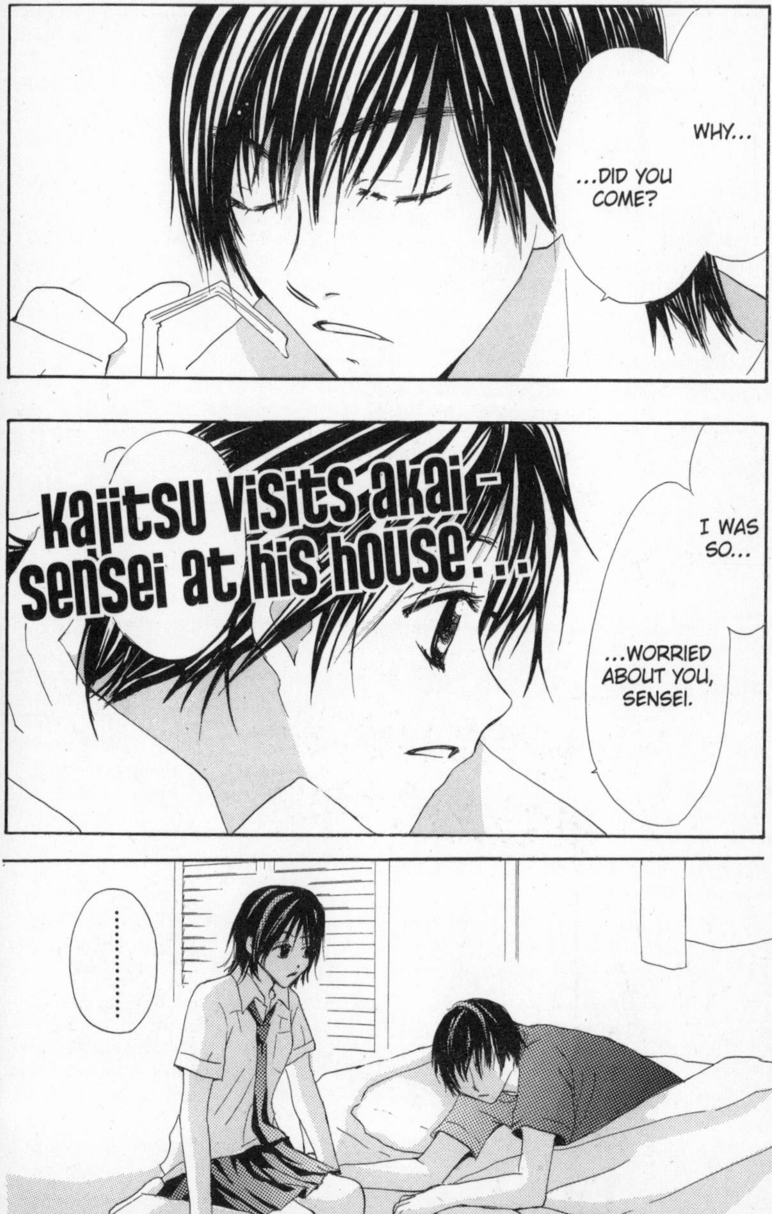
WHY...
...DID YOU COME?
I WAS SO...
...WORRIED ABOUT YOU, SENSEI.
Kajitsu visits Akai-sensei at his house...
....

crossroad

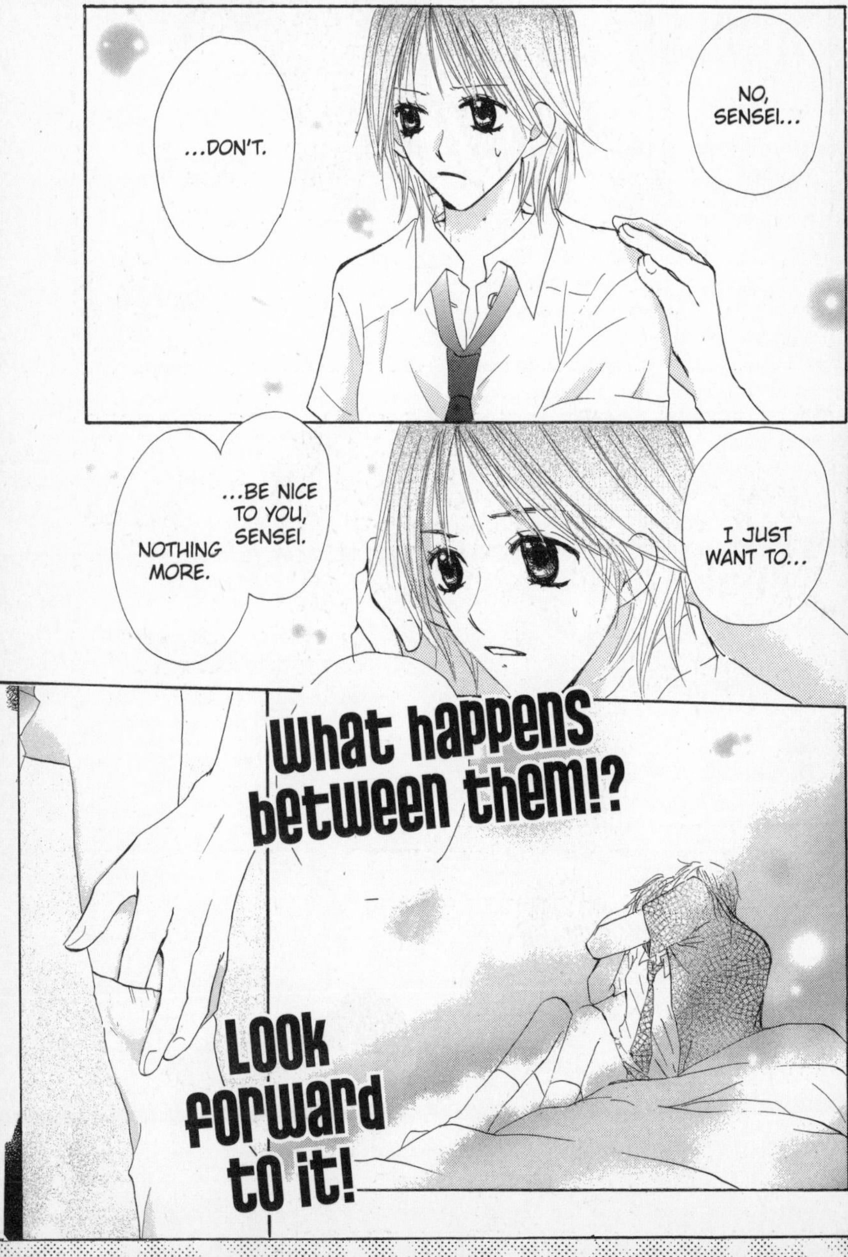
NO, SENSEI...
...DON'T.
I JUST WANT TO...
...BE NICE TO YOU, SENSEI.
NOTHING MORE.
What happens between them!?
Look forward to it!

Transator's notes

Pg. 85

Kabuki-niku – Kabuki-niku is a type of restaurant where you're seated at a table with a grill in it and you're given a bunch of meat and other cool stuff to cook up yourself right on the grill.

Pg. 126

Judy Ongg is a star who was raised in Japan but born in Taiwan, so one could say that her heart is split between two countries. Likewise, Tokihito seems to be dividing his heart between two girls.

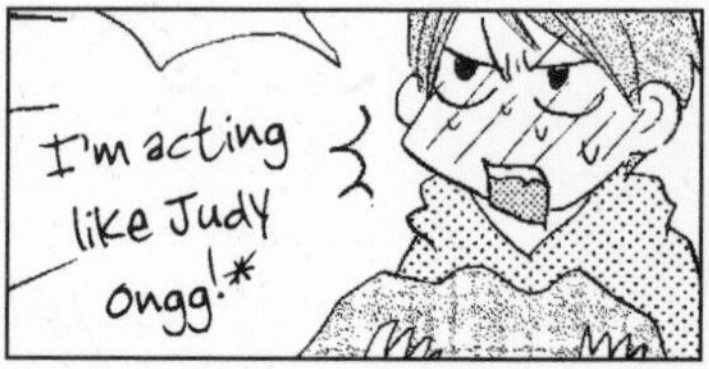
I'm acting like Judy Ongg!*

Pg. 126

Even if I -- Cough -- I Am Alone, is the name of a play by Yamashita Zen. It won the Kyoto Arts Center Theatre Award in 2004.

Pg. 164

Chat room plans are common in Japan. Cell phone users can pay money to message with their friends in a chat room-like environment, but it'll end up costing the user a ton of money.

Pg. 180

The Fukai, also known as "The Sea of Corruption," is a wasteland tainted with poison in Hayao Miyazaki's epic anime *Nausicaa* (for which he also wrote a dense, dramatic manga version). The heroine of the story, Nausicaa, finds out in the course of the story that the wasteland was created by an apocalyptic war that poisoned the earth centuries before. The Fukai, creeping ever closer to what remains of human civilization, can only be kept at bay temporarily with the use of fire.

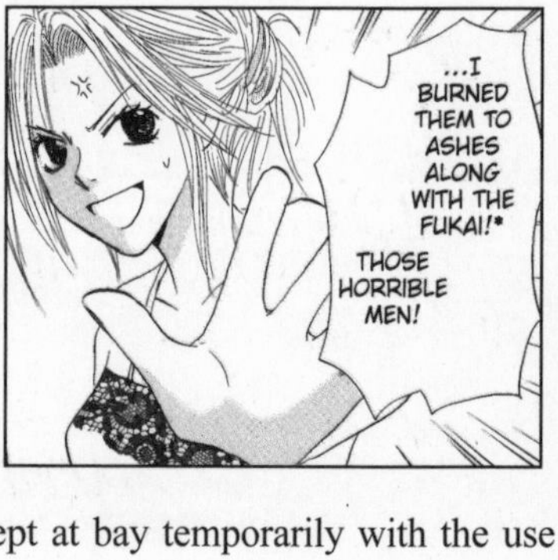
...I BURNED THEM TO ASHES ALONG WITH THE FUKAI!*
THOSE HORRIBLE MEN!

Fan art

I said NO Incest!

Shinoga
11/10/05

AMANDA S.
ABALINE, TX

Fan art

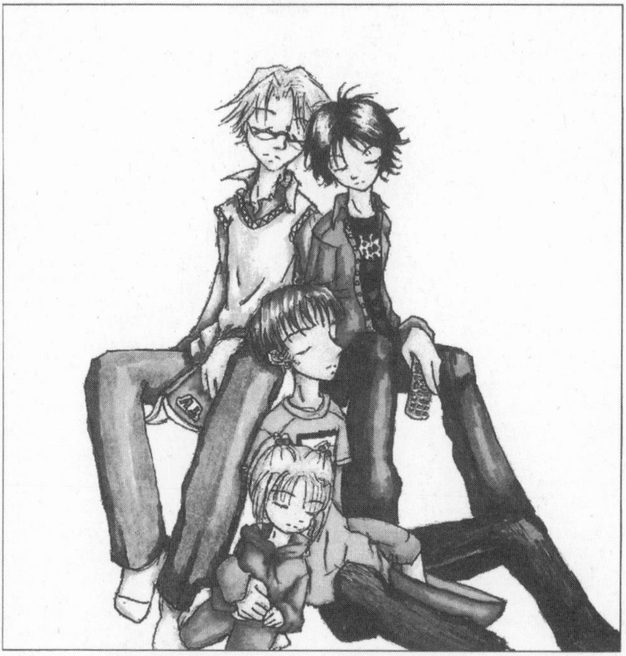

No Incest Allowed

LANI E.
KAMLAH, ID

GO! COMI IS NOW TAKING FAN ART FOR FUTURE VOLUMES OF CROSSROAD! ALL ARTWORK SUBMITTED WILL NOT BE RETURNED, SO IF IT'S IMPORTANT TO YOU, MAKE SURE TO SEND A COPY. IF YOU'RE UNDER 18, PLEASE INCLUDE YOUR PARENT'S WRITTEN PERMISSION FOR US TO PUBLISH THE ART. ALL SUBMISSIONS BECOME THE PROPERTY OF GO! MEDIA ENTERTAINMENT LLC.

SEND YOUR FAN ART AND LETTERS TO:

GO! MEDIA ENTERTAINMENT
ATTN: CROSSROAD
5737 KANAN RD. #591
AGOURA HILLS, CA 91301

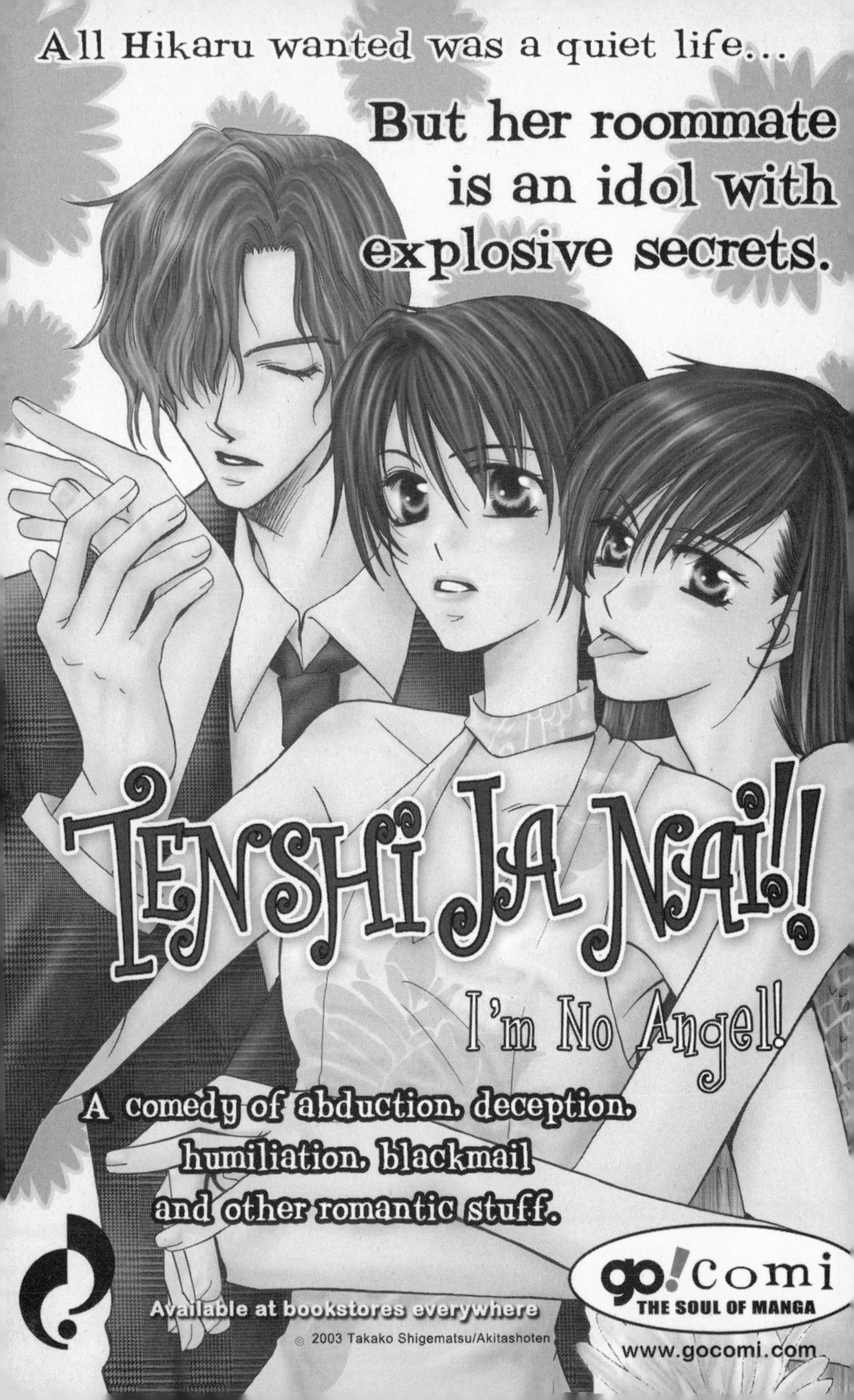
All Hikaru wanted was a quiet life...
But her roommate is an idol with explosive secrets.
TENSHI JA NAI!!
I'm No Angel!
A comedy of abduction, deception, humiliation, blackmail and other romantic stuff.
Available at bookstores everywhere
© 2003 Takako Shigematsu/Akitashoten
go!comi
THE SOUL OF MANGA
www.gocomi.com

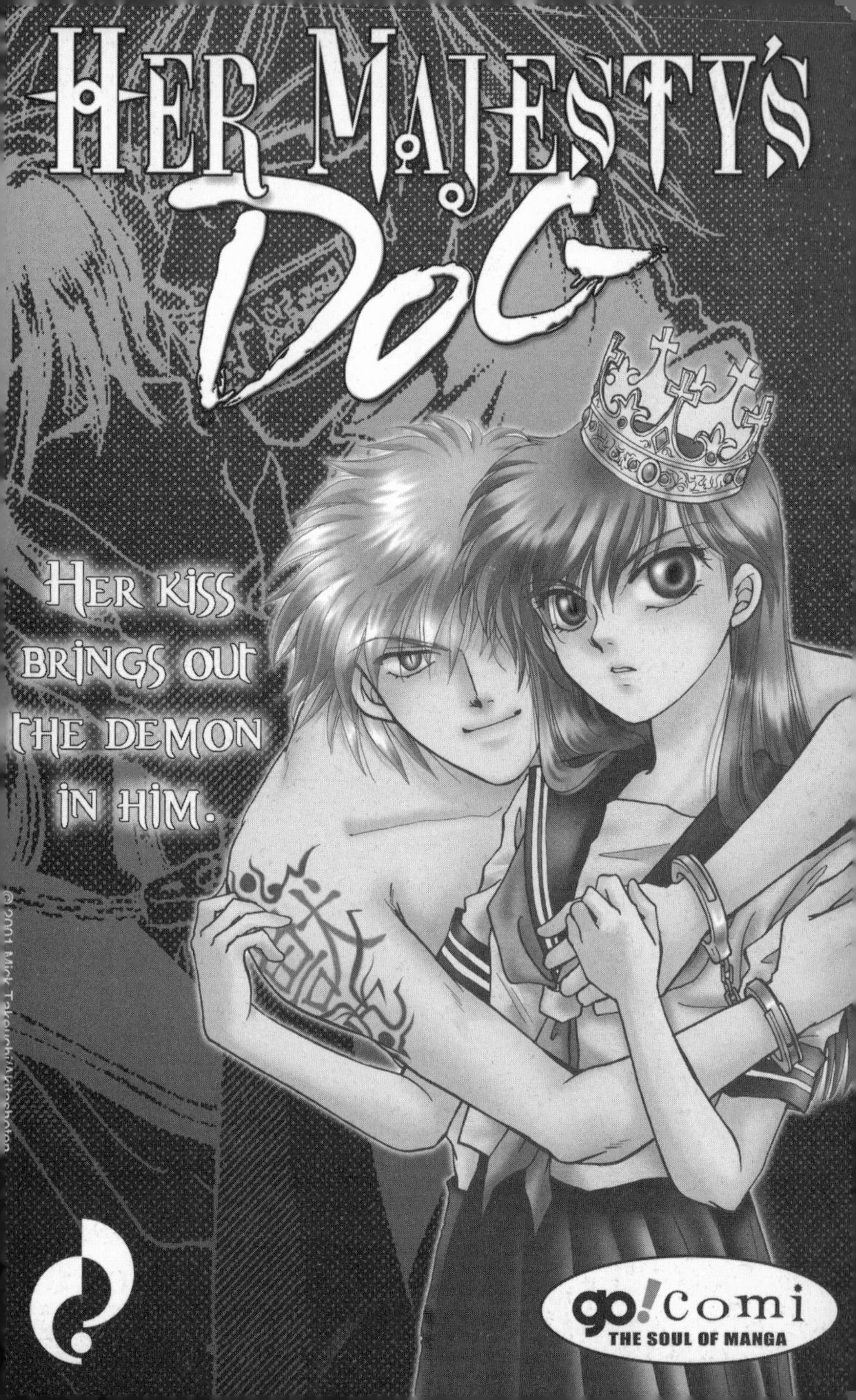

HER MAJESTY'S DOG
HER KISS BRINGS OUT THE DEMON IN HIM.
©2001 Mick Takeuchi/Akitashoten
go!comi
THE SOUL OF MANGA

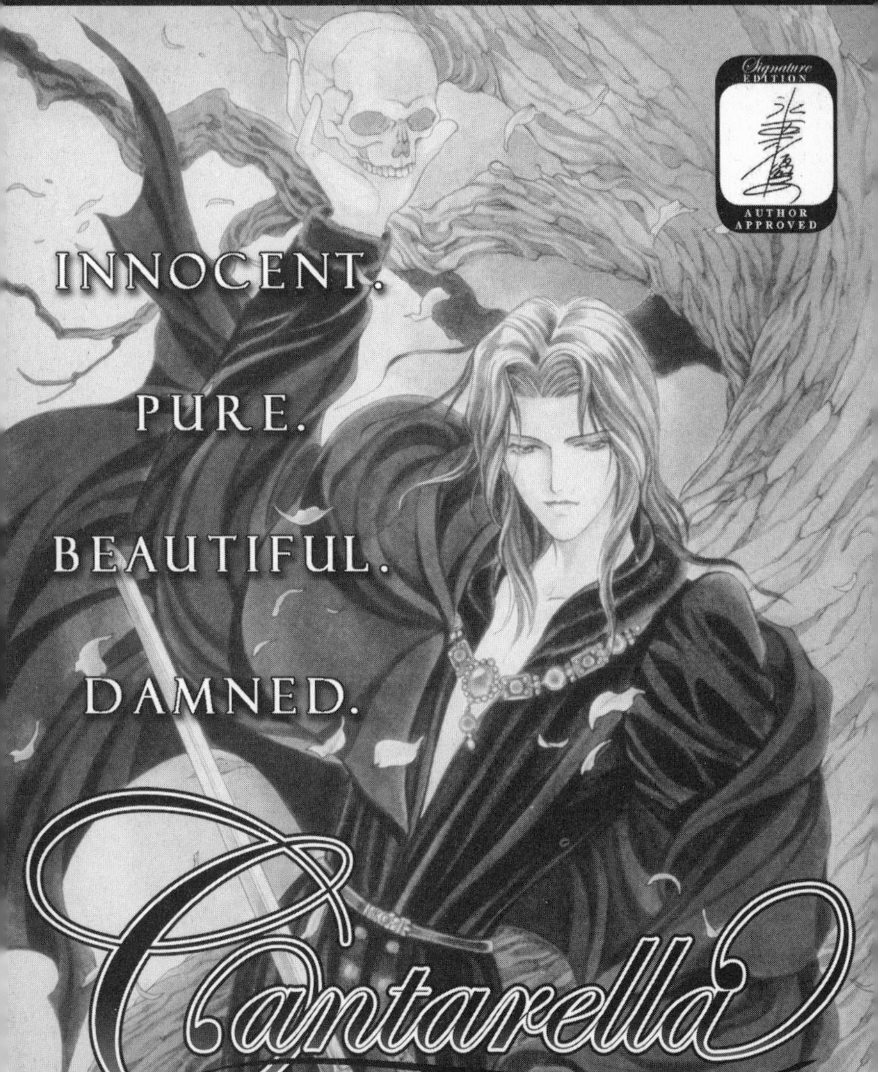
Signature EDITION
AUTHOR APPROVED
INNOCENT.
PURE.
BEAUTIFUL.
DAMNED.
Cantarella
© 2001 You Higuri/Akitashoten

Author's Note

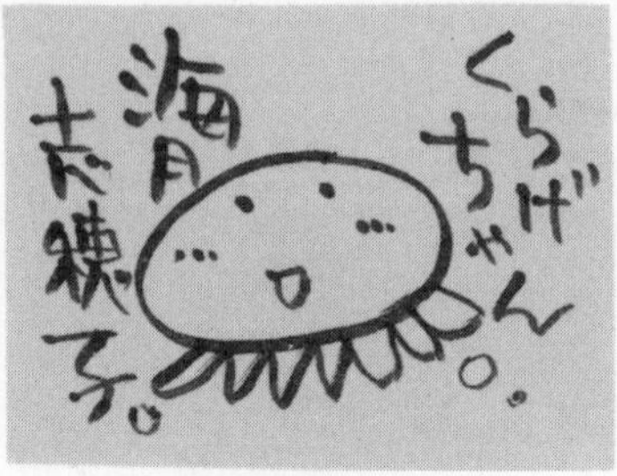
くらげちゃん。
海月志穂子。

Shioko Mizuki

Jellyfish-chan

Shioko Mizuki

About this "Jellyfish-chan" thing... I've been using the same self-portrait ever since I first debuted, so I thought it was about time I tried something new. I've had this picture for years (it's a portrait of me drawn by manga-ka Ozawa Kaoru) so I decided to use it. But I wish that Kaoru-chan would draw me something new! Please! (I'm not going to draw it myself.)

Other Works by Shioko Mizuki

(only available in Japan)

CAN THREE PEOPLE BE IN LOVE?

<5 VOLS>

LOVE FRUITS

<1 VOL>

Visit the manga-ka online at www.shioko.com